Bertolt Brecht
Collected Plays: Five

Life of Galileo
Mother Courage and her Children

The fifth volume in the Collected Plays series contains two of Brecht's best-known plays, *Life of Galileo* and *Mother Courage and her Children*. *Life of Galileo* examines the problems that face not only the scientist but the whole spirit of free inquiry when brought into conflict with the requirements of government or official ideology. Written in exile in 1937–9 it was first staged in English in 1947 in a version jointly prepared by Brecht and Charles Laughton, who played the title role. A complete translation by John Willett is printed here and the much shorter Laughton version is included in full as an appendix.

Along with Galileo, the character of Mother Courage is one of Brecht's great creations: she follows the armies back and forth across Europe in this 'chronicle play of the Thirty Years War', selling provisions and liquor from her canteen wagon. One by one she loses her children to the war but will not part from her livelihood – the wagon.

Edited by John Willett and Ralph Manheim, the volume includes Brecht's own notes and relevant texts as well as an extensive introduction and commentary.

Bertolt Brecht was born in Augsburg on 10 February 1898 and died in Berlin on 14 August 1956. He grew to maturity as a playwright in the frenetic years of the twenties and early thirties, with such plays as *Man equals Man*, *The Threepenny Opera* and *The Mother*. He left Germany when Hitler came to power in 1933, eventually reaching the United States in 1941, where he remained until 1947. It was during this period of exile that such masterpieces as *Life of Galileo*, *Mother Courage* and *The Caucasian Chalk Circle* were written. Shortly after his return to Europe in 1947 he founded the Berliner Ensemble, and from then until his death was mainly occupied in producing his own plays.

BRECHT COLLECTED PLAYS
Series Editors: John Willett, Ralph Manheim and Tom Kuhn

Brecht Collected Plays: One
Baal
Drums in the Night
In the Jungle of Cities
The Life of Edward II of England
A Respectable Wedding
The Beggar or The Dead Dog
Driving Out a Devil
Lux in Tenebris
The Catch

Brecht Collected Plays: Two
Man equals Man
The Elephant Calf
The Threepenny Opera
The Rise and Fall of the City of Mahagonny
The Seven Deadly Sins

Brecht Collected Plays: Three
Lindbergh's Flight
The Baden-Baden Lesson on Consent
He Said Yes/He Said No
The Decision
The Mother
The Exception and the Rule
The Horatians and the Curiatians
St Joan of the Stockyards

Brecht Collected Plays: Four*
Round Heads and Pointed Heads
Dansen
How Much Is Your Iron?
The Trial of Lucullus
Fear and Misery of the Third Reich
Señora Carrar's Rifles

Brecht Collected Plays: Five
Life of Galileo
Mother Courage and her Children

Brecht Collected Plays: Six
The Good Person of Szechwan
The Resistible Rise of Arturo Ui
Mr Puntila and his Man Matti

Brecht Collected Plays: Seven
The Visions of Simone Machard
Schweyk in the Second World War
The Caucasian Chalk Circle
The Duchess of Malfi

Brecht Collected Plays: Eight*

* in preparation

BERTOLT BRECHT

Collected Plays: Five

Life of Galileo
translated by John Willett

Mother Courage and her Children
translated by John Willett

Edited and introduced by
John Willett and Ralph Manheim

Methuen Drama

METHUEN WORLD CLASSICS

10 9 8 7

This edition first published in Great Britain in 1995
by Methuen Drama
Reissued with a new cover in 1999
by Methuen Publishing Ltd
215 Vauxhall Bridge Road, London SW1V 1EJ
by arrangement with Suhrkamp Verlag, Frankfurt am Main

Translation copyright for the plays and texts by Brecht © 1980 by Stefan S. Brecht
Introduction and editorial notes copyright © 1980 by Eyre Methuen Ltd, 1995 by
Methuen Drama

Life of Galileo first published in this translation in Great Britain in hardback and
paperback 1980 by Eyre Methuen Ltd
Original work entitled *Leben des Galilei*. Copyright © 1940 by Arvid Englind
Teaterforlag, a.b., renewed June 1967 by Stefan S. Brecht. Copyright © 1955 by
Suhrkamp Verlag, Frankfurt am Main. Charles Laughton's translation of *Galileo*
(in appendix) copyright © 1952 by Bertolt Brecht

Mother Courage and her Children first published in this translation in Great
Britain in hardback and paperback 1980 by Eyre Methuen Ltd
Original work entitled *Mutter Courage und ihre Kinder*. Copyright © 1940 by
Arvid Englind Teaterforlag, a.b., renewed June 1967 by Stefan S. Brecht.
Copyright © 1949 by Suhrkamp Verlag, Frankfurt am Main

All rights reserved

Methuen Publishing Limited Reg. No. 3543167

A CIP catalogue record for this book is available from the British Library

ISBN 0 413 69970 6

Printed in Great Britain by Cox & Wyman Ltd, Reading, Berkshire

CAUTION
These plays are fully protected by copyright. All enquiries concerning the rights
for professional stage production of the plays should be directed to Alan Brodie
Representation Ltd, 211 Piccadilly, London W1V 9LD and those for amateur stage
production to Samuel French Ltd, 52 Fitzroy Street, London W1P 6JR. In the United
States and Canada enquiries concerning all the plays should be directed to Jerold
L. Couture, Fitelson, Lasky, Aslan & Couture, 551 Fifth Avenue, New York,
NY 10176–0078.

Enquiries concerning music for the plays should also be directed as above.

Enquiries about use of any material other than in performance should be directed
to the publishers.

Contents

Introduction

In all Brecht's work there is no more substantial and significant landmark than the first version of *Galileo*, which he wrote in three weeks of November 1938, not long after the Munich agreement had opened the door of Eastern Europe to Hitler. As is well known, it inaugurated the series of major plays whose writing occupied him until his return to Germany some ten years later: from *Mother Courage* to *The Days of the Commune*, those great works of his forties on which his reputation largely rests. At the same time it marks the virtual end of his efforts to write plays and poems of instant political relevance, such as the Spanish Civil War one-acter *Señora Carrar's Rifles* or the loose sequence of anti-Nazi scenes known variously as *99%, The Private Life of the Master Race* and *Fear and Misery of the Third Reich*. Short satirical poems designed for the exiles' cabarets or for broadcasting (notably by the Communist-run German Freedom Radio) now give way to something at once more personal and more pessimistic. The *Lenin Cantata* set by Eisler for the twentieth anniversary of the October Revolution is followed during 1938 by 'To Those Born Later' and the great Lao-Tse poem. All along the line Brecht appears to be backing away from the kind of close political engagement which had occupied him since the crisis years of 1929, as also from the didactic and agitational forms to which this gave rise. Walter Benjamin, who visited him in his Danish cottage that June and stayed till after Munich, found him at once more isolated and more mellow than he had been four years earlier. 'It's a good thing', he notes Brecht as saying, 'when someone who has taken up an extreme position then goes into a period of reaction. That way he arrives at a half-way house.'

Though such a change might seem compatible with the new aesthetic traditionalism being preached from Moscow after the Writers' Congress of 1934 – with *Galileo* itself as part of the same historicising trend as led to Heinrich Mann's Henri IV novels and Friedrich Wolf's play *Beaumarchais* – it primarily relates to something very different: to Brecht's shuddering consciousness of what he called 'the dark times'. The phrase was first used by him in a poem of 1937 and from then on it overshadows much of his writing right up to the crucial German defeats at Stalingrad and El Alamein in the autumn of 1942. For it was a desperate period, and the despair could be felt on at least three different levels. First of all there was the relentless progress of Fascism (intervention in Spain, Japanese invasion of China, the Austrian Anschluss, the annexation of the German-speaking areas of Czechoslovakia) aided by British appeasement and the fall of the French Popular Front. Overlapping these events, and in many ways closer to Brecht personally, was the great Soviet purge which by the time of Benjamin's visit had already carried away such friends of theirs as Tretiakoff, Ottwalt, Carola Neher and the Reichs, as well as Brecht's two Comintern contacts Béla Kun and Vilis Knorin, to as yet unclear fates. Linked with the new Russian spy mania, itself shot through with xenophobia, was the increasingly strict imposition of the Socialist Realist aesthetic whose German-language spokesmen were Alfred Kurella and Georg Lukács. With Meyerhold deprived of his allegedly 'alien' theatre in January 1938, Brecht that summer wrote a number of ripostes to Lukács which he seemingly thought wiser not to publish, even in the Moscow magazine *Das Wort* of which he was a nominal editor. 'They want to play the *apparatchik* and exercise control over the other people', he told Benjamin. 'Every one of their criticisms contains a threat.'

In the *Journals* (*Arbeitsjournal*) which he now began keeping, the place of *Galileo* is very clear. In October a short entry reflects on the unwillingness of any of the major powers, including Russia, to risk war for Czechoslovakia. In January 1939 another reports the arrest in Moscow of *Das Wort*'s sponsor Mikhail Koltsov – 'my last link with that place' – and concludes that the right Marxist attitude to Stalinism was that of Marx himself to German social-democracy: 'constructively critical'. Between these two pages comes the entry of 23 November, recording that this hitherto unmentioned play has taken three weeks to write. Before and after come biting comments on Lukács and the 'Realism controversy'. It must already have been in Brecht's mind ('for some while', so his collaborator Margarete Steffin wrote to Benjamin in the letter cited on p. 235); and certainly he had done a good deal of preliminary reading: of the standard German biography by Emil Wohlwill, for instance, as well as of nineteenth-century translations of the *Discorsi* and Bacon's *Novum Organum* (from which a number of key ideas were derived) and works by modern physicists such as Eddington and Jeans. But an important contributing factor was his decision, evidently taken around this time, to follow Hanns Eisler's example and apply for a quota visa to the United States, where he hoped that a work about the great physicist would make him some money. This idea crystallised just after Munich as a result of a visit by his American friend Ferdinand Reyher, a Hollywood script writer whom he had first met in Berlin at the time of *The Threepenny Opera*. Arriving in Copenhagen on 28 October, Reyher suggested that Brecht should start by writing *Galileo* as a film story which he, Reyher, could market for him. Though Brecht in the event found himself writing the play instead (see Letter 373 of 2 December), and never even embarked on the film project, he said from the outset that it was 'really intended for New York'.

This original *Galileo*, revised with some minor changes in the first few weeks of 1939, was initially called *The Earth Moves*. Its full German text was first published under its subsequent title *Leben des Galilei* by Suhrkamp in 1988. In February Reyher wrote from Hollywood to say that while he would discuss its screen possibilities with the director William Dieterle – himself an old acquaintance of Brecht's from the early 1920s – he felt some measure of adaptation was needed to fit it for the American stage. With Brecht's permission, accordingly, he proposed not just to do a straight translation but to introduce a little more speed':

> a sharpened drive, because our mode of thinking and our interests are gaited to a more nervous tempo, and what induces us to think in this country is not ideas, but action.

Brecht never seems to have agreed to this; nor do we know how Dieterle reacted to the film idea. Meantime, however, copies of the script were going to a number of other recipients: among them Piscator, Hanns Eisler and Fritz Lang in the United States, Brecht's publisher Wieland Herzfelde in Prague, his translator Desmond Vesey in London, the main German-language theatres in Basle and Zurich, and Pierre Abraham and Walter Benjamin in Paris. Not long before leaving Denmark that spring he began writing his *Messingkauf Dialogues* on the model of Galileo's *Discorsi* dialogues. Characteristically, he had already become dissatisfied with the play, which he saw as 'far too opportunist' and conventionally atmospheric, like the deliberately Aristotelian 'empathy drama' *Señora Carrar's Rifles*, for which he was still praised by the Party aestheticians. He even thought of remodelling the whole thing in a more didactic form, based on the example of the big unfinished *Fatzer* and *Breadshop* schemes of the late 1920s. However, there is no evidence that he did this except a rough outline for a 'version for workers'; and instead the project slumbered while he wrote the next four of the major plays. Only in Moscow was there a review of the play in *Sovietski Isskusstvo* (18 August 1939) and some suggestion of an illustrated edition for which his new friend Hans Tombrock was to make the etchings. This too never materialised, though it prompted the vivid description of Galileo's appearance which we cite on p. 193.

*   *   *

The Brechts eventually moved to the United States in the summer of 1941, leaving via Moscow and Vladivostock a matter of days before the German invasion of the USSR. By then France, Poland, Yugoslavia and Greece had all fallen to

Hitler; Benjamin had committed suicide on the Franco–Spanish frontier; Margarete Steffin was left in Moscow to die of tuberculosis. Settling in California in the hope of finding work in the film industry, Brecht was soon seeing both Dieterle and Reyher, who had by now evidently completed a straight translation of the play. The idea of a film version seems not to have been resumed. That autumn he discussed the script with the physicist Hans Reichenbach, a pupil of Einstein's then teaching in Los Angeles at the University of California, who congratulated him on the accuracy of its scientific and historical aspects. Then at the end of the year he tried to interest his old friend Oskar Homolka, and for a time Homolka toyed with the idea of playing the part: something that made Brecht feel

> as if I were recalling a strange sunken theatre of a bygone age on continents that had been submerged.

A similar sense of unreality must have seized him in September 1943, when the Zurich Schauspielhaus finally gave the play its world première some two and a half years after that of *Mother Courage*. How he reacted to the news of the production – or when, indeed, he heard it – remains unclear; he never even alludes to it in his diary. Soberly interpreted by Leonard Steckel, who not only played Galileo but was also the director, it was greatly applauded despite its lack of dramatic effects: 'a Lehrstück or a play for reading', one critic called it. What was not clear, however, in a generally clear performance, was whether Galileo recanted out of cowardice or as part of a deliberate plan to complete his life's work on behalf of human reason and smuggle it out to the free world. This ambiguity (which led so experienced a critic as Bernhard Diebold to favour the second, more topically anti-Nazi interpretation) is of course built into the first version of the play, where Galileo has already been conspiring with the stove-fitter (symbol of the workers) to send his manuscript abroad in the penultimate scene even before Andrea appears. (In Zurich this was in fact the last scene, that at the frontier being, as usual, cut.)

It was only in the spring of 1944 that the play seems once

more to have become a reality to Brecht. Wintering in New York, he had discussed the possibility of a production with Jed Harris, the backer of Thornton Wilder's *Our Town*, and on getting back to Santa Monica he looked at *Galileo* with a fresh eye, re-checking its moral content, so he noted in his journal,

since it had always worried me. just because i was trying to follow the historical story, without being morally concerned, a moral content emerged and i'm not happy about it. g. can no more resist stating the truth than eating an appetising dish; to him it's a matter of sensual enjoyment. and he constructs his own personality as wisely and passionately as he does his image of the world. actually he falls twice. the first time is when he suppresses or recants the truth because he is in mortal danger, the second when despite the mortal danger he once again seeks out the truth and disseminates it. he is destroyed by his own productivity. and it upsets me to be told that i approve of his publicly recanting so as to be able to carry on his work in secret. that's too banal and too cheap. g., after all, destroyed not only himself as a person but also the most valuable part of his scientific work. the church (i.e. the authorities) defended the teachings of the bible purely as a way of defending itself, its authority and its power of oppression and exploitation. the sole reason why the people became interested in g.'s ideas about the planets was that they were chafing under church domination. g. threw all real progress to the wolves when he recanted. he abandoned the people, and astronomy once again became an affair for specialists, the exclusive concern of scholars, unpolitical, cut off. the church made a distinction between these celestial 'problems' and those of the earth, consolidated its rule and then cheerfully went on to acknowledge the new solutions.

It was during that March that Brecht first met Charles Laughton, who was then living within walking distance in a street called Corona del Mar above the Pacific Coast Highway.

Both men were friends of Berthold Viertel's wife Salka (best known perhaps as Greta Garbo's preferred script writer), and it seems to have been through her that they learnt to appreciate one another's company. As Laughton's biographer Charles Higham has put it, they found they had certain likes and dislikes in common:

> They both shared a sympathy and concern for ordinary people, a dislike of pomp and circumstance and the attitudes and actions of the European ruling class. They both disliked elaborate artifice in the theatre, as exemplified by the spangles-and-tinsel of Max Reinhardt's stage and film productions of *A Midsummer Night's Dream* . . .

Laughton had last acted in the theatre in 1934, and since playing Rembrandt in Alexander Korda's 1936 film of that name (for which Brecht's old friend Carl Zuckmayer wrote the script) he had had a surfeit of supporting roles in second- and third-rate Hollywood films. During the spring and summer of 1944 he read the rough translation of Brecht's *Schweik in the Second World War* and greatly enjoyed it, while Brecht for his part wrote the long poem 'Garden in Progress' to commemorate, not without irony, the landslide which sent part of the Laughtons' beautifully tended garden sliding down the cliff face to the road below. By then the actor had evidently learnt enough about *Galileo*, whether through Brecht's description or from the Vesey and Reyher translations, to decide that it might well be the masterpiece to carry him back to the live stage. With Brecht's agreement he now commissioned a fresh translation by a young writer called Brainerd Duffield, who had been working with Alfred Döblin and other German exiles employed by MGM. By the end of November Duffield and his contemporary Emerson Crocker had once again translated Brecht's original script and produced a third text which both Laughton and the Brechts evidently approved. A fortnight later actor and playwright together were getting down to what the former terms 'systematic work on the translation and stage

version of the *Life of the Physicist Galileo*'. Whatever the
original intention, it was in effect to be a new play.

*   *   *

Brecht later called the work with Laughton a 'zweijähriger
Spass', a two-year escapade, and undoubtedly it covers more
paper than did any other of his writings, so that altogether it
represents a prodigal expenditure of both men's time. But he
also saw it as the classic collaboration between a great
dramatist and a great actor, and the loving account which he
gives in 'Building up a part' (p. 206 ff.) seems to have been
filtered through a warm Californian haze rather than the
wintry greys of Berlin. Inevitably there were long interruptions
before a first script was ready. From February to May 1945
Laughton was off playing in the pirate film *Captain Kidd*
(Brecht meantime consoling himself by trying to put the
Communist Manifesto into Lucretian hexameters); then in
June and July Brecht was in New York for a none too
successful production of *The Private Life of the Master Race* in
Eric Bentley's translation, directed initially by Piscator and
finally by Viertel on Brecht's intervention. Generally however
they worked as described by Brecht, with him reshaping the
play in a mixture of German and English – his typescript drafts
contain many instances of this, of which one is cited on p. 237
– and both men then trying to get the English working right.
This reshaping often followed Laughton's suggestions, which
went much further than the basic cutting and streamlining
which were his most obvious contribution. Thus it was he who
proposed the elimination of the Doppone character (see
p. 239), the 'positive entry' of the iron founder in scene 2, the
argument between Ludovico and Galileo in the sunspot scene
and the shifting of the handing-over of the *Discorsi* so that
Galileo's great speech of self-abasement should come after it
and offset it. Brecht too worked to make this self-abasement
seem more of a piece with Galileo's concern for his own
comforts, which were now to include thinking. In this, as in the
new emphasis on Galileo's sensuality, he was aided by Laughton's character, of which Eric Bentley has written that

It is unlikely that anyone again will combine as he did every appearance of intellectual brilliance with every appearance of physical self-indulgence.

If the 1938 version derived its political relevance from the need to smuggle the truth out of Nazi Germany, this new version was given an extra edge of topicality by the dropping of the first atomic bomb on 6 August 1945. Not that any significant change was needed apart from the addition of the passage about 'a universal cry of fear' in the penultimate scene. The notion of a Hippocratic oath for scientists had still to be worked in. So before leaving the US Brecht drafted the relevant passage (see p. 270), which could indeed have been in his mind from the inception of the play, the idea itself having been put forward by Lancelot Law White in *Nature* in 1938 and discussed at the time in an editorial in the *New York Times*.

On 1 December 1945 the new, 'American' text was complete enough for Laughton to read it to the Brechts, Eisler, Reichenbach, Salka Viertel and other friends. About a week later he also read it to Orson Welles, whom both he and Brecht seem already to have had in mind for some while as the right director for the production towards which they were working. Welles instantly accepted the job, and a few days after that the three men saw Laughton's agents Berg-Allenberg to discuss whether to open in the spring or the summer. This question was bound up with their choice of producer, which seems to have veered initially between Welles himself, the film impresario Mike Todd and Elisabeth Bergner's husband Paul Czinner, for whom Brecht was already working on the *Duchess of Malfi* adaptation. Czinner was not congenial to Laughton, and once the idea of a spring production was abandoned he dropped out. Welles for his part apparently disliked Brecht; nevertheless for a time the intention was that he and Todd should combine forces; then a mixture of uncertainty about dates and dislike of the kind of teamwork proposed by Laughton and Brecht made Welles drop out after the middle of 1946, leaving Todd as sole producer. After that various directors were suggested: Elia Kazan, who had a particular appeal for Brecht because he did not claim to know all the answers; Harold Clurman, whom Brecht respected as 'an intelligent critic and interested in theoretical issues' but saw primarily as a 'Stanislavsky man' unlikely to let him have any say. He even inquired about Alfred Lunt. Meantime a great deal of detailed revision of the new Brecht–Laughton text went on, with Brecht and Reyher totally overhauling it in New York, then Laughton and Brecht again reworking it in California. Versions of the ballad-singer's song were made by Reyher and by Abe Burrows (of *Guys and Dolls* fame) while the inter-scene verses seem to have involved a whole host of collaborators including Brecht himself and his daughter Barbara; the only programme credit, however, for the 'lyrics' went to a Santa Monica poet called Albert Brush. The eventual director chosen was Joseph Losey, who had met Brecht in Moscow in 1935 and thereafter made his name with the Living Newspaper programmes of the Federal Theatre. Finally Todd too dropped out after offering (in Losey's words) to 'dress the production in Renaissance furniture from the Hollywood warehouses', an idea that was unacceptable to Brecht, Laughton and Losey alike. With this the hope of any kind of production in 1946 disappeared.

Briefly Brecht hoped that he and Losey might be able to stage a try-out at Berkeley under the auspices of Henry Schnitzler, son of the Austrian playwright, but time was too short. Instead the three partners decided to turn to a new smaller management headed by Norman Lloyd and John Houseman, who were then about to take over the Coronet Theatre on La Cienega Boulevard, Los Angeles. They agreed to put on *Galileo* as their second production, with the 'extremely decent' (said Brecht) T. Edward Hambleton as its principal backer. Though Brecht was unable to get his old collaborator Caspar Neher over from Europe as he wished, the substitute designer Robert Davison accepted his and Laughton's ideas for an unmonumental, non-naturalistic setting; Helene Weigel helped with the costumes. Eisler (who actually preferred the first version of the play) wrote the music in a fortnight; Lotte Goslar did the choreography. Rehearsals were scheduled to start at the end of May 1947, when Laughton would have finished a film; the opening would be on 1 July. Though this had to be put off till the last day of the month everything otherwise seems – amazingly enough – to have gone according to plan. Losey not only justified Reyher's recommendation of him –

> He knows casting, has the feel for it; he knows what to do with actors; he can get a crowd sense without numbers, and movement that isn't just confusion, and keep the whole of a play in mind.

– but worked so closely with Brecht that the latter ever afterwards treated the production as his own. Laughton, exceptionally nervous before the première, resisted any temptation to overact, and concentrated on bringing out the contradictory elements with which they had enriched Galileo's character; the one point that still resisted him, according to Brecht, being the logic of the deep self-abasement manifested in his 'Welcome to the gutter' speech near the end of the play. Not that such refinements would have been particularly appreciated by the critics, for both *Variety* and the *New York Times* complained that the production was too flat and colourless. Charlie Chaplin too – who never really knew what to make of Brecht – sat next to Eisler at the opening and dined with him afterwards; he found that the play was not theatrical enough and said it should have been mounted differently. 'When I told him', said Eisler later,

> that Brecht never wants to 'mount' things, he simply couldn't understand.

To Hella Wuolijoki in Finland Losey would write after the New York production that

> working with Brecht has spoilt me for any other kind of theatre . . .

And from then on he was lost to the cinema. For Brecht himself however it was certainly the most important and satisfying theatrical occasion since he first went into exile in 1933:

The stage and the production were strongly reminiscent of the Schiffbauerdamm Theatre in Berlin; likewise the intellectual part of the audience.

So he wrote to Reyher (Letter 543). Whether or not it played to such full houses as he later claimed, the whole achievement was an astonishing tribute to the actor's courage, the director's commitment and the writer's relentless perfectionism: one of the great events in Brecht's life.

*   *   *

In the long struggle to stage the 'American' version it might seem that Brecht hardly noticed that the Second World War was over. Thus his poem to Laughton 'concerning the work on the play *The Life of Galileo*' (*Poems 1913–1956*, p. 405):

Still your people and mine were tearing each other to pieces
    when we
Pored over those tattered exercise books, looking
Up words in dictionaries, and time after time
Crossed out our texts and then
Under the crossings-out excavated
The original turns of phrase. Bit by bit –
While the housefronts crashed down in our capitals –
The façades of language gave way. Between us
We began following what characters and actions dictated:
New text.

Again and again I turned actor, demonstrating
A character's gestures and tone of voice, and you
Turned writer. Yet neither I nor you
Stepped outside his profession.

In fact however he had begun to prepare his return to Germany as early as 1944 (when the FBI reported him visiting the Czech consulate for the purpose), and in December 1945 he wrote in his journal, 'maybe I'll no longer be here, next autumn'. The *Galileo* discussions apart, this was the beginning of a curiously blank year in Brecht's biography (see *Journals*, editorial note to

5 January 1946), by the end of which he had had some kind of invitation to work in the Soviet sector of Berlin, once again at the Theater am Schiffbauerdamm. Early in 1947 he was trying to organise a common front with Piscator and Friedrich Wolf (who was already back there) with a view to rehabilitating the Berlin theatre; by March he and Weigel had got their papers to go to Switzerland. The machinations of the House Un-American Activities Committee (from May onwards) thus had less effect on his movements than is sometimes thought. Hanns Eisler was interrogated by one of their subcommittees that month and the FBI file on Brecht reopened, while Eisler's brother Gerhart was on trial during much of the *Galileo* rehearsals; finally Brecht himself appeared before the committee a day or two before leaving for Switzerland in September. But these words did probably affect the fortunes of the New York production, which Hambleton had delayed (according to Higham) in order to add the 'passion, excitement, colour' which the critics had felt to be lacking. Further cuts were made there to give us the text as we now print it (see the appendix, p. 333 ff.), the odd facetious line was worked in; the cast was entirely new. Again however the reviews were bad, Brooks Atkinson in the *New York Times* dismissing the production as 'stuffed with hokum'. 'The New York press', noted Brecht in Zurich,

> seems to have missed exactly what laughton's catholic friend missed in GALILEO: a scientist agonising under duress whom we can empathise with. well, galileo's bad conscience is shown in right proportion in the play, but this is not nearly enough for the bourgeoisie; having come to power it wishes to see the higher spiritual movements of those whom it compels to act against their consciences displayed larger than life so as to embellish the overall picture of their world.

The run was a very short one – six performances, suggests the 1988 edition. Higham blames the difficulty of finding another theatre to which to transfer. But Laughton's earlier biographer Kurt Singer gave a somewhat different interpretation, writing (with an exaggeration indicative of the temper of those times) that

> The trouble lay in the political affiliations of the playwright. Berthold Brecht was a dyed-in-the-wool Communist. On the point of being deported from the United States for his Communist activities, he escaped and turned up again in East Germany, where be became the Soviet's pet author, supervising the literary life of the Soviet-controlled zone and turning out odes to Stalin on the various state holidays. The musical score for the play on Galileo had been composed by Hanns Eisler, another convinced Communist who had composed many propaganda songs, including *The Comintern March*. Several actors in the cast turned out to be Communists too . . .

Whether or not this put Laughton himself off the play, as Singer suggests, Brecht continued to count on the actor's collaboration in a proposed film version to be made in Italy. The producer who had initiated this scheme was Rod E. Geiger, who apparently had funds in that country as a result of his earnings on Rossellini's *Open City*. Negotiations continued while Brecht was in Switzerland, and a scheme was worked out with the approval of Laughton and his agents by which the former would come to London for a production of the play around the end of 1948, after which work on the film would follow. Brecht and Reyher would write the script, which Geiger felt must give more emphasis to the relationship between Virginia and her fiancé Ludovico. However, everything was conditional on Laughton's involvement, and he blew hot and cold, his own nervousness of Communist associations being no doubt aggravated by the warnings of his agent. So it all fell through – possibly prompting Brecht to the satirical 'Obituary for Ch.L' which he wrote around this time (*Poems 1913–1956*, p. 418):

> Speak of the weather
> Be thankful he's dead

Who before he had spoken
Took back what he said.

At any rate this put paid for the moment to all further plans,
since the play could hardly be staged by Brecht's own company, the Berliner Ensemble, till they had a suitable actor and a
revised German text. Brecht himself in Zurich had made a start
and translated about half the Laughton text; he seems to have
discussed a Berlin production outside the programme of that
company, with Kortner or Steckel in the title part. Then in
1953 he set his collaborators (Hauptmann, Besson, Berlau) to
work translating and expanding the 'American' version so as
to include certain elements of that of 1938, notably the plague
scenes and the great introductory speech about the 'new time'
in scene 1. He then went over the results himself, also adding
German versions of the ballad, the poems and the inter-scene
verses. In 1955 all this but for the verses was given its première
in Cologne in West Germany, after which he at last – in the
final year of his life – began preparing to stage the play with the
Berliner Ensemble.

In ten years a lot had changed. The text had grown longer by
half, the production envisaged (with Neher as designer) was
more lavish, there was no actor of Laughton's calibre available. Brecht himself was to direct it, but he could only conduct
rehearsals from mid-December up to the end of March 1956
when he became too ill to go on. As Galileo he cast his old
Communist friend Ernst Busch, who had been in *The Mother,
Kuhle Wampe* and the *Threepenny Opera* film before 1933,
had sung Brecht–Eisler songs to the troops in Spain, been
interned by the French, then handed over to the Gestapo and
wounded in the bombing of Berlin. Since returning to the
German stage Busch had tended to specialise in cunning or
lovable rogues: Mephisto and Iago for the Deutsches Theater,
Azdak and the Cook (in *Mother Courage*) for Brecht. A much
less intellectual actor than Laughton, he found it even more
difficult to alienate the audience's sympathies at the end of the
play; and when Erich Engel took over the production after
Brecht's death he was allowed to present the handing-over of

the *Discorsi* as a piece of justified foxiness which made his recantation ultimately forgiveable. Brecht himself had underlined two points in connection with this production: the first, his view that the recantation was an absolute crime (see p. 205), the second, that Galileo's line in scene 9 'My object is not to establish that I was right but to find out if I am' is the most important sentence in the play. Others have stressed that the new version followed the manufacture and testing of the hydrogen bomb, so that the social responsibility of the scientist became a particularly topical theme. It is difficult however to see this play as a member of an East European audience without feeling that it is above all about scientific enquiry and the human reason. For the parallels are too clear: the Catholic Church is the Communist Party, Aristotle is Marxism–Leninism with its incontrovertible scriptures, the late 'reactionary' pope is Joseph Stalin, the Inquisition the KGB. Obviously Brecht did not write it to mean this, and if he had seen how the local context prompted this interpretation he might have been less keen for the production to go on. But as things turned out it proved to be among the most successful of all his plays in the Communist world.

*   *   *

In our view *Galileo* is Brecht's greatest play, and it is worth tracing its long and involved history in order to understand why. Not just one, but three crucial moments of our recent history helped to give it its multiple relevance to our time: Hitler's triumphs in 1938, the dropping of the first nuclear bomb in 1945, the death of Stalin in 1953. Each found Brecht writing or rewriting his play. And on each occasion the conditions of work were different: thus it was first written in his measured, stylish yet utterly down-to-earth German, then re-thought in English for Anglo-Saxon tongues and ears, then put back into German so as to combine the strengths of both. At none of these three stages was its form in any way mannered or gimmicky: sprawl as it might, particularly in the two German versions, it was outwardly a straightforward chronicle of seventeenth-century intellectual history, sticking surprisingly closely to the known facts. This was not 'opportunist' as Brecht at one moment termed it, even if it did represent a reaction against the conventionally realistic small-scale forms which he had used in 1937. Undoubtedly however his new approach made for accessibility, and as a result almost any competent and unpretentious production of the play will grab the audience's attention and get the meaning across.

What is that meaning? In fact there are several that can be read into the play, nor is this surprising when you think that Brecht's active concern with it covered nearly twenty years. So the problem for the modern director is to sift out those that matter from those that don't. First of all, this is not only a hymn to reason, but one that centres specifically on the need to be sceptical, to doubt. The theme is one that recurs more briefly in others of Brecht's writings of the later 1930s – for instance the poems 'The Doubter' and 'In Praise of Doubt' and the 'On Doubt' section of the as yet untranslated *Me-Ti* – and it very clearly conflicts with the kind of 'positive' thinking called for by both Nazis and the more rigid-minded of the Communists, which must not be critical ('negative') but optimistic. This notion of Brecht's that doubt and even self-doubt can be highly productive – that 'disbelief can move mountains', as he later put it in the *Short Organum* – is deeply engrained in the play; and although it ties in with his doctrine of 'alienation' or the need to take nothing for granted it also surely represents a reaction against the orthodox Socialist Realist view. How far it can be attributed to the historical Galileo is another matter. As Eric Bentley and, more recently, Paul Feierabend have pointed out, Galileo's reliance on the evidence of his senses was largely limited to the observations which he made with the telescope; elsewhere he was more speculative and less rational than Brecht suggests. What is true however is the conflict between authority and free scientific enquiry, both on the institutional level and within Galileo's own character (for he was indeed a believing Catholic). If anything, the former's position is presented too reasonably, both Barberini and the Inquisitor having in fact behaved much worse than Brecht let them do.

Brecht all along was writing about attitudes which he could

understand and even sympathise with; it is a play that contains very little element of caricature. This does not turn his Galileo into the self-portrait it is sometimes alleged to be, particularly by those who wish to present Brecht as a 'survivor' – as if surviving was not a very reputable thing for him to have done. Nor does it bear out Isaac Deutscher's interpretation of the first version as an apologia for those who, like Brecht himself, supported Stalin whilst disliking many aspects of his regime. Not that such autobiographical considerations – which can of course be clamped on to almost any play – are much help to the director, who has first and foremost to take the work at its face value. What matters here is the overlaying of the original message, about the need at all costs to establish and communicate the truth in defiance of authority, by Brecht's growing recognition of the losses that this may involve: for instance, the creation of such a cleft between the intellectual and the average man that the former eventually comes to overlook the social consequences of his research. The intertwining of these two contradictory morals has presented problems to actor and director alike, and of course it devalues the original happy ending. None the less it represents a considerable enrichment both of the Galileo figure and of the story; while taking away nothing from the vividness with which the scientific attitude is depicted, it cuts down the improbabilities and brings the whole thing closer to the uneasy compromises of real life. The problem in production, then, is how to compress the play into a length appropriate to its audience without losing essential elements of so carefully thought-out a mixture. As a reading text it has a balance which needs also to be achieved under the very different conditions of the stage.

By turning it back, finally, into something of a meditation on the notion of a 'new time', Brecht re-emphasised another general theme of particular significance to himself. Between 1929 and 1933 (and even, less pardonably, for two or three years afterwards) the German Communists thought that the Revolution was round the corner, and men like Brecht were stimulated much as he describes in the Foreword on p. 189. At the end of the 1930s, however, when he wrote the poem 'To

Those Born Later' (*Poems 1913–1956*, pp. 318–320), their goal

> Lay far in the distance
> It was clearly visible, though I myself
> Was hardly likely to reach it.

'Terrible is the disappointment', says the Foreword, when the new time fails to arrive and the old times prove stronger than anyone thought. For what had actually arrived was the 'dark times' of the first line of 'To Those Born Later', and with this the whole concept of 'old' and 'new' got confused. 'So the Old strode in disguised as the New', says the prose poem 'Parade of the Old New' which he wrote at the time of the first version as one of five 'Visions' foreshadowing the coming war. The temptation was to look nostalgically backwards, as the end of the Foreword suggests:

> Is that why I occupy myself with that epoch of the flowering of the arts and sciences three hundred years ago? I hope not.

And in this hope he was determined to hold on to his old belief in the New, writing for instance to Karin Michaelis in March 1942, when the war was still going Hitler's way, that

> the time we live in is an excellent time for fighters. Was there ever a time when Reason had such a chance?

What is significant in the final version is not just that it reinstates and even extends Galileo's opening 'aria' of 1938 on the new age – that Elizabethan-Jacobean age which always fascinated Brecht, not least because of Germany's failure to benefit from it. The really crucial remark, rather, comes in the final summing up of the same idea, which differs subtly from one version to another. 'Reason', says Galileo in the first version, 'is not coming to an end but beginning.

> And I still believe that this is a new age. It may look like a blood-stained old harridan, but if so that must be the way new ages look.'

In the American version, which omits the reference to Reason, Andrea asks Galileo outright if he doesn't now think that this 'new age' was an illusion, and is again given the same answer. In the third version, far more tellingly, he gets the almost indifferent response 'Doch' – 'On the contrary', almost implying 'despite all' – followed by a quick change of subject. And it is this one word, with all its overtones from the history of Brecht's own time – at once so new and so dark – that wryly wraps up the whole optimistic tragedy, pinning the beginning and the end together with a single jab.

That Hitler meant war was clear to Brecht by the beginning of 1937. During the previous November the German and Italian fascist regimes had banded together to form the 'Rome–Berlin axis'; Franco, whose rebellious armies were on the outskirts of Madrid, was recognised by them as the legitimate ruler of Spain; an anti-Comintern alliance was forged between Japan, then on the point of invading China, and the Germans. Hitler, who had already got away with the re-militarisation of the Rhineland in defiance of the Versailles Treaty, henceforward had no reason to moderate his aggressive aims. As Brecht put in one of the 'German War Primer' series of 'Svendborg Poems' which he wrote on Fünen Island less than fifty miles across the Baltic from Germany:

> ON THE CALENDAR THE DAY IS NOT YET SHOWN
> Every month, every day
> Lies open still. One of these days
> Is going to be marked with a cross.

For him it was the start of 'the dark times': a phrase that from now on permeates his poetry. Austria fell in March 1938, the German-speaking areas of Czechoslovakia that September, Prague and the remainder of Czechoslovakia in March 1939, Memel in Lithuania the same month, Madrid and the Spanish Republic with it. Then Hitler offered Denmark a non-aggression pact.

In April 1939, with Fascist Italy in its turn starting to invade Albania, Brecht took advantage of a lecture invitation to move to Sweden, where he was lent a sculptress's house on the island of Lidingö outside Stockholm. From now on he and his immediate entourage were even more isolated than they had been in Denmark; while their object was no longer to await the collapse of the Nazis but to move on to the United States, where Piscator, Fritz Lang and Ferdinand Reyher had already begun working on their behalf. This isolation was also in part political, starting back in 1937 when Brecht largely gave up writing those committed plays and poems which had reflected the day-to-day Communist Party line. Three things then combined to give him a much more sceptical attitude towards the Soviet Union and Stalin's leadership. The first and most painful was the purges of 1936–39; the second, unpleasantly interwoven with the purges, was the imposition of the Socialist Realist aesthetic preached by his old adversary Georg Lukács, which forbade any kind of 'formalism' in the arts; this became a serious factor from 1937 on. Finally there was the switch in foreign policy which led to the Soviet–Nazi pact and the partition of Poland. The Soviet Union, noted Brecht at the time, had thereby saved itself, 'but at the cost of leaving the workers of the world without slogans, hopes or support'.

The day marked with a cross proved to be 1 September 1939, when Brecht somewhat uncharacteristically attended a lunch in honour of Thomas Mann at Stockholm Town Hall. That day the Soviet–Nazi pact was announced, and the Nazis invaded Poland; forty-eight hours later Britain and France declared war on Germany. At first Brecht carried on working at his old project *Love is the Goods*, which he had taken up before leaving Denmark and renamed *The Good Person of Szechwan*; he had also brought with him the unfinished Julius Caesar novel and *The Messingkauf Dialogues*, a by-product of the revision of *Galileo*. But within ten days he found work grinding to a halt. The Szechwan play was laid aside; three diary entries comment disillusionedly on the 'singularly Napoleonic' Russian invasion of Eastern Poland, with its 'usurpation of all the Fascist hypocrisy about "blood brotherhood" '; then for nearly seven weeks, from 21 September to 7 November, the diary too goes blank.

During this interval, and in clear reaction to events, Brecht wrote his great play about a war which would range devastatingly across great tracts of Europe, creating heroes and profiteers, imposing order and ideologies, and leaving the self-sentimentalising 'little people' – particularly of Germany – as blindly unaware as they were at its start.

*   *   *

Mother Courage was written under pressure. In the words of a later note to Scandinavian audiences,

> As I wrote I imagined that the playwright's warning voice would be heard from the stages of various great cities, proclaiming that he who would sup with the devil must have a long spoon. This may have been naïve of me, but I do not consider being naïve a disgrace. Such productions never materialised. Writers cannot write as rapidly as governments can make war, because writing demands hard thought.

And the effort to speak out quickly made it one of the most spontaneous and, despite its length, most concentrated of all Brecht's plays. It bears virtually no trace of any preliminary work or preparatory reading; there is none of the major rewriting that characterises so many of the other plays; there is for once no mention of any collaborator, nor any element of borrowing or adaptation; there are just two original type-scripts, the one a straightforward revise of the other. As a feat of deeply felt anticipation it is amazing. Though there is nothing to bear out Brecht's claim (p. 321) that the play was written in 1938 or (as the note to the 1949 edition had it) 'before the outbreak of the Second World War' it undoubtedly dates from well before the start of any major fighting. This was still the period of 'We'll hang out the washing on the Siegfried Line', of the phoney war, what Brecht termed 'the war that isn't waged'. At that time some kind of peace seemed quite possible, whether as a return to the prewar policy of appeasement or by means of an appeal to the German people over the heads of their government, as wishfully proposed by the Communists. Few foresaw the mass bombings, the deportations, the torture of resistants, the extermination of the Jews; those vast tragedies which any modern audience tends to assume as the understood background to Brecht's 'chronicle play'.

Where did his vision come from? It is rooted, certainly, in his particular feeling for the seventeenth century, the period in which he had already set *The Life of Galileo* with its proclamation of faith in a 'new age' (even if that age might, in the words of its Danish version, look like 'a blood-stained old harridan'). That last leap forward of the Renaissance – one of whose forms, the Shakespearean History, he adopted for the play – failed in his view to make a modern nation of Germany because of the catastrophic effects of the Thirty Years War, which thus became the natural analogy for his pessimistic warnings. The obvious dramatic precedent here was Schiller's *Wallenstein's Camp* with its picture of a mongrel seventeenth-century army milling round the canteen tents; and indeed there are two engravings showing a camp and Wallenstein's siege of Stralsund in one of the earliest scripts. Stylistically however, and to some extent structurally too, Brecht's example seems to have been the earlier German writer Grimmelshausen, who himself served in the Thirty Years War before publishing his rambling picaresque novel *Simplicissimus* in 1669. From a lesser offshoot of that wartime saga, published separately as *Die Landestörzerin Courasche*, came the name of the play and of its central figure, though in fact Grimmelshausen's Amazonian adventuress sprang from a higher social class than Brecht's canteen woman and enjoyed a career closer to that of Yvette. 'A horrific picture of war', the critic Bernhard Diebold termed it, 'written about with deliberate detachment and seen from *below*: a frog's-eye view.' The Swedish actress Naima Wifstrand, whom Brecht wanted to play the leading part, also introduced him to the figure of Lotta Svård, a canteen woman in Johan Ludvig Runeberg's early nineteenth-century ballads about the Russian–Swedish war. But she, very unlike Brecht's character, was 'a pearl on the pathway of war', always up with the troops. 'And the dear young soldiers' heroic mood / she loved in its full display.' (Thus G. B. Shaw's translation.)

Brueghel, of whom Brecht had two books of reproductions, may have contributed something; his *Dulle Griet* is gummed into another script. Peter Weiss in his *Ästhetik des Widerstandes* describes Brecht speaking of Franco's victory in summer 1939 and turning to this figure whose 'devastated world' was part of what was starting to take place:

the Fury defending her pathetic household goods with the sword. The world at the end of its tether. Little cruelty, much hypersensitivity.

Callot too is visually relevant, with his *Misères de la Guerre*, even though Brecht nowhere mentions them.

The character of Brecht's Mother Courage, however, like her way of speaking, comes primarily from that other great war novelist Jaroslav Hašek; indeed Brecht saw his own *Schweyk* play, when he came to write it four years later, as a 'companion play'. Moreover there were also other significant links within Brecht's own work. Thus in one sense Mother Courage, battling to save her children, can be compared and contrasted with his earlier Señora Carrar, whom Naima Wifstrand had translated into Swedish and acted. In another she is much closer to the Widow Begbick, the tough itinerant hostess of *Man equals Man* and *Rise and Fall of the City of Mahagonny*, two roles already associated with Helene Weigel. Her language looks forward to the consciously Schweik-like dialogue of *Puntila* and the *Conversations Between Exiles*. And the whole inverted morality of the play, with its suggestion that the conventional virtues sometimes have the opposite effect from what moralists imagine, is close to that of *The Seven Deadly Sins* and *The Threepenny Opera*. This perhaps is why Brecht could think of including 'Surabaya-Johnny' as well as the 'Solomon Song'.

*   *   *

Quickly as the play was written, in Brecht's view it came too late to serve as the intended warning. 'The great bandit [i.e. Hitler] got his hooks on the theatres much too soon.' His immediate hope had been that it could be staged in Stockholm with Wifstrand as Courage and Helene Weigel in the nonspeaking part of Kattrin, who is supposed to have been made dumb so that Weigel could play her. That winter, while Russia invaded Finland, Weigel gave some classes in Wifstrand's acting school, for which Brecht wrote his Shakespearean *Practice Scenes for Actors*; meanwhile Brecht, on a commission from Stockholm Radio, wrote *The Trial of Lucullus* for the composer Hilding Rosenberg to set. Given the threat represented by the Nazis, however, neither work was performed in Sweden; and in April the police searched the Lidingö house, the German forces moved into Denmark and Norway, and Brecht thought it wise to move on. The plan for a *Mother Courage* production was then resumed in Finland, where the Brechts lived for a further year before the last of the party's American visas came through. The aim there was to secure a production in the Helsinki Swedish-language theatre during the winter of 1940–41. To this end Brecht worked on the songs with the Finnish composer Simon Parmet, who appears to have dropped out for fear of echoing Weill too closely. Once again, however, the reason for the play's rejection was evidently the increasing Nazi pressure, and that January Brecht listed it as one of his six unstaged plays 'which cannot at present be performed'.

In German-speaking Switzerland the Zurich Schauspielhaus was less inhibited. Cut off from the dramatist himself by the war, this predominantly German company contained a high proportion of anti-Nazi actors of whom some, like Leonard Steckel and the director Leopold Lindtberg, had worked in Berlin with Piscator, while Wolfgang Langhoff of the Rhineland Agitprop Truppe im Westen had subsequently been in a concentration camp. Under the sympathetic management of Ferdinand Rieser and Oskar Wälterlin they had given the premières of a number of plays unacceptable in Nazi Germany, notably Ferdinand Bruckner's *Die Rassen* and Friedrich Wolf's *Professor Mamlock* (both about anti-Semitism) as well as others by Kaiser, Horváth, Zuckmayer and such Anglo-American authors as Wilder, O'Neill, Priestley and Shaw. On 19 April 1941, a month before the Brechts left Helsinki on their long trip to California, the company now gave the première of *Mother Courage* before a predominantly Swiss and German émigré audience, among those who saw the production being Thornton Wilder.

This was one of the great theatrical events of the Second World War, and the play itself made a great impact, thanks above all to the performance of Therese Giehse (who oddly enough was a British subject) in the title part and to the setting devised by Teo Otto, who had worked with Brecht before 1933. Lindtberg directed, and the Swiss composer Paul Burkhard wrote a new score. Langhoff and the Austrian Karl Paryla played the two sons, Wolfgang Heinz the Cook. Meanwhile Sigfrit Steiner, the Chaplain of this production, was staging the far more directly political *Mother* for the first time in Switzerland with a cast of amateurs. And yet there were only ten performances, and Brecht, appreciative as he was, felt that to some extent his intentions had been traduced. Thus the *Basler Nachrichten* saw Courage as a model example of how to get through a terrible time in the face of human crudeness, while Elisabeth Thommen in the Basel *National-Zeitung* wrote that 'all women should be grateful to Bert Brecht for his portrayal of this strong female character'. It was only Brecht himself whose notes (p. 271) referred to the figure of Niobe, daughter of Tantalus, as the classic example of maternal grief. But even Bernhard Diebold, who had been one of the outstanding German theatre critics before 1933, wrote in *Die Tat* that this Courage, far from being primarily a 'hyaena of the battlefield' (as the Chaplain calls her), made her commercial toughness 'almost too subsidiary' to the strength of her maternal feelings; while as for Lindtberg's direction, it 'either failed to take enough account of the crude earthiness of the period and Brecht's own malicious sarcasm, or else it deliberately softened them'.

As it turned out, this was the play's sole wartime production. It was not one of those works which Brecht expected to see put on in the USA, nor did he make any of the efforts which he and his friends there devoted to *Fear and Misery of the Third Reich*, *Galileo* and *The Good Person of Szechwan*, let alone the plays which he wrote after arriving. Early in 1941, at the latest, the poet H. R. Hays had made a translation from a copy lent him by Hanns Eisler (to whom Brecht sent one of the first scripts), but although this appeared in *New Directions* the same year there never seems to have been any move to stage it, not even as a college production. Almost it might be said that Brecht had decided to shelve *Mother Courage* as he shelved so many of his works, putting them out of his mind for years at a time. In 1943, however, he met the composer Paul Dessau, whose musical background was in some ways comparable to those of Weill and Eisler, and who had written some music for the original Paris production of *Fear and Misery of the Third Reich* in which Weigel had acted. At a Brecht recital given at the New School in New York that March, Dessau sang one of his Brecht settings with such verve that Brecht encouraged him to write more, first inviting him to come and work in California, then at some undefined date asking him to write new settings for the *Mother Courage* songs. These were completed by 1946, when the Zurich company used them for its guest performances in Vienna, and they became the standard music for the play. For the moment it seems that they, like the play itself, were really being reserved for the day when Brecht should return to the German-language theatre and stage the kind of performance which he and Helene Weigel had in mind.

Though there is evidence in the FBI files of his intention to return from as early as 1944, it seems to have been at least a year after the ending of the war that he began to make serious plans. Then he wrote to his old collaborator the designer Caspar Neher (who had remained in Germany) to announce his conviction that 'we shall build up a theatre once more', followed by his decision to come to Zurich during 1947 and prepare his return to Berlin, where he had been offered the use of the Theater am Schiffbauerdamm 'for certain things'. This theatre, the original home of *The Threepenny Opera*, had now been made an offshoot of the revived Volksbühne, the great popular theatre organisation which the Nazis had suppressed thirteen years earlier. The Deutsches Theater, where Brecht had worked for Max Reinhardt on first coming to Berlin, had been put under Langhoff of the Zurich *Mother Courage*; both theatres were in the Soviet sector.

Early in 1947 Brecht and Piscator started corresponding with a view to a joint descent on that city. They were in some measure encouraged in this by Friedrich Wolf, who had returned with the Red Army and now hoped to draw Piscator back to the Volksbühne. Before Piscator made up his mind, however, the division of Berlin had occurred, and in the event he remained in New York for another three years. Meanwhile the Brechts carried out their plan of going to Zurich, and immediately on arrival began discussing plans with Neher. Within a month the two friends in collaboration had completed the adaptation of *Antigone* which they proposed to stage at the small theatre in Chur managed by Klemperer's former dramaturg Hans Curjel. The object of this brilliant but short-lived exercise, so Brecht noted in his diary on 16 December, was 'to do preparatory work with Weigel and Cas [Neher] on *Courage* for Berlin'. For Weigel had not acted on the professional stage for fifteen years, and the Schauspielhaus apparently had nothing for her.

The *Antigone* production took place on 15 February 1948, five days after Brecht's fiftieth birthday. The same occasion was celebrated in Berlin by a programme organised by Langhoff, who had staged a short version of *Fear and Misery of the Third Reich* only a fortnight or so earlier. Thereafter it was agreed that the Zurich Schauspielhaus would give the first production of *Puntila*, the fourth and last of their Brecht premières and the first to be staged with Brecht's own participation (as unofficial director); this took place in June, with Leonard Steckel acting the name part. After that the Brechts' attention was again focused on Berlin (Salzburg being an alternative bet), and the main problem was how to get there. Eventually the necessary Austrian and Czech permits came through, allowing them to travel to the Soviet Zone of Germany in late October (the US authorities having refused them leave to cross Bavaria). Straightaway Brecht began holding auditions at Langhoff's theatre, then on 8 November his co-director Erich Engel arrived from Munich and two months of intensive rehearsal began. Brecht's idea at this time was to set up his own ensemble under the wing of the Deutsches Theater and invite prominent outsiders to act with it; he had in mind figures like Fritz Kortner and Peter Lorre as well as Therese Giehse from Zurich.

In mid-December he discussed this scheme with Langhoff, seemingly still in the expectation of being able to use the Theater am Schiffbauerdamm. Then three weeks later he was hauled out of a rehearsal to attend a formal meeting with the party authorities, the East Berlin mayor Friedrich Ebert (son of the former Social-Democratic President), Langhoff and the Schiffbauerdamm *Intendant* Fritz Wisten. Here he was told that the Schiffbauerdamm was needed for the Volksbühne; the mayor, who never addressed a word to him, spoke slightingly of half-baked schemes which might upset existing arrangements; and, in the words of the diary 'for the first time since coming here I felt the foetid breath of provincialism'.

Within a few days, however, everything fell into the background as the white half-curtain of the Deutsches Theater fluttered open on a brilliantly lit stage. The band struck up 'You captains, tell the drums to slacken', and the dusty, tattered family came rolling on with its cart. Suddenly, in this still devastated city hovering between peace and war, the world could see one of the unforgettable images of our time.

*   *   *

From that moment dates Brecht's postwar reputation as a great director, which for non-Germans has even overshadowed his reputation as a playwright. It was a formidable comeback planned from three overlapping aspects, and its triple success was stunning. First of all, here was a largely unknown German masterpiece, written in language of tremendous vitality and still with many shrewd things to say about war and people's reactions to it. Second was an outstanding acting performance from a virtually forgotten actress, whose striking voice and features have become almost inseparable from the Mother Courage figure; that night a legendary character, as well as a star, was born. Finally, embracing everything else, there was a new, outwardly subdued but inwardly authoritative spirit emanating from the whole production and from the new Berliner Ensemble which the Brechts went on to found upon it. The object of this entire operation was of course rather different from Brecht's original aim when he wrote the play. For he made it very clear in his notes and jottings that he wished not only to make his countrymen think about their blind involvement in Hitler's war but also to help rebuild their shattered culture and bridge the long gap back to the progressive ideas of the Weimar Republic, thereby bringing on a new generation of actors and directors who would not have been debased by too much experience of Nazi methods. Given that he meant to tackle these worthwhile tasks from within the Communist orbit, in his old spirit of sceptical allegiance, he had to establish his constructive intentions, which he set himself to do soon after his arrival by writing some slightly vapid political songs. At the same time he had to overcome or get round the obstacles to any kind of formal innovation embodied in the revived Socialist Realism now being preached by the Russians, the Party spokesman Fritz Erpenbeck and, once again, Georg Lukács. As he put it in the foreword to *Antigone*, 'it may not be easy to create progressive art in the period of reconstruction'. But nobody was better placed to do it than he.

The criticisms of the play which now came from both right and left arose from a feeling that Brecht, having created a great human character, had deliberately stunted her, thereby stifling much of the emotion natural both to himself as the creator and also to his audience. Some, like Friedrich Wolf in the dialogue printed on pp. 226–9 of *Brecht on Theatre*, felt that by the end of the play Courage should have seen the light – that is, the futility of war – thereby emerging as (in Communist aesthetic jargon) a 'positive' figure. Others, on both sides of the barriers, pointed to what they considered a theoretical inconsistency between Brecht's ideas of 'epic' or 'alienated' acting and the undoubted empathy experienced by audiences at emotional high spots like the death of Kattrin. This notion that Brecht, for purely intellectual reasons, was. denying certain powerful elements which he had (or should have) instinctively put into the original play, was reinforced, if not actually sparked off, by the textual changes which he confesses to on pp. 271–4 of his notes. Indeed to judge from some commentators' reactions one might imagine that he had rewritten the Zurich version as extensively as he did so many of his other plays. In fact, of course, only two of his four alterations are significant – the first, where Courage's salesmanship distracts her from her son's enlistment, and the second, which makes her less ready than before to give her goods for humanitarian ends – and even they would scarcely have been noticed if he had not drawn attention to them himself. What he worked much harder to correct was not only 'softness' in the actual play but those features of Lindtberg's production on which Diebold had commented nearly eight years earlier, along with a certain 'curious aura of harmlessness' which he found emanating from his own first Berlin rehearsals. This, with its smudging-over of all sense of background or development, he blamed on the bland conformism of the Nazi theatre.

But it is true that the point of the play had in some measure changed, and the audiences who saw it in Berlin and Munich (where he re-staged it with Giehse as Courage and a new cast), or during the Berliner Ensemble's various tours, were very different from that in wartime Zurich. For these people had been through a European war; they did not have to be warned about it; they were actually beginning to experience the consequences, including some which Brecht had not foretold. None the less he remained convinced that his countrymen were a long way from understanding how far they had contributed to the horror, the chaos and the suffering – their own included. Doubtful whether they had learnt anything, he was convinced that it would be misleading to make Courage finish up any less short-sighted than they. In fact the surprising thing, to anyone familiar with Brecht's restless revaluation of his own plays, is that he did not alter the text more. Perhaps the reason for this is that his chronic itch to revise could in this case be worked out on the (alas, unrealised) film version, whose making by the East German DEFA was decided as early as September 1949.

Initially the work on its script was done by Emil Hesse Burri, Brecht's old collaborator of the mid-1920s, who had been a scriptwriter in Munich under the Nazis; and the intention was that Engel should direct it. When Engel fell out some time during 1951 he was replaced by the forty-five-year-old Wolfgang Staudte, a former Piscator trainee whose DEFA film *Die Mörder sind unter uns* had been the first great postwar success. Though Brecht himself did not actually do any of the writing, he was in on the planning, and many of the changes were in line with his suggestions. The film, said his first notes for DEFA, 'must bring out even more clearly than the play how reality punishes [Mother Courage] for her failure to learn'. The treatment was simplified to distinguish her from the 'little people' and show her marked urge to go forward and profit from the war; later the 'little people' too were criticised as 'the worst of the lot. Why? The big shots plan it, and the little people carry it out'. Kattrin in turn was given a lover, a young miller whose vision of popular resistance to the rulers and their foreign mercenaries is echoed during the scene of her death, when the peasants in the besieged town take up improvised arms and drive out the attackers (now made Croats in order to seem more alien). This is clearly in accordance with the criticism made of the play by Wolf and others, who wanted a greater element of optimism at the end; though the old woman herself, her eyes lighting up 'with an expression of greed and desperate hope' as she hears the troops marching off, finishes up more incorrigible than ever. After Burri had completed this first script he and Brecht agreed to make the story relevant to the postwar occupation of Germany by stressing the contrast between the German protagonists (Eilif and Yvette were now to be Germans, like Courage and Kattrin) and their motley foreign invaders; there would be control barriers everywhere and a 'Babylonian' mixture of strange tongues. Evidence too would be given of persistent foreign attempts to recruit Germans (including the young miller) for continued wars. Brecht's feelings at this point are well summed up in the poem 'Germany 1952' which was worked into the final script, where a group of deserters led by the young miller throw down their

weapons in an abandoned house full of bourgeois comforts
and one of them sings:

> O Germany, so torn in pieces
> And never left alone!
> The cold and dark increases
> While each see to his own.
> Such lovely fields you'd have
> Such cities thronged and gay;
> If you'd but trust yourself
> All would be child's play.

But this film was never made. The trouble seems to have
been that DEFA, instead of setting out from the Brecht–Engel
production and the actors associated with it, wished to make a
grand international co-production with star appeal. Simone
Signoret was booked as Yvette, whose part was then dispro-
portionately inflated; the French actor Bernard Blier became
the Cook. Angelika Hurwicz, the unforgettable stage Kattrin,
was replaced by Sigrid Roth; difficulties were made over
Helene Weigel, who had to be cast as Courage on Brecht's
insistence. In many other ways, too, Brecht's vision and
Staudte's proved deeply incompatible. Staudte wanted to use
colour, Brecht to achieve 'daguerreotype-like' effects in black
and white; Staudte commissioned period costumes, Brecht
rejected them as too operatic; Staudte's French designer
provided the heavy baronial setting seen in the surviving stills
and located the camp scenes in a sandy waste, Brecht objected
that the Thirty Years War didn't take place in a desert.
Staudte's verdict was that Brecht was 'utterly hostile to the
cinema'. Shooting nevertheless began, apparently on the
assumption that Brecht would feel forced to accept designs
which had only been put before him at the very last moment.
He did not, and as a result the whole operation had to be called
off after about a fortnight's unhappy work. It was never
resumed, though plans for some kind of *Mother Courage* film
continued to be discussed, this time with Engel and Burri, right
up to Brecht's death in August 1956. The film which DEFA did
finally realise some four years later was made on an entirely

different basis, for it was a largely static film version, made in a studio and photographed in Cinemascope of the Berliner Ensemble stage production: a kind of Model-book in motion, preserving Brecht's original vision with minor changes. Its directors were Brecht's young assistants Manfred Wekwerth and Peter Palitzsch, who subsequently directed, respectively, the Berliner Ensemble itself and the Frankfurt city theatres.

* * *

It was one of Brecht's endless inconsistencies (or 'contradictions') that, while believing firmly in the need for change, he established certain standard productions which other directors of his plays were expected to study before deciding their own interpretations. *Mother Courage* was a prime candidate for this treatment, thanks on the one hand to its high reputation with other theatres throughout the globe and on the other to the critical disagreements which it provoked. The 'Mother Courage Model' therefore consists not only of the notes which we print on pp. 277–323 but of a series of carefully-keyed photographs of the Berliner Ensemble production which exists in a published version but was originally made as a much fuller and more detailed album for loan to prospective directors. Brecht's purpose here has often been regarded as absurdly rigid, and the Ensemble itself has been accused of putting Brecht's works into some kind of airless museum showcase. On the one hand there have been instances of lifeless copying or resentful friction whenever the standard model was imposed; on the other it has shocked more jealously 'original' producers to go as far as they can in some alternative, if not actually opposite, direction. Seldom has any director done what Brecht really had in mind: that is, gone through the 'model' to see exactly what problems Brecht was trying to solve in each detail of his production, and how he arrived at his answers, and then gone on to think out an approach of his own based on the same understanding of the play. So the use of Model-books has proved to be a somewhat two-edged device, hindering as much as helping the assimilation of this great play, particularly by non-German theatres.

Certainly *Mother Courage* has never become securely established in the English-speaking countries, where the size of the
cast and the length of the play present a more formidable initial
problem than they do in the German subsidised theatres.
Generally it has proved a box-office disaster, and the one
production to enjoy a long run – Richard Schechner's with the
Performance Group off-Broadway – seems to have done so
more because of its original treatment of the audience than by
its conception and performance of the text; it became a vivid,
sharply biting Courage experience, almost a happening. The
odd thing is that this overall failure in the professional theatre
has not impaired the play's critical and academic reputation,
nor even its attraction for amateurs, to whom of course a large
cast often seems an advantage. As a result *Mother Courage* is
still somehow lurking in the wings as an enormous challenge,
even something of a reproach to our finest directors and actors.
Why have they never been able to communicate its pessimism,
its savagery and its force? A large part of the reason surely lies
in the language, which in the original is unique, the invention
of a major poet who chose neither to imitate seventeenth-
century dialogue nor to reproduce modern everyday speech
but devised his own curt, sardonic lingo, full of elisions and
with few conjunctions, vividly conveying not only Courage's
own character but also the hard pressures of the war. This is
established in the very first speeches, and from then on it
becomes the principal dynamic force of what is otherwise a
stragglingly episodic play. Those directors who have enough
German to appreciate it have generally treated it as untransla-
table, thereby losing their main chance of holding the
audience's attention; the sense has been communicated at the
cost of Brecht's imaginative assault on the ear. Our translation
therefore sets out to tackle this key problem by using a
somewhat analogous artificial diction, based this time on those
north English cadences which can reflect a similarly dry,
gloomily humorous approach to great events. It could have
been done in other ways – by a Welsh or Irish writer perhaps,
or one versed in Lallans – but so far it has not. The aim must be
to find a language which will keep the play moving across

twelve years of history, a great slice of devastated Europe and, last but not least, three or four hours in the theatre.

Add this to the barriers sometimes presented by the 'Model', plus the widespread feeling among actors that performing Brecht demands outlandish technical methods, and there is some danger of *Mother Courage* appearing a horribly complicated play. You only have to read it to see that it is not. Even the changes which Brecht made to it are only designed to clarify and bring out more strongly what was already meant to be there; they were correctives, not major switches of direction. All this belongs in the background, to be digested and understood certainly, but not to obstruct the story of the play and the long chain of small, conflicting episodes which goes to make it up. The stage must be cleared, as Brecht cleared it in 1950 to tell German children 'The story of Mother Courage':

> There once was a mother
> Mother Courage they called her
> In the Thirty Years War
> She sold victuals to soldiers.
>
> The war did not scare her
> From making her cut
> Her three children went with her
> And so got their bit.
>
> Her first son died a hero
> The second an honest lad
> A bullet found her daughter
> Whose heart was too good.

In the end it has to be as simple as that.

THE EDITORS

Chronology

1898 10 February: Eugen Berthold Friedrich Brecht born in Augsburg.

1917 Autumn: Bolshevik revolution in Russia. Brecht to Munich university.

1918 Work on his first play, *Baal*. In Augsburg Brecht is called up as medical orderly till end of year. Elected to Soldiers' Council as Independent Socialist (USPD) following Armistice.

1919 Brecht writing second play, *Drums in the Night*. In January Spartacist Rising in Berlin. Rosa Luxemburg murdered. April–May: Bavarian Soviet. Summer: Weimar Republic constituted. Birth of Brecht's illegitimate son Frank Banholzer.

1920 May: death of Brecht's mother in Augsburg.

1921 Brecht leaves university without a degree. Reads Rimbaud.

1922 A turning point in the arts. End of utopian Expressionism; new concern with technology. Brecht's first visit to Berlin, seeing theatres, actors, publishers and cabaret. He writes 'Of Poor BB' on the return journey. Autumn: becomes a dramaturg in Munich. Première of *Drums in the Night*, a prize-winning national success. Marries Marianne Zoff, an opera singer.

1923 Galloping German inflation stabilised by November currency reform. In Munich Hitler's new National Socialist party stages unsuccessful 'beer-cellar putsch'.

1924 'Neue Sachlichkeit' exhibition at Mannheim gives its name to the new sobriety in the arts. Brecht to Berlin as assistant in Max Reinhardt's Deutsches Theater.

1925 Field-Marshal von Hindenburg becomes President. Elisabeth Hauptmann starts working with Brecht. Two seminal films: Chaplin's *The Gold Rush* and Eisenstein's *The Battleship Potemkin*. Brecht writes birthday tribute to Bernard Shaw.

1926 Première of *Man equals Man* in Darmstadt. Now a freelance; starts reading Marx. His first book of poems, the *Devotions*, includes the 'Legend of the Dead Soldier'.

1927 After reviewing the poems and a broadcast of *Man equals Man*, Kurt Weill approaches Brecht for a libretto. Result is the text of *Mahagonny*, whose 'Songspiel' version is performed in a boxing-ring at Hindemith's Baden-Baden music festival in July. In Berlin he helps adapt *The Good Soldier Schweik* for Piscator's high-tech theatre.

1928 August 31: première of *The Threepenny Opera* by Brecht and Weill, based on Gay's *The Beggar's Opera*.

1929 Start of Stalin's policy of 'socialism in one country'. Divorced from Marianne, Brecht now marries the actress Helene Weigel. May 1: Berlin police break up banned KPD demonstration, witnessed by Brecht. Summer: Brecht writes two didactic music-theatre pieces with Weill and Hindemith, and neglects *The Threepenny Opera*'s successor *Happy End*, which is a flop. From now on he stands by the KPD. Autumn: Wall Street crash initiates world economic crisis. Cuts in German arts budgets combine with renewed nationalism to create cultural backlash.

1930 Nazi election successes; end of parliamentary government. Unemployed 3 million in first quarter, about 5 million at end of the year. March: première of the full-scale *Mahagonny* opera in Leipzig Opera House.

1931 German crisis intensifies. Aggressive KPD arts policy: agitprop theatre, marching songs, political photomontage. In Moscow the Comintern forms international associations of revolutionary artists, writers, musicians and theatre people.

1932 Première of Brecht's agitational play *The Mother* (after Gorky) with Eisler's music. *Kuhle Wampe*, his militant film with Eisler, is held up by the censors. He meets Sergei Tretiakov at the film's première in Moscow. Summer: the Nationalist Von Papen is made Chancellor. He denounces 'cultural bolshevism', and deposes the SPD-led Prussian administration.

1933   January 30: Hitler becomes Chancellor with Papen as his deputy. The Prussian Academy is purged; Goering becomes Prussian premier. A month later the Reichstag is burnt down, the KPD outlawed. The Brechts instantly leave via Prague; at first homeless. Eisler is in Vienna, Weill in Paris, where he agrees to compose a ballet with song texts by Brecht: *The Seven Deadly Sins*, premièred there in June. In Germany Nazi students burn books; all parties and trade unions banned; first measures against the Jews. Summer: Brecht in Paris works on anti-Nazi publications. With the advance on his *Threepenny Novel*, he buys a house on Fyn island, Denmark, overlooking the Svendborg Sound, where the family will spend the next six years. Margarete Steffin, a young Berlin Communist, goes with them. Autumn: he meets the Danish Communist actress Ruth Berlau, a doctor's wife.

1934   Spring: suppression of Socialist rising in Austria. Eisler stays with Brecht to work on *Round Heads and Pointed Heads* songs. Summer: Brecht misses the first Congress of Soviet Writers, chaired by Zhdanov along the twin lines of Socialist Realism and Revolutionary Romanticism. October: in London with Eisler.

1935   Italy invades Ethiopia. Hitler enacts the Nuremberg Laws against the Jews. March–May: Brecht to Moscow for international theatre conference. Meets Kun and Knorin of Comintern Executive. Eisler becomes president of the International Music Bureau. At the 7th Comintern Congress Dimitrov calls for all antifascist parties to unite in Popular Fronts against Hitler and Mussolini. Autumn: Brecht with Eisler to New York for Theatre Union production of *The Mother*.

1936   Soviet purges lead to arrests of many Germans in USSR, most of them Communists; among them Carola Neher and Ernst Ottwalt, friends of the Brechts. International cultural associations closed down. Official campaign against 'Formalism' in the arts. Mikhail Koltsov, the Soviet journalist, founds *Das Wort* as a literary magazine for the German emigration, with Brecht as one of the editors. Popular Front government in Spain resisted by Franco and other generals, with the support of the Catholic hierarchy. The Spanish Civil War becomes a great international cause.

1937 Summer: in Munich, opening of Hitler's House of German Art. Formally, the officially approved art is closely akin to Russian 'Socialist Realism'. In Russia Tretiakov is arrested as a Japanese spy, interned in Siberia and later shot. October: Brecht's Spanish war play *Señora Carrar's Rifles*, with Weigel in the title part, is performed in Paris, and taken up by antifascist and amateur groups in many countries.

1938 January: in Moscow Meyerhold's avant-garde theatre is abolished. March: Hitler takes over Austria without resistance. It becomes part of Germany. May 21: première of scenes from Brecht's *Fear and Misery of the Third Reich* in a Paris hall. Autumn: Munich Agreement, by which Britain, France and Italy force Czechoslovakia to accept Hitler's demands. In Denmark Brecht writes the first version of *Galileo*. In Moscow Koltsov disappears into arrest after returning from Spain.

1939 March: Hitler takes over Prague and the rest of the Czech territories. Madrid surrenders to Franco; end of the Civil War. Eisler has emigrated to New York. April: the Brechts leave Denmark for Stockholm. Steffin follows. May: Brecht's *Svendborg Poems* published. His father dies in Germany. Denmark accepts Hitler's offer of a Non-Aggression Pact. August 23: Ribbentrop and Molotov agree Nazi-Soviet Pact. September 1: Hitler attacks Poland and unleashes Second World War. Stalin occupies Eastern Poland, completing its defeat in less than three weeks. All quiet in the West. Autumn: Brecht writes *Mother Courage* and the radio play *Lucullus* in little over a month. November: Stalin attacks Finland.

1940 Spring: Hitler invades Norway and Denmark. In May his armies enter France through the Low Countries, taking

Paris in mid-June. The Brechts hurriedly leave for Finland, taking Steffin with them. They aim to travel on to the US, where Brecht has been offered a teaching job in New York at the New School. July: the Finnish writer Hella Wuolijoki invites them to her country estate, which becomes the setting for *Puntila*, the comedy she and Brecht write there.

1941   April: première of *Mother Courage* in Zurich. May: he gets US visas for the family and a tourist visa for Steffin. On 15th they leave with Berlau for Moscow to take the Trans-Siberian railway. In Vladivostok they catch a Swedish ship for Los Angeles, leaving just nine days before Hitler, in alliance with Finland, invades Russia. June: Steffin dies of tuberculosis in a Moscow sanatorium, where they have had to leave her. July: once in Los Angeles, the Brechts decide to stay there in the hope of film work. December: Japanese attack on Pearl Harbor brings the US into the war. The Brechts become 'enemy aliens'.

1942   Spring: Eisler arrives from New York. He and Brecht work on Fritz Lang's film *Hangmen Also Die*. Brecht and Feuchtwanger write *The Visions of Simone Machard*; sell rights to MGM. Ruth Berlau takes a job in New York. August: the Brechts rent a pleasant house and garden in Santa Monica. Autumn: Germans defeated at Stalingrad and El Alamein. Turning point of World War 2.

1943   Spring: Brecht goes to New York for three months – first visit since 1935 – where he stays with Berlau till May and plans a wartime *Schweik* play with Kurt Weill. In Zurich the Schauspielhaus gives world premières of *The Good Person of Szechwan* and *Galileo*. November: his first son Frank is killed on the Russian front.

1944   British and Americans land in Normandy (June); Germans driven out of France by end of the year. Heavy bombing of Berlin, Hamburg and other German cities. Brecht works on *The Caucasian Chalk Circle*, and with H. R. Hays on *The Duchess of Malfi*. His son by Ruth Berlau, born prematurely in Los Angeles, lives only a few days. Start of collaboration with Charles Laughton on English version of *Galileo*.

1945 Spring: Russians enter Vienna and Berlin. German surrender; suicide of Hitler; Allied military occupation of Germany and Austria, each divided into four Zones. Roosevelt dies; succeeded by Truman; Churchill loses elections to Attlee. June: *Private Life of the Master Race* (wartime adaptation of *Fear and Misery* scenes) staged in New York. August: US drops atomic bombs on Hiroshima and Nagasaki. Japan surrenders. Brecht and Laughton start discussing production of *Galileo*.

1946 Ruth Berlau taken to hospital after a violent breakdown in New York. Work with Auden on *Duchess of Malfi*, which is finally staged there in mid-October – not well received. The Brechts have decided to return to Germany. Summer: A. A. Zhdanov reaffirms Stalinist art policies: Formalism bad, Socialist Realism good. Eisler's brother Gerhart summoned to appear before the House Un-American Activities Committee. November: the Republicans win a majority in the House. Cold War impending.

1947 FBI file on Brecht reopened in May. Rehearsals begin for Los Angeles production of *Galileo*, with Laughton in the title part and music by Eisler; opens July 31. Brecht's HUAC hearing October 30; a day later he leaves the US for Zurich.

1948 In Zurich renewed collaboration with Caspar Neher. Production of *Antigone* in Chur, with Weigel. Berlau arrives from US. Summer: *Puntila* world première at Zurich Schauspielhaus. Brecht completes his chief theoretical work, the *Short Organum*. Travel plans hampered because he is not allowed to enter US Zone (which includes Augsburg and Munich). Russians block all land access to Berlin. October: the Brechts to Berlin via Prague, to establish contacts and prepare production of *Mother Courage*.

1949 January: success of *Mother Courage* leads to establishment of the Berliner Ensemble. Collapse of Berlin blockade in May followed by establishment of West and East German states. Eisler, Dessau and Elisabeth Hauptmann arrive from US and join the Ensemble.

1 Chronology

1950   Brecht gets Austrian nationality in connection with plan to involve him in Salzburg Festival. Long drawn-out scheme for *Mother Courage* film. Spring: he and Neher direct Lenz's *The Tutor* with the Ensemble. Autumn: he directs *Mother Courage* in Munich; at the end of the year *The Mother* with Weigel, Ernst Busch and the Ensemble.

1951   Selection of *A Hundred Poems* is published in East Berlin. Brecht beats off Stalinist campaign to stop production of Dessau's opera version of *Lucullus*.

1952   Summer: at Buckow, east of Berlin, Brecht starts planning a production of *Coriolanus* and discusses Eisler's project for a *Faust* opera.

1953   Spring: Stalin dies, aged 73. A 'Stanislavsky conference' in the East German Academy, to promote Socialist Realism in the theatre, is followed by meetings to discredit Eisler's libretto for the *Faust* opera. June: quickly suppressed rising against the East German government in Berlin and elsewhere. Brecht at Buckow notes that 'the whole of existence has been alienated' for him by this. Khrushchev becomes Stalin's successor.

1954   January: Brecht becomes an adviser to the new East German Ministry of Culture. March: the Ensemble at last gets its own theatre on the Schiffbauerdamm. July: its production of *Mother Courage* staged in Paris. December: Brecht awarded a Stalin Peace Prize by the USSR.

1955   August: shooting at last begins on *Mother Courage* film, but is broken off after ten days and the project abandoned. Brecht in poor health.

1956   Khrushchev denounces Stalin's dictatorial methods and abuses of power to the Twentieth Party Congress in Moscow. A copy of his speech reaches Brecht. May: Brecht in the Charité hospital to shake off influenza. August 14: he dies in the Charité of a heart infarct.

1957   *The Resistible Rise of Arturo Ui*, *The Visions of Simone Machard* and *Schweyk in the Second World War* produced for the first time in Stuttgart, Frankfurt and Warsaw respectively.

Life of Galileo

Play

Collaborator: M. STEFFIN

Translator: JOHN WILLETT

Characters

GALILEO GALILEI
ANDREA SARTI
MRS SARTI, *Galileo's housekeeper, Andrea's mother*
LUDOVICO MARSILI, *a rich young man*
THE PROCURATOR OF PADUA UNIVERSITY, *Mr Priuli*
SAGREDO, *Galileo's friend*
VIRGINIA, *Galileo's daughter*
FEDERZONI, *a lens-grinder, Galileo's assistant*
THE DOGE
SENATORS
COSIMO DE MEDICI, *Grand Duke of Florence*
THE COURT CHAMBERLAIN
THE THEOLOGIAN
THE PHILOSOPHER
THE MATHEMATICIAN
THE OLDER COURT LADY
THE YOUNGER COURT LADY
GRAND-DUCAL FOOTMAN
TWO NUNS
TWO SOLDIERS
THE OLD WOMAN
A FAT PRELATE
TWO SCHOLARS
TWO MONKS
TWO ASTRONOMERS
A VERY THIN MONK
THE VERY OLD CARDINAL
FATHER CHRISTOPHER CLAVIUS, *astonomer*
THE LITTLE MONK

THE CARDINAL INQUISITOR
CARDINAL BARBERINI, *subsequently Pope Urban VIII*
CARDINAL BELLARMIN
TWO CLERICAL SECRETARIES
TWO YOUNG LADIES
FILIPPO MUCIUS, *a scholar*
MR GAFFONE, *Rector of the University of Pisa*
THE BALLAD-SINGER
HIS WIFE
VANNI, *an ironfounder*
AN OFFICIAL
A HIGH OFFICIAL
AN INDIVIDUAL
A MONK
A PEASANT
A FRONTIER GUARD
A CLERK
Men, women, children

Galileo Galilei, a teacher of mathematics at Padua, sets out to prove Copernicus's new cosmogony

In the year sixteen hundred and nine
Science's light began to shine.
At Padua city in a modest house
Galileo Galilei set out to prove
The sun is still, the earth is on the move.

Galileo's rather wretched study in Padua. It is morning. A boy, Andrea, the housekeeper's son, brings in a glass of milk and a roll.

GALILEO *washing down to the waist, puffing and cheerful*: Put that milk on the table, and don't you shut any of those books.

ANDREA: Mother says we must pay the milkman. Or he'll start making a circle round our house, Mr Galilei.

GALILEO: Describing a circle, you mean, Andrea.

ANDREA: Whichever you like. If we don't pay the bill he'll start describing a circle round us, Mr Galilei.

GALILEO: Whereas when Mr Cambione the bailiff comes straight for us what sort of distance between two points is he going to pick?

ANDREA *grinning*: The shortest.

GALILEO: Right. I've got something for you. Look behind the star charts.

Andrea rummages behind the star charts and brings out a big wooden model of the Ptolemaic system.

ANDREA: What is it?

GALILEO: That's an armillary sphere. It's a contraption to

show how the planets move around the earth, according to our forefathers.

ANDREA: How?

GALILEO: Let's examine it. Start at the beginning. Description?

ANDREA: In the middle there's a small stone.

GALILEO: That's the earth.

ANDREA: Round it there are rings, one inside another.

GALILEO: How many?

ANDREA: Eight.

GALILEO: That's the crystal spheres.

ANDREA: Stuck to the rings are little balls.

GALILEO: The stars.

ANDREA: Then there are bands with words painted on them.

GALILEO: What sort of words?

ANDREA: Names of stars.

GALILEO: Such as . . .

ANDREA: The lowest ball is the moon, it says. Above that's the sun.

GALILEO: Now start the sun moving.

ANDREA *moves the rings*: That's great. But we're so shut in.

GALILEO *drying himself*: Yes, I felt that first time I saw one of those. We're not the only ones to feel it. *He tosses the towel to Andrea, for him to dry his back with.* Walls and spheres and immobility! For two thousand years people have believed that the sun and all the stars of heaven rotate around mankind. Pope, cardinals, princes, professors, captains, merchants, fishwives and schoolkids thought they were sitting motionless inside this crystal sphere. But now we are breaking out of it, Andrea, at full speed. Because the old days are over and this is a new time. For the last hundred years mankind has seemed to be expecting something.

Our cities are cramped, and so are men's minds. Superstition and the plague. But now the word is 'that's how things are, but they won't stay like that'. Because everything is in motion, my friend.

I like to think that it began with the ships. As far as men could remember they had always hugged the coast, then suddenly they abandoned the coast line and ventured out across the seas. On our old continent a rumour sprang up: there might be new ones. And since our ships began sailing to them the laughing continents have got the message: the great ocean they feared, is a little puddle. And a vast desire has sprung up to know the reasons for everything: why a stone falls when you let it go and why it rises when you toss it up. Each day something fresh is discovered. Men of a hundred, even, are getting the young people to bawl the latest example into their ear. There have been a lot of discoveries, but there is still plenty to be found out. So future generations should have enough to do.

As a young man in Siena I watched a group of building workers argue for five minutes, then abandon a thousand-year-old method of shifting granite blocks in favour of a new and more efficient arrangement of the ropes. Then and there I knew, the old days are over and this is a new time. Soon humanity is going to understand its abode, the heavenly body on which it dwells. What is written in the old books is no longer good enough. For where faith has been enthroned for a thousand years doubt now sits. Everyone says: right, that's what it says in the books, but let's have a look for ourselves. The most solemn truths are being familiarly nudged; what was never doubted before is doubted now.

This has created a draught which is blowing up the gold-embroidered skirts of the prelates and princes, revealing the fat and skinny legs underneath, legs like our own. The heavens, it turns out, are empty. Cheerful laughter is our response. But the waters of the earth drive the new spinning machines, while in the shipyards, the ropewalks and sail-lofts five hundred hands are moving together in a new system.

It is my prophecy that our own lifetime will see astronomy being discussed in the marketplaces. Even the fishwives' sons will hasten off to school. For these novelty-seeking people in our cities will be delighted with a new astronomy that sets the earth moving too. The old idea was always that the stars were fixed to a crystal vault to stop them falling down.

Today we have found the courage to let them soar through space without support; and they are travelling at full speed just like our ships, at full speed and without support.

And the earth is rolling cheerfully around the sun, and the fishwives, merchants, princes, cardinals and even the Pope are rolling with it.

The universe has lost its centre overnight, and woken up to find it has countless centres. So that each one can now be seen as the centre, or none at all. Suddenly there is a lot of room.

Our ships sail far overseas, our planets move far out into space, in chess too the rooks have begun sweeping far across the board.

What does the poet say? O early morning of beginnings . . .

ANDREA:

O early morning of beginnings
O breath of wind that
Cometh from new shores!

And you'd better drink up your milk, because people are sure to start arriving soon.

GALILEO: Have you understood what I told you yesterday?

ANDREA: What? All about Copper Knickers and turning?

GALILEO: Yes.

ANDREA: No. What d'you want me to understand that for? It's very difficult, and I'm not even eleven till October.

GALILEO: I particularly want you to understand it. Getting people to understand it is the reason why I go on working and buying expensive books instead of paying the milkman.

ANDREA: But I can see with my own eyes that the sun goes down in a different place from where it rises. So how can it stay still? Of course it can't.

GALILEO: You can see, indeed! What can you see? Nothing at all. You just gawp. Gawping isn't seeing. *He puts the iron washstand in the middle of the room.* Right: this is the sun. Sit down. *Andrea sits on one of the chairs, Galileo stands behind him.* Where's the sun, right or left of you?

ANDREA: Left.

GALILEO: And how does it get to be on your right?

ANDREA: By you carrying it to my right, of course.

GALILEO: Isn't there any other way? *He picks him up along with the chair and makes an about-turn.* Now where's the sun?

ANDREA: On my right.

GALILEO: Did it move?

ANDREA: Not really.

GALILEO: So what did move?

ANDREA: Me.

GALILEO *bellows*: Wrong! You idiot! The chair!

ANDREA: But me with it!

GALILEO: Of course. The chair's the earth. You're sitting on it.

MRS SARTI *has entered in order to make the bed. She has been watching*: Just what are you up to with my boy, Mr Galilei?

GALILEO: Teaching him to see, Mrs Sarti.

MRS SARTI: What, by lugging him round the room?

ANDREA: Lay off, mother. You don't understand.

MRS SARTI: Oh, don't I? And you do: is that it? There's a young gentleman wants some lessons. Very well dressed, got a letter of introduction too. *Hands it over.* You'll have Andrea believing two and two makes five any minute now, Mr Galilei. As if he didn't already muddle up everything you tell him. Only last night he was arguing that the earth goes round the sun. He's got it into his head that some gentleman called Copper Knickers worked that one out.

ANDREA: Didn't Copper Knickers work it out, Mr Galilei? You tell her.

MRS SARTI: You surely can't tell him such stories? Making him trot it all out at school so the priests come and see me because he keeps on coming out with blasphemies. You should be ashamed of yourself, Mr Galilei.

GALILEO *eating his breakfast*: In consequence of our researches, Mrs Sarti, and as a result of intensive arguments, Andrea and I have made discoveries which we can no longer hold back from the world. A new time has begun, a time it's a pleasure to live in.

MRS SARTI: Well. Let's hope your new time will allow us to

pay the milkman, Mr Galilei. *Indicating the letter of introduction.* Just do me a favour and don't send this man away. I'm thinking of the milk bill.

GALILEO *laughing*: Let me at least finish my milk! *To Andrea*: So you did understand something yesterday?

ANDREA: I only told her to wake her up a bit. But it isn't true. All you did with me and that chair was turn it sideways, not like this. *He makes a looping motion with his arm.* Or I'd have fallen off, and that's a fact. Why didn't you turn the chair over? Because it would have proved I'd fall off if you turned it that way. So there.

GALILEO: Look, I proved to you . . .

ANDREA: But last night I realised that if the earth turned that way I'd be hanging head downwards every night, and that's a fact.

GALILEO *takes an apple from the table*: Right, now this is the earth.

ANDREA: Don't keep on taking that sort of example, Mr Galilei. They always work.

GALILEO *putting back the apple*: Very well.

ANDREA: Examples always work if you're clever. Only I can't lug my mother round in a chair like you did me. So you see it's a rotten example really. And suppose your apple is the earth like you say? Nothing follows.

GALILEO *laughing*: You just don't want to know.

ANDREA: Pick it up again. Why don't I hang head downwards at night, then?

GALILEO: Right: here's the earth and here's you standing on it. *He takes a splinter from a piece of firewood and sticks it into the apple.* Now the earth's turning round.

ANDREA: And now I'm hanging head downwards.

GALILEO: What d'you mean? Look at it carefully. Where's your head?

ANDREA *pointing*: There. Underneath.

GALILEO: Really? *He turns it back*: Isn't it in precisely the same position? Aren't your feet still underneath? You don't stand like this when I turn it, do you? *He takes out the splinter and puts it in upside down.*

ANDREA: No. Then why don't I notice it's turning?

GALILEO: Because you're turning with it. You and the air above you and everything else on this ball.

ANDREA: Then why does it look as if the sun's moving?

GALILEO *turns the apple and the splinter round again*: Right: you're seeing the earth below you; that doesn't change, it's always underneath you and so far as you're concerned it doesn't move. But then look what's above you. At present the lamp's over your head, but once I've turned the apple what's over it now; what's above?

ANDREA *turns his head similarly*: The stove.

GALILEO: And where's the lamp?

ANDREA: Underneath.

GALILEO: Ha.

ANDREA: That's great: that'll give her something to think about. *Enter Ludovico Marsili, a rich young man.*

GALILEO: This place is getting like a pigeon loft.

LUDOVICO: Good morning, sir. My name is Ludovico Marsili.

GALILEO *reading his letter of introduction*: So you've been in Holland?

LUDOVICO: Where they were all speaking about you, Mr Galilei.

GALILEO: Your family owns estates in the Campagna?

LUDOVICO: Mother wanted me to have a look-see, find out what's cooking in the world and all that.

GALILEO: And in Holland they told you that in Italy, for instance, I was cooking?

LUDOVICO: And since Mother also wanted me to have a look-see in the sciences . . .

GALILEO: Private tuition: ten scudi a month.

LUDOVICO: Very well, sir.

GALILEO: What are your main interests?

LUDOVICO: Horses.

GALILEO: Ha.

LUDOVICO: I've not got the brains for science, Mr Galilei.

GALILEO: Ha. In that case we'll make it fifteen scudi a month.

LUDOVICO: Very well, Mr Galilei.

GALILEO: I'll have to take you first thing in the morning. That'll be your loss, Andrea. You'll have to drop out of course. You don't pay, see?

ANDREA: I'm off. Can I have the apple?

GALILEO: Yes.

Exit Andrea.

LUDOVICO: You'll have to be patient with me. You see, everything in the sciences goes against a fellow's good sound commonsense. I mean, look at that queer tube thing they're selling in Amsterdam. I gave it a good looking-over. A green leather casing and a couple of lenses, one this way – *he indicates a concave lens* – and the other that way – *he indicates a convex lens.* One of them's supposed to magnify and the other reduces. Anyone in his right mind would expect them to cancel out. They don't. The thing makes everything appear five times the size. That's science for you.

GALILEO: What appears five times the size?

LUDOVICO: Church spires, pigeons, anything that's a long way off.

GALILEO: Did you yourself see church spires magnified in this way?

LUDOVICO: Yes, sir.

GALILEO: And this tube has two lenses? *He makes a sketch on a piece of paper.* Did it look like that? *Ludovico nods.* How old's this invention?

LUDOVICO: Not more than a couple of days, I'd say, when I left Holland; at least that's how long it had been on the market.

GALILEO *almost friendly*: And why does it have to be physics? Why not horsebreeding?

Enter Mrs Sarti unobserved by Galileo.

LUDOVICO: Mother thinks you can't do without a bit of science. Nobody can drink a glass of wine without science these days, you know.

GALILEO: Why didn't you pick a dead language or theology? That's easier. *Sees Mrs Sarti.* Right, come along on Tuesday morning. *Ludovico leaves.*

GALILEO: Don't give me that look. I accepted him.

MRS SARTI: Because I caught your eye in time. The procurator of the university is out there.

GALILEO: Show him in, he matters. There may be 500 scudi in this. I wouldn't have to bother with pupils.

Mrs Sarti shows in the procurator. Galileo has finished dressing, meanwhile jotting down figures on a piece of paper.

GALILEO: Good morning. Lend us half a scudo. *The procurator digs a coin out of his purse and Galileo gives it to Sarti.* Sarti, tell Andrea to go to the spectacle-maker's and get two lenses: there's the prescription.

Exit Mrs Sarti with the paper.

PROCURATOR: I have come in connection with your application for a rise in salary to 1000 scudi. I regret that I cannot recommend it to the university. As you know, courses in mathematics do not attract new students. Mathematics, so to speak, is an unproductive art. Not that our Republic doesn't esteem it most highly. It may not be so essential as philosophy or so useful as theology, but it nonetheless offers infinite pleasures to its adepts.

GALILEO *busy with his papers*: My dear fellow, I can't manage on 500 scudi.

PROCURATOR: But, Mr Galilei, your week consists of two two-hour lectures. Given your outstanding reputation you can certainly get plenty of pupils who can afford private lessons. Haven't you got private pupils?

GALILEO: Too many, sir. I teach and I teach, and when am I supposed to learn? God help us, I'm not half as sharp as those gentlemen in the philosophy department. I'm stupid. I understand absolutely nothing. So I'm compelled to fill the gaps in my knowledge. And when am I supposed to do that? When am I to get on with my research? Sir, my branch of knowledge is still avid to know. The greatest problems still find us with nothing but hypotheses to go on. Yet we keep asking ourselves for proofs. How am I to provide them if I can only maintain my home by having to take any thickhead who can afford the money and din it into him that parallel lines meet at infinity?

PROCURATOR: Don't forget that even if the Republic pays less well than certain princes it does guarantee freedom of research. In Padua we even admit Protestants to our lectures. And give them doctors' degrees too. In Mr Cremonini's case we not only failed to hand him over to the Inquisition when he was proved, proved, Mr Galilei – to have made irreligious remarks, but actually granted him a rise in salary. As far as Holland Venice is known as the republic where the Inquisition has no say. That should mean something to you, being an astronomer, that's to say operating in a field where for some time now the doctrines of the church have hardly been treated with proper respect.

GALILEO: You people handed Mr Giordano Bruno over to Rome. Because he was propagating the ideas of Copernicus.

PROCURATOR: Not because he was propagating the ideas of Mr Copernicus, which anyway are wrong, but because he was not a Venetian citizen and had no regular position here. So you needn't drag in the man they burned. Incidentally, however free we are, I wouldn't go around openly citing a name like his, which is subject to the express anathema of the church: not even here, not even here.

GALILEO: Your protection of freedom of thought is pretty good business, isn't it? By showing how everywhere else the Inquisition prevails and burns people, you get good teachers cheap for this place. You make up for your attitude to the Inquisition by paying lower salaries than anyone.

PROCURATOR: That's most unfair. What use would it be to you to have limitless spare time for research if any ignorant monk in the Inquisition could just put a ban on your thoughts? Every rose has its thorn, Mr Galilei, and every ruler has his monks.

GALILEO: So what's the good of free research without free time to research in? What happens to its results? Perhaps you'd kindly show this paper about falling bodies to the gentlemen at the Signoria – *he indicates a bundle of manuscript* – and ask them if it isn't worth a few extra scudi.

PROCURATOR: It's worth infinitely more than that, Mr Galilei.

GALILEO: Sir, not infinitely more, a mere 500 scudi more.

PROCURATOR: What is worth scudi is what brings scudi in. If you want money you'll have to produce something else. When you're selling knowledge you can't ask more than the buyer is likely to make from it. Philosophy, for instance, as taught by Mr Colombe in Florence, nets the prince at least 10,000 scudi a year. I know your laws on falling bodies have made a stir. They've applauded you in Prague and Paris. But the people who applaud don't pay Padua University what you cost it. You made an unfortunate choice of subject, Mr Galilei.

GALILEO: I see. Freedom of trade, freedom of research. Free trading in research, is that it?

PROCURATOR: Really, Mr Galilei, what a way of looking at it! Allow me to tell you that I don't quite understand your flippant remarks. Our Republic's thriving foreign trade hardly strikes me as a matter to be sneered at. And speaking from many years of experience as procurator of this university I would be even more disinclined to speak of scientific research in what I would term with respect, so frivolous a manner. *While Galileo glances longingly at his work table*: Consider the conditions that surround us. The slavery under whose whips the sciences in certain places are groaning. Whips cut from old leather bindings. Nobody there needs to know how a stone falls, merely what Aristotle wrote about it. Eyes are only for reading with. Why investigate falling bodies, when it's laws governing grovelling bodies that count? Contrast the infinite joy with which our Republic welcomes your ideas, however daring they may be. Here you have a chance to research, to work. Nobody supervises you, nobody suppresses you. Our merchants know the value of better linen in their struggle with their competitors in Florence; they listen interestedly to your cry for better physics, and physics in turn owes much to their cry for better looms. Our most prominent citizens take an interest in your researches, call on you, get you to demonstrate your findings: men whose time is precious. Don't underrate trade, Mr Galilei. Nobody here would stand for the slightest interference with your work or let outsiders make difficulties for you. This is a place where you can work, Mr Galilei, you have to admit it.

GALILEO *in despair*: Yes.

PROCURATOR: As for the material aspects: why can't you give us another nice piece of work like those famous proportional compasses of yours, the ones that allow complete mathematical dunces to trace lines, reckon compound interest on capital, reproduce a land survey on varying scales and determine the weight of cannon balls?

GALILEO: Kids' stuff.

PROCURATOR: Here's something that fascinated and astonished our top people and brought in good money, and you call it kids' stuff. I'm told even General Stefano Gritti can work out square roots with your instrument.

GALILEO: A real miracle. – All the same, Priuli, you've given me something to think about. Priuli, I think I might be able to let you have something of the kind you want. *He picks up the paper with the sketch.*

PROCURATOR: Could you? That would be the answer. *Gets up*: Mr Galilei, we realise that you are a great man. A great but dissatisfied man, if I may say so.

GALILEO: Yes, I am dissatisfied, and that's what you'd be paying me for if you had any brains. Because I'm dissatisfied with myself. But instead of doing that you force me to be dissatisfied with you. I admit I enjoy doing my stuff for you gentlemen of Venice in your famous arsenal and in the shipyards and cannon foundries. But you never give me the time to follow up the hunches which come to me there and which are important for my branch of science. That way you muzzle the threshing ox. I am 46 years old and have achieved nothing that satisfies me.

PROCURATOR: I mustn't interrupt you any longer.

GALILEO: Thank you.

Exit the Procurator.

Galileo is left alone for a moment or two and begins to work. Then Andrea hurries in.

GALILEO *working*: Why didn't you eat the apple?

ANDREA: I need it to convince her that it turns.

GALILEO: Listen to me, Andrea: don't talk to other people about our ideas.

ANDREA: Why not?

GALILEO: The big shots won't allow it.

ANDREA: But it's the truth.

GALILEO: But they're forbidding it. – And there's something more. We physicists may think we have the answer, but that doesn't mean we can prove it. Even the ideas of a great man like Copernicus still need proving. They are only hypotheses. Give me those lenses.

ANDREA: Your half scudo wasn't enough. I had to leave my coat. As security.

GALILEO: How will you manage without a coat this winter? *Pause. Galileo arranges the lenses on the sheet with the sketch on it.*

ANDREA: What's a hypothesis?

GALILEO: It's when you assume that something's likely, but haven't any facts. Look at Felicia down there outside the basket-maker's shop breastfeeding her child: it remains a hypothesis that she's giving it milk and not getting milk from it, till one actually goes and sees and proves it. Faced with the stars we are like dull-eyed worms that can hardly see at all. Those old constructions people have believed in for the last thousand years are hopelessly rickety: vast buildings most of whose wood is in the buttresses propping them up. Lots of laws that explain very little, whereas our new hypothesis has very few laws that explain a lot.

ANDREA: But you proved it all to me.

GALILEO: No, only that that's how it could be. I'm not saying it isn't a beautiful hypothesis; what's more there's nothing against it.

ANDREA: I'd like to be a physicist too, Mr Galilei.

GALILEO: That's understandable, given the million and one questions in our field still waiting to be cleared up. *He has gone to the window and looked through the lenses. Mildly interested*: Have a look through that, Andrea.

ANDREA: Holy Mary, it's all quite close. The bells in the

campanile very close indeed. I can even read the copper
letters: GRACIA DEI.

GALILEO: That'll get us 500 scudi.

2

Galileo presents the Venetian Republic with a new invention

No one's virtue is complete:
Great Galileo liked to eat.
You will not resent, we hope
The truth about his telescope.

The great arsenal of Venice, alongside the harbour.

*Senators, headed by the Doge. To one side, Galileo's friend
Sagredo and the fifteen-year-old Virginia Galilei with a velvet
cushion on which rests a two-foot-long telescope in a crimson
leather case. On a dais, Galileo. Behind him the telescope's
stand, supervised by Federzoni the lens-grinder.*

GALILEO: Your Excellency; august Signoria! In my capacity as
mathematics teacher at your university in Padua and director of your great arsenal here in Venice I have always seen it
as my job not merely to fulfil my exalted task as a teacher but
also to provide useful inventions that would be of exceptional advantage to the Venetian Republic. Today it is with
deep joy and all due deference that I find myself able to
demonstrate and hand over to you a completely new
instrument, namely my spyglass or telescope, fabricated in
your world-famous Great Arsenal on the loftiest Christian
and scientific principles, the product of seventeen years of
patient research by your humble servant. *Galileo leaves the
dais and stands alongside Sagredo. Applause. Galileo bows.*

GALILEO *softly to Sagredo*: Waste of time.

SAGREDO *softly*: You'll be able to pay the butcher, old boy.

GALILEO: Yes, they'll make money on this. *He bows again.*

PROCURATOR *steps on to the dais*: Your Excellency, august Signoria! Once again a glorious page in the great book of the arts is inscribed in a Venetian hand. *Polite applause.* Today a world-famous scholar is offering you, and you alone, a highly marketable tube, for you to manufacture and sell as and how you wish. *Louder applause.* What is more, has it struck you that in wartime this instrument will allow us to distinguish the number and types of the enemy's ships at least two hours before he does ours, with the result that we shall know how strong he is and be able to choose whether to pursue, join battle or run away? *Very loud applause.* And now, your Excellency, august Signoria, Mr Galileo invites you to accept this instrument which he has invented, this testimonial to his intuition, at the hand of his enchanting daughter.

Music. Virginia steps forward, bows and hands the telescope to the Procurator, who passes it to Federzoni. Federzoni puts it on the stand and focusses it. Doge and Senators mount the dais and look through the tube.

GALILEO *softly*: I'm not sure how long I'll be able to stick this circus. These people think they're getting a lucrative plaything, but it's a lot more than that. Last night I turned it on the moon.

SAGREDO: What did you see?

GALILEO: The moon doesn't generate its own light.

SAGREDO: What?

SENATORS: I can make out the fortifications of Santa Rosita, Mr Galilei. – They're having their dinner on that boat. Fried fish. Makes me feel peckish.

GALILEO: I'm telling you astronomy has stagnated for the last thousand years because they had no telescope.

SENATOR: Mr Galilei!

SAGREDO: They want you.

SENATOR: That contraption lets you see too much. I'll have to tell my women they can't take baths on the roof any longer.

GALILEO: Know what the Milky Way consists of?

SAGREDO: No.

GALILEO: I do.

SENATOR: One should be able to ask 10 scudi for a thing like that, Mr Galilei. *Galileo bows.*

VIRGINIA *leading Ludovico up to her father*: Ludovico wants to congratulate you, Father.

LUDOVICO *embarrassed*: I congratulate you, sir.

GALILEO: I've improved it.

LUDOVICO: Yes, sir. I see you've made the casing red. In Holland it was green.

GALILEO *turning to Sagredo*: I've even begun to wonder if I couldn't use it to prove a certain theory.

SAGREDO: Watch your step.

PROCURATOR: Your 500 scudi are in the bag, Galileo.

GALILEO *disregarding him*: Of course I'm sceptical about jumping to conclusions.

The Doge, a fat unassuming man, has come up to Galileo and is trying to address him with a kind of dignified awkwardness.

PROCURATOR: Mr Galilei, His Excellency the Doge.

The Doge shakes Galileo's hand.

GALILEO: Of course, the 500! Are you satisfied, your Excellency?

DOGE: I'm afraid our republic always has to have some pretext before the city fathers can do anything for our scholars.

PROCURATOR: But what other incentive can there be, Mr Galilei?

DOGE *smiling*: We need that pretext.

The Doge and the Procurator lead Galileo towards the Senators, who gather round him. Virginia and Ludovico slowly go away.

VIRGINIA: Did I do all right?

LUDOVICO: Seemed all right to me.

VIRGINIA: What's the matter?

LUDOVICO: Nothing, really. I suppose a green casing would have been just as good.

VIRGINIA: It strikes me they're all very pleased with Father.

LUDOVICO: And it strikes me I'm starting to learn a thing or two about science.

3

10 January 1610. Using the telescope, Galileo discovers celestial phenomena that confirm the Copernican system. Warned by his friend of the possible consequences of his research, Galileo proclaims his belief in human reason

> January ten, sixteen ten:
> Galileo Galilei abolishes heaven.

Galileo's study in Padua. Night. Galileo and Sagredo at the telescope, wrapped in heavy overcoats.

SAGREDO *looking through the telescope, half to himself*: The crescent's edge is quite irregular, jagged and rough. In the dark area, close to the luminous edge, there are bright spots. They come up one after the other. The light starts from the spots and flows outwards over bigger and bigger surfaces, where it merges into the larger luminous part.

GALILEO: What's your explanation of these bright spots?

SAGREDO: It's not possible.

GALILEO: It is. They're mountains.

SAGREDO: On a star?

GALILEO: Huge mountains. Whose peaks are gilded by the rising sun while the surrounding slopes are still covered by night. What you're seeing is the light spreading down into the valleys from the topmost peaks.

SAGREDO: But this goes against two thousand years of astronomy.

GALILEO: It does. What you are seeing has been seen by no mortal except myself. You are the second.

SAGREDO: But the moon can't be an earth complete with mountains and valleys, any more than the earth can be a star.

GALILEO: The moon can be an earth complete with mountains and valleys, and the earth can be a star. An ordinary celestial body, one of thousands. Take another look. Does the dark part of the moon look completely dark to you?

SAGREDO: No. Now that I look at it, I can see a feeble ashy-grey light all over it.

GALILEO: What sort of light might that be?

SAGREDO: ?

GALILEO: It comes from the earth.

SAGREDO: You're talking through your hat. How can the earth give off light, with all its mountains and forests and waters; it's a cold body.

GALILEO: The same way the moon gives off light. Both of them are lit by the sun, and so they give off light. What the moon is to us, we are to the moon. It sees us sometimes as a crescent, sometimes as a half-moon, sometimes full and sometimes not at all.

SAGREDO: In other words, there's no difference between the moon and earth.

GALILEO: Apparently not.

SAGREDO: Ten years ago in Rome they burnt a man at the stake for that. His name was Giordano Bruno, and that is what he said.

GALILEO: Exactly. And that's what we can see. Keep your eye glued to the telescope, Sagredo, my friend. What you're seeing is the fact that there is no difference between heaven and earth. Today is 10 January 1610. Today mankind can write in its diary: Got rid of Heaven.

SAGREDO: That's frightful.

GALILEO: There is another thing I discovered. Perhaps it's more appalling still.

MRS SARTI *quietly*: Mr Procurator.

The Procurator rushes in.

PROCURATOR: I'm sorry to come so late. Do you mind if I speak to you alone?

GALILEO: Mr Sagredo can listen to anything I can, Mr Priuli.

PROCURATOR: But you may not exactly be pleased if the gentleman hears what has happened. Unhappily it is something quite unbelievable.

GALILEO: Mr Sagredo is quite used to encountering the unbelievable when I am around, let me tell you.

PROCURATOR: No doubt, no doubt. *Pointing at the telescope*: Yes, that's the famous contraption. You might just as well throw it away. It's useless, utterly useless.

SAGREDO *who has been walking around impatiently*: Why's that?

PROCURATOR: Are you aware that this invention of yours which you said was the fruit of seventeen years of research can be bought on any street corner in Italy for a few scudi? Made in Holland, what's more. There is a Dutch merchantman unloading 500 telescopes down at the harbour at this very moment.

GALILEO: Really?

PROCURATOR: I find your equanimity hard to understand, sir.

SAGREDO: What are you worrying about? Thanks to this instrument, let me tell you, Mr Galilei has just made some revolutionary discoveries about the universe.

GALILEO *laughing*: Have a look, Priuli.

PROCURATOR: And let me tell you it's quite enough for me to have made my particular discovery, after getting this unspeakable man's salary doubled, what's more. It's a pure stroke of luck that the gentlemen of the Signoria, in their confidence that they had secured the republic a monopoly of this instrument, didn't look through it and instantly see an ordinary streetseller at the nearest corner, magnified to the power of seven and hawking an identical tube for twice nothing. *Galileo laughs resoundingly.*

SAGREDO: My dear Mr Priuli. I may not be competent to judge this instrument's value for commerce but its value for philosophy is so boundless that . . .

PROCURATOR: For philosophy indeed. What's a mathematician like Mr Galilei got to do with philosophy? Mr Galilei, you did once invent a very decent water pump for the city and your irrigation system works well. The weavers too report favourably on your machine. So how was I to expect something like this?

GALILEO: Not so fast, Priuli. Sea passages are still long, hazardous and expensive. We need a clock in the sky we can rely on. A guide for navigation, right? Well, I have reason to believe that the telescope will allow us to make clear sightings of certain stars that execute extremely regular movements. New star charts might save our shipping several million scudi, Priuli.

PROCURATOR: Don't bother. I've listened too long already. In return for my help you've made me the laughing-stock of the city. I'll go down to history as the procurator who fell for a worthless telescope. It's all very well for you to laugh. You've got your 500 scudi. But I'm an honourable man, and I tell you this world turns my stomach.

He leaves, slamming the door.

GALILEO: He's really quite likeable when he's angry. Did you hear that? A world where one can't do business turns his stomach.

SAGREDO: Did you know about these Dutch instruments?

GALILEO: Of course, by hearsay. But the one I made these skinflints in the Signoria was twice as good. How am I supposed to work with the bailiffs in the house? And Virginia will soon have to have a dowry: she's not bright. Then I like buying books about other things besides physics, and I like a decent meal. Good meals are when I get most of my ideas. A degraded age! They were paying me less than the carter who drives their wine barrels. Four cords of firewood for two courses on mathematics. Now I've managed to squeeze 500 scudi out of them, but I've still got debts, including some dating from twenty years back. Give me five years off to research, and I'd have proved it all. I'm going to show you another thing.

SAGREDO *is reluctant to go to the telescope*: I feel something not all that remote from fear, Galileo.

GALILEO: I'm about to show you one of the shining milk-white clouds in the Milky Way. Tell me what it's made up of.

SAGREDO: They're stars, an infinite number.

GALILEO: In Orion alone there are 500 fixed stars. Those are the countless other worlds, the remote stars the man they burned talked about. He never saw them, he just expected them to be there.

SAGREDO: But even supposing our earth is a star, that's still a long way from Copernicus's view that it goes round the sun. There's not a star in the sky that has another star going round it. But the moon does go round the earth.

GALILEO: Sagredo, I wonder. I've been wondering since yesterday. Here we have Jupiter. *He focusses on it.* Round it we have four smaller neighbouring stars that are invisible except through the tube. I saw them on Monday but without bothering to note their position. Yesterday I looked again. I could swear the position of all four had changed. I noted them down. They've changed again. What's this? I saw four. *Agitated*: Have a look.

SAGREDO: I can see three.

GALILEO: Where's the fourth? There are the tables. We must work out what movements they might have performed. *Excited, they sit down to work. The stage darkens, but Jupiter and its accompanying stars can be seen on the cyclorama. As it grows light once more they are still sitting there in their winter coats.*

GALILEO: That's the proof. The fourth one can only have gone behind Jupiter, where it can't be seen. So here you've a star with another one going round it.

SAGREDO: What about the crystal sphere Jupiter is attached to?

GALILEO: Yes, where has it got to? How can Jupiter be attached if other stars circle round it? It's not some kind of prop in the sky, some base in the universe. It's another sun.

SAGREDO: Calm down. You're thinking too quickly.

GALILEO: What d'you mean, quickly? Wake up, man! You're seeing something nobody has ever seen before. They were right.

SAGREDO: Who, Copernicus and his lot?

GALILEO: And the other fellow. The whole world was against them, and they were right. Andrea must see this! *In great excitement he hurries to the door and shouts*: Mrs Sarti! Mrs Sarti!

SAGREDO *turns the telescope away*: Stop bellowing like an idiot.

GALILEO: Stop standing there like a stuffed dummy when the truth has been found.

SAGREDO: I'm not standing like a stuffed dummy; I'm trembling with fear that it may be the truth.

GALILEO: Uh?

SAGREDO: Have you completely lost your head? Don't you realise what you'll be getting into if what you see there is true? And if you go round telling all and sundry that the earth is a planet and not the centre of the universe?

GALILEO: Right, and that the entire universe full of stars isn't turning around our tiny little earth, anyone could guess.

SAGREDO: In other words that it's just a lot of stars. Then where's God.

GALILEO: What d'you mean?

SAGREDO: God! Where is God?

GALILEO *angrily*: Not there anyway. Any more than he'd be here on earth, suppose there were creatures out there wanting to come and look for him.

SAGREDO: So where is God?

GALILEO: I'm not a theologian. I'm a mathematician.

SAGREDO: First and foremost you're a human being. And I'm asking: where is God in your cosmography?

GALILEO: Within ourselves or nowhere.

SAGREDO *shouting*: Like the man they burned said?

GALILEO: Like the man they burned said.

SAGREDO: That's what they burned him for. Less than ten years back.

GALILEO: Because he couldn't prove it. Because it was just a hypothesis. Mrs Sarti!

SAGREDO: Galileo, ever since I've known you you've known how to cover yourself. For seventeen years here in Padua and three more in Pisa you have been patiently teaching the

Ptolemaic system proclaimed by the Church and confirmed by the writings the Church is based on. Like Copernicus you thought it was wrong but you taught it just the same.

GALILEO: Because I couldn't prove anything.

SAGREDO *incredulously*: And do you imagine that makes any difference!

GALILEO: A tremendous difference. Look, Sagredo, I believe in Humanity, which means to say I believe in human reason. If it weren't for that belief each morning I wouldn't have the power to get out of bed.

SAGREDO: Then let me tell you something. I don't. Forty years spent among human beings has again and again brought it home to me that they are not open to reason. Show them a comet with a red tail, scare them out of their wits, and they'll rush out of their houses and break their legs. But try making one rational statement to them, and back it up with seven proofs, and they'll just laugh at you.

GALILEO: That's quite untrue, and it's a slander. I don't see how you can love science if that's what you believe. Nobody who isn't dead can fail to be convinced by proof.

SAGREDO: How can you imagine their pathetic shrewdness has anything to do with reason?

GALILEO: I'm not talking about their shrewdness. I know they call a donkey a horse when they want to sell it and a horse a donkey when they want to buy. That's the kind of shrewdness you mean. But the horny-handed old woman who gives her mule an extra bundle of hay on the eve of a journey, the sea captain who allows for storms and doldrums when laying in stores, the child who puts on his cap once they have convinced him that it may rain: these are the people I pin my hopes to, because they all accept proof. Yes, I believe in reason's gentle tyranny over people. Sooner or later they have to give in to it. Nobody can go on indefinitely watching me – *he drops a pebble on the ground* – drop a pebble, then say it doesn't fall. No human being is capable of that. The lure of a proof is too great. Nearly everyone succumbs to it; sooner or later we all do. Thinking is one of the chief pleasures of the human race.

MRS SARTI *enters*: Do you want something, Mr Galilei?

GALILEO *who is back at his telescope making notes; in a very friendly voice*: Yes, I want Andrea.

MRS SARTI: Andrea? He's asleep in bed.

GALILEO: Can't you wake him up?

MRS SARTI: Why d'you want him?

GALILEO: I want to show him something he'll appreciate. He's to see something nobody but us two has seen since the earth was made.

MRS SARTI: Something more through your tube?

GALILEO: Something through my tube, Mrs Sarti.

MRS SARTI: And I'm to wake him up in the middle of the night for that? Are you out of your mind? He's got to have his sleep. I wouldn't think of waking him.

GALILEO: Definitely not?

MRS SARTI: Definitely not.

GALILEO: In that case, Mrs Sarti, perhaps you can help me. You see, a question has arisen where we can't agree, probably because both of us have read too many books. It's a question about the heavens, something to do with the stars. This is it: are we to take it that the greater goes round the smaller, or does the smaller go round the greater?

MRS SARTI *cautiously*: I never know where I am with you. Mr Galilei. Is that a serious question, or are you pulling my leg again?

GALILEO: A serious question.

MRS SARTI: Then I'll give you a quick answer. Do I serve your dinner or do you serve mine?

GALILEO: You serve mine. Yesterday it was burnt.

MRS SARTI: And why was it burnt? Because I had to fetch you your shoes in the middle of my cooking. Didn't I fetch you your shoes?

GALILEO: I suppose so.

MRS SARTI: You see, you're the one who has studied and is able to pay.

Mrs Sarti, amused, goes off.

GALILEO: Don't tell me people like that can't grasp the truth. They grab at it.

The bell has begun sounding for early morning mass. Enter Virginia in a cloak, carrying a shielded light.

VIRGINIA: Good morning, Father.

GALILEO: Why are you up at this hour?

VIRGINIA: Mrs Sarti and I are going to early mass. Ludovico's coming too. What sort of night was it, Father?

GALILEO: Clear.

VIRGINIA: Can I have a look?

GALILEO: What for? *Virginia does not know what to say.* It's not a toy.

VIRGINIA: No, Father.

GALILEO: Anyhow the tube is a flop, so everybody will soon be telling you. You can get it for 3 scudi all over the place and the Dutch invented it ages ago.

VIRGINIA: Hasn't it helped you see anything fresh in the sky?

GALILEO: Nothing in your line. Just a few dim little spots to the left of a large planet; I'll have to do something to draw attention to them. *Talking past his daughter to Sagredo*: I might christen them 'the Medicean Stars' after the Grand-Duke of Florence. *Again to Virginia*: You'll be interested to hear, Virginia, that we'll probably be moving to Florence. I've written to them to ask if the Grand Duke can use me as his court mathematician.

VIRGINIA *radiant*: At Court?

SAGREDO: Galileo!

GALILEO: My dear fellow, I'll need time off. I need proofs. And I want the fleshpots. And here's a job where I won't have to take private pupils and din the Ptolemaic system into them, but shall have the time, time, time, time, time – to work out my proofs; because what I've got so far isn't enough. It's nothing, just wretched odds and ends. I can't take on the whole world with that. There's not a single shred of proof to show that any heavenly body whatever goes round the sun. But I am going to produce the proofs, proofs for everyone, from Mrs Sarti right up to the Pope. The only thing that worries me is whether the court will have me.

VIRGINIA: Of course they'll have you, Father, with your new stars and all that.

GALILEO: Run along to your mass.

Exit Virginia.

GALILEO: I'm not used to writing to important people. *He hands Sagredo a letter.* Do you think this is well expressed?

SAGREDO *reads out the end of the letter*: 'My most ardent desire is to be closer to you, the rising sun that will illuminate this age.' The grand duke of Florence is aged nine.

GALILEO: That's it. I see; you think my letter is too submissive. I'm wondering if it is submissive enough – not too formal, lacking in authentic servility. A reticent letter would be all right for someone whose distinction it is to have proved Aristotle correct, but not for me. A man like me can only get a halfway decent job by crawling on his belly. And you know what I think of people whose brains aren't capable of filling their stomachs.

Mrs Sarti and Virginia pass the men on their way to mass.

SAGREDO: Don't go to Florence, Galileo.

GALILEO: Why not?

SAGREDO: Because it's run by monks.

GALILEO: The Florentine Court includes eminent scholars.

SAGREDO: Flunkeys.

GALILEO: I'll take them by the scruff of the neck and I'll drag them to the telescope. Even monks are human beings, Sagredo. Even they are subject to the seduction of proof. Copernicus, don't forget, wanted them to believe his figures; but I only want them to believe their eyes. If the truth is too feeble to stick up for itself then it must go over to the attack. I'm going to take them by the scruff of the neck and force them to look through this telescope.

SAGREDO: Galileo, I see you embarking on a frightful road. It is a disastrous night when mankind sees the truth. And a delusive hour when it believes in human reason. What kind of person is said to go into things with his eyes open? One who is going to his doom. How could the people in power give free rein to somebody who knows the truth, even if it concerns the remotest stars? Do you imagine the Pope will hear the truth when you tell him he's wrong, and not just hear that he's wrong? Do you imagine he will merely note in his diary: January 10th 1610 – got rid of heaven? How can you propose to leave the Republic with the truth in your pocket, risking the traps set by monks and princes and brandishing your tube. You may be a sceptic in science, but you're childishly credulous as soon as anything seems likely to help you to pursue it. You don't believe in Aristotle, but you do believe in the Grand Duke of Florence. Just now, when I was watching you at the telescope and you were watching those new stars, it seemed to me I was watching you stand on blazing faggots; and when you said you believed in proof I smelt burnt flesh. I am fond of science, my friend, but I am fonder of you. Don't go to Florence, Galileo.

GALILEO: If they'll have me I shall go.

On a curtain appears the last page of his letter:

In giving the noble name of the house of Medici to the new stars which I have discovered I realise that whereas the old gods and heroes were immortalised by being raised to the realm of the stars in this case the noble name of Medici will ensure that these stars are remembered for ever. For my own part I commend myself to you as one of your loyalest and most humble servants who considers it the height of privilege to have been born as your subject.

There is nothing for which I long more ardently than to be closer to you, the rising sun which will illuminate this epoch.

Galileo Galilei.

4

Galileo has exchanged the Venetian Republic for the Court of Florence. His discoveries with the telescope are not believed by the court scholars

> The old says: What I've always done I'll always do.
> The new says: If you're useless you must go.

Galileo's house in Florence. Mrs Sarti is preparing Galileo's study for the reception of guests. Her son Andrea is sitting tidying the star charts.

MRS SARTI: There has been nothing but bowing and scraping ever since we arrived safe and sound in this marvellous Florence. The whole city files past the tube, with me mopping the floor after them. If there was anything to all these discoveries the clergy would be the first to know. I spent four years in service with Monsignor Filippo without ever managing to get all his library dusted. Leather bound books up to the ceiling — and no slim volumes of poetry either. And that good Monsignor had a whole cluster of sores on his bottom from sitting and poring over all that learning; d'you imagine a man like that doesn't know the answers? And today's grand visit will be such a disaster that I'll never be able to meet the milkman's eye tomorrow. I knew what I was about when I advised him to give the gentlemen a good supper first, a proper joint of lamb, before they inspect his tube. But no: *she imitates Galileo*: 'I've got something else for them.'
There is knocking downstairs.
MRS SARTI *looks through the spyhole in the window*: My goodness, the Grand Duke's arrived. And Galileo is still at the University.
She hurries down the stairs and admits the Grand Duke of Tuscany, Cosimo de Medici, together with his chamberlain and two court ladies.

COSIMO: I want to see that tube.

CHAMBERLAIN: Perhaps your Highness will possess himself until Mr Galilei and the other university gentlemen have arrived. *To Mrs Sarti*: Mr Galilei was going to ask our astronomers to test his newly discovered so-called Medicean stars.

COSIMO: They don't believe in the tube, not for one moment. So where is it?

MRS SARTI: Upstairs in the study.

The boy nods, points up the staircase and runs up it at a nod from Mrs Sarti.

CHAMBERLAIN *a very old man*: Your Highness! *To Mrs Sarti*: Have we *got* to go up there? I wouldn't have come at all if his tutor had not been indisposed.

MRS SARTI: The young gentleman will be all right. My own boy is up there.

COSIMO *entering above*: Good evening!

The two boys bow ceremoniously to each other. Pause. Then Andrea turns back to his work.

ANDREA *very like his master*: This place is getting like a pigeon loft.

COSIMO: Plenty of visitors?

ANDREA: Stump around here staring, and don't know the first thing.

COSIMO: I get it. That the . . . ? *Pointing to the telescope.*

ANDREA: Yes, that's it. Hands off, though.

COSIMO: And what's that? *He points to the wooden model of the Ptolemaic system.*

ANDREA: That's Ptolemy's thing.

COSIMO: Showing how the sun goes round, is that it?

ANDREA: So they say.

COSIMO *sitting down on a chair, takes the model on his lap*: My tutor's got a cold. I got off early. It's all right here.

ANDREA *shambles around restlessly and irresolutely shooting doubtful looks at the unknown boy, then finds that he cannot hold out any longer, and brings out a second model from behind the maps, one representing the Copernican system*: But really it's like this.

COSIMO: What's like this?

ANDREA *pointing at Cosimo's model*: That's how people think it is and – *pointing at his own* – this is how it is really. The earth turns round the sun, get it?

COSIMO: D'you really mean that?

ANDREA: Sure, it's been proved.

COSIMO: Indeed? I'd like to know why I'm never allowed to see the old man now. Yesterday he came to supper again.

ANDREA: They don't believe it, do they?

COSIMO: Of course they do.

ANDREA *suddenly pointing at the model on Cosimo's lap*: Give it back: you can't even understand that one.

COSIMO: Why should you have two?

ANDREA: Just you hand it over. It's not a toy for kids.

COSIMO: No reason why I shouldn't give it to you, but you need to learn some manners, you know.

ANDREA: You're an idiot, and to hell with manners, just give it over or you'll start something.

COSIMO: Hands off, I tell you.

They start brawling and are soon tangled up on the floor.

ANDREA: I'll teach you to handle a model properly! Say 'pax'.

COSIMO: It's broken. You're twisting my hand.

ANDREA: We'll see who's right. Say it turns or I'll bash you.

COSIMO: Shan't. Stop it, Ginger. I'll teach you manners.

ANDREA: Ginger: who are you calling Ginger?

They go on brawling in silence. Enter Galileo and a group of university professors downstairs. Federzoni follows.

CHAMBERLAIN: Gentlemen, his highness's tutor Mr Suri has a slight indisposition and was therefore unable to accompany his highness.

THEOLOGIAN: I hope it's nothing serious.

CHAMBERLAIN: Not in the least.

GALILEO *disappointed*: Isn't his highness here?

CHAMBERLAIN: His highness is upstairs. I would ask you gentlemen not to prolong matters. The court is so very eager to know what our distinguished university thinks about Mr Galilei's remarkable instrument and these amazing new stars.

They go upstairs.

The boys are now lying quiet, having heard the noise downstairs.

COSIMO: Here they are. Let me get up.

They stand up quickly.

THE GENTLEMEN *on their way upstairs*: No, there's nothing whatever to worry about. – Those cases in the old city: our faculty of medicine says there's no question of it being plague. Any miasmas would freeze at this temperature. – The worst possible thing in such a situation is to panic. – It's just the usual incidence of colds for this time of year. – Every suspicion has been eliminated. – Nothing whatever to worry about.

Greetings upstairs.

GALILEO: Your highness, I am glad to be able to introduce the gentlemen of your university to these new discoveries in your presence.

Cosimo bows formally in all directions, including Andrea's.

THEOLOGIAN *noticing the broken Ptolemaic model on the floor*: Something seems to have got broken here.

Cosimo quickly stoops down and politely hands Andrea the model. Meantime Galileo unobtrusively shifts the model to one side.

GALILEO *at the telescope*: As your highness no doubt realises, we astronomers have been running into great difficulties in our calculations for some while. We have been using a very ancient system which is apparently consistent with our philosophy but not, alas, with the facts. Under this ancient, Ptolemaic system the motions of the stars are presumed to be extremely complex. The planet Venus, for instance, is supposed to have an orbit like this. *On a board he draws the epicyclical orbit of Venus according to the Ptolemaic hypothesis.* But even if we accept the awkwardness of such motions we are still unable to predict the position of the stars accurately. We do not find them where in principle they ought to be. What is more, some stars perform motions which the Ptolemaic system just cannot explain. Such motions, it seems to me, are performed by certain small stars which I have recently discovered around the planet Jupiter. Would you gentlemen care to start by observing these satellites of Jupiter, the Medicean stars?

ANDREA *indicating the stool by the telescope*: Kindly sit here.

PHILOSOPHER: Thank you, my boy. I fear things are not quite so simple. Mr Galilei, before turning to your famous tube, I wonder if we might have the pleasure of a disputation? Its subject to be: Can such planets exist?

MATHEMATICIAN: A formal dispute.

GALILEO: I was thinking you could just look through the telescope and convince yourselves?

ANDREA: This way, please.

MATHEMATICIAN: Of course, of course. I take it you are familiar with the opinion of the ancients that there can be no stars which turn round centres other than the earth, nor any which lack support in the sky?

GALILEO: I am.

PHILOSOPHER: Moreover, quite apart from the very possibility of such stars, which our mathematicians – *he turns towards the mathematician* – would appear to doubt, I would like in all humility to pose the philosophical question: are such stars necessary? *Aristotelis divini universum* . . .

GALILEO: Shouldn't we go on using the vernacular? My colleague Mr Federzoni doesn't understand Latin.

PHILOSOPHER: Does it matter if he understands us or not?

GALILEO: Yes.

PHILOSOPHER: I am so sorry. I thought he was your lens-grinder.

ANDREA: Mr Federzoni is a lens-grinder and a scholar.

PHILOSOPHER: Thank you, my boy. Well, if Mr Federzoni insists . . .

GALILEO: I insist.

PHILOSOPHER: The argument will be less brilliant, but it's your house. The universe of the divine Aristotle, with the mystical music of its spheres and its crystal vaults, the orbits of its heavenly bodies, the slanting angle of the sun's course, the secrets of the moon tables, the starry richness catalogued in the southern hemisphere and the transparent structure of the celestial globe add up to an edifice of such exquisite proportions that we should think twice before disrupting its harmony.

GALILEO: How about your highness now taking a look at his impossible and unnecessary stars through this telescope?

MATHEMATICIAN: One might be tempted to answer that, if your tube shows something which cannot be there, it cannot be an entirely reliable tube, wouldn't you say?

GALILEO: What d'you mean by that?

MATHEMATICIAN: It would be rather more appropriate, Mr Galilei, if you were to name your reasons for assuming that there could be free-floating stars moving about in the highest sphere of the unalterable heavens.

PHILOSOPHER: Your reasons, Mr Galilei, your reasons.

GALILEO: My reasons! When a single glance at the stars themselves and my own notes makes the phenomenon evident? Sir, your disputation is becoming absurd.

MATHEMATICIAN: If one could be sure of not over-exciting you one might say that what is in your tube and what is in the skies is not necessarily the same thing.

PHILOSOPHER: That couldn't be more courteously put.

FEDERZONI: They think we painted the Medicean stars on the lens.

GALILEO: Are you saying I'm a fraud?

PHILOSOPHER: How could we? In his highness's presence too.

MATHEMATICIAN: Your instrument – I don't know whether to call it your brainchild or your adopted brainchild – is most ingeniously made, no doubt of that.

PHILOSOPHER: And we are utterly convinced, Mr Galilei, that neither you nor anyone else would bestow the illustrious name of our ruling family on stars whose existence was not above all doubt. *All bow deeply to the grand duke.*

COSIMO *turns to the ladies of the court*: Is something the matter with my stars?

THE OLDER COURT LADY: There is nothing the matter with your highness's stars. It's just that the gentlemen are wondering if they are really and truly there.
Pause.

THE YOUNGER COURT LADY: I'm told you can actually see the wheels on the Plough.

FEDERZONI: Yes, and all kinds of things on the Bull.

GALILEO: Well, are you gentlemen going to look through it or not?

PHILOSOPHER: Of course, of course.

MATHEMATICIAN: Of course.

Pause. Suddenly Andrea turns and walks stiffly out across the whole length of the room. His mother stops him.

MRS SARTI: What's the matter with you?

ANDREA: They're stupid. *He tears himself away and runs off.*

PHILOSOPHER: A lamentable boy.

CHAMBERLAIN: Your highness: gentlemen: may I remind you that the state ball is due to start in three quarters of an hour.

MATHEMATICIAN: Let's not beat about the bush. Sooner or later Mr Galilei will have to reconcile himself to the facts. Those Jupiter satellites of his would penetrate the crystal spheres. It is as simple as that.

FEDERZONI: You'll be surprised: the crystal spheres don't exist.

PHILOSOPHER: Any textbook will tell you that they do, my good man.

FEDERZONI: Right, then let's have new textbooks.

PHILOSOPHER: Your highness, my distinguished colleague and I are supported by none less than the divine Aristotle himself.

GALILEO *almost obsequiously*: Gentlemen, to believe in the authority of Aristotle is one thing, tangible facts are another. You are saying that according to Aristotle there are crystal spheres up there, so certain motions just cannot take place because the stars would penetrate them. But suppose those motions could be established? Mightn't that suggest to you that those crystal spheres don't exist? Gentlemen, in all humility I ask you to go by the evidence of your eyes.

MATHEMATICIAN: My dear Galileo, I may strike you as very old-fashioned, but I'm in the habit of reading Aristotle now and again, and there, I can assure you, I trust the evidence of my eyes.

GALILEO: I am used to seeing the gentlemen of the various faculties shutting their eyes to every fact and pretending that nothing has happened. I produce my observations and everyone laughs: I offer my telescope so they can see for themselves, and everyone quotes Aristotle.

FEDERZONI: The fellow had no telescope.

MATHEMATICIAN: That's just it.

PHILOSOPHER *grandly*: If Aristotle is going to be dragged in the mud – that's to say an authority recognized not only by every classical scientist but also by the chief fathers of the church – then any prolonging of this discussion is in my view a waste of time. I have no use for discussions which are not objective. Basta.

GALILEO: Truth is born of the times, not of authority. Our ignorance is limitless: let us lop one cubic millimetre off it. Why try to be clever now that we at last have a chance of being just a little less stupid? I have had the unimaginable luck to get my hands on a new instrument that lets us observe one tiny corner of the universe a little, but not all that much, more exactly. Make use of it.

PHILOSOPHER: Your highness, ladies and gentlemen, I just wonder where all this is leading?

GALILEO: I should say our duty as scientists is not to ask where truth is leading.

PHILOSOPHER *agitatedly*: Mr Galilei, truth might lead us anywhere!

GALILEO: Your highness. At night nowadays telescopes are being pointed at the sky all over Italy. Jupiter's moons may not bring down the price of milk. But they have never been seen before, and yet all the same they exist. From this the man in the street concludes that a lot else might exist if only he opened his eyes. It is your duty to confirm this. What has made Italy prick up its ears is not the movements of a few distant stars but the news that hitherto unquestioned dogmas have begun to totter – and we all know that there are too many of those. Gentlemen, don't let us fight for questionable truths.

FEDERZONI: You people are teachers: you should be stimulating the questions.

PHILOSOPHER: I would rather your man didn't tell us how to conduct a scholarly disputation.

GALILEO: Your highness! My work in the Great Arsenal in Venice brought me into daily contact with draughtsmen, builders and instrument mechanics. Such people showed me a lot of new approaches. They don't read much, but rely on the evidence of their five senses, without all that much fear as to where such evidence is going to lead them . . .

PHILOSOPHER: Oho!

GALILEO: Very much like our mariners who a hundred years ago abandoned our coasts without knowing what other coasts they would encounter, if any. It looks as if the only way today to find that supreme curiosity which was the real glory of classical Greece is to go down to the docks.

PHILOSOPHER: After what we've heard so far I'm not surprised that Mr Galilei finds admirers at the docks.

CHAMBERLAIN: Your highness, I am dismayed to note that this exceptionally instructive conversation has become a trifle prolonged. His highness must have some repose before the court ball.

At a sign, the grand duke bows to Galileo. The court quickly gets ready to leave.

MRS SARTI *blocks the grand duke's way and offers him a plate of biscuits*: A biscuit, your highness? *The older court lady leads the grand duke out.*

GALILEO *hurrying after them*: But all you gentlemen need do is look through the telescope!

CHAMBERLAIN: His highness will not fail to submit your ideas to our greatest living astronomer: Father Christopher Clavius, chief astronomer at the papal college in Rome.

5

Undeterred even by the plague, Galileo carries on with his researches

(a)

Early morning. Galileo at the telescope, bent over his notes. Enter Virginia with a travelling bag.

GALILEO: Virginia! Has something happened?

VIRGINIA: The convent's shut; they sent us straight home. Arcetri has had five cases of plague.

GALILEO *calls*: Sarti!

VIRGINIA: Market Street was barricaded off last night. Two people have died in the old town, they say, and there are three more dying in hospital.

GALILEO: As usual they hushed it all up till it was too late.

MRS SARTI *entering*: What are you doing here?

VIRGINIA: The plague.

MRS SARTI: God alive! I'll pack. *Sits down.*

GALILEO: Pack nothing. Take Virginia and Andrea. I'll get my notes.

He hurries to his table and hurriedly gathers up papers. Mrs Sarti puts Andrea's coat on him as he runs up, then collects some food and bed linen. Enter a grand-ducal footman.

FOOTMAN: In view of the spread of the disease his highness has left the city for Bologna. However, he insisted that Mr Galilei too should be offered a chance to get to safety. The carriage will be outside your door in two minutes.

MRS SARTI *to Virginia and Andrea*: Go outside at once. Here, take this.

ANDREA: What for? If you don't tell my why I shan't go.

MRS SARTI: It's the plague, my boy.

VIRGINIA: We'll wait for Father.

MRS SARTI: Mr Galilei, are you ready?

GALILEO *wrapping the telescope in the tablecloth*: Put Virginia and Andrea in the carriage. I won't be a moment.

VIRGINIA: No, we're not going without you. Once you start packing up your books you'll never finish.

MRS SARTI: The coach is there.

GALILEO: Have some sense, Virginia, if you don't take your seats the coachman will drive off. Plague is no joking matter.

VIRGINIA *protesting, as Mrs Sarti and Andrea escort her out*: Help him with his books, or he won't come.

MRS SARTI *from the main door*: Mr Galilei, the coachman says he can't wait.

GALILEO: Mrs Sarti, I don't think I should go. It's all such a mess, you see: three months' worth of notes which I might as well throw away if I can't spend another night or two on them. Anyway this plague is all over the place.

MRS SARTI: Mr Galilei! You must come now! You're crazy.

GALILEO: You'll have to go off with Virginia and Andrea. I'll follow.

MRS SARTI: Another hour, and nobody will be able to get away. You must come. *Listens*. He's driving off. I'll have to stop him.

Exit.

Galileo walks up and down. Mrs Sarti re-enters, very pale, without her bundle.

GALILEO: What are you still here for? You'll miss the children's carriage.

MRS SARTI: They've gone. Virginia had to be held in. The children will get looked after in Bologna. But who's going to see you get your meals?

GALILEO: You're crazy. Staying in this city in order to cook! *Picking up his notes*: Don't think I'm a complete fool, Mrs Sarti. I can't abandon these observations. I have powerful enemies and I must collect proofs for certain hypotheses.

MRS SARTI: You don't have to justify yourself. But it's not exactly sensible.

(b)

Outside Galileo's house in Florence. Galileo steps out and looks down the street. Two nuns pass by.

GALILEO *addresses them*: Could you tell me, sisters, where I can buy some milk? The milk woman didn't come this morning, and my housekeeper has left.

ONE NUN: The only shops open are in the lower town.

THE OTHER NUN: Did you come from here? *Galileo nods.* This is the street!
The two nuns cross themselves, mumble a Hail Mary and hurry away. A man goes by.

GALILEO *addresses him*: Aren't you the baker that delivers our bread to us? *The man nods.* Have you seen my housekeeper? She must have left last night. She hasn't been around all day. *The man shakes his head. A window is opened across the way and a woman looks out.*

WOMAN *yelling*: Hurry! They've got the plague opposite! *The man runs off horrified.*

GALILEO: Have you heard anything about my housekeeper?

WOMAN: Your housekeeper collapsed in the street up there. She must have realised. That's why she went. So inconsiderate!
She slams the window shut.
Children come down the street. They see Galileo and run away screaming. Galileo turns round; two soldiers hurry up, encased in armour.

SOLDIERS: Get right back indoors!
They push Galileo back into his house with their long pikes. They bolt the door behind him.

GALILEO *at the window*: Can you tell me what happened to the woman?

SOLDIERS: They throw them on the heap.

WOMAN *reappears at the window*: That whole street back there is infected. Why can't you close it off?
The soldiers rope the street off.

WOMAN: But that way nobody can get into our house. This part doesn't have to be closed off. This part's all right. Stop it! Stop! Can't you listen? My husband's still in town, he won't be able to get through to us. You animals! *She can be heard inside weeping and screaming. The soldiers leave. At another window an old woman appears.*

GALILEO: That must be a fire back there.

THE OLD WOMAN: They've stopped putting them out where there's any risk of infection. All they can think about is the plague.

GALILEO: Just like them. It's their whole system of government. Chopping us off like the diseased branch of some barren figtree.

THE OLD WOMAN: That's not fair. It's just that they're powerless.

GALILEO: Are you the only one in your house?

THE OLD WOMAN: Yes. My son sent me a note. Thank God he got a message last night to say somebody back there had died, so he didn't come home. There were eleven cases in our district during the night.

GALILEO: I blame myself for not making my housekeeper leave in time. I had some urgent work, but she had no call to stay.

THE OLD WOMAN: We can't leave either. Who's to take us in? No need for you to blame yourself. I saw her. She left early this morning, around seven o'clock. She must have been ill; when she saw me coming out to fetch in the bread she deliberately kept away from me. She didn't want them to close off your house. But they're bound to find out.

A rattling sound is heard.

GALILEO: What's that?

THE OLD WOMAN: They're trying to make noises to drive away the clouds with the plague seeds in them.

Galileo roars with laughter.

THE OLD WOMAN: Fancy being able to laugh now.

A man comes down the street and finds it roped off.

GALILEO: Hey, you! This street's closed off and I've nothing to eat. Hey! Hey!

The man has quickly hurried away.

THE OLD WOMAN: They may bring something. If not I can

leave a jug of milk outside your door tonight, if you're not scared.

GALILEO: Hey! Hey! Can't anybody hear us?

All of a sudden Andrea is standing by the rope. He looks desperate.

GALILEO: Andrea! How did you get here?

ANDREA: I was here first thing. I knocked but you didn't open your door. They told me you . . .

GALILEO: Didn't you go off in the carriage?

ANDREA: Yes. But I managed to jump out. Virginia went on. Can't I come in?

THE OLD WOMAN: No, you can't. You'll have to go to the Ursulines. Your mother may be there.

ANDREA: I've been. But they wouldn't let me see her. She's too ill.

GALILEO: Did you walk the whole way back? It's three days since you left, you know.

ANDREA: It took all that time. Don't be cross with me. They arrested me once.

GALILEO *helplessly*: Don't cry. You know, I've found out lots of things since you went. Shall I tell you? *Andrea nods between his sobs.* Listen carefully or you won't understand. You remember me showing you the planet Venus? Don't bother about that noise, it's nothing. Can you remember? You know what I saw? It's like the moon! I've seen it as a half circle and I've seen it as a sickle. What d'you say to that? I can demonstrate the whole thing to you with a lamp and a small ball. That proves it's yet another planet with no light of its own. And it turns round the sun in a simple circle; isn't that marvellous?

ANDREA *sobbing*: Yes, and that's a fact.

GALILEO *quietly*: I never asked her to stay.

Andrea says nothing.

GALILEO: But of course if I hadn't stayed myself it wouldn't have happened.

ANDREA: They'll have to believe you now, won't they?

GALILEO: I've got all the proofs I need now. Once this is over, I tell you, I shall go to Rome and show them.

Down the street come two masked men with long poles and buckets. They use these to pass bread through the window to Galileo and the old woman.

THE OLD WOMAN: And there's a woman across there with three children. Leave something for her too.

GALILEO: But I've got nothing to drink. There's no water left in the house. *The two shrug their shoulders.* Will you be coming back tomorrow?

ONE MAN *in a muffled voice, since he has a rag over his mouth*: Who knows what'll happen tomorrow?

GALILEO: If you do come, could you bring me a small book I need for my work?

THE MAN *gives a stifled laugh*: As if a book could make any difference. You'll be lucky if you get bread.

GALILEO: But this boy is my pupil, and he'll be there and can give it you for me. It's the chart giving the periodicity of Mercury, Andrea: I've mislaid it. Can you get me one from the school.

The men have gone on.

ANDREA: Of course. I'll get it, Mr Galilei. *Exit. Galileo likewise goes in. The old woman comes out of the house opposite and puts a jug outside Galileo's door.*

6

1616. The Vatican research institute, the Collegium Romanum, confirms Galileo's findings

Things take indeed a wondrous turn
When learned men do stoop to learn.
Clavius, we are pleased to say
Upheld Galileo Galilei.

Hall of the Collegium Romanum in Rome. It is night-time. High ecclesiastics, monks and scholars in groups. On his own,

to one side, Galileo. The atmosphere is extremely hilarious.
Before the beginning of the scene a great wave of laughter is
heard.

A FAT PRELATE *clasps his belly with laughing*: Stupidity!
Stupidity! I'd like to hear a proposition that people won't
believe.

A SCHOLAR: For instance: that you have an incurable aversion
to meals, Monsignor.

A FAT PRELATE: They'd believe it; they'd believe it. Things
have to make sense to be disbelieved. That Satan exists:
that's something they doubt. But that the earth spins round
like a marble in the gutter; that's believed all right. O sancta
simplicitas!

A MONK *play-acting*: I'm getting giddy. The earth's spinning
round too fast. Permit me to hold on to you, professor. *He*
pretends to lurch and clutches one of the scholars.

THE SCHOLAR *following suit*: Yes, the old girl has been on the
bottle again.

He clutches another.

THE MONK: Stop, stop! We're skidding off. Stop, I said!

A SECOND SCHOLAR: Venus is all askew. I can only see one
half of her backside. Help!

A group of laughing monks forms, acting as if they were
doing their best not to be swept off a ship's deck in a storm.

A SECOND MONK: As long as we aren't flung on to the moon!
It's said to have terribly sharp peaks, my brethren.

THE FIRST SCHOLAR: Dig your heels in and resist.

THE FIRST MONK: And don't look down. I'm losing my
balance.

THE FAT PRELATE *intentionally loudly, aiming at Galileo*: Oh,
that's impossible. Nobody is unbalanced in the Collegium
Romanum.

Much laughter. Two of the Collegium astronomers enter
from a door. There is a silence.

A MONK: Are you still going over it? That's scandalous.

THE FIRST ASTRONOMER *angrily*: Not us.

THE SECOND ASTRONOMER: What's this meant to lead to? I

don't understand Clavius's attitude ... One can't treat everything as gospel that has been put forward in the past fifty years. In 1572 a new star appeared in the eighth and highest sphere, the sphere of the fixed stars, which seemed larger and more brilliant than all the stars round it, and within eighteen months it had gone out and been annihilated. Does that mean we must question the eternity and immutability of the heavens?

PHILOSOPHER: Give them half a chance and they'll smash up the whole starry sky.

THE FIRST ASTRONOMER: Yes, what are we coming to? Five years later Tycho Brahe in Denmark established the course of a comet. It started above the moon and broke through one crystal sphere after another, the solid supports on which all the moving of the heavenly bodies depend. It encountered no obstacles, there was no deflection of its light. Does that mean we must doubt the existence of the spheres?

THE PHILOSOPHER: It's out of the question. As Italy's and the Church's greatest astronomer, how can Christopher Clavius stoop to examine such a proposition?

THE FAT PRELATE: Outrageous.

THE FIRST ASTRONOMER: He is examining it, though. He's sitting in there staring through that diabolical tube.

THE SECOND ASTRONOMER: Principiis obsta! It all started when we began reckoning so many things – the length of the solar year, the dates of solar and lunar eclipses, the position of the heavenly bodies – according to the tables established by Copernicus, who was a heretic.

A MONK: Which is better, I ask you: to have an eclipse of the moon happen three days later than the calendar says, or never to have eternal salvation at all?

A VERY THIN MONK *comes forward with an open Bible, fanatically thrusting his finger at a certain passage*: What do the Scriptures say? "Sun, stand thou still on Gibeon and thou, moon, in the valley of Ajalon." How can the sun stand still if it never moves at all as suggested by this heretic? Are the Scriptures lying?

THE FIRST ASTRONOMER: No, and that's why we walked out.

THE SECOND ASTRONOMER: There *are* phenomena that present difficulties for us astronomers, but does mankind have to understand everything? *Both go out.*

THE VERY THIN MONK: They degrade humanity's dwelling place to a wandering star. Men, animals, plants and the kingdoms of the earth get packed on a cart and driven in a circle round an empty sky. Heaven and earth are no longer distinct, according to them. Heaven because it is made of earth, and earth because it is just one more heavenly body. There is no more difference between top and bottom, between eternal and ephemeral. That we are short-lived we know. Now they tell us that heaven is short-lived too. There are sun, moon and stars, and we live on the earth, it used to be said, and so the Book has it; but now these people are saying the earth is another star. Wait till they say man and animal are not distinct either, man himself is an animal, there's nothing but animals!

THE FIRST SCHOLAR *to Galileo*: Mr Galilei, you've let something fall.

GALILEO *who had meanwhile taken his stone from his pocket, played with it and finally allowed it to drop on the floor, bending to pick it up*: Rise, monsignor; I let it rise.

THE FAT PRELATE *turning round*: An arrogant fellow.

Enter a very old cardinal supported by a monk. They respectfully make way for him.

THE VERY OLD CARDINAL: Are they still in there? Can't they settle such a trivial matter more quickly? Clavius must surely know his astronomy. I am told that this Mr Galilei moves mankind away from the centre of the universe and dumps it somewhere on the edge. Clearly this makes him an enemy of the human race. We must treat him as such. Mankind is the crown of creation, as every child knows, God's highest and dearest creature. How could He take something so miraculous, the fruit of so much effort, and lodge it on a remote, minor, constantly elusive star? Would he send His Son to such a place? How can there be people so perverse as to pin their faith to these slaves of the multiplication table! Which of God's creatures would stand for anything like that?

THE FAT PRELATE *murmurs*: The gentleman is present.

THE VERY OLD CARDINAL *to Galileo*: It's you, is it? You know, my eyesight is not what it was, but I can still see one thing: that you bear a remarkable likeness to what's-his-name, you know, the man we burned.

THE MONK: Your Eminence should avoid excitement. The doctor . . .

THE VERY OLD CARDINAL *shakes him off. To Galileo*: You want to debase the earth even though you live on it and derive everything from it. You are fouling your own nest. But I for one am not going to stand for that. *He pushes the monk away and begins proudly striding to and fro.* I am not just any old creature on any insignificant star briefly circling in no particular place. I am walking with a firm step, on a fixed earth, it is motionless, it is the centre of the universe, I am at the centre and the eye of the Creator falls upon me and me alone. Round about me, attached to eight crystal spheres, revolve the fixed stars and the mighty sun which has been created to light my surroundings. And myself too, that God may see me. In this way everything comes visibly and incontrovertibly to depend on me, mankind, God's great effort, the creature on whom it all centres, made in God's own image, indestructible and . . . *He collapses.*

THE MONK: Your Eminence has overstrained himself.

At this moment the door at the back opens and the great Clavius enters at the head of his astronomers. Swiftly and in silence he crosses the hall without looking to one side or the other and addresses a monk as he is on the way out.

CLAVIUS: He's right. *He leaves, followed by the astronomers. The door at the back remains open. Deadly silence. The very old cardinal recovers consciousness.*

THE VERY OLD CARDINAL: What's that? Have they reached a conclusion?

Nobody dares tell him.

THE MONK: Your Eminence must be taken home. *The old man is assisted out. All leave the hall, worried. A little monk from Clavius's committee of experts pauses beside Galileo.*

THE LITTLE MONK *confidentially*: Mr Galilei, before he left

Father Clavius said: Now it's up to the theologians to see
how they can straighten out the movements of the heavens
once more. You've won. *Exit.*

GALILEO *tries to hold him back*: It has won. Not me: reason
has won.

*The little monk has already left. Galileo too starts to go. In
the doorway he encounters a tall cleric, the Cardinal
Inquisitor, who is accompanied by an astronomer. Galileo
bows. Before going out he whispers a question to the guard
at the door.*

GUARD *whispers back*: His Eminence the Cardinal Inquisitor.
*The astronomer leads the Cardinal Inquisitor up to the
telescope.*

7

But the Inquisition puts Copernicus's teachings on the Index (March 5th, 1616)

When Galileo was in Rome
A cardinal asked him to his home.
He wined and dined him as his guest
And only made one small request.

*Cardinal Bellarmin's house in Rome. A ball is in progress. In
the vestibule, where two clerical secretaries are playing chess
and making notes about the guests, Galileo is received with
applause by a small group of masked ladies and gentlemen. He
arrives accompanied by his daughter Virginia and her fiancé
Ludovico Marsili.*

VIRGINIA: I'm not dancing with anybody else, Ludovico.
LUDOVICO: Your shoulder-strap's undone.

GALILEO:
> Fret not, daughter, if perchance
> You attract a wanton glance.
> The eyes that catch a trembling lace
> Will guess the heartbeat's quickened pace.
> Lovely woman still may be
> Careless with felicity.

VIRGINIA: Feel my heart.

GALILEO *puts his hand on her heart*: It's thumping.

VIRGINIA: I'd like to look beautiful.

GALILEO: You'd better, or they'll go back to wondering whether it turns or not.

LUDOVICO: Of course it doesn't turn. *Galileo laughs.* Rome is talking only of you. But after tonight, sir, they will be talking about your daughter.

GALILEO: It's supposed to be easy to look beautiful in the Roman spring. Even I shall start looking like an overweight Adonis. *To the secretaries*: I am to wait here for his Eminence the Cardinal. *To the couple*: Go off and enjoy yourselves. *Before they leave for the ball offstage Virginia again comes running back.*

VIRGINIA: Father, the hairdresser in the Via del Trionfo took me first, and he made four other ladies wait. He knew your name right away. *Exit.*

GALILEO *to the secretaries as they play chess*: How can you go on playing old-style chess? Cramped, cramped. Nowadays the play is to let the chief pieces roam across the whole board. The rooks like this – *he demonstrates* – and the bishops like that and the Queen like this and that. That way you have enough space and can plan ahead.

FIRST SECRETARY: It wouldn't go with our small salaries, you know. We can only do moves like this. *He makes a small move.*

GALILEO: You've got it wrong, my friend, quite wrong. If you live grandly enough you can afford to sweep the board. One has to move with the times, gentlemen. Not just hugging the coasts; sooner or later one has to venture out. *The very old cardinal from the previous scene crosses the stage, led by his*

*monk. He notices Galileo, walks past him, turns round
hesitantly and greets him. Galileo sits down. From the
ballroom boys' voices are heard singing Lorenzo di Medici's
famous poem on transience,*

> I who have seen the summer's roses die
> And all their petals pale and shrivelled lie
> Upon the chilly ground, I know the truth:
> How evanescent is the flower of youth.

GALILEO: Rome – A large party?

THE FIRST SECRETARY: The first carnival since the plague
years. All Italy's great families are represented here tonight.
The Orsinis, the Villanis, the Nuccolis, the Soldanieris, the
Canes, the Lecchis, the d'Estes, the Colombinis . . .

SECOND SECRETARY *interrupting*: Their Eminences Cardinals
Bellarmin and Barberini.

*Enter Cardinal Bellarmin and Cardinal Barberini. They are
holding sticks with the masks of a lamb and a dove over their
faces.*

BARBERINI *pointing at Galileo*: 'The sun also ariseth, and the
sun goeth down, and hasteth to his place where he arose.' So
says Solomon, and what does Galileo say?

GALILEO: When I was so high – *he indicates with his hand* –
your Eminence, I stood on a ship and called out 'The shore is
moving away.' Today I realise that the shore was standing
still and the ship moving away.

BARBERINI: Ingenious, ingenious – what our eyes see, Bellarmin, in other words the rotation of the starry heavens, is not
necessarily true – witness the ship and the shore. But what is
true – i.e. the rotation of the earth – cannot be perceived.
Ingenious. But his moons of Jupiter are a tough nut for our
astronomers to crack. Unfortunately I once studied some
astronomy, Bellarmin. It sticks to you like the itch.

BELLARMIN: We must move with the times, Barberini. If new
star charts based on a new hypothesis help our mariners to
navigate, then they should make use of them. We only
disapprove of such doctrines as run counter to the Scriptures.
He waves toward the ballroom in greeting.

GALILEO: The Scriptures . . . 'He that withholdeth corn, the people shall curse him.' Proverbs of Solomon.

BARBERINI: 'A prudent man concealeth knowledge.' Proverbs of Solomon.

GALILEO: 'Where no oxen are the crib is clean: but much increase is by the strength of the ox.'

BARBERINI: 'He that ruleth his spirit is better than he that taketh a city.'

GALILEO: 'But a broken spirit drieth the bones.' *Pause.* 'Doth not wisdom cry?'

BARBERINI: 'Can one go upon hot coals, and his feet not be burned?' – Welcome to Rome, Galileo my friend. You know its origins? Two little boys, so runs the legend, were given milk and shelter by a she-wolf. Since that time all her children have had to pay for their milk. The she-wolf makes up for it by providing every kind of pleasure, earthly and heavenly, ranging from conversations with my friend Bellarmin to three or four ladies of international repute; let me point them out to you . . .

He takes Galileo upstage to show him the ballroom. Galileo follows reluctantly.

BARBERINI: No? He would rather have a serious discussion. Right. Are you sure, Galileo my friend, that you astronomers aren't merely out to make astronomy simpler for yourselves? *He leads him forward once more.* You think in circles and ellipses and constant velocities, simple motions such as are adapted to your brains. Suppose it had pleased God to make his stars more like this? *With his finger he traces an extremely complicated course at an uneven speed.* What would that do to your calculations?

GALILEO: Your Eminence, if God had constructed the world like that – *he imitates Barberini's course* – then he would have gone on to construct our brains like that, so that they would regard such motions as the simplest. I believe in men's reason.

BARBERINI: I think men's reason is not up to the job. Silence. He's too polite to go on and say he thinks mine is not up to the job.

Laughs and walks back to the balustrade.

BELLARMIN: Men's reason, my friend, does not take us very far. All around us we see nothing but crookedness, crime and weakness. Where is truth?

GALILEO *angrily*: I believe in men's reason.

BARBERINI *to the secretaries*: You needn't take this down; it's a scientific discussion among friends.

BELLARMIN: Think for an instant how much thought and effort it cost the Fathers of the Church and their countless successors to put some sense into this appalling world of ours. Think of the brutality of the landowners in the Campagna who have their half-naked peasants flogged to work, and of the stupidity of those poor people who kiss their feet in return.

GALILEO: Horrifying. As I was driving here I saw . . .

BELLARMIN: We have shifted the responsibility for such occurrences as we cannot understand – life is made up of them – to a higher Being, and argued that all of them contribute to the fulfilment of certain intentions, that the whole thing is taking place according to a great plan. Admittedly this hasn't satisfied everybody, but now you come along and accuse this higher Being of not being quite clear how the stars move, whereas you yourself are. Is that sensible?

GALILEO *starts to make a statement*: I am a faithful son of the Church . . .

BARBERINI: He's a terrible man. He cheerfully sets out to convict God of the most elementary errors in astronomy. I suppose God hadn't got far enough in his studies before he wrote the Bible; is that it? My *dear* fellow . . .

BELLARMIN: Wouldn't you also think it possible that the Creator had a better idea of what he was making than those he has created?

GALILEO: But surely, gentlemen, mankind may not only get the motions of the stars wrong but the Bible too?

BELLARMIN: But isn't interpreting the Bible the business of Holy Church and her theologians, wouldn't you say?

Galileo is silent.

BELLARMIN: You have no answer to that, have you? *He makes a sign to the secretaries*: Mr Galilei, tonight the Holy Office decided that the doctrine of Copernicus, according to which the sun is motionless and at the centre of the cosmos, while the earth moves and is not at the centre of the cosmos, is foolish, absurd, heretical and contrary to our faith. I have been charged to warn you that you must abandon this view.

GALILEO: What does this mean?

From the ballroom boys can be heard singing a further verse of the madrigal.

I said: This lovely springtime cannot last
So pluck your roses before May is past.

Barberini gestures Galileo not to speak till the song is finished. They listen.

GALILEO: And the facts? I understand that the Collegium Romanum had approved my observations.

BELLARMIN: And expressed their complete satisfaction, in terms very flattering to you.

GALILEO: But the moons of Jupiter, the phases of Venus . . .

BELLARMIN: The Holy Congregation took its decision without going into such details.

GALILEO: In other words, all further scientific research . . .

BELLARMIN: Is explicitly guaranteed, Mr Galilei. In line with the Church's view that it is impossible for us to know, but legitimate for us to explore. *He again greets a guest in the ballroom.* You are also at liberty to treat the doctrine in question mathematically, in the form of a hypothesis. Science is the rightful and much-loved daughter of the Church, Mr Galilei. None of us seriously believes that you want to shake men's faith in the Church.

GALILEO *angrily*: What destroys faith is invoking it.

BARBERINI: Really? *He slaps him on the shoulder with a roar of laughter. Then he gives him a keen look and says in a not unfriendly manner*: Don't tip the baby out with the bathwater, Galileo my friend. We shan't. We need you more than you need us.

BELLARMIN: I cannot wait to introduce Italy's greatest mathematician to the Commissioner of the Holy Office, who has the highest possible esteem for you.

BARBERINI *taking Galileo's other arm*: At which he turns himself back into a lamb. You too, my dear fellow, ought really to have come disguised as a good orthodox thinker. It's my own mask that permits me certain freedoms today. Dressed like this I might be heard to murmur: If God didn't exist we should have to invent him. Right, let's put on our masks once more. Poor old Galileo hasn't got one. *They put Galileo between them and escort him into the ballroom.*

FIRST SECRETARY: Did you get that last sentence?

SECOND SECRETARY: Just doing it. *They write rapidly.* Have you got that bit where he said he believes in men's reason? *Enter the Cardinal Inquisitor.*

THE INQUISITOR: Did the conversation take place?

FIRST SECRETARY *mechanically*: To start with Mr Galilei arrived with his daughter. She has become engaged today to Mr . . . *The Inquisitor gestures him not to go on.* Mr Galilei then told us about the new way of playing chess in which, contrary to all the rules, the pieces are moved right across the board.

THE INQUISITOR *with a similar gesture*: The transcript. *A secretary hands him the transcript and the cardinal sits down and skims through it. Two young ladies in masks cross the stage; they curtsey to the cardinal.*

ONE YOUNG LADY: Who's that?

THE OTHER: The Cardinal Inquisitor.

They giggle and go off. Enter Virginia, looking around for something.

THE INQUISITOR *from his corner*: Well, my daughter?

VIRGINIA *gives a slight start, not having seen him*: Oh, your Eminence . . .

Without looking up, the Inquisitor holds out his right hand to her. She approaches and kisses his ring.

THE INQUISITOR: A splendid night. Permit me to congratulate you on your engagement. Your future husband comes from a distinguished family. Are you staying long in Rome?

VIRGINIA: Not this time, your Eminence. A wedding takes so much preparing.

THE INQUISITOR: Ah, then you'll be returning to Florence like your father. I am glad of that. I expect that your father needs you. Mathematics is not the warmest of companions in the home, is it? Having a creature of flesh and blood around makes all the difference. It's easy to get lost in the world of the stars, with its immense distances, if one is a great man.

VIRGINIA *breathlessly*: You are very kind, your Eminence. I really understand practically nothing about such things.

THE INQUISITOR: Indeed? *He laughs.* In the fisherman's house no one eats fish, eh? It will tickle your father to hear that almost all your knowledge about the world of the stars comes ultimately from me, my child. *Leafing through the transcript*: It says here that our innovators, whose acknowledged leader is your father – a great man, one of the greatest – consider our present ideas about the significance of the dear old earth to be a little exaggerated. Well, from Ptolemy's time – and he was a wise man of antiquity – up to the present day we used to reckon that the whole of creation – in other words the entire crystal ball at whose centre the earth lies – measured about twenty thousand diameters of the earth across. Nice and roomy, but not large enough for innovators. Apparently they feel that it is unimaginably far-flung and that the earth's distance from the sun – quite a respectable distance, we always found it – is so minute compared with its distance from the fixed stars on the outermost sphere that our calculations can simply ignore it. So who can say that the innovators themselves aren't living on a very grand scale?

Virginia laughs. So does the Inquisitor.

THE INQUISITOR: True enough, there are a few gentlemen of the Holy Office who have started objecting, as it were, to such a view of the world, compared with which our picture so far has been a little miniature such as one might hang round the neck of certain young ladies. What worries them is that a prelate or even a cardinal might get lost in such vast distances and the Almighty might lose sight of the Pope himself. Yes, it's very amusing, but I am glad to know that you will remain close to your great father whom we all esteem so highly, my dear child. By the way, do I know your Father Confessor . . . ?

VIRGINIA: Father Christophorus of Saint Ursula.

THE INQUISITOR: Ah yes, I am glad that you will be going with your father. He will need you; perhaps you cannot imagine this, but the time will come. You are still so young and so very much flesh and blood, and greatness is occasionally a difficult burden for those on whom God has bestowed it; it can be. No mortal is so great that he cannot be contained in a prayer. But I am keeping you, my dear child, and I'll be making your fiancé jealous and maybe your father too by telling you something about the stars which is possibly out of date. Run off and dance; only mind you remember me to Father Christophorus.

Virginia makes a deep bow and goes.

8

A conversation

> Galileo, feeling grim,
> A young monk came to visit him.
> The monk was born of common folk.
> It was of science that they spoke.

In the Florentine Ambassador's palace in Rome Galileo is listening to the little monk who whispered the papal astronomer's remark to him after the meeting of the Collegium Romanum.

GALILEO: Go on, go on. The habit you're wearing gives you the right to say whatever you want.

THE LITTLE MONK: I studied mathematics, Mr Galilei.

GALILEO: That might come in handy if it led you to admit that two and two sometimes makes four.

THE LITTLE MONK: Mr Galilei, I have been unable to sleep for three days. I couldn't see how to reconcile the decree I had read with the moons of Jupiter which I had observed. Today I decided to say an early mass and come to you.

GALILEO: In order to tell me Jupiter has no moons?

THE LITTLE MONK: No. I have managed to see the wisdom of the decree. It has drawn my attention to the potential dangers for humanity in wholly unrestricted research, and I have decided to give astronomy up. But I also wanted to explain to you the motives which can make even an astronomer renounce pursuing that doctrine any further.

GALILEO: I can assure you that such motives are familiar to me.

THE LITTLE MONK: I understand your bitterness. You have in mind certain exceptional powers of enforcement at the Church's disposal.

GALILEO: Just call them instruments of torture.

THE LITTLE MONK: But I am referring to other motives. Let me speak about myself. My parents were peasants in the Campagna, and I grew up there. They are simple people. They know all about olive trees, but not much else. As I study the phases of Venus I can visualise my parents sitting round the fire with my sister, eating their curded cheese. I see the beams above them, blackened by hundreds of years of smoke, and I see every detail of their old worn hands and the little spoons they are holding. They are badly off, but even their misfortunes imply a certain order. There are so many cycles, ranging from washing the floor, through the seasons of the olive crop to the paying of taxes. There is a regularity about the disasters that befall them. My father's back does not get bent all at once, but more and more each spring he spends in the olive groves; just as the successive childbirths that have made my mother increasingly sexless have followed well-defined intervals. They draw the strength they need to carry their baskets sweating up the stony tracks, to bear children and even to eat, from the feeling of stability and necessity that comes of looking at the soil, at the annual greening of the trees and at the little church, and of listening to the Bible passages read there every Sunday. They have been assured that God's eye is always on them – probingly, even anxiously – that the whole drama of the world is constructed around them so that they, the performers, may prove themselves in their greater or lesser roles. What would my people say if I told them that they happen to be on a small knob of stone twisting endlessly through the void round a second-rate star, just one among myriads? What would be the value or necessity then of so much patience, such understanding of their own poverty? What would be the use of Holy Scripture, which has explained and justified it all – the sweat, the patience, the hunger, the submissiveness – and now turns out to be full of errors? No: I can see their eyes wavering, I can see them letting their spoons drop, I can see how betrayed and deceived they will feel. So nobody's eye is on us, they'll say. Have we got to look after ourselves, old, uneducated and worn-out as we are? The only part anybody has devised for us is this wretched, earthly one, to be played out on a tiny star wholly dependent on others, with nothing revolving round it. Our poverty has no meaning: hunger is no trial of strength, it's merely not having eaten: effort is no virtue, it's just bending and carrying. Can you see now why I read into the Holy Congregation's decree a noble motherly compassion; a vast goodness of soul?

GALILEO: Goodness of soul! Aren't you really saying that there's nothing for them, the wine has all been drunk, their lips are parched, so they had better kiss the cassock? Why is there nothing for them? Why does order in this country mean the orderliness of a bare cupboard, and necessity nothing but the need to work oneself to death? When there are teeming vineyards and cornfields on every side? Your Campagna peasants are paying for the wars which the representative of gentle Jesus is waging in Germany and Spain. Why does he make the earth the centre of the universe? So that the See of St Peter can be the centre of the

earth! That's what it is all about. You're right, it's not about
the planets, it's about the peasants of the Campagna. And
don't talk to me about the beauty given to phenomena by the
patina of age! You know how the Margaritifera oyster
produces its pearl? By a mortally dangerous disease which
involves taking some unassimilable foreign body, like a grain
of sand, and wrapping it in a slimy ball. The process all but
kills it. To hell with the pearl, give me the healthy oyster.
Virtues are not an offshoot of poverty, my dear fellow. If
your people were happy and prosperous they could develop
the virtues of happiness and prosperity. At present the
virtues of exhaustion derive from exhausted fields, and I
reject them. Sir, my new pumps will perform more miracles
in that direction than all your ridiculous superhuman slaving. – 'Be fruitful and multiply', since your fields are not
fruitful and you are being decimated by wars. Am I supposed
to tell your people lies?

THE LITTLE MONK *much agitated*: We have the highest of all
motives for keeping our mouths shut – the peace of mind of
the less fortunate.

GALILEO: Would you like me to show you a Cellini clock that
Cardinal Bellarmin's coachman brought round this morning? My dear fellow, authority is rewarding me for not
disturbing the peace of mind of people like your parents, by
offering me the wine they press in the sweat of their
countenance which we all know to have been made in God's
image. If I were to agree to keep my mouth shut my motives
would be thoroughly low ones: an easy life, freedom from
persecution, and so on.

THE LITTLE MONK: Mr Galilei, I am a priest.

GALILEO: You're also a physicist. And you can see that Venus
has phases. Here, look out there! *He points at the window.*
Can you see the little Priapus on the fountain next the laurel
bush? The god of gardens, birds and thieves, rich in two
thousand years of bucolic indecency. Even he was less of a
liar. All right, let's drop it. I too am a son of the Church. But
do you know the eighth Satire of Horace? I've been rereading
it again lately, it acts as a kind of counterweight. *He picks up*

a small book. He makes his Priapus speak — a little statue which was then in the Esquiline gardens. Starting:

> Stump of a figtree, useless kind of wood
> Was I once; then the carpenter, not sure
> Whether to make a Priapus or a stool
> Opted for the god . . .

Can you imagine Horace being told not to mention stools and agreeing to put a table in the poem instead? Sir, it offends my sense of beauty if my cosmogony has a Venus without phases. We cannot invent mechanisms to pump water up from rivers if we are not to be allowed to study the greatest of all mechanisms right under our nose, that of the heavenly bodies. The sum of the angles in a triangle cannot be varied to suit the Vatican's convenience. I can't calculate the courses of flying bodies in such a way as also to explain witches taking trips on broomsticks.

THE LITTLE MONK: But don't you think that the truth will get through without us, so long as it's true?

GALILEO: No, no, no. The only truth that gets through will be what we force through: the victory of reason will be the victory of people who are prepared to reason, nothing else. Your picture of the Campagna peasants makes them look like the moss on their own huts. How can anyone imagine that the sum of the angles in a triangle conflicts with *their* needs? But unless they get moving and learn how to think, they will find even the finest irrigation systems won't help them. Oh, to hell with it: I see your people's divine patience, but where is their divine anger?

THE LITTLE MONK: They are tired.

GALILEO *tosses him a bundle of manuscripts*: Are you a physicist, my son? Here you have the reasons why the ocean moves, ebbing and flowing. But you're not supposed to read it, d'you hear? Oh, you've already started. You are a physicist, then? *The little monk is absorbed in the papers.*

GALILEO: An apple from the tree of knowledge! He's wolfing it down. He is damned for ever, but he has got to wolf it down, the poor glutton. I sometimes think I'll have myself shut up in a dungeon ten fathoms below ground in complete darkness if only it will help me to find out what light is. And the worst thing is that what I know I have to tell people, like a lover, like a drunkard, like a traitor. It is an absolute vice and leads to disaster. How long can I go on shouting it into the void, that's the question.

THE LITTLE MONK *indicating a passage in the papers*: I don't understand this sentence.

GALILEO: I'll explain it to you, I'll explain it to you.

9

After keeping silent for eight years, Galileo is encouraged by the accession of a new pope, himself a scientist, to resume his researches into the forbidden area: the sunspots

Eight long years with tongue in cheek
Of what he knew he did not speak.
Then temptation grew too great
And Galileo challenged fate.

Galileo's home in Florence. Galileo's pupils – Federzoni, the little monk and Andrea Sarti, a young man now – have gathered to see an experiment demonstrated. Galileo himself is standing reading a book. Virginia and Mrs Sarti are sewing her trousseau.

VIRGINIA: Sewing one's trousseau is fun. That one's for entertaining at the long table; Ludovico likes entertaining. It's got to be neat, though; his mother can spot every loose thread. She doesn't like Father's books. Nor does Father Christophorus.

MRS SARTI: He hasn't written a book for years.

VIRGINIA: I think he realises he was wrong. A very high church person in Rome told me a lot about astronomy. The distances are too great.

ANDREA *writing the day's programme on the board*: 'Thursday p.m. Floating bodies' – as before, ice, bucket of water, balance, iron needle, Aristotle.

He fetches these thing.

The others are reading books.

Enter Filippo Mucius, a scholar in middle age. He appears somewhat distraught.

MUCIUS: Could you tell Mr Galilei that he has got to see me? He is condemning me unheard.

MRS SARTI: But he won't receive you.

MUCIUS: God will recompense you if you will only ask. I must speak to him.

VIRGINIA *goes to the stairs*: Father!

GALILEO: What is it?

VIRGINIA: Mr Mucius.

GALILEO *looking up sharply, goes to the head of the stairs, followed by his pupils*: What do you want?

MUCIUS: Mr Galilei, may I be allowed to explain those passages from my book which seem to contain a condemnation of Copernicus's theories about the rotation of the earth? I have . . .

GALILEO: What do you want to explain? You are fully in line with the Holy Congregation's decree of 1616. You cannot be faulted. You did of course study mathematics here, but that's no reason why we should need to hear you say that two and two makes four. You are quite within your rights in saying that this stone – *he takes a little stone from his pocket and throws it down to the hall* – has just flown up to the ceiling.

MUCIUS: Mr Galilei, there are worse things than the plague.

GALILEO: Listen to me: someone who doesn't know the truth is just thick-headed. But someone who does know it and calls it a lie is a crook. Get out of my house.

MUCIUS *tonelessly*: You're quite right.

He goes out.

Galileo goes back into his work room.

FEDERZONI: I am afraid so. He's not a great man and no one would take him seriously for one moment if he hadn't been your pupil. Now of course people are saying 'he's heard everything Galileo had to teach and he's forced to admit that it's all nonsense'.

MRS SARTI: I'm sorry for the poor gentleman.

VIRGINIA: Father was too good to him.

MRS SARTI: I really wanted to talk to you about your marriage, Virginia. You're such a child still, and got no mother, and your father keeps putting those little bits of ice on water. Anyhow I wouldn't ask him anything to do with your marriage if I were you. He'd keep on for days saying the most dreadful things, preferably at meals and when the young people are there, because he hasn't got half a scudo's worth of shame in his make-up, and never had. But I'm not talking about that kind of thing, just about how the future will turn out. Not that I'm in a position to know anything myself. I'm not educated. But nobody goes blindly into a serious affair like this. I really think you ought to go to a proper astronomer at the university and get him to cast your horoscope so you know what you're in for. Why are you laughing?

VIRGINIA: Because I've been.

MRS SARTI *very inquisitive*: What did he say?

VIRGINIA: For three months I'll have to be careful, because the sun will be in Aries, but then I shall get a particularly favourable ascendant and the clouds will part. So long as I keep my eye on Jupiter I can travel as much as I like, because I'm an Aries.

MRS SARTI: And Ludovico?

VIRGINIA: He's a Leo. *After a little pause*: That's supposed to be sensual. *Pause.*

VIRGINIA: I know whose step that is. It's Mr Gaffone, the Rector.

Enter Mr Gaffone, Rector of the University.

GAFFONE: I'm just bringing a book which I think might interest your father. For heaven's sake please don't disturb him. I can't help it; I always feel that every moment stolen from that great man is a moment stolen from Italy. I'll lay it neatly and daintily in your hands and slip away, on tiptoe. *He goes. Virginia gives the book to Federzoni.*

GALILEO: What's it about?

FEDERZONI: I don't know. *Spelling out*: 'De maculis in sole'.

ANDREA: About sunspots. Yet another.
Federzoni irritably passes it on to him.

ANDREA: Listen to the dedication. 'To the greatest living authority on physics, Galileo Galilei.'
Galileo is once more deep in his book.

ANDREA: I've read the treatise on sunspots which Fabricius has written in Holland. He thinks they are clusters of stars passing between the earth and the sun.

THE LITTLE MONK: Doubtful, don't you think, Mr Galilei?
Galileo does not answer.

ANDREA: In Paris and in Prague they think they are vapours from the sun.

FEDERZONI: Hm.

ANDREA: Federzoni doubts it.

FEDERZONI: Leave me out of it, would you? I said 'Hm', that's all. I'm your lens-grinder, I grind lenses and you make observations of the sky through them and what you see isn't spots but 'maculis'. How am I to doubt anything? How often do I have to tell you I can't read the books, they're in Latin? *In his anger he gesticulates with the scales. One of the pans falls to the floor. Galileo goes over and picks it up without saying anything.*

THE LITTLE MONK: There's happiness in doubting: I wonder why.

ANDREA: Every sunny day for the past two weeks I've gone up to the attic, under the roof. The narrow chinks between the shingles let just a thin ray of light through. If you take a sheet of paper you can catch the sun's image upside down. I saw a spot as big as a fly, as smudged as a cloud. It was moving. Why aren't we investigating those spots, Mr Galilei?

GALILEO: Because we're working on floating bodies.

ANDREA: Mother's got great baskets full of letters. The whole of Europe wants to know what you think, you've such a reputation now, you can't just say nothing.

GALILEO: Rome allowed me to get a reputation because I said nothing.

FEDERZONI: But you can't afford to go on saying nothing now.

GALILEO: Nor can I afford to be roasted over a wood fire like a ham.

ANDREA: Does that mean you think the sunspots are part of this business?

Galileo does not answer.

ANDREA: All right, let's stick to our bits of ice, they can't hurt you.

GALILEO: Correct. – Our proposition, Andrea?

ANDREA: As for floating, we assume that it depends not on a body's form but on whether it is lighter or heavier than water.

GALILEO: What does Aristotle say?

THE LITTLE MONK: 'Discus latus platique . . .'

GALILEO: For God's sake translate it.

THE LITTLE MONK: 'A broad flat piece of ice will float on water whereas an iron needle will sink.'

GALILEO: Why does the ice not sink, in Aristotle's view?

THE LITTLE MONK: Because it is broad and flat and therefore cannot divide the water.

GALILEO: Right. *He takes a piece of ice and places it in the bucket.* Now I am pressing the ice hard against the bottom of the bucket. I release the pressure of my hands. What happens?

THE LITTLE MONK: It shoots up to the top again.

GALILEO: Correct. Apparently it can divide the water all right as it rises. Fulganzio!

THE LITTLE MONK: But why can it float in the first place? It's heavier than water, because it is concentrated water.

GALILEO: Suppose it were thinned-down water?

ANDREA: It has to be lighter than water, or it wouldn't float.

GALILEO: Aha.

ANDREA: Any more than an iron needle can float. Everything lighter than water floats and everything heavier sinks. QED.

GALILEO: Andrea, you must learn to think cautiously. Hand me the needle. A sheet of paper. Is iron heavier than water?

ANDREA: Yes.

Galileo lays the needle on a piece of paper and launches it on the water. A pause.

GALILEO: What happens?

FEDERZONI: The needle's floating. Holy Aristotle, they never checked up on him!

They laugh.

GALILEO: One of the main reasons why the sciences are so poor is that they imagine they are so rich. It isn't their job to throw open the door to infinite wisdom but to put a limit to infinite error. Make your notes.

VIRGINIA: What is it?

MRS SARTI: Whenever they laugh it gives me a turn. What are they laughing about, I ask myself.

VIRGINIA: Father says theologians have their bells to ring: physicists have their laughter.

MRS SARTI: Anyway I'm glad he isn't looking through his tube so often these days. That was even worse.

VIRGINIA: All he's doing now is put bits of ice in water: that can't do much harm.

MRS SARTI: I don't know.

Enter Ludovico Marsili in travelling clothes, followed by a servant carrying items of luggage. Virginia runs up and throws her arms round him.

VIRGINIA: Why didn't you write and say you were coming?

LUDOVICO: I happened to be in the area, inspecting our vineyards at Buccioli, and couldn't resist the chance.

GALILEO *as though short-sighted*: Who is it?

VIRGINIA: Ludovico.

THE LITTLE MONK: Can't you see him?

GALILEO: Ah yes, Ludovico. *Goes towards him.* How are the horses?

LUDOVICO: Doing fine, sir.

GALILEO: Sarti, we're celebrating. Get us a jug of that Sicilian wine, the old sort.

Exit Mrs Sarti with Andrea.

LUDOVICO *to Virginia*: You look pale. Country life will suit you. My mother is expecting you in September.

VIRGINIA: Wait a moment, I'll show you my wedding dress. *Runs out.*

GALILEO: Sit down.

LUDOVICO: I'm told there are over a thousand students going to your lectures at the university, sir. What are you working at just now?

GALILEO: Routine stuff. Did you come through Rome?

LUDOVICO: Yes. – Before I forget: my mother congratulates you on your remarkable tact in connection with those sunspot orgies the Dutch have been going in for lately.

GALILEO *drily*: Very kind of her.

Mrs Sarti and Andrea bring wine and glasses. Everyone gathers round the table.

LUDOVICO: I can tell you what all the gossip will be about in Rome this February. Christopher Clavius said he's afraid the whole earth-round-the-sun act will start up again because of these sunspots.

ANDREA: No chance.

GALILEO: Any other news from the Holy City, aside from hopes of fresh lapses on my part?

LUDOVICO: I suppose you know that His Holiness is dying?

THE LITTLE MONK: Oh.

GALILEO: Who do they think will succeed him?

LUDOVICO: The favourite is Barberini.

GALILEO: Barberini.

ANDREA: Mr Galilei knows Barberini.

THE LITTLE MONK: Cardinal Barberini is a mathematician.

FEDERZONI: A mathematician at the Holy See!

Pause.

GALILEO: Well: so now they need people like Barberini who have read a bit of mathematics! Things are beginning to move. Federzoni, we may yet see the day when we no longer have to look over our shoulder like criminals every time we say two and two equals four. *To Ludovico*: I like this wine, Ludovico. What do you think of it?

LUDOVICO: It's good.

GALILEO: I know the vineyard. The hillside is steep and stony, the grapes almost blue. I love this wine.

LUDOVICO: Yes, sir.

GALILEO: It has got little shadows in it. And it is almost sweet but just stops short of it. – Andrea, clear all that stuff away, the ice, needle and bucket. – I value the consolations of the flesh. I've no use for those chicken-hearts who see them as weaknesses. Pleasure takes some achieving, I'd say.

THE LITTLE MONK: What have you in mind?

FEDERZONI: We're starting up the earth-round-the-sun act again.

ANDREA *hums*:

> It's fixed, the Scriptures say. And so
> Orthodox science proves.
> The Holy Father grabs its ears, to show
> It's firmly held. And yet it moves.

Andrea, Federzoni and the little monk hurry to the work table and clear it.

ANDREA: We might find that the sun goes round too. How would that suit you, Marsili?

LUDOVICO: What's the excitement about?

MRS SARTI: You're not going to start up that devilish business again, surely, Mr Galilei?

GALILEO: Now I know why your mother sent you to me. Barberini in the ascendant! Knowledge will become a passion and research an ecstasy. Clavius is right, those sunspots interest me. Do you like my wine, Ludovico?

LUDOVICO: I told you I did, sir.

GALILEO: You really like it?

LUDOVICO *stiffly*: I like it.

GALILEO: Would you go so far as to accept a man's wine or his daughter without asking him to give up his profession? What has my astronomy got to do with my daughter? The phases of Venus can't alter my daughter's backside.

MRS SARTI: Don't be so vulgar. I am going to fetch Virginia.

LUDOVICO *holding her back*: Marriages in families like ours are not based on purely sexual considerations.

GALILEO: Did they stop you from marrying my daughter for eight years because I had a term of probation to serve?

LUDOVICO: My wife will also have to take her place in our pew in the village church.

GALILEO: You think your peasants will go by the saintliness of their mistress in deciding whether to pay rent or not?

LUDOVICO: In a sense, yes.

GALILEO: Andrea, Fulganzio, get out the brass reflector and the screen! We will project the sun's image on it so as to protect our eyes; that's your method, Andrea.

Andrea and the little monk fetch reflector and screen.

LUDOVICO: You did sign a declaration in Rome, you know, sir, saying you would have nothing more to do with this earth-round-the-sun business.

GALILEO: Oh that. In those days we had a reactionary pope.

MRS SARTI: Had! And His Holiness not even dead yet!

GALILEO: Almost. Put a grid of squares on the screen. We will do this methodically. And then we'll be able to answer their letters, won't we, Andrea?

MRS SARTI: 'Almost' indeed. The man'll weigh his pieces of ice fifty times over, but as soon as it's something that suits his book he believes it blindly.

The screen is set up.

LUDOVICO: If His Holiness does die, Mr Galilei, irrespective who the next pope is and how intense his devotion to the sciences, he will also have to take into account the devotion felt for him by the most respected families in the land.

THE LITTLE MONK: God made the physical world, Ludovico; God made the human brain; God will permit physics.

MRS SARTI: Galileo, I am going to say something to you. I have watched my son slipping into sin with all those 'experiments' and 'theories' and 'observations' and there was nothing I could do about it. You set yourself up against the authorities and they have already warned you once. The highest cardinals spoke to you like a sick horse. That worked for a time, but then two months ago, just after the Feast of the Immaculate Conception, I caught you secretly starting your 'observations' again. In the attic. I didn't say much but I knew what to do. I ran and lit a candle to St Joseph. It's more than I can cope with. When I get you on your own you show vestiges of sense and tell me you know you've got to behave or else it'll be dangerous; but two days of experiments and you're just as bad as before. If I choose to forfeit eternal bliss by sticking with a heretic that's my business, but you have no right to trample all over your daughter's happiness with your great feet.

GALILEO *gruffly*: Bring the telescope.

LUDOVICO: Giuseppe, take our luggage back to the coach.

The servant goes out.

MRS SARTI: She'll never get over this. You can tell her yourself.

Hurries off, still carrying the jug.

LUDOVICO: I see you have made your preparations. Mr Galilei, my mother and I spend three quarters of each year on our estate in the Campagna, and we can assure you that our peasants are not disturbed by your papers on Jupiter and its moons. They are kept too busy in the fields. But they could be upset if they heard that frivolous attacks on the church's sacred doctrines were in future to go unpunished. Don't forget that the poor things are little better than animals and get everything muddled up. They truly are like beasts, you can hardly imagine it. If rumour says a pear has been seen on an apple tree they will drop their work and hurry off to gossip about it.

GALILEO: *interested*: Really?

LUDOVICO: Beasts. If they come up to the house to make some minor complaint or other, my mother is forced to have a dog whipped before their eyes, as the only way to recall them to discipline and order and a proper respect. You, Mr Galilei, may see rich cornfields from your coach as you pass, you eat our olives and our cheese, without a thought, and you have no idea how much trouble it takes to produce them, how much supervision.

GALILEO: Young man, I do not eat my olives without a

thought. *Roughly*: You're holding me up. *Calls through the door*: Got the screen?

ANDREA: Yes. Are you coming?

GALILEO: You whip other things than dogs for the sake of discipline, don't you, Marsili?

LUDOVICO: Mr Galilei. You have a marvellous brain. Pity.

THE LITTLE MONK *amazed*: He's threatening you.

GALILEO: Yes, I might stir up his peasants to think new thoughts. And his servants and his stewards.

FEDERZONI: How? None of them can read Latin.

GALILEO: I might write in the language of the people, for the many, rather than in Latin for the few. Our new thoughts call for people who work with their hands. Who else cares about knowing the causes of things? People who only see bread on their table don't want to know how it got baked; that lot would sooner thank God than thank the baker. But the people who make the bread will understand that nothing moves unless it has been made to move. Your sister pressing olives, Fulganzio, won't be astounded but will probably laugh when she hears that the sun isn't a golden coat of arms but a motor: that the earth moves because the sun sets it moving.

LUDOVICO: You will always be the slave of your passions. Make my excuses to Virginia; I think it will be better if I don't see her.

GALILEO: Her dowry will remain available to you, at any time.

LUDOVICO: Good day. *He goes.*

ANDREA: And our kindest regards to all the Marsilis.

FEDERZONI: Who command the earth to stand still so their castles shan't tumble down.

ANDREA: And the Cenzis and the Villanis!

FEDERZONI: The Cervillis!

ANDREA: The Lecchis!

FEDERZONI: The Pirleonis!

ANDREA: Who are prepared to kiss the pope's toe only if he uses it to kick the people with!

THE LITTLE MONK *likewise at the instruments*: The new pope is going to be an enlightened man.

GALILEO: So let us embark on the examination of those spots on the sun in which we are interested, at our own risk and without banking too much on the protection of a new pope.

ANDREA *interrupting*: But fully convinced that we shall dispel Mr Fabricius's star shadows along with the sun vapours of Paris and Prague, and establish the rotation of the sun.

GALILEO: Somewhat convinced that we shall establish the rotation of the sun. My object is not to establish that I was right but to find out if I am. Abandon hope, I say, all ye who enter on observation. They may be vapours, they may be spots, but before we assume that they are spots – which is what would suit us best – we should assume that they are fried fish. In fact we shall question everything all over again. And we shall go forward not in seven-league boots but at a snail's pace. And what we discover today we shall wipe off the slate tomorrow and only write it up again once we have again discovered it. And whatever we wish to find we shall regard, once found, with particular mistrust. So we shall approach the observation of the sun with an irrevocable determination to establish that the earth does *not* move. Only when we have failed, have been utterly and hopelessly beaten and are licking our wounds in the profoundest depression, shall we start asking if we weren't right after all, and the earth does go round. *With a twinkle*: But once every other hypothesis has crumbled in our hands then there will be no mercy for those who failed to research, and who go on talking all the same. Take the cloth off the telescope and point it at the sun!

He adjusts the brass reflector.

THE LITTLE MONK: I knew you had begun working on this. I knew when you failed to recognise Mr Marsili.

In silence they begin their observations. As the sun's flaming image appears on the screen Virginia comes running in in her wedding dress.

VIRGINIA: You sent him away, Father.

She faints. Andrea and the little monk hurry to her side.

GALILEO: I've got to know.

10

During the next decade Galileo's doctrine spreads among the common people. Ballad-singers and pamphleteers everywhere take up the new ideas. In the carnival of 1632 many Italian cities choose astronomy as the theme of their guilds' carnival processions.

A half-starved couple of fairground people with a baby and a five-year-old girl enter a market-place where a partly masked crowd is awaiting the carnival procession. The two of them are carrying bundles, a drum and other utensils.

THE BALLAD-SINGER *drumming*: Honoured inhabitants, ladies and gentlemen! To introduce the great carnival procession of the guilds we are going to perform the latest song from Florence which is now being sung all over north Italy and has been imported by us at vast expense. It is called: Ye horrible doctrine and opinions of Messer Galileo Galilei, physicist to the court, or A Foretaste of ye Future. *He sings*:

> When the Almighty made the universe
> He made the earth and then he made the sun.
> Then round the earth he bade the sun to turn –
> That's in the Bible, Genesis, Chapter One.
> And from that time all creatures here below
> Were in obedient circles meant to go.
>
> So the circles were all woven:
> Around the greater went the smaller
> Around the pace-setter the crawler
> On earth as it is in heaven.
> Around the pope the cardinals
> Around the cardinals the bishops
> Around the bishops the secretaries
> Around the secretaries the aldermen

> Around the aldermen the craftsmen
> Around the craftsmen the servants
> Around the servants the dogs, the chickens and the
>   beggars.

That, good people, is the Great Order of things, ordo ordinum as the theologians call it, regula aeternis, the rule of rules; but what, dear people, happened?
Sings:

> Up stood the learned Galilei
> (Chucked away the Bible, whipped out his telescope, took a
> quick look at the universe.)
> And told the sun 'Stop there.
> From now the whole creatio dei
> Will turn as I think fair:
> The boss starts turning from today
> His servants stand and stare.'

> Now that's no joke, my friends, it is no matter small.
> Each day our servants' insolence increases
> But one thing's true, pleasures are few. I ask you all:
> Who wouldn't like to say and do just as he pleases?

Honourable inhabitants, such doctrines are utterly impossible.
He sings:

> The serf stays sitting on his arse.
> This turning's turned his head.
> The altar boy won't serve the mass
> The apprentice lies in bed.

> No, no, my friends, the Bible is no matter small
> Once let them off the lead indeed all loyalty ceases
> For one thing's true, pleasures are few. I ask you all:
> Who wouldn't like to say and do just as he pleases?

Good people all, kindly take a glance at the future as foretold by the learned Doctor Galileo Galilei:

Two housewives standing buying fish
Don't like the fish they're shown
The fishwife takes a hunk of bread
And eats them up alone.
The mason clears the building site
And hauls the builders' stone.
And when the house is finished quite
He keeps it as his own.

Can such things be, my friends? It is no matter small
For independent spirit spreads like foul diseases.
But one thing's true, pleasures are few. I ask you all:
Who wouldn't like to say and do just as he pleases?

The tenant gives his landlord hell
Not caring in the least.
His wife now feeds her children well
On the milk she fed the priest.

No, no, my friends, the Bible is no matter small
Once let them off the lead indeed all loyalty ceases.
But one thing's true, pleasures are few. I ask you all:
Who wouldn't like to say and do just as he pleases?

THE SINGER'S WIFE:
    I lately went a bit too far
    And told my husband I'd see
    If I could get some other fixed star
    To do what he does for me.
BALLAD-SINGER:
    No, no, no, no, no, no! Stop, Galileo, stop.
    Once take a mad dog's muzzle off it spreads diseases
    People must keep their place, some down and some on
        top.
    (Although it's nice for once to do just as one pleases.)
BOTH:
    Good people who have trouble here below
    In serving cruel lords and gentle Jesus
    Who bid you turn the other cheek just so
    They're better placed to strike the second blow:

Obedience isn't going to cure your woe
So each of you wake up, and do just as he pleases!

THE BALLAD-SINGER: Honoured inhabitants, you will now see Galileo Galilei's amazing discovery: the earth circling round the sun!

He belabours the drum violently. The woman and child step forward. The woman holds a crude image of the sun while the child, with a pumpkin over its head to represent the earth, circles round her. The singer points elatedly at the child as if it were performing a dangerous leap as it takes jerky steps to single beats on the drum. Then comes the drumming from the rear.

A DEEP VOICE *calls*: The procession!

Enter two men in rags pulling a little cart. On an absurd throne sits the 'Grand Duke of Florence', a figure with a cardboard crown dressed in sacking and looking through a telescope. Above his throne a sign saying 'Looking for trouble'. Then four masked men march in carrying a big tarpaulin. They stop and toss a puppet representing a cardinal into the air. A dwarf has taken up position to one side with a sign saying 'The new age'. In the crowd a beggar gets up on his crutches and dances, stamping the ground till he crashes to earth. Enter an over-lifesize puppet, Galileo Galilei, bowing to the audience. Before it goes a boy carrying a gigantic Bible, open, with crossed-out pages.

THE BALLAD-SINGER: Galileo Galilei, the Bible-buster!

Huge laughter among the crowd.

11

1633: The Inquisition summons the world-famous scientist to Rome

> The depths are hot, the heights are chill
> The streets are loud, the court is still.

Antechamber and staircase in the Medici palace in Florence. Galileo and his daughter are waiting to be admitted by the Grand Duke.

VIRGINIA: This is taking a long time.

GALILEO: Yes.

VIRGINIA: There's that fellow again who followed us here.
She points out an individual who walks past without looking at them.

GALILEO *whose eyes have suffered*: I don't know him.

VIRGINIA: I've seen him several times in the past few days, though. He gives me the creeps.

GALILEO: Rubbish. We're in Florence, not among Corsican bandits.

VIRGINIA: Here's Rector Gaffone.

GALILEO: He makes me want to run. That idiot will involve me in another of his interminable talks.
Down the stairs comes Mr Gaffone, rector of the university. He is visibly alarmed on seeing Galileo and walks stiffly past them barely nodding, his head awkwardly averted.

GALILEO: What's got into the man? My eyes are bad again. Did he even greet us?

VIRGINIA: Barely. What's in your book? Could it be thought heretical maybe?

GALILEO: You're wasting too much time in church. You'll spoil what's left of your complexion with all this early rising and scurrying off to mass. You're praying for me, is that it?

VIRGINIA: Here's Mr Vanni the ironfounder you designed the furnace for. Don't forget to thank him for those quails.

A man has come down the stairs.

VANNI: Were those good quails I sent you, Mr Galilei?

GALILEO: The quails were first-rate, Messer Vanni, many thanks again.

VANNI: Your name was mentioned upstairs. They're blaming you for those pamphlets against the Bible that have been selling all over the place lately.

GALILEO: I know nothing about pamphlets. The Bible and Homer are my preferred reading.

VANNI: Even if that weren't so I'd like to take this chance to say that we manufacturers are behind you. I'm not the sort of fellow that knows much about the stars, but to me you're the man who's battling for freedom to teach what's new. Take that mechanical cultivator from Germany you were describing to me. In the past year alone five books on agriculture have been published in London. We'd be glad enough to have a book on the Dutch canals. The same sort of people as are trying to block you are stopping the Bologna doctors from dissecting bodies for medical research.

GALILEO: Your voice can be heard, Vanni.

VANNI: I should hope so. Do you realise that they've now got money markets in Amsterdam and London? Commercial schools too. Regularly printed papers with news in them. In this place we haven't even the freedom to make money. They're against ironfoundries because they imagine putting too many workers in one place leads to immorality. I sink or swim with people like you, Mr Galilei. If anybody ever tries launching anything against you, please remember you've friends in every branch of business. You've got the north Italian cities behind you, sir.

GALILEO: As far as I know nobody's thinking of launching anything against me.

VANNI: No?

GALILEO: No.

VANNI: I think you'd be better off in Venice. Fewer clerics. You could take up the cudgels from there. I've a travelling coach and horses, Mr Galilei.

GALILEO: I don't see myself as a refugee. I like my comforts.

VANNI: Surely. But from what I heard upstairs I'd say there was a hurry. It's my impression they'd be glad to know you weren't in Florence just now.

GALILEO: Nonsense. The Grand Duke is my pupil, and what's more the pope himself would never stand for any kind of attempt to trap me.

VANNI: I'm not sure you're good at distinguishing your friends from your enemies, Mr Galilei.

GALILEO: I can distinguish power from impotence. *He goes off brusquely.*

VANNI: Right. I wish you luck. *Exit.*

GALILEO *returning to Virginia*: Every local Tom, Dick and Harry with an axe to grind wants me to be his spokesman, particularly in places where it's not exactly helpful to me. I've written a book about the mechanics of the universe, that's all. What people make of it or don't make of it isn't my business.

VIRGINIA *loudly*: If they only knew how you condemned all those incidents at last carnival-time!

GALILEO: Yes. Give a bear honey and if the brute's hungry you risk losing your arm.

VIRGINIA *quietly*: Did the Grand Duke actually send for you today?

GALILEO: No, but I had myself announced. He wants to have the book, he has paid for it. Ask that official and tell him we don't like being kept waiting.

VIRGINIA: *followed by the same individual, goes and addresses an official*: Mr Mincio, has his Highness been told my father wishes to speak with him?

THE OFFICIAL: How am I to know?

VIRGINIA: I don't call that an answer.

THE OFFICIAL: Don't you?

VIRGINIA: You're supposed to be polite.

The official half turns his back on her and yawns as he looks at the individual.

VIRGINIA *returning*: He says the Grand Duke is still occupied.

GALILEO: I heard you say something about 'polite'. What was it?

VIRGINIA: I was thanking him for his polite answer, that's all. Can't you just leave the book here? You could use the time.

GALILEO: I'm beginning to wonder how much my time is worth. Perhaps I'll accept Sagredo's invitation to spend a few weeks in Padua after all. My health's not what it was.

VIRGINIA: You couldn't live without your books.

GALILEO: We could take a crate or two of that Sicilian wine in the coach with us.

VIRGINIA: You've always said it doesn't travel. And the court owes you three months' salary. They'll never forward it.

GALILEO: That's true.

The Cardinal Inquisitor comes down the stairs.

VIRGINIA: The Cardinal Inquisitor.

As he walks past he makes a deep bow to Galileo.

VIRGINIA: What's the Cardinal Inquisitor doing in Florence, Father?

GALILEO: I don't know. He behaved quite respectfully. I knew what I was doing when I came to Florence and kept quiet for all those years. They've paid me such tributes that now they're forced to accept me as I am.

THE OFFICIAL *calls out*: His Highness the Grand Duke!

Cosimo de Medici comes down the staircase. Galileo goes to meet him. Cosimo stops somewhat embarrassedly.

GALILEO: I wanted to bring my Dialogues on Two World Systems to your . . .

COSIMO: Ah, yes. How are your eyes?

GALILEO: Not too good, your Highness. If your Highness permits, I have the book . . .

COSIMO: The state of your eyes worries me. It worries me, truly. It shows me that you've been a little too eager to use that admirable tube of yours, haven't you?

He walks on without accepting the book.

GALILEO: He didn't take the book, did he?

VIRGINIA: Father, I'm scared.

GALILEO *firmly, in a low voice*: Control your feelings. We're not going home after this, we're going to Volpi the glazier's. I've fixed with him to have a cart full of empty barrels

standing permanently in the yard of the wine house next
door, ready to take me out of the city.

VIRGINIA: So you knew . . .

GALILEO: Don't look round.

They start to go.

A HIGH OFFICIAL *comes down the stairs*: Mr Galilei, I have
been charged to tell you that the court of Florence is no
longer in a position to oppose the Holy Inquisition's wish to
interrogate you in Rome. The coach of the Holy Inquisition
awaits you, Mr Galilei.

12

The Pope

*Room in the Vatican. Pope Urban VIII (formerly Cardinal
Barberini) has received the Cardinal Inquisitor. In the course
of the audience he is robed. Outside is heard the shuffling of
many feet.*

THE POPE *very loudly*: No! No! No!

THE INQUISITOR: So it is your Holiness's intention to go
before this gathering of doctors from every faculty, representatives of every order and the entire clergy, all with their
naive faith in the word of God as set down in the Scriptures,
who are now assembling here to have that trust confirmed by
your Holiness, and tell them that those Scriptures can no
longer be regarded as true?

THE POPE: I am not going to have the multiplication table
broken. No!

THE INQUISITOR: Ah, it's the multiplication table, not the
spirit of insubordination and doubt: that's what these people
will tell you. But it isn't the multiplication table. No, a
terrible restlessness has descended on the world. It is the
restlessness of their own brain which these people have

transferred to the unmoving earth. They shout 'But look at the figures'. But where do their figures come from? Everybody knows they originate in doubt. These people doubt everything. Are we to base human society on doubt and no longer on faith? 'You are my lord, but I doubt if that's a good thing.' 'This is your house and your wife, but I doubt if they shouldn't be mine.' Against that we have your Holiness's love of art, to which we owe our fine collections, being subjected to such disgraceful interpretations as we see scrawled on the walls of Roman houses: 'The Barberinis take what the Barbarians left'. And abroad? Your Holiness's Spanish policy has been misinterpreted by short-sighted critics, its antagonising of the Emperor regretted. For the last fifteen years Germany has been running with blood, and men have quoted the Bible as they hacked each other to pieces. And at this moment, just when Christianity is being shrivelled into little enclaves by plague, war and the Reformation, a rumour is going through Europe that you have made a secret pact with protestant Sweden in order to weaken the Catholic emperor. So what do these wretched mathematicians do but go and point their tubes at the sky and inform the whole world that your Holiness is hopelessly at sea in the one area nobody has yet denied you? There's every reason to be surprised at this sudden interest in an obscure subject like astronomy. Who really cares how these spheres rotate? But thanks to the example of this wretched Florentine all Italy, down to the last stable boy, is now gossiping about the phases of Venus, nor can they fail at the same time to think about a lot of other irksome things that schools and others hold to be incontrovertible. Given the weakness of their flesh and their liability to excesses of all kinds, what would the effect be if they were to believe in nothing but their own reason, which this maniac has set up as the sole tribunal? They would start by wondering if the sun stood still over Gibeon, then extend their filthy scepticism to the offertory box. Ever since they began voyaging across the seas – and I've nothing against that – they have placed their faith in a brass ball they call a compass, not in

God. This fellow Galileo was writing about machines even when he was young. With machines they hope to work miracles. What sort? God anyhow is no longer necessary to them, but what kind of miracle is it to be? The abolition of top and bottom, for one. They're not needed any longer. Aristotle, whom they otherwise regard as a dead dog, has said – and they quote this – that once the shuttle weaves by itself and the plectrum plays the zither of its own accord, then masters would need no apprentice and lords no servants. And they think they are already there. This evil man knows what he is up to when he writes his astronomical works not in Latin but in the idiom of fishwives and wool merchants.

THE POPE: That's very bad taste; I shall tell him.

THE INQUISITOR: He agitates some of them and bribes others. The north Italian ports are insisting more and more that they must have Mr Galilei's star charts for their ships. We'll have to give in to them, material interests are at stake.

THE POPE: But those star charts are based on his heretical theories. They presuppose certain motions on the part of the heavenly bodies which are impossible if you reject his doctrine. You can't condemn the doctrine and accept the charts.

THE INQUISITOR: Why not? It's the only way.

THE POPE: This shuffling is getting on my nerves. I cannot help listening to it.

THE INQUISITOR: It may speak to you more persuasively than I can, your Holiness. Are all these people to leave here with doubt in their hearts?

THE POPE: After all the man is the greatest physicist of our time, the light of Italy, and not just any old crank. He has friends. There is Versailles. There's the Viennese Court. They'll call Holy Church a cesspool of decomposing prejudices. Hands off him!

THE INQUISITOR: Practically speaking one wouldn't have to push it very far with him. He is a man of the flesh. He would give in immediately.

THE POPE: He enjoys himself in more ways than any man I

have ever met. His thinking springs from sensuality. Give him an old wine or a new idea, and he cannot say no. But I won't have any condemnation of the physical facts, no war cries of 'Up the Church' 'Up Reason'. I let him write his book on condition that he finished it by saying that the last word lay with faith, not science. He met that condition.

THE INQUISITOR: But how? His book shows a stupid man, representing the view of Aristotle of course, arguing with a clever one who of course represents Mr Galilei's own; and which do you think, your Holiness, delivers the final remark?

THE POPE: What did you say? Well, which of them expresses our view?

THE INQUISITOR: Not the clever one.

THE POPE: Yes, that is an impertinence. All this stamping in the corridors is really unbearable. Is the whole world coming here?

THE INQUISITOR: Not the whole of it but its best part.
Pause. The Pope is now in his full robes.

THE POPE: At the very most he can be shown the instruments.

THE INQUISITOR: That will be enough, your Holiness. Instruments are Mr Galilei's speciality.

13

Before the Inquisition, on June 22nd 1633, Galileo recants his doctrine of the motion of the earth

> June twenty-second, sixteen thirty-three
> A momentous day for you and me.
> Of all the days that was the one
> An age of reason could have begun.

In the Florentine ambassador's palace in Rome. Galileo's pupils are waiting for news. Federzoni and the little monk are playing new-style chess with its sweeping moves. In one corner Virginia kneels saying the Ave Maria.

THE LITTLE MONK: The Pope wouldn't receive him. No more discussions about science.

FEDERZONI: That was his last hope. It's true what he told him years back in Rome when he was still Cardinal Barberini: We need you. Now they've got him.

ANDREA: They'll kill him. The Discorsi will never get finished.

FEDERZONI *gives him a covert look*: You think so?

ANDREA: Because he'll never recant.

Pause.

THE LITTLE MONK: You keep getting quite irrelevant thoughts when you can't sleep. Last night for instance I kept on thinking, he ought never to have left the Venetian Republic.

ANDREA: He couldn't write his book there.

FEDERZONI: And in Florence he couldn't publish it.

Pause.

THE LITTLE MONK: I also wondered if they'd let him keep his little stone he always carries in his pocket. His proving stone.

FEDERZONI: You don't wear pockets where they'll be taking him.

ANDREA *shouting*: They daren't do that! And even if they do he'll not recant. 'Someone who doesn't know the truth is just thick-headed. But someone who does know it and calls it a lie is a crook.'

FEDERZONI: I don't believe it either and I wouldn't want to go on living if he did it. But they do have the power.

ANDREA: Power can't achieve everything.

FEDERZONI: Perhaps not.

THE LITTLE MONK *softly*: This is his twenty-fourth day in prison. Yesterday was the chief hearing. And today they're sitting on it. *Aloud, as Andrea is listening*: That time I came to see him here two days after the decree we sat over there and he showed me the little Priapus by the sundial in the garden – you can see it from here – and he compared his own work with a poem by Horace which cannot be altered either. He talked about his sense of beauty, saying that was what forced him to look for the truth. And he quoted the motto 'Hieme et aestate, et prope et procul, usque dum vivam et ultra'. And he was referring to truth.

ANDREA *to the little monk*: Have you told him the way he stood in the Collegium Romanum when they were testing his tube? Tell him! *The little monk shakes his head.* He behaved just as usual. He had his hands on his hams, thrust out his tummy and said 'I would like a bit of reason, please, gentlemen.'
Laughing, he imitates Galileo.
Pause.

ANDREA *referring to Virginia*: She is praying that he'll recant.

FEDERZONI: Leave her alone. She's been all confused ever since they spoke to her. They brought her father confessor down from Florence.
The individual from the Grand-Ducal palace in Florence enters.

INDIVIDUAL: Mr Galilei will be here shortly. He may need a bed.

FEDERZONI: Have they released him?

INDIVIDUAL: It is expected that Mr Galilei will recant around five o'clock at a full sitting of the Inquisition. The great bell of St Mark's will be rung and the text of his recantation will be proclaimed in public.

ANDREA: I don't believe it.

INDIVIDUAL: In view of the crowds in the streets Mr Galilei will be brought to the garden gate here at the back of the palace.
Exit.

ANDREA *suddenly in a loud voice*: The moon is an earth and has no light of its own. Likewise Venus has no light of its own and is like the earth and travels round the sun. And four moons revolve round the planet Jupiter which is on a level with the fixed stars and is unattached to any crystal sphere. And the sun is the centre of the cosmos and motionless, and the earth is not the centre and not motionless. And he is the one who showed us this.

THE LITTLE MONK: And no force will help them to make what has been seen unseen.

Silence.

FEDERZONI *looks at the sundial in the garden*: Five o'clock.

Virginia prays louder.

ANDREA: I can't wait any more. They're beheading the truth. *He puts his hands over his ears, as does the little monk. But the bell is not rung. After a pause filled only by Virginia's murmured prayers, Federzoni shakes his head negatively. The others let their hands drop.*

FEDERZONI *hoarsely*: Nothing. It's three minutes past the hour.

ANDREA: He's holding out.

THE LITTLE MONK: He's not recanting.

FEDERZONI: No. Oh, how marvellous for us!

They embrace. They are ecstatically happy.

ANDREA: So force won't do the trick. There are some things it can't do. So stupidity has been defeated, it's not invulnerable. So man is not afraid of death.

FEDERZONI: This truly is the start of the age of knowledge. This is the hour of its birth. Imagine if he had recanted.

THE LITTLE MONK: I didn't say, but I was worried silly. O ye of little faith!

ANDREA: But I knew.

FEDERZONI: Like nightfall in the morning, it would have been.

ANDREA: As if the mountain had said 'I'm a lake'.

THE LITTLE MONK *kneels down weeping*: Lord, I thank thee.

ANDREA: But today everything is altered. Man, so tormented, is lifting his head and saying 'I can live'. Such a lot is won when even a single man gets to his feet and says No. *At this moment the bell of Saint Mark's begins to toll. All stand rigid.*

VIRGINIA *gets up*: The bell of Saint Mark's. He is not damned! *From the street outside we hear the crier reading Galileo's recantation*:

CRIER'S VOICE: 'I, Galileo Galilei, teacher of mathematics and physics in Florence, abjure what I have taught, namely that

the sun is the centre of the cosmos and motionless and the
earth is not the centre and not motionless. I foreswear, detest
and curse, with sincere heart and unfeigned faith, all these
errors and heresies as also any error and any further opinion
repugnant to Holy Church.'
It grows dark.
When the light returns the bell is still tolling, but then stops.
Virginia has left. Galileo's pupils are still there.

FEDERZONI: You know, he never paid you for your work.
You could never publish your own stuff or buy yourself new
breeches. You stood for it because it was 'working for the
sake of science'.

ANDREA *loudly*: Unhappy the land that has no heroes!
*Galileo has entered, so completely changed by his trial as to
be almost unrecognisable. He has heard Andrea's remark.
For a few moments he stands at the gate waiting to be
greeted. When he is not, and his pupils back away from him,
he goes slowly and, on account of his bad eyes, uncertainly
forward till he finds a stool and sits down.*

ANDREA: I can't look at him. Get him away.

FEDERZONI: Calm down.

ANDREA *yells at Galileo*: Wine-pump! Snail-eater! Did you
save your precious skin? *Sits down*: I feel ill.

GALILEO *quietly*: Give him a glass of water.
*The little monk fetches Andrea a glass of water from outside.
The others do nothing about Galileo, who sits on his stool
and listens. Outside the crier's voice can again be heard in
the distance.*

ANDREA: I think I can walk with a bit of help.
*They escort him to the door. At this juncture Galileo starts
to speak.*

GALILEO: No. Unhappy the land where heroes are needed.
A reading before the curtain:
Is it not obvious that a horse falling from a height of three
or four ells will break its legs, whereas a dog would not
suffer any damage, nor would a cat from a height of eight
or nine ells, nor a cricket from a tower nor an ant even if it
were to fall from the moon? And just as smaller animals

are comparatively stronger than larger ones, so small plants too stand up better: an oak tree two hundred ells high cannot sustain its branches in the same proportion as a small oak tree, nor can nature let a horse grow as large as twenty horses or produce a giant ten times the size of man unless it changes all the proportions of the limbs and especially of the bones, which would have to be strengthened far beyond the size demanded by mere proportion. – The common assumption that large and small machines are equally durable is apparently erroneous.

Galileo. Discorsi.

14

1633–1642. Galileo Galilei lives in a house in the country near Florence, a prisoner of the Inquisition till he dies. The 'Discorsi'

A large room with table, leather chair and globe. Galileo, old now and half blind, is carefully experimenting with a bent wooden rail and a small ball of wood. In the antechamber sits a monk on guard. There is a knock at the door. The monk opens it and a peasant comes in carrying two plucked geese. Virginia emerges from the kitchen. She is now about forty years old.

THE PEASANT: They told me to deliver these.
VIRGINIA: Who? I didn't order any geese.
THE PEASANT: They told me to say it was someone passing through. *Virginia looks at the geese in amazement. The monk takes them from her and examines them dubiously. Then he gives them back to her, satisfied, and she carries them by their necks to Galileo in the large room.*
VIRGINIA: Somebody passing through has sent us a present.

GALILEO: What is it?

VIRGINIA: Can't you see?

GALILEO: No. *He walks over.* Geese. Any name on them?

VIRGINIA: No.

GALILEO *takes one of the geese from her*: Heavy. I could eat some of that.

VIRGINIA: Don't tell me you're hungry again; you've just had your supper. And what's wrong with your eyes this time? You should have been able to see them from where you are.

GALILEO: You're in the shadow.

VIRGINIA: I'm not in the shadow. *She takes the geese out.*

GALILEO: Put thyme with them, and apples.

VIRGINIA *to the monk*: We'll have to get the eye doctor in. Father couldn't see the geese from his table.

THE MONK: Not till I've cleared it with Monsignor Carpula. Has he been writing again?

VIRGINIA: No. He dictated his book to me, as you know. You've had pages 131 and 132, and those were the last.

THE MONK: He's an old fox.

VIRGINIA: He's doing nothing contrary to instructions. His repentance is genuine. I'll keep an eye on him. Tell them in the kitchen they're to fry the liver with an apple and an onion. *She goes back into the large room.* And now let's consider our eyes and leave that ball alone and dictate just a bit more of our weekly letter to the archbishop.

GALILEO: I'm not well enough. Read me some Horace.

VIRGINIA: Only last week Monsignor Carpula was telling me – and we owe him so much, you know; another lot of vegetables only the other day – that the archbishop keeps asking him what you think of those questions and quotations he sends you.

She has sat down to take dictation.

GALILEO: Where had I got to?

VIRGINIA: Section four: with respect to Holy Church's policy concerning the unrest in the Arsenal in Venice I agree with the attitude adopted by Cardinal Spoletti towards the disaffected rope-makers . . .

GALILEO: Yes. *He dictates*: I agree with the attitude adopted by Cardinal Spoletti towards the disaffected rope-makers, namely that it is better to hand out soup to them in the name of Christian brotherly love than to pay them more for their hawsers and bell ropes. Especially as it seems wiser to encourage their faith rather than their acquisitiveness. The apostle Paul says 'Charity never faileth'. – How's that?

VIRGINIA: That's wonderful, Father.

GALILEO: You don't think a suspicion of irony might be read into it?

VIRGINIA: No, the archbishop will be delighted. He is so practical.

GALILEO: I trust your judgement. What's next?

VIRGINIA: A most beautiful saying: 'When I am weak then I am strong'.

GALILEO: No comment.

VIRGINIA: Why not?

GALILEO: What's next?

VIRGINIA: 'And to know the love of Christ, which passeth knowledge'. Saint Paul's Epistle to the Ephesians, iii, 19.

GALILEO: I am particularly grateful to your Eminence for the splendid quotation from the Epistle to the Ephesians. Stimulated by it I looked in our incomparable *Imitation* and found the following. *He quotes by heart*: 'He to whom speaketh the eternal word is free from much questioning.' May I take this opportunity to refer to my own affairs? I am still blamed for once having written an astronomical work in the language of the market-place. It was not my intention thereby to propose or approve the writing of books on infinitely more important matters, such as theology, in the jargon of pasta merchants. The argument for holding services in Latin – that it is a universal language and allows every nationality to hear holy mass in exactly the same way – seems to me a shade unfortunate in that our ever-present cynics might say this prevents any nationality from understanding the text. That sacred matters should be made cheaply understandable is something I can gladly do without. The church's Latin, which protects its eternal verities from the curiosity of the ignorant, inspires confidence when spoken by the priestly sons of the lower classes in the accents of the appropriate local dialect. No, strike that out.

VIRGINIA: All of it?

GALILEO: Everything after pasta merchants.

There is a knock at the door. Virginia goes into the antechamber. The monk opens. It is Andrea Sarti. He is now a man in his middle years.

ANDREA: Good evening. I am leaving Italy to do research in Holland and they asked me to look him up on the way through so I can say how he is.

VIRGINIA: I don't know that he'll want to see you. You never came.

ANDREA: Ask him. *Galileo has recognised his voice. He sits motionless. Virginia goes in to him.*

GALILEO: Is that Andrea?

VIRGINIA: Yes. Shall I send him away?

GALILEO *after a moment*: Show him in.

Virginia brings Andrea in.

VIRGINIA *to the monk*: He's harmless. Used to be his pupil. So now he's his enemy.

GALILEO: Leave us, Virginia.

VIRGINIA: I want to hear what he's got to say. *She sits down.*

ANDREA *coolly*: How are you?

GALILEO: Come closer. What are you doing now? Tell us about your work. I'm told you're on hydraulics.

ANDREA: Fabricius in Amsterdam has commissioned me to inquire about your health.

Pause.

GALILEO: My health is good. They pay me every attention.

ANDREA: I am glad I can report that your health is good.

GALILEO: Fabricius will be glad to hear it. And you can tell him that I live in corresponding comfort. The depth of my repentance has earned me enough credit with my superiors to be permitted to conduct scientific studies on a modest scale under clerical supervision.

ANDREA: That's right. We too heard that the church is more than pleased with you. Your utter capitulation has been effective. We understand the authorities are happy to note that not a single paper expounding new theories has been published in Italy since you toed the line.

GALILEO *listening*: Unhappily there are still countries not under the wing of the church. I'm afraid the condemned doctrines are being pursued there.

ANDREA: There too your recantation caused a setback most gratifying to the church.

GALILEO: Really? *Pause.* Nothing from Descartes? No news from Paris.

ANDREA: On the contrary. When he heard about your recantation he shoved his treatise on the nature of light away in a drawer.

Long pause.

GALILEO: I feel concern for certain scientific friends whom I led into error. Did they learn anything from my recantation?

ANDREA: The only way I can do research is by going to Holland. They won't permit the ox anything that Jove won't permit himself.

GALILEO: I see.

ANDREA: Federzoni is back to grinding lenses in some shop in Milan.

GALILEO *laughs*: He doesn't know Latin.

ANDREA: Fulganzio, our little monk, has given up science and gone back to the bosom of the church.

GALILEO: Yes. *Pause.*

GALILEO: My superiors hope to achieve a spiritual cure in my case too. I am progressing better than anyone expected.

ANDREA: Indeed.

VIRGINIA: The Lord be praised.

GALILEO *roughly*: See to the geese, Virginia.

Virginia goes out angrily. The monk speaks to her as she passes.

THE MONK: I don't like that man.

VIRGINIA: He's harmless. You heard them. *Walking away*: There's some fresh goats-milk cheese arrived.

The monk follows her out.

ANDREA: I have to travel all night if I'm to cross the frontier early tomorrow. May I go?

GALILEO: I don't know why you came, Sarti. Was it to unsettle me? I've been living prudently and thinking prudently since coming here. Even so I get relapses.

ANDREA: I have no wish to arouse you, Mr Galilei.

GALILEO: Barberini called it the itch. He wasn't entirely free of it himself. I've been writing again.

ANDREA: Indeed.

GALILEO: I finished the 'Discorsi'.

ANDREA: What? The 'Discourses Concerning Two New Sciences: Mechanics and Local Motion'? Here?

GALILEO: Oh, they let me have pens and paper. My masters aren't stupid. They realise that deeply engrained vices can't be snapped off just like that. They shield me from any undesirable consequences by locking the pages away as I write them.

ANDREA: O God!

GALILEO: Did you say something?

ANDREA: They're making you plough water. They allow you pens and paper to keep you quiet. How can you possibly write when you know that's the purpose?

GALILEO: Oh, I'm a creature of habit.

ANDREA: The 'Discorsi' in the hands of the monks! With Amsterdam and London and Prague all slavering for it!

GALILEO: I can hear Fabricius grumbling away, insisting on his pound of flesh, meanwhile sitting safe and sound himself in Amsterdam.

ANDREA: Two new branches of science as good as lost!

GALILEO: It will no doubt relieve him and one or two others to hear that I've been risking the last pathetic remnants of my own comfort by making a transcript, more or less behind my back, by squeezing the very last ounce of light out of each reasonably clear night for the past six months.

ANDREA: You've got a transcript?

GALILEO: So far my vanity has stopped me destroying it.

ANDREA: Where is it?

GALILEO: 'If thine eye offend thee, pluck it out'. Whoever wrote that knew more about comfort than me. I suppose it's the height of folly to part with it. However, as I haven't managed to keep clear of scientific work you people might as well have it. The transcript is inside that globe. Should you think of taking it to Holland you would of course have to bear the entire responsibility. In that case you would have bought it from someone who had access to the original in the Holy Office.

Andrea has gone to the globe. He takes out the transcript.

ANDREA: The 'Discorsi'! *He leafs through the manuscript. Reads:* 'It is my purpose to establish an entirely new science in regard to a very old problem, namely, motion. By means of experiments I have discovered some of its properties, which are worth knowing.'

GALILEO: I had to do something with my time.

ANDREA: This will found a new physics.

GALILEO: Stuff it under your coat.

ANDREA: And we thought you had deserted! No voice against you was louder than mine!

GALILEO: Very proper. I taught you science and I denied the truth.

ANDREA: This alters everything. Everything.

GALILEO: Really?

ANDREA: You were hiding the truth. From the enemy. Even in matters of ethics you were centuries ahead of us.

GALILEO: Elaborate that, will you, Andrea?

ANDREA: Like the man in the street we said 'He'll die, but he'll never recant.' You came back: 'I've recanted, but I'm going to live.' – 'Your hands are stained', we said. You're saying: 'Better stained than empty'.

GALILEO: Better stained than empty. Sounds realistic. Sounds like me. New science, new ethics.

ANDREA: I of all people should have known. I was eleven when you sold another man's telescope to the Venetian Senate. And I saw you put that instrument to immortal use. Your friends shook their heads when you bowed to that boy in Florence: science gained an audience. Even then you used to laugh at heroes. 'People who suffer are boring,' you said. 'Misfortune comes from miscalculation'. And 'When there are obstacles the shortest line betweeen two points may be a crooked one.'

GALILEO: I remember.

ANDREA: So in '33 when you chose to recant a popular point in your doctrine I ought to have known that you were simply backing out of a hopeless political wrangle in order to get on with the real business of science.

GALILEO: Which is . . .

ANDREA: Studying the properties of motion, mother of those machines which alone are going to make the earth so good to live on that heaven can be cleared away.

GALILEO: Aha.

ANDREA: You gained the leisure to write a scientific work which could be written by nobody else. If you had ended up at the stake in a halo of flames the other side would have won.

GALILEO: They did win. And there is no scientific work that can only be written by one particular man.

ANDREA: Why did you recant, then?

GALILEO: I recanted because I was afraid of physical pain.

ANDREA: No!

GALILEO: They showed me the instruments.

ANDREA: So it wasn't planned?

GALILEO: It was not.

Pause.

ANDREA *loudly*: Science makes only one demand: contribution to science.

GALILEO: And I met it. Welcome to the gutter, brother in science and cousin in betrayal! Do you eat fish? I have fish. What stinks is not my fish but me. I sell out, you are a buyer. O irresistible glimpse of the book, the sacred commodity! The mouth waters and curses drown. The great whore of Babylon, the murderous beast, the scarlet woman, opens her thighs and everything is altered. Blessed be our horse-trading, whitewashing, death-fearing community!

ANDREA: Fearing death is human. Human weaknesses don't matter to science.

GALILEO: Don't they? – My dear Sarti, even as I now am I

think I can still give you a tip or two as to what matters to that science you have dedicated yourself to.

A short pause.

GALILEO *professorially, folding his hands over his stomach*: In my spare time, of which I have plenty, I have gone over my case and considered how it is going to be judged by that world of science of which I no longer count myself a member. Even a wool merchant has not only to buy cheap and sell dear but also to ensure that the wool trade continues unimpeded. The pursuit of science seems to me to demand particular courage in this respect. It deals in knowledge procured through doubt. Creating knowledge for all about all, it aims to turn all of us into doubters. Now the bulk of the population is kept by its princes, landlords and priests in a pearly haze of superstition and old saws which cloak what these people are up to. The poverty of the many is as old as the hills, and from pulpit and lecture platform we hear that it is as hard as the hills to get rid of. Our new art of doubting delighted the mass audience. They tore the telescope out of our hands and trained it on their tormentors, the princes, landlords and priests. These selfish and domineering men, having greedily exploited the fruits of science, found the cold eye of science had been turned on a primaeval but contrived poverty that could clearly be swept away if they were swept away themselves. They showered us with threats and bribes, irresistible to feeble souls. But can we deny ourselves to the crowd and still remain scientists? The movements of the heavenly bodies have become more comprehensible, but the peoples are as far as ever from calculating the moves of their rulers. The battle for a measurable heaven has been won thanks to doubt; but thanks to credulity the Rome house-wife's battle for milk will be lost time and time again. Science, Sarti, is involved in both these battles. A human race which shambles around in a pearly haze of superstition and old saws, too ignorant to develop its own powers, will never be able to develop those powers of nature which you people are revealing to it. To what end are you working? Presumably for the principle that science's sole aim must be to lighten the burden of human existence. If the scientists, brought to heel by self-interested rulers, limit themselves to piling up knowledge for knowledge's sake, then science can be crippled and your new machines will lead to nothing but new impositions. You may in due course discover all that there is to discover, and your progress will nonetheless be nothing but a progress away from mankind. The gap between you and it may one day become so wide that your cry of triumph at some new achievement will be echoed by a universal cry of horror. – As a scientist I had a unique opportunity. In my day astronomy emerged into the market-place. Given this unique situation, if one man had put up a fight it might have had tremendous repercussions. Had I stood firm the scientists could have developed something like the doctors' Hippocratic oath, a vow to use their knowledge exclusively for mankind's benefit. As things are, the best that can be hoped for is a race of inventive dwarfs who can be hired for any purpose. What's more, Sarti, I have come to the conclusion that I was never in any real danger. For a few years I was as strong as the authorities. And I handed my knowledge to those in power for them to use, fail to use, misuse – whatever best suited their objectives.

Virginia has entered with a dish and come to a standstill.

GALILEO: I betrayed my profession. A man who does what I did cannot be tolerated in the ranks of science.

VIRGINIA: You are accepted in the ranks of the faithful.

She moves on and puts the dish on the table.

GALILEO: Correct. – Now I must eat.

Andrea holds out his hand. Galileo sees the hand but does not take it.

GALILEO: You're a teacher yourself now. Can you afford to take a hand like mine? *He goes to the table.* Somebody passing through sent me some geese. I still enjoy eating.

ANDREA: So you no longer believe a new age has started?

GALILEO: On the contrary – Look out for yourself when you pass through Germany, with the truth under your coat.

ANDREA *unable to tear himself away*: About your opinion of the author we were talking about. I don't know how to answer. But I cannot think your devastating analysis will be the last word.

GALILEO: Thank you very much, sir. *He begins eating.*

VIRGINIA *escorting Andrea out*: We don't like visitors from the past. They excite him.

Andrea leaves. Virginia comes back.

GALILEO: Got any idea who might have sent the geese?

VIRGINIA: Not Andrea.

GALILEO: Perhaps not. What's the night like?

VIRGINIA *at the window*: Clear.

15

Galileo's book, the 'Discorsi', crosses the Italian frontier

> The great book o'er the border went
> And, good folk, that was the end.
> But we hope you'll keep in mind
> He and I were left behind.
> May you now guard science's light
> Kindle it and use it right
> Lest it be a flame to fall
> Downward to consume us all.
> Yes, us all.

Little Italian frontier town in the early morning. Children are playing by the barrier. Andrea, standing beside a coachman, is waiting to have his papers checked by the frontier guards. He is sitting on a small box reading Galileo's manuscript. On the other side of the barrier stands the coach.

THE CHILDREN *sing*:

> Mary, Mary sat her down
> Had a little old pink gown

Gown was shabby and bespattered.
But when chilly winter came
Gown went round her just the same.
Bespattered don't mean tattered.

THE FRONTIER GUARD: Why are you leaving Italy?

ANDREA: I'm a scholar.

THE FRONTIER GUARD *to his clerk*: Put under 'reason for leaving': scholar.
I must examine your luggage.
He does so.

THE FIRST BOY *to Andrea*: Better not sit there. *He points to the hut outside which Andrea is sitting*. There's a witch lives inside.

THE SECOND BOY: Old Marina's no witch.

THE FIRST BOY: Want me to twist your wrist?

THE THIRD BOY: Course she's one. She flies through the air at night.

THE FIRST BOY: And why won't anyone in the town let her have a jug of milk even, if she's not a witch?

THE SECOND BOY: Who says she flies through the air? It can't be done. *To Andrea*: Can it?

THE FIRST BOY *referring to the second*: That's Giuseppe. He doesn't know a thing because he doesn't go to school because his trousers need patching.

THE FRONTIER GUARD: What's that book you've got?

ANDREA *without looking up*: It's by Aristotle, the great philosopher.

THE FRONTIER GUARD *suspiciously*: Who's he when he's at home?

ANDREA: He's been dead for years.
The boys mock Andrea's reading by walking round as if they were meanwhile reading books.

THE FRONTIER GUARD *to the clerk*: Have a look if there's anything about religion in it.

THE CLERK *turning the pages*: I can't see nothing.

THE FRONTIER GUARD: All this searching's a bit of a waste of time anyway. Nobody who wanted to hide something would put it under our noses like that. *To Andrea:* You're to sign that we've examined it all.

Andrea gets up reluctantly and accompanies the frontier guard into the house, still reading.

THE THIRD BOY *to the clerk, pointing at the box:* There's that too, see?

THE CLERK: Wasn't it there before?

THE THIRD BOY: The devil put it there. It's a box.

THE SECOND BOY: No, it belongs to that foreigner.

THE THIRD BOY: I wouldn't touch it. She put the evil eye on old Passi's horses. I looked through the hole in the roof made by the blizzard and heard them coughing.

THE CLERK *who was almost at the box, hesitates and turns back:* Devil's tricks, what? Well, we can't check everything. We'd never get done.

Andrea comes back with a jug of milk. He sits down on the box once more and goes on reading.

THE FRONTIER GUARD *following him with papers:* Shut the boxes. Is that everything?

THE CLERK: Yes.

THE SECOND BOY *to Andrea:* So you're a scholar. Tell us, can people fly through the air?

ANDREA: Wait a moment.

THE FRONTIER GUARD: You can go through.

The coachman has taken the luggage. Andrea picks up the box and is about to go.

THE FRONTIER GUARD: Halt! What's in that box?

ANDREA *taking up his book again:* Books.

THE FIRST BOY: It's the witch's.

THE FRONTIER GUARD: Nonsense. How could she bewitch a box?

THE THIRD BOY: She could if the devil helped.

THE FRONTIER GUARD *laughs:* That wouldn't work here.
To the clerk: Open it.
The box is opened.

THE FRONTIER GUARD *unenthusiastically:* How many are there?

ANDREA: Thirty-four.

THE FRONTIER GUARD *to the clerk*: How long will they take to go through?

THE CLERK *who has begun superficially rummaging through the box*: Nothing but printed stuff. It'll mean you miss your breakfast, and when am I going to get over to Passi's stables to collect the road tax due on the sale of his house if I'm to go through this lot?

THE FRONTIER GUARD: Right, we need that money. *He kicks at the books*: After all, what can there be in those?
To the coachman: Off with you!
Andrea crosses the frontier with the coachman carrying the box. Once across, he puts Galileo's manuscript in his travelling bag.

THE THIRD BOY *points at the jug which Andrea has left behind*: Look!

THE FIRST BOY: The box has gone too! Didn't I tell you it was the devil?

ANDREA *turning round*: No, it was me. You should learn to use your eyes. The milk's paid for, the jug too. The old woman can keep it. Oh, and I didn't answer your question, Giuseppe. People can't fly through the air on a stick. It'd have to have a machine on it, to say the least. But there's no machine like that so far. Maybe there never will be, as a human being's too heavy. But of course one never knows. There are a lot of things we don't know yet, Giuseppe. We're really just at the beginning.

Mother Courage
and Her Children

A Chronicle of the Thirty Years War

Translator: JOHN WILLETT

Characters

MOTHER COURAGE
KATTRIN, *her dumb daughter*
EILIF, *the elder son*
SWISS CHEESE, *the younger son*
THE RECRUITER
THE SERGEANT
THE COOK
THE GENERAL
THE CHAPLAIN
THE ARMOURER
YVETTE POTTIER
THE MAN WITH THE PATCH
ANOTHER SERGEANT
THE ANCIENT COLONEL
A CLERK
A YOUNG SOLDIER
AN OLDER SOLDIER
A PEASANT
THE PEASANT'S WIFE
THE YOUNG MAN
THE OLD WOMAN
ANOTHER PEASANT
HIS WIFE
THE YOUNG PEASANT
THE ENSIGN
Soldiers
A Voice

I

Spring 1624. The Swedish Commander-in-Chief Count Oxenstierna is raising troops in Dalecarlia for the Polish campaign. The canteen woman Anna Fierling, known under the name of Mother Courage, loses one son

Country road near a town.
A sergeant and a recruiter stand shivering.

RECRUITER: How can you muster a unit in a place like this? I've been thinking about suicide, sergeant. Here am I, got to find our commander four companies before the twelfth of the month, and people round here are so nasty I can't sleep nights. S'pose I get hold of some bloke and shut my eye to his pigeon chest and varicose veins, I get him proper drunk, he signs on the line, I'm just settling up, he goes for a piss, I follow him to the door because I smell a rat; bob's your uncle, he's off like a flea with the itch. No notion of word of honour, loyalty, faith, sense of duty. This place has shattered my confidence in the human race, sergeant.

SERGEANT: It's too long since they had a war here; stands to reason. Where's their sense of morality to come from? Peace – that's just a mess; takes a war to restore order. Peacetime, the human race runs wild. People and cattle get buggered about, who cares? Everyone eats just as he feels inclined, a hunk of cheese on top of his nice white bread, and a slice of fat on top of the cheese. How many young blokes and good horses in that town there, nobody knows; they never thought of counting. I been in places ain't seen a war for nigh seventy years: folks hadn't got names to them, couldn't tell one another apart. Takes a war to get proper nominal rolls and inventories – shoes in bundles and corn in bags, and man and beast properly numbered and carted off, cause it stands to reason: no order, no war.

RECRUITER: Too true.

SERGEANT: Same with all good things, it's a job to get a war going. But once it's blossomed out there's no holding it; folk start fighting shy of peace like punters what can't stop for fear of having to tot up what they lost. Before that it's war they're fighting shy of. It's something new to them.

RECRUITER: Hey, here's a cart coming. Two tarts with two young fellows. Stop her, sergeant. If this one's a flop I'm not standing around in your spring winds any longer, I can tell you.

Sound of a jew's-harp. Drawn by two young fellows, a covered cart rolls in. On it sit Mother Courage and her dumb daughter Kattrin.

MOTHER COURAGE: Morning, sergeant.

SERGEANT *blocking the way*: Morning, all. And who are you?

MOTHER COURAGE: Business folk. *Sings*:

> You captains, tell the drums to slacken
> And give your infanteers a break:
> It's Mother Courage with her waggon
> Full of the finest boots they make.
> With crawling lice and looted cattle
> With lumbering guns and straggling kit –
> How can you flog them into battle
> Unless you get them boots that fit?
>> The new year's come. The watchmen shout.
>> The thaw sets in. The dead remain.
>> Wherever life has not died out
>> It staggers to its feet again.
>
> Captains, how can you make them face it –
> Marching to death without a brew?
> Courage has rum with which to lace it
> And boil their souls and bodies through.
> Their musket primed, their stomach hollow –

Captains, your men don't look so well.
So feed them up and let them follow
While you command them into hell.
  The new year's come. The watchmen shout.
  The thaw sets in. The dead remain.
  Wherever life has not died out
  It staggers to its feet again.

SERGEANT: Halt! Who are you with, you trash?

THE ELDER SON: Second Finnish Regiment.

SERGEANT: Where's your papers?

MOTHER COURAGE: Papers?

THE YOUNGER SON: What, mean to say you don't know Mother Courage?

SERGEANT: Never heard of her. What's she called Courage for?

MOTHER COURAGE: Courage is the name they gave me because I was scared of going broke, sergeant, so I drove me cart right through the bombardment of Riga with fifty loaves of bread aboard. They were going mouldy, it was high time, hadn't any choice really.

SERGEANT: Don't be funny with me. Your papers.

MOTHER COURAGE *pulling a bundle of papers from a tin box and climbing down off the cart*: That's all my papers, sergeant. You'll find a whole big missal from Altötting in Bavaria for wrapping gherkins in, and a road map of Moravia, the Lord knows when I'll ever get there, might as well chuck it away, and here's a stamped certificate that my horse hasn't got foot-and-mouth, only he's dead worse luck, cost fifteen florins he did – not me luckily. That enough paper for you?

SERGEANT: You pulling my leg? I'll knock that sauce out of you. S'pose you know you got to have a licence.

MOTHER COURAGE: Talk proper to me, do you mind, and don't you dare say I'm pulling your leg in front of my unsullied children, 'tain't decent, I got no time for you. My honest face, that's me licence with the Second Regiment, and if it's too difficult for you to read there's nowt I can do about it. Nobody's putting a stamp on that.

RECRUITER: Sergeant, methinks I smell insubordination in this individual. What's needed in our camp is obedience.

MOTHER COURAGE: Sausage, if you ask me.

SERGEANT: Name.

MOTHER COURAGE: Anna Fierling.

SERGEANT: You all called Fierling then?

MOTHER COURAGE: What d'you mean? It's me's called Fierling, not them.

SERGEANT: Aren't all this lot your children?

MOTHER COURAGE: You bet they are, but why should they all have to be called the same, eh? *Pointing to her elder son*: For instance, that one's called Eilif Nojocki – Why? his father always claimed he was called Kojocki or Mojocki or something. The boy remembers him clearly, except that the one he remembers was someone else, a Frenchie with a little beard. Aside from that he's got his father's wits; that man knew how to snitch a peasant's pants off his bum without him noticing. This way each of us has his own name, see.

SERGEANT: What, each one different?

MOTHER COURAGE: Don't tell me you ain't never come across that.

SERGEANT: So I s'pose he's a Chinaman? *Pointing to the younger son.*

MOTHER COURAGE: Wrong. Swiss.

SERGEANT: After the Frenchman?

MOTHER COURAGE: What Frenchman? I never heard tell of no Frenchman. You keep muddling things up, we'll be hanging around here till dark. A Swiss, but called Fejos, and the name has nowt to do with his father. He was called something quite different and was a fortifications engineer, only drunk all the time.

Swiss Cheese beams and nods; dumb Kattrin too is amused.

SERGEANT: How in hell can he be called Fejos?

MOTHER COURAGE: I don't like to be rude, sergeant, but you ain't got much imagination, have you? Course he's called Fejos, because when he arrived I was with a Hungarian, very decent fellow, had terrible kidney trouble though he never touched a drop. The boy takes after him.

SERGEANT: But he wasn't his father . . .

MOTHER COURAGE: Took after him just the same. I call him Swiss Cheese cause he's good at pulling cart. *Pointing to her daughter*: And that's Kattrin Haupt, she's half German.

SERGEANT: Nice family, I must say.

MOTHER COURAGE: Aye, me cart and me have seen the world.

SERGEANT: I'm writing all this down. *He writes*. And you're from Bamberg in Bavaria; how d'you come to be here?

MOTHER COURAGE: Can't wait till war chooses to visit Bamberg, can I?

RECRUITER *to Eilif*: You two should be called Jacob Ox and Esau Ox, pulling the cart like that. I s'pose you never get out of harness?

EILIF: Ma, can I clobber him one? I wouldn't half like to.

MOTHER COURAGE: And I says you can't; just you stop where you are. And now two fine officers like you, I bet you could use a good pistol, or a belt buckle, yours is on its last legs, sergeant.

SERGEANT: I could use something else. Those boys are healthy as young birch trees, I observe: chests like barrels, solid leg muscles. So why are they dodging their military service, may I ask?

MOTHER COURAGE *quickly*: Nowt doing, sergeant. Yours is no trade for my kids.

RECRUITER: But why not? There's good money in it, glory too. Flogging boots is women's work. *To Eilif*: Come here, let's see if you've muscles in you or if you're a chicken.

MOTHER COURAGE: He's a chicken. Give him a fierce look, he'll fall over.

RECRUITER: Killing a young bull that happens to be in his way. *Wants to lead him off*.

MOTHER COURAGE: Let him alone, will you? He's nowt for you folk.

RECRUITER: He was crudely offensive and talked about clobbering me. The two of us are going to step into that field and settle it man to man.

EILIF: Don't you worry, mum, I'll fix him.

MOTHER COURAGE: Stop there! You varmint! I know you, nowt but fights. There's a knife down his boot. A slasher, that's what he is.

RECRUITER: I'll draw it out of him like a milk-tooth. Come along, sonny.

MOTHER COURAGE: Sergeant, I'll tell the colonel. He'll have you both in irons. The lieutenant's going out with my daughter.

SERGEANT: No rough stuff, chum. *To Mother Courage*: What you got against military service? Wasn't his own father a soldier? Died a soldier's death, too? Said it yourself.

MOTHER COURAGE: He's nowt but a child. You want to take him off to slaughterhouse, I know you lot. They'll give you five florins for him.

RECRUITER: First he's going to get a smart cap and boots, eh?

EILIF: Not from you.

MOTHER COURAGE: Let's both go fishing, said angler to worm. *To Swiss Cheese*: Run off, call out they're trying to kidnap your brother. *She pulls a knife*: Go on, you kidnap him, just try. I'll slit you open, trash. I'll teach you to make war with him. We're doing an honest trade in ham and linen, and we're peaceable folk.

SERGEANT: Peaceable I don't think; look at your knife. You should be ashamed of yourself; put that knife away, you old harridan. A minute back you were admitting you live off the war, how else should you live, what from? But how's anyone to have war without soldiers?

MOTHER COURAGE: No need for it to be my kids.

SERGEANT: Oh, you'd like war to eat the pips but spit out the apple? It's to fatten up your kids, but you won't invest in it. Got to look after itself, eh? And you called Courage, fancy that. Scared of the war that keeps you going? Your sons aren't scared of it, I can see that.

EILIF: Take more than a war to scare me.

SERGEANT: And why? Look at me: has army life done all that badly by me? Joined up at seventeen.

MOTHER COURAGE: Still got to reach seventy.

SERGEANT: I don't mind waiting.

MOTHER COURAGE: Under the sod, eh?

SERGEANT: You trying to insult me, saying I'll die?

MOTHER COURAGE: S'pose it's true? S'pose I can see the mark's on you? S'pose you look like a corpse on leave to me? Eh?

SWISS CHEESE: She's got second sight, Mother has.

RECRUITER: Go ahead, tell the sergeant's fortune, might amuse him.

MOTHER COURAGE: Gimme helmet. *He gives it to her.*

SERGEANT: It don't mean a bloody sausage. Anything for a laugh though.

MOTHER COURAGE *taking out a sheet of parchment and tearing it up*: Eilif, Swiss Cheese and Kattrin, may all of us be torn apart like this if we lets ourselves get too mixed up in the war. *To the sergeant*: Just for you I'm doing it for free. Black's for death. I'm putting a big black cross on this slip of paper.

SWISS CHEESE: Leaving the other one blank, see?

MOTHER COURAGE: Then I fold them across and shake them. All of us is jumbled together like this from our mother's womb, and now draw a slip and you'll know. *The sergeant hesitates.*

RECRUITER *to Eilif*: I don't take just anybody, they all know I'm choosey, but you got the kind of fire I like to see.

SERGEANT *fishing in the helmet*: Too silly. Load of eyewash.

SWISS CHEESE: Drawn a black cross, he has. Write him off.

RECRUITER: They're having you on; not everybody's name's on a bullet.

SERGEANT *hoarsely*: You've put me in the shit.

MOTHER COURAGE: Did that yourself the day you became a soldier. Come along, let's move on now. 'Tain't every day we have a war, I got to get stirring.

SERGEANT: God damn it, you can't kid me. We're taking that bastard of yours for a soldier.

EILIF: Swiss Cheese'd like to be a soldier too.

MOTHER COURAGE: First I've heard of that. You'll have to

draw too, all three of you. *She goes to the rear to mark crosses on further slips.*

RECRUITER *to Eilif*: One of the things they say against us is that it's all holy-holy in the Swedish camp; but that's a malicious rumour to do us down. There's no hymn-singing but Sundays, just a single verse, and then only for those got voices.

MOTHER COURAGE *coming back with the slips, which she drops into the sergeant's helmet*: Trying to get away from their ma, the devils, off to war like calves to salt-lick. But I'm making you draw lots, and that'll show you the world is no vale of joys with 'Come along, son, we need a few more generals'. Sergeant, I'm so scared they won't get through the war. Such dreadful characters, all three of them. *She hands the helmet to Eilif.* Hey, come on, fish out your slip. *He fishes one out, unfolds it. She snatches it from him.* There you are, it's a cross. Oh, wretched mother that I am, o pain-racked giver of birth! Shall he die? Aye, in the springtime of life he is doomed. If he becomes a soldier he shall bite the dust, it's plain to see. He is foolhardy, like his dad was. And if he ain't sensible he'll go the way of all flesh, his slip proves it. *Shouts at him*: You going to be sensible?

EILIF: Why not?

MOTHER COURAGE: Sensible thing is stay with your mother, never mind if they poke fun at you and call you chicken, just you laugh.

RECRUITER: If you're pissing in your pants I'll make do with your brother.

MOTHER COURAGE: I told you laugh. Go on, laugh. Now you draw, Swiss Cheese. I'm not so scared on your account, you're honest. *He fishes in the helmet.* Oh, why look at your slip in that strange way? It's got to be a blank. There can't be any cross on it. Surely I'm not going to lose *you*. *She takes the slip.* A cross? What, you too? Is that because you're so simple, perhaps? O Swiss Cheese, you too will be sunk if you don't stay utterly honest all the while, like I taught you from childhood when you brought the change back from the baker's. Else you can't save yourself. Look, sergeant, that's a black cross, ain't it?

SERGEANT: A cross, that's right. Can't think how I come to get one. I always stay in the rear. *To the recruiter*: There's no catch. Her own family get it too.

SWISS CHEESE: I get it too. But I listen to what I'm told.

MOTHER COURAGE *to Kattrin*: And now you're the only one I know's all right, you're a cross yourself; got a kind heart you have. *Holds the helmet up to her on the cart, but takes the slip out herself.* No, that's too much. That can't be right; must have made a mistake shuffling. Don't be too kind-hearted, Kattrin, you'll have to give it up, there's a cross above your path too. Lie doggo, girl, it can't be that hard once you're born dumb. Right, all of you know now. Look out for yourselves, you'll need to. And now up we get and on we go. *She climbs on to the cart.*

RECRUITER *to the sergeant*: Do something.

SERGEANT: I don't feel very well.

RECRUITER: Must of caught a chill taking your helmet off in that wind. Involve her in a deal. *Aloud*: Might as well have a look at that belt-buckle, sergeant. After all, our friends here have to live by their business. Hey, you people, the sergeant wants to buy that belt-buckle.

MOTHER COURAGE: Half a florin. Two florins is what a belt like that's worth. *Climbs down again.*

SERGEANT: 'Tain't new. Let me get out of this damned wind and have a proper look at it. *Goes behind the cart with the buckle.*

MOTHER COURAGE: Ain't what I call windy.

SERGEANT: I s'pose it might be worth half a florin, it's silver.

MOTHER COURAGE *joining him behind the cart*: It's six solid ounces.

RECRUITER *to Eilif*: And then we men'll have one together. Got your bounty money here, come along. *Eilif stands undecided.*

MOTHER COURAGE: Half a florin it is.

SERGEANT: It beats me. I'm always at the rear. Sergeant's the safest job there is. You can send the others up front, cover themselves with glory. Me dinner hour's properly spoiled. Shan't be able to hold nowt down, I know.

MOTHER COURAGE: Mustn't let it prey on you so's you can't eat. Just stay at the rear. Here, take a swig of brandy, man. *Gives him a drink.*

RECRUITER *has taken Eilif by the arm and is leading him away up stage*: Ten florins bounty money, then you're a gallant fellow fighting for the king and women'll be after you like flies. And you can clobber me for free for insulting you. *Exeunt both.*

Dumb Kattrin leans down from the cart and makes hoarse noises.

MOTHER COURAGE: All right, Kattrin, all right. Sergeant's just paying., *Bites the half-florin.* I got no faith in any kind of money. Burnt child, that's me, sergeant. This coin's good, though. And now let's get moving. Where's Eilif?

SWISS CHEESE: Went off with the recruiter.

MOTHER COURAGE *stands quite still, then*: You simpleton. *To Kattrin*: 'Tain't your fault, you can't speak, I know.

SERGEANT: Could do with a swig yourself, ma. That's life. Plenty worse things than being a soldier. Want to live off war, but keep yourself and family out of it, eh?

MOTHER COURAGE: You'll have to help your brother pull now, Kattrin.

Brother and sister hitch themselves to the cart and start pulling. Mother Courage walks alongside. The cart rolls on.

SERGEANT *looking after them*:

Like the war to nourish you?
Have to feed it something too.

2

In the years 1625 and 1626 Mother Courage crosses Poland in the train of the Swedish armies. Before the fortress of Wallhof she meets her son again. Successful sale of a capon and heyday of her dashing son

The general's tent.

Beside it, his kitchen. Thunder of cannon. The cook is arguing with Mother Courage, who wants to sell him a capon.

THE COOK: Sixty hellers for a miserable bird like that?

MOTHER COURAGE: Miserable bird? This fat brute? Mean to say some greedy old general — and watch your step if you got nowt for his dinner — can't afford sixty hellers for him?

THE COOK: I can get a dozen like that for ten hellers just down the road.

MOTHER COURAGE: What, a capon like this you can get just down the road? In time of siege, which means hunger that tears your guts. A rat you might get: 'might' I say because they're all being gobbled up, five men spending best part of day chasing one hungry rat. Fifty hellers for a giant capon in time of siege!

THE COOK: But it ain't us having the siege, it's t'other side. We're conducting the siege, can't you get that in your head?

MOTHER COURAGE: But we got nowt to eat too, even worse than them in the town. Took it with them, didn't they? They're having a high old time, everyone says. And look at us! I been to the peasants, there's nowt there.

THE COOK: There's plenty. They're sitting on it.

MOTHER COURAGE *triumphantly*: They ain't. They're bust, that's what they are. Just about starving. I saw some, were grubbing up roots from sheer hunger, licking their fingers after they boiled some old leather strap. That's way it is. And me got a capon here and supposed to take forty hellers for it.

THE COOK: Thirty, not forty. I said thirty.

MOTHER COURAGE: Here, this ain't just any old capon. It was such a gifted beast, I been told, it could only eat to music, had a military march of its own. It could count, it was that intelligent. And you say forty hellers is too much? General will make mincemeat of you if there's nowt on his table.

THE COOK: See what I'm doing? *He takes a piece of beef and puts his knife to it.* Here I got a bit of beef, I'm going to roast it. Make up your mind quick.

MOTHER COURAGE: Go on, roast it. It's last year's.

THE COOK: Last night's. That animal was still alive and kicking, I saw him myself.

MOTHER COURAGE: Alive and stinking, you mean.

THE COOK: I'll cook him five hours if need be. I'll just see if he's still tough. *He cuts into it.*

MOTHER COURAGE: Put plenty of pepper on it so his lordship the general don't smell the pong.

The general, a chaplain and Eilif enter the tent.

THE GENERAL *slapping Eilif on the shoulder*: Now then, Eilif my son, into your general's tent with you and sit thou at my right hand. For you accomplished a deed of heroism, like a pious cavalier; and doing what you did for God, and in a war of religion at that, is something I commend in you most highly, you shall have a gold bracelet as soon as we've taken this town. Here we are, come to save their souls for them, and what do those insolent dung-encrusted yokels go and do? Drive their beef away from us. They stuff it into those priests of theirs all right, back and front, but you taught 'em manners, ha! So here's a pot of red wine for you, the two of us'll knock it back at one gulp. *They do so.* Piss all for the chaplain, the old bigot. And now, what would you like for dinner, my darling?

EILIF: A bit of meat, why not?

THE GENERAL: Cook! Meat!

THE COOK: And then he goes and brings guests when there's nowt there.

Mother Courage silences him so she can listen.

EILIF: Hungry job cutting down peasants.

MOTHER COURAGE: Jesus Christ, it's my Eilif.

THE COOK: Your what?

MOTHER COURAGE: My eldest boy. It's two years since I lost sight of him, they pinched him from me on the road, must think well of him if the general's asking him to dinner, and what kind of a dinner can you offer? Nowt. You heard what the visitor wishes to eat: meat. Take my tip, you settle for the capon, it'll be a florin.

THE GENERAL *has sat down with Eilif, and bellows*: Food, Lamb, you foul cook, or I'll have your hide.

THE COOK: Give it over, dammit, this is blackmail.

MOTHER COURAGE: Didn't someone say it was a miserable bird?

THE COOK: Miserable; give it over, and a criminal price, fifty hellers.

MOTHER COURAGE: A florin, I said. For my eldest boy, the general's guest, no expense is too great for me.

THE COOK *gives her the money*: You might at least pluck it while I see to the fire.

MOTHER COURAGE *sits down to pluck the fowl*: He won't half be surprised to see me. He's my dashing clever son. Then I got a stupid one too, he's honest though. The girl's nowt. One good thing, she don't talk.

THE GENERAL: Drink up, my son, this is my best Falernian; only got a barrel or two left, but that's nothing to pay for a sign that there's still true faith to be found in my army. As for that shepherd of souls he can just look on, because all he does is preach, without the least idea how it's to be carried out. And now, my son Eilif, tell us more about the neat way you smashed those yokels and captured the twenty oxen. Let's hope they get here soon.

EILIF: A day or two at most.

MOTHER COURAGE: Thoughtful of our Eilif not to bring the oxen in till tomorrow, else you lot wouldn't have looked twice at my capon.

EILIF: Well, it was like this, see. I'd heard peasants had been driving the oxen they'd hidden, out of the forest into one particular wood, on the sly and mostly by night. That's where people from the town were s'posed to come and pick them up. So I holds off and lets them drive their oxen together, reckoning they'd be better than me at finding 'em. I had my blokes slavering after the meat, cut their emergency rations even further for a couple of days till their mouths was watering at the least sound of any word beginning with 'me-', like 'measles' say.

THE GENERAL: Very clever of you.

EILIF: Possibly. The rest was a piece of cake. Except that the peasants had cudgels and outnumbered us three to one and made a murderous attack on us. Four of 'em shoved me into a thicket, knocked my sword from my hand and bawled out 'Surrender!' What's the answer, I wondered; they're going to make mincemeat of me.

THE GENERAL: What did you do?

EILIF: I laughed.

THE GENERAL: You did what?

EILIF: Laughed. So we got talking. I put it on a business footing from the start, told them 'Twenty florins a head's too much. I'll give you fifteen'. As if I was meaning to pay. That threw them, and they began scratching their heads. In a flash I'd picked up my sword and was hacking 'em to pieces. Necessity's the mother of invention, eh, sir?

THE GENERAL: What is your view, pastor of souls?

THE CHAPLAIN: That phrase is not strictly speaking in the Bible, but when Our Lord turned the five loaves into five hundred there was no war on and he could tell people to love their neighbours as they'd had enough to eat. Today it's another story.

THE GENERAL *laughs*: Quite another story. You can have a swig after all for that, you old Pharisee. *To Eilif*: Hacked 'em to pieces, did you, so my gallant lads can get a proper bite to eat? What do the Scriptures say? 'Whatsoever thou doest for the least of my brethren, thou doest for me'. And what did you do for them? Got them a good square meal of beef, because they're not accustomed to mouldy bread, the old way was to fix a cold meal of rolls and wine in your helmet before you went out to fight for God.

EILIF: Aye, in a flash I'd picked up my sword and was hacking them to pieces.

THE GENERAL: You've the makings of a young Caesar. You ought to see the King.

EILIF: I have from a distance. He kind of glows. I'd like to model myself on him.

THE GENERAL: You've got something in common already. I appreciate soldiers like you, Eilif, men of courage. Somebody like that I treat as I would my own son. *He leads him over to the map.* Have a look at the situation, Eilif; it's a long haul still.

MOTHER COURAGE *who has been listening and now angrily plucks the fowl*: That must be a rotten general.

THE COOK: He's ravenous all right, but why rotten?

MOTHER COURAGE: Because he's got to have men of courage, that's why. If he knew how to plan a proper campaign what would he be needing men of courage for? Ordinary ones would do. It's always the same; whenever there's a load of special virtues around it means something stinks.

THE COOK: I thought it meant things is all right.

MOTHER COURAGE: No, that they stink. Look, s'pose some general or king is bone stupid and leads his men up shit creek, then those men've got to be fearless, there's another virtue for you. S'pose he's stingy and hires too few soldiers, then they got to be a crowd of Hercules's. And s'pose he's slapdash and don't give a bugger, then they got to be clever as monkeys else their number's up. Same way they got to show exceptional loyalty each time he gives them impossible jobs. Nowt but virtues no proper country and no decent king or general would ever need. In decent countries folk don't have to have virtues, the whole lot can be perfectly ordinary, average intelligence, and for all I know cowards.

THE GENERAL: I'll wager your father was a soldier.

EILIF: A great soldier, I been told. My mother warned me about it. There's a song I know.

THE GENERAL: Sing it to us. *Roars*: When's that dinner coming?

EILIF: It's called The Song of the Girl and the Soldier.
He sings it, dancing a war dance with his sabre:

> The guns blaze away, and the bay'nit'll slay
> And the water can't hardly be colder.
> What's the answer to ice? Keep off's my advice!
> That's what the girl told the soldier.
> Next thing the soldier, wiv' a round up the spout
> Hears the band playing and gives a great shout:
> Why, it's marching what makes you a soldier!
> So it's down to the south and then northwards once more:
> See him catching that bay'nit in his naked paw!
> That's what his comrades done told her.
>
> Oh, do not despise the advice of the wise
> Learn wisdom from those that are older
> And don't try for things that are out of your reach –
> That's what the girl told the soldier.
> Next thing the soldier, his bay'nit in place
> Wades into the river and laughs in her face
> Though the water comes up to his shoulder.
> When the shingle roof glints in the light o' the moon
> We'll be wiv' you again, not a moment too soon!
> That's what his comrades done told her.

MOTHER COURAGE *takes up the song in the kitchen, beating on a pot with her spoon:*

> You'll go out like a light! And the sun'll take flight
> For your courage just makes us feel colder.
> Oh, that vanishing light! May God see that it's right! –
> That's what the girl told the soldier.

EILIF: What's that?
MOTHER COURAGE *continues singing:*

> Next thing the soldier, his bay'nit in place
> Was caught by the current and went down without trace
> And the water couldn't hardly be colder.

The shingle roof froze in the light o' the moon
As both soldier and ice drifted down to their doom –
And d'you know what his comrades done told her?

He went out like a light. And the sunshine took flight
For his courage just made 'em feel colder.
Oh, do not despise the advice of the wise!
That's what the girl told the soldier.

THE GENERAL: The things they get up to in my kitchen these days.

EILIF *has gone into the kitchen. He flings his arms round his mother*: Fancy seeing you again, ma! Where's the others?

MOTHER COURAGE *in his arms*: Snug as a bug in a rug. They made Swiss Cheese paymaster of the Second Finnish; any road he'll stay out of fighting that way, I couldn't keep him out altogether.

EILIF: How's the old feet?

MOTHER COURAGE: Bit tricky getting me shoes on of a morning.

THE GENERAL *has joined them*: So you're his mother, I hope you've got plenty more sons for me like this one.

EILIF: Ain't it my lucky day? You sitting out there in the kitchen, ma, hearing your son commended . . .

MOTHER COURAGE: You bet I heard. *Slaps his face.*

EILIF *holding his cheek*: What's that for? Taking the oxen?

MOTHER COURAGE: No. Not surrendering when those four went for you and wanted to make mincemeat of you. Didn't I say you should look after yourself? You Finnish devil!

The general and the chaplain stand in the doorway laughing.

3

Three years later Mother Courage is taken prisoner along with elements of a Finnish regiment. She manages to save her daughter, likewise her covered cart, but her honest son is killed

Military camp.
Afternoon. A flagpole with the regimental flag. From her cart, festooned now with all kinds of goods, Mother Courage has stretched a washing line to a large cannon, across which she and Kattrin are folding the washing. She is bargaining at the same time with an armourer over a sack of shot. Swiss Cheese, now wearing a paymaster's uniform, is looking on.
   A comely person, Yvette Pottier, is sewing a gaily coloured hat, a glass of brandy before her. She is in her stockinged feet, having laid aside her red high-heeled boots.

THE ARMOURER: I'll let you have that shot for a couple of florins. It's cheap at the price, I got to have the money because the colonel's been boozing with his officers since two days back, and the drink's run out.

MOTHER COURAGE: That's troops' munitions. They catch me with that, I'm for court-martial. You crooks flog the shot, and troops got nowt to fire at enemy.

THE ARMOURER: Have a heart, can't you; you scratch my back and I'll scratch yours.

MOTHER COURAGE: I'm not taking army property. Not at that price.

THE ARMOURER: You can sell it on the q.t. tonight to the Fourth Regiment's armourer for five florins, eight even, if you let him have a receipt for twelve. He's right out of ammunition.

MOTHER COURAGE: Why not you do it?

THE ARMOURER: I don't trust him, he's a pal of mine.

MOTHER COURAGE *takes the sack*: Gimme. *To Kattrin*: Take

it away and pay him a florin and a half. *The armourer protests.* I said a florin and a half. *Kattrin drags the sack upstage, the armourer following her. Mother Courage addresses Swiss Cheese:* Here's your woollies, now look after them, it's October and autumn may set in any time. I ain't saying it's got to, cause I've learned nowt's got to come when you think it will, not even seasons of the year. But your regimental accounts got to add up right, come what may. Do they add up right?

SWISS CHEESE: Yes, mother.

MOTHER COURAGE: Don't you forget they made you pay-master cause you was honest, not dashing like your brother, and above all so stupid I bet you ain't even thought of clearing off with it, no not you. That's a big consolation to me. And don't lose those woollies.

SWISS CHEESE: No, mother, I'll put them under my mattress. *Begins to go.*

THE ARMOURER: I'll go along with you, paymaster.

MOTHER COURAGE: And don't you start learning him none of your tricks.

The armourer leaves with Swiss Cheese without any farewell gesture.

YVETTE *waving to him*: No reason not to say goodbye, armourer.

MOTHER COURAGE *to Yvette*: I don't like to see them together. He's wrong company for our Swiss Cheese. Oh well, war's off to a good start. Easily take four, five years before all countries are in. A bit of foresight, don't do nothing silly, and business'll flourish. Don't you know you ain't s'posed to drink before midday with your complaint?

YVETTE: Complaint, who says so, it's a libel.

MOTHER COURAGE: They all say so.

YVETTE: Because they're all telling lies, Mother Courage, and me at my wits' end cause they're all avoiding me like something the cat brought in thanks to those lies, what the hell am I remodelling my hat for? *She throws it away.* That's why I drink before midday. Never used to, gives you crows' feet, but now what the hell? All the Second Finnish know me.

Ought to have stayed at home when my first fellow did me wrong. No good our sort being proud. Eat shit, that's what you got to do, or down you go.

MOTHER COURAGE: Now don't you start up again about that Pieter of yours and how it all happened, in front of my innocent daughter too.

YVETTE: She's the one should hear it, put her off love.

MOTHER COURAGE: Nobody can put 'em off that.

YVETTE: Then I'll go on, get if off my chest. It all starts with yours truly growing up in lovely Flanders, else I'd never of seen him and wouldn't be stuck here now in Poland, cause he was an army cook, fair-haired, a Dutchman but thin for once. Kattrin, watch out for the thin ones, only in those days I didn't know that, or that he'd got a girl already, or that they all called him Puffing Piet cause he never took his pipe out of his mouth when he was on the job, it meant that little to him. *She sings the Song of Fraternisation:*

When I was only sixteen
The foe came into our land.
He laid aside his sabre
And with a smile he took my hand.
After the May parade
The May light starts to fade.
The regiment dressed by the right
The drums were beaten, that's the drill.
The foe took us behind the hill
And fraternised all night.

There were so many foes then
But mine worked in the mess.
I loathed him in the daytime.
At night I loved him none the less.
After the May parade
The May light starts to fade.
The regiment dressed by the right
The drums were beaten, that's the drill.

The foe took us behind the hill
And fraternised all night.

The love which came upon me
Was wished on me by fate.
My friends could never grasp why
I found it hard to share their hate.
The fields were wet with dew
When sorrow first I knew.
The regiment dressed by the right
The drums were beaten, that's the drill.
And then the foe, my lover still
Went marching out of sight.

I followed him, fool that I was, but I never found him, and that was five years back. *She walks unsteadily behind the cart.*

MOTHER COURAGE: You left your hat here.

YVETTE: Anyone wants it can have it.

MOTHER COURAGE: Let that be a lesson, Kattrin. Don't you start anything with them soldiers. Love makes the world go round, I'm warning you. Even with fellows not in the army it's no bed of roses. He says he'd like to kiss the ground your feet walk on – reminds me, did you wash them yesterday? – and after that you're his skivvy. Be thankful you're dumb, then you can't contradict yourself and won't be wanting to bite your tongue off for speaking the truth; it's a godsend, being dumb is. And here comes the general's cook, now what's he after?

Enter the cook and the chaplain.

THE CHAPLAIN: I have a message for you from your son Eilif, and the cook has come along because you made such a profound impression on him.

THE COOK: I just came along to get a bit of air.

MOTHER COURAGE: That you can always do here if you behave yourself, and if you don't I can deal with you. What does he want? I got no spare cash.

THE CHAPLAIN: Actually I had a message for his brother the paymaster.

MOTHER COURAGE: He ain't here now nor anywhere else neither. He ain't his brother's paymaster. He's not to lead him into temptation nor be clever at his expense. *Giving him money from the purse slung round her*: Give him this, it's a sin, he's banking on mother's love and ought to be ashamed of himself.

THE COOK: Not for long, he'll have to be moving off with the regiment, might be to his death. Give him a bit extra, you'll be sorry later. You women are tough, then later on you're sorry. A little glass of brandy wouldn't have been a problem, but it wasn't offered and, who knows, a bloke may lie beneath the green sod and none of you people will ever be able to dig him up again.

THE CHAPLAIN: Don't give way to your feelings, cook. To fall in battle is a blessing, not an inconvenience, and why? It is a war of faith. None of your common wars but a special one, fought for the faith and therefore pleasing to God.

THE COOK: Very true. It's a war all right in one sense, what with requisitioning, murder and looting and the odd bit of rape thrown in, but different from all the other wars because it's a war of faith; stands to reason. But it's thirsty work at that, you must admit.

THE CHAPLAIN *to Mother Courage, indicating the cook*: I tried to stop him, but he says he's taken a shine to you, you figure in his dreams.

THE COOK *lighting a stumpy pipe*: Just want a glass of brandy from a fair hand, what harm in that? Only I'm groggy already cause the chaplain here's been telling such jokes all the way along you bet I'm still blushing.

MOTHER COURAGE: Him a ciergyman too. I'd best give the pair of you a drink or you'll start making me immoral suggestions cause you've nowt else to do.

THE CHAPLAIN: Behold a temptation, said the court preacher, and fell. *Turning back to look at Kattrin as he leaves*: And who is this entrancing young person?

MOTHER COURAGE: That ain't an entrancing but a decent young person. *The chaplain and the cook go behind the cart with Mother Courage. Kattrin looks after them, then walks away from her washing towards the hat. She picks it up and sits down, pulling the red boots towards her. Mother Courage can be heard in the background talking politics with the chaplain and the cook.*

MOTHER COURAGE: Those Poles here in Poland had no business sticking their noses in. Right, our king moved in on them, horse and foot, but did they keep the peace? no, went and stuck their noses into their own affairs, they did, and fell on king just as he was quietly clearing off. They committed a breach of peace, that's what, so blood's on their own head.

THE CHAPLAIN: All our king minded about was freedom. The emperor had made slaves of them all, Poles and Germans alike, and the king had to liberate them.

THE COOK: Just what I say, your brandy's first rate, I weren't mistaken in your face, but talk of the king, it cost the king dear trying to give freedom to Germany, what with giving Sweden the salt tax, what cost the poor folk a bit, so I've heard, on top of which he had to have the Germans locked up and drawn and quartered cause they wanted to carry on slaving for the emperor. Course the king took a serious view when anybody didn't want to be free. He set out by just trying to protect Poland against bad people, particularly the emperor, then it started to become a habit till he ended up protecting the whole of Germany. They didn't half kick. So the poor old king's had nowt but trouble for all his kindness and expenses, and that's something he had to make up for by taxes of course, which caused bad blood, not that he'd let a little matter like that depress him. One thing he had on his side, God's word, that was a help. Because otherwise folk would of been saying he done it all for himself and to make a bit on the side. So he's always had a good conscience, which was the main point.

MOTHER COURAGE: Anyone can see you're no Swede or you wouldn't be talking that way about the Hero King.

THE CHAPLAIN: After all he provides the bread you eat.

THE COOK: I don't eat it, I bake it.

MOTHER COURAGE: They'll never beat him, and why, his men got faith in him. *Seriously*: To go by what the big shots say, they're waging war for almighty God and in the name of everything that's good and lovely. But look closer, they ain't so silly, they're waging it for what they can get. Else little folk like me wouldn't be in it at all.

THE COOK: That's the way it is.

THE CHAPLAIN: As a Dutchman you'd do better to glance at the flag above your head before venting your opinions here in Poland.

MOTHER COURAGE: All good Lutherans here. Prosit!

Kattrin has put on Yvette's hat and begun strutting around in imitation of her way of walking.

Suddenly there is a noise of cannon fire and shooting. Drums. Mother Courage, the cook and the chaplain rush out from behind the cart, the two last-named still carrying their glasses. The armourer and another soldier run up to the cannon and try to push it away.

MOTHER COURAGE: What's happening? Wait till I've taken my washing down, you louts! *She tries to rescue her washing.*

THE ARMOURER: The Catholics! Broken through. Don't know if we'll get out of here. *To the soldier*: Get that gun shifted! *Runs on.*

THE COOK: God, I must find the general. I'll drop by in a day or two for another talk.

MOTHER COURAGE: Wait, you forgot your pipe.

THE COOK *in the distance*: Keep it for me. I'll be needing it.

MOTHER COURAGE: Would happen just as we're making a bit of money.

THE CHAPLAIN: Ah well, I'll be going too. Indeed, if the enemy is so close as that it might be dangerous. Blesséd are the peacemakers is the motto in wartime. If only I had a cloak to cover me.

MOTHER COURAGE: I ain't lending no cloaks, not on your life. I been had too often.

THE CHAPLAIN: But my faith makes it particularly dangerous for me.

MOTHER COURAGE *gets him a cloak*: Goes against my conscience, this does. Now you run along.

THE CHAPLAIN: Thank you, dear lady, that's very generous of you, but I think it might be wiser for me to remain seated here; it could arouse suspicion and bring the enemy down on me if I were seen to run.

MOTHER COURAGE *to the soldier*: Leave it, you fool, who's going to pay you for that! I'll look after it for you, you're risking your neck.

THE SOLDIER *running away*: You can tell 'em I tried.

MOTHER COURAGE: Cross my heart. *Sees her daughter with the hat*. What you doing with that strumpet's hat? Take that lid off, you gone crazy? And the enemy arriving any minute! *Pulls the hat off Kattrin's head*. Want 'em to pick you up and make a prostitute of you? And she's gone and put those boots on, whore of Babylon! Off with those boots! *Tries to tug them off her*. Jesus Christ, chaplain, gimme a hand, get those boots off her, I'll be right back. *Runs to the cart*.

YVETTE *arrives, powdering her face*: Fancy that, the Catholics are coming. Where's my hat? Who's been kicking it around? I can't go about looking like this if the Catholics are coming. What'll they think of me? No mirror either. *To the chaplain*: How do I look? Too much powder?

THE CHAPLAIN: Exactly right.

YVETTE: And where are them red boots? *Fails to find them as Kattrin hides her feet under her skirt*. I left them here all right. Now I'll have to get to me tent barefoot. It's an outrage. *Exit*.

Swiss Cheese runs in carrying a small box.

MOTHER COURAGE *arrives with her hands full of ashes. To Kattrin*: Here some ashes. *To Swiss Cheese*: What's that you're carrying?

SWISS CHEESE: Regimental cash box.

MOTHER COURAGE: Chuck it away. No more paymastering for you.

SWISS CHEESE: I'm responsible. *He goes to the rear*.

MOTHER COURAGE *to the chaplain*: Take your clerical togs off, padre, or they'll spot you under that cloak. *She rubs Kattrin's face with ash*. Keep still, will you? There you are, a bit of muck and you'll be safe. What a disaster. Sentries were drunk. Hide your light under a bushel, it says. Take a soldier, specially a Catholic one, add a clean face, and there's your instant whore. For weeks they get nowt to eat, then soon as they manage to get it by looting they're falling on anything in skirts. That ought to do. Let's have a look. Not bad. Looks like you been grubbing in muckheap. Stop trembling. Nothing'll happen to you like that. *To Swiss Cheese*: Where d'you leave cash box?

SWISS CHEESE: Thought I'd put it in cart.

MOTHER COURAGE *horrified*: What, my cart? Sheer criminal idiocy. Only take me eyes off you one instant. Hang us all three, they will.

SWISS CHEESE: I'll put it somewhere else then, or clear out with it.

MOTHER COURAGE: You sit on it, it's too late now.

THE CHAPLAIN *who is changing his clothes downstage*: For heaven's sake, the flag!

MOTHER COURAGE *hauls down the regimental flag*: Bozhe moi! I'd given up noticing it were there. Twenty-five years I've had it.

The thunder of cannon intensifies.

A morning three days later. The cannon has gone. Mother Courage, Kattrin, the chaplain and Swiss Cheese are sitting gloomily over a meal.

SWISS CHEESE: That's three days I been sitting around with nowt to do, and sergeant's always been kind to me but any moment now he'll start asking where's Swiss Cheese with the pay box?

MOTHER COURAGE: You thank your stars they ain't after you.

THE CHAPLAIN: What can I say? I can't even hold a service here, it might make trouble for me. Whosoever hath a full heart, his tongue runneth over, it says, but heaven help me if mine starts running over.

MOTHER COURAGE: That's how it goes. Here they sit, one with his faith and the other with his cash box. Dunno which is more dangerous.

THE CHAPLAIN: We are all of us in God's hands.

MOTHER COURAGE: Oh, I don't think it's as bad as that yet, though I must say I can't sleep nights. If it weren't for you, Swiss Cheese, things'd be easier. I think I got meself cleared. I told 'em I didn't hold with Antichrist, the Swedish one with horns on, and I'd observed left horn was a bit unserviceable. Half way through their interrogation I asked where I could get church candles not too dear. I knows the lingo cause Swiss Cheese's dad were Catholic, often used to make jokes about it, he did. They didn't believe me all that much, but they ain't got no regimental canteen lady. So they're winking an eye. Could turn out for the best, you know. We're prisoners, but same like fleas on dog.

THE CHAPLAIN: That's good milk. But we'll need to cut down our Swedish appetites a bit. After all, we've been defeated.

MOTHER COURAGE: Who's been defeated? Look, victory and defeat ain't bound to be same for the big shots up top as for them below, not by no means. Can be times the bottom lot find a defeat really pays them. Honour's lost, nowt else. I remember once up in Livonia our general took such a beating from enemy I got a horse off our baggage train in the confusion, pulled me cart seven months, he did, before we won and they checked up. As a rule you can say victory and defeat both come expensive to us ordinary folk. Best thing for us is when politics get bogged down solid. *To Swiss Cheese*: Eat up.

SWISS CHEESE: Got no appetite for it. What's sergeant to do when pay day comes round?

MOTHER COURAGE: They don't have pay days on a retreat.

SWISS CHEESE: It's their right, though. They needn't retreat if they don't get paid. Needn't stir a foot.

MOTHER COURAGE: Swiss Cheese, you're that conscientious it makes me quite nervous. I brought you up to be honest, you not being clever, but you got to know where to stop. Chaplain and me, we're off now to buy Catholic flag and some meat. Dunno anyone so good at sniffing meat, like sleepwalking it is, straight to target. I'd say he can pick out a good piece by the way his mouth starts watering. Well, thank goodness they're letting me go on trading. You don't ask tradespeople their faith but their prices. And Lutheran trousers keep cold out too.

THE CHAPLAIN: What did the mendicant say when he heard the Lutherans were going to turn everything in town and country topsy-turvy? 'They'll always need beggars'. *Mother Courage disappears into the cart.* So she's still worried about the cash box. So far they've taken us all for granted as part of the cart, but how long for?

SWISS CHEESE: I can get rid of it.

THE CHAPLAIN: That's almost more dangerous. Suppose you're seen. They have spies. Yesterday a fellow popped up out of the ditch in front of me just as I was relieving myself first thing. I was so scared I only just suppressed an ejaculatory prayer. That would have given me away all right. I think what they'd like best is to go sniffing people's excrement to see if they're Protestants. The spy was a little runt with a patch over one eye.

MOTHER COURAGE *clambering out of the cart with a basket*: What have I found, you shameless creature? *She holds up the red boots in triumph.* Yvette's red high-heeled boots! Coolly went and pinched them, she did. Cause you put it in her head she was an enchanting young person. *She lays them in the basket.* I'm giving them back. Stealing Yvette's boots! She's wrecking herself for money. That's understandable. But you'd do it for nothing, for pleasure. What did I tell you: you're to wait till it's peace. No soldiers for you. You're not to start exhibiting yourself till it's peacetime.

THE CHAPLAIN: I don't find she exhibits herself.

MOTHER COURAGE: Too much for my liking. Let her be like a stone in Dalecarlia, where there's nowt else, so folk say 'Can't see that cripple', that's how I'd lief have her. Then nowt'll happen to her. *To Swiss Cheese*: You leave that box where it is, d'you hear? And keep an eye on your sister, she needs it. The pair of you'll have me in grave yet. Sooner be minding a bagful of fleas.

She leaves with the chaplain. Kattrin clears away the dishes.

SWISS CHEESE: Won't be able to sit out in the sun in shirtsleeves much longer. *Kattrin points at a tree.* Aye, leaves turning yellow. *Kattrin asks by gestures if he wants a drink.* Don't want no drink. I'm thinking. *Pause.* Said she can't sleep. Best if I got rid of that box, found a good place for it. All right, let's have a glass. *Kattrin goes behind the cart.* I'll stuff it down the rat-hole by the river for the time being. Probably pick it up tonight before first light and take it to Regiment. How far can they have retreated in three days? Bet sergeant's surprised. I'm agreeably disappointed in you, Swiss Cheese, he'll say. I make you responsible for the cash, and you go and bring it back.

As Kattrin emerges from behind the cart with a full glass in her hand, two men confront her. One is a sergeant, the other doffs his hat to her. He has a patch over one eye.

THE MAN WITH THE PATCH: God be with you, mistress. Have you seen anyone round here from Second Finnish Regimental Headquarters?

Kattrin, badly frightened, runs downstage, spilling the brandy. The two men look at one another, then withdraw on seeing Swiss Cheese sitting there.

SWISS CHEESE *interrupted in his thoughts*: You spilt half of it. What are those faces for? Jabbed yourself in eye? I don't get it. And I'll have to be off, I've thought it over, it's the only way. *He gets up. She does everything possible to make him realise the danger. He only shrugs her off.* Wish I knew what you're trying to say. Sure you mean well, poor creature, just can't get words out. What's it matter your spilling my brandy, I'll drink plenty more glasses yet, what's one more or less? *He gets the box from the cart and takes it under his tunic.* Be back in a moment. Don't hold me up now, or I'll be angry. I know you mean well. Too bad you can't speak.

As she tries to hold him back he kisses her and tears himself away. Exit. She is desperate, running hither and thither uttering little noises. The chaplain and Mother Courage return. Kattrin rushes to her mother.

MOTHER COURAGE: What's all this? Pull yourself together, love. They done something to you? Where's Swiss Cheese? Tell it me step by step, Kattrin. Mother understands you.

What, so that bastard did take the box? I'll wrap it round his ears, the little hypocrite. Take your time and don't gabble, use your hands, I don't like it when you howl like a dog, what'll his reverence say? Makes him uncomfortable. What, a one-eyed man came along?

THE CHAPLAIN: That one-eyed man is a spy. Have they arrested Swiss Cheese? *Kattrin shakes her head, shrugs her shoulders.* We're done for.

MOTHER COURAGE *fishes in her basket and brings out a Catholic flag, which the chaplain fixes to the mast*: Better hoist new flag.

THE CHAPLAIN *bitterly*: All good Catholics here.
  Voices are heard from the rear. The two men bring in Swiss Cheese.

SWISS CHEESE: Let me go, I got nowt. Don't twist my shoulder, I'm innocent.

SERGEANT: Here's where he came from. You know each other.

MOTHER COURAGE: Us? How?

SWISS CHEESE: I don't know her. Got no idea who she is, had nowt to do with them. I bought me dinner here, ten hellers it cost. You might have seen me sitting here, it was too salty.

SERGEANT: Who are you people, eh?

MOTHER COURAGE: We're law-abiding folk. That's right, he bought a dinner. Said it was too salty.

SERGEANT: Trying to pretend you don't know each other, that it?

MOTHER COURAGE: Why should I know him? Can't know everyone. I don't go asking 'em what they're called and are they a heretic; if he pays he ain't a heretic. You a heretic?

SWISS CHEESE: Go on.

THE CHAPLAIN: He sat there very properly, never opening his mouth except when eating. Then he had to.

SERGEANT: And who are you?

MOTHER COURAGE: He's just my potboy. Now I expect you gentlemen are thirsty, I'll get you a glass of brandy, you must be hot and tired with running.

SERGEANT: No brandy on duty. *To Swiss Cheese*: You were

carrying something. Must have hidden it by the river. Was a bulge in your tunic when you left here.

MOTHER COURAGE: You sure it was him?

SWISS CHEESE: You must be thinking of someone else. I saw someone bounding off with a bulge in his tunic. I'm the wrong man.

MOTHER COURAGE: I'd say it was a misunderstanding too, such things happen. I'm a good judge of people, I'm Courage, you heard of me, everyone knows me, and I tell you that's an honest face he has.

SERGEANT: We're on the track of the Second Finnish Regiment's cash box. We got the description of the fellow responsible for it. Been trailing him two days. It's you.

SWISS CHEESE: It's not me.

SERGEANT: And you better cough it up, or you're a goner, you know. Where is it?

MOTHER COURAGE *urgently*: Of course he'd give it over rather than be a goner. Right out he'd say: I got it, here it is, you're too strong. He ain't all that stupid. Speak up, stupid idiot, here's the sergeant giving you a chance.

SWISS CHEESE: S'pose I ain't got it.

SERGEANT: Then come along. We'll get it out of you. *They lead him off.*

MOTHER COURAGE *calls after them*: He'd tell you. He's not that stupid. And don't you twist his shoulder! *Runs after them.*

Evening of the same day. The chaplain and dumb Kattrin are cleaning glasses and polishing knives.

THE CHAPLAIN: Cases like that, where somebody gets caught, are not unknown in religious history. It reminds me of the Passion of Our Lord and Saviour. There's an old song about that. *He sings the Song of the Hours:*

> In the first hour Jesus mild
> Who had prayed since even
> Was betrayed and led before
> Pontius the heathen.

Pilate found him innocent
Free from fault and error
Therefore, having washed his hands
Sent him to King Herod.

In the third hour he was scourged
Stripped and clad in scarlet
And a plaited crown of thorns
Set upon his forehead.

On the Son of Man they spat
Mocked him and made merry.
Then the cross of death was brought
Given him to carry.

At the sixth hour with two thieves
To the cross they nailed him
And the people and the thieves
Mocked him and reviled him.

This is Jesus King of Jews
Cried they in derision
Till the sun withdrew its light
From that awful vision.

At the ninth hour Jesus wailed
Why hast thou me forsaken?
Soldiers brought him vinegar
Which he left untaken.

Then he yielded up the ghost
And the earth was shaken
Rended was the temple's veil
And the saints were wakened.

Soldiers broke the two thieves' legs
As the night descended
Thrust a spear in Jesus' side
When his life had ended.

Still they mocked, as from his wound
Flowed the blood and water
And blasphemed the Son of Man
With their cruel laughter.*

MOTHER COURAGE *entering excitedly*: It's touch and go. They say sergeant's open to reason though. Only we mustn't let on it's Swiss Cheese else they'll say we helped him. It's a matter of money, that's all. But where's money to come from? Hasn't Yvette been round? I ran into her, she's got her hooks on some colonel, maybe he'd buy her a canteen business.

THE CHAPLAIN: Do you really wish to sell?

MOTHER COURAGE: Where's money for sergeant to come from?

THE CHAPLAIN: What'll you live on, then?

MOTHER COURAGE: That's just it.

Yvette Pottier arrives with an extremely ancient colonel.

YVETTE *embracing Mother Courage*: My dear Courage, fancy seeing you so soon. *Whispers*: He's not unwilling. *Aloud*: This is my good friend who advises me in business matters. I happened to hear you wanted to sell your cart on account of circumstances. I'll think it over.

MOTHER COURAGE: Pledge it, not sell, just not too much hurry, 'tain't every day you find a cart like this in wartime.

YVETTE *disappointed*: Oh, pledge. I thought it was for sale. I'm not so sure I'm interested. *To the colonel*: How do you feel about it?

THE COLONEL: Just as you feel, pet.

MOTHER COURAGE: I'm only pledging it.

YVETTE: I thought you'd got to have the money.

MOTHER COURAGE *firmly*: I got to have it, but sooner run myself ragged looking for a bidder than sell outright. And why? The cart's our livelihood. It's a chance for you, Yvette; who knows when you'll get another like it and have a special friend to advise you, am I right?

YVETTE: Yes, my friend thinks I should clinch it, but I'm not

*Song translated by Ralph Manheim.

sure. If it's only a pledge . . . so you agree we ought to buy outright?

THE COLONEL: I agree, pet.

MOTHER COURAGE: Best look and see if you can find anything for sale then; maybe you will if you don't rush it, take your friend along with you, say a week or fortnight, might find something suits you.

YVETTE: Then let's go looking. I adore going around looking for things, I adore going around with you, Poldi, it's such fun, isn't it? No matter if it takes a fortnight. How soon would you pay the money back if you got it?

MOTHER COURAGE: I'd pay back in two weeks, maybe one.

YVETTE: I can't make up my mind, Poldi chéri, you advise me. *Takes the colonel aside*: She's got to sell, I know, no problem there. And there's that ensign, you know, the fair-haired one, he'd be glad to lend me the money. He's crazy about me, says there's someone I remind him of. What do you advise?

THE COLONEL: You steer clear of him. He's no good. He's only making use of you. I said I'd buy you something, didn't I, pussykins?

YVETTE: I oughtn't to let you. Of course if you think the ensign might try to take advantage . . . Poldi, I'll accept it from you.

THE COLONEL: That's how I feel too.

YVETTE: Is that your advice?

THE COLONEL: That is my advice.

YVETTE *to Courage once more*: My friend's advice would be to accept. Make me out a receipt saying the cart's mine once two weeks are up, with all its contents, we'll check it now, I'll bring the two hundred florins later. *To the colonel*: You go back to the camp, I'll follow, I got to check it all and see there's nothing missing from my cart. *She kisses him. He leaves. She climbs up on the cart.* Not all that many boots, are there?

MOTHER COURAGE: Yvette, it's no time for checking your cart, s'posing it is yours. You promised you'd talk to sergeant about Swiss Cheese, there ain't a minute to lose, they say in an hour he'll be court-martialled.

YVETTE: Just let me count the shirts.

MOTHER COURAGE *pulling her down by the skirt*: You bloody vampire. Swiss Cheese's life's at stake. And not a word about who's making the offer, for God's sake, pretend it's your friend, else we're all done for cause we looked after him.

YVETTE: I fixed to meet that one-eyed fellow in the copse, he should be there by now.

THE CHAPLAIN: It doesn't have to be the whole two hundred either, I'd go up to a hundred and fifty, that may be enough.

MOTHER COURAGE: Since when has it been your money? You kindly keep out of this. You'll get your hotpot all right, don't worry. Hurry up and don't haggle, it's life or death. *Pushes Yvette off.*

THE CHAPLAIN: Far be it from me to interfere, but what are we going to live on? You're saddled with a daughter who can't earn her keep.

MOTHER COURAGE: I'm counting on regimental cash box, Mr Clever. They'll allow it as his expenses.

THE CHAPLAIN: But will she get the message right?

MOTHER COURAGE: It's her interest I should spend her two hundred so she gets the cart. She's set on that, God knows how long that colonel of hers'll last. Kattrin, polish the knives, there's the pumice. And you, stop hanging round like Jesus on Mount of Olives, get moving, wash them glasses, we'll have fifty or more of cavalry in tonight and I don't want to hear a lot of 'I'm not accustomed to having to run about, oh my poor feet, we never ran in church'. Thank the Lord they're corruptible. After all, they ain't wolves, just humans out for money. Corruption in humans is same as compassion in God. Corruption's our only hope. Long as we have it there'll be lenient sentences and even an innocent man'll have a chance of being let off.

YVETTE *comes in panting*: They'll do it for two hundred. But it's got to be quick. Soon be out of their hands. Best thing is I go right away to my colonel with the one-eyed man. He's admitted he had the box, they put the thumbscrews on him. But he chucked it in the river soon as he saw they were on his track. The box is a write-off. I'll go and get the money from my colonel, shall I?

MOTHER COURAGE: Box is a write-off? How'm I to pay back two hundred then?

YVETTE: Oh, you thought you'd get it from the box, did you? And I was to be Joe Soap I suppose? Better not count on that. You'll have to pay up if you want Swiss Cheese back, or would you sooner I dropped the whole thing so's you can keep your cart?

MOTHER COURAGE: That's something I didn't allow for. Don't worry, you'll get your cart, I've said goodbye to it, had it seventeen years, I have. I just need a moment to think, it's bit sudden, what'm I to do, two hundred's too much for me, pity you didn't beat 'em down. Must keep a bit back, else any Tom, Dick and Harry'll be able to shove me in ditch. Go and tell them I'll pay hundred and twenty florins, else it's all off, either way I'm losing me cart.

YVETTE: They won't do it. That one-eyed man's impatient already, keeps looking over his shoulder, he's so worked up. Hadn't I best pay them the whole two hundred?

MOTHER COURAGE *in despair*: I can't pay that. Thirty years I been working. She's twenty-five already, and no husband. I got her to think of too. Don't push me, I know what I'm doing. Say a hundred and twenty, or it's off.

YVETTE: It's up to you. *Rushes off.*

Without looking at either the chaplain or her daughter, Mother Courage sits down to help Kattrin polish knives.

MOTHER COURAGE: Don't smash them glasses, they ain't ours now. Watch what you're doing, you'll cut yourself. Swiss Cheese'll be back, I'll pay two hundred if it comes to the pinch. You'll get your brother, love. For eighty florins we could fill a pack with goods and start again. Plenty of folk has to make do.

THE CHAPLAIN: The Lord will provide, it says.

MOTHER COURAGE: See they're properly dry. *She cleans knives in silence. Kattrin suddenly runs behind the cart, sobbing.*

YVETTE *comes running in*: They won't do it. I told you so. The one-eyed man wanted to leave right away, said there was no point. He says he's just waiting for the drum-roll; that means sentence has been pronounced. I offered a hundred and fifty. He didn't even blink. I had to convince him to stay there so's I could have another word with you.

MOTHER COURAGE: Tell him I'll pay the two hundred. Hurry! *Yvette runs off. They sit in silence. The chaplain has stopped polishing the glasses.* I reckon I bargained too long. *In the distance drumming is heard. The chaplain gets up and goes to the rear. Mother Courage remains seated. It grows dark. The drumming stops. It grows light once more. Mother Courage is sitting exactly as before.*

YVETTE *arrives, very pale*: Well, you got what you asked for, with your haggling and trying to keep your cart. Eleven bullets they gave him, that's all. You don't deserve I should bother any more about you. But I did hear they don't believe the box really is in the river. They've an idea it's here and anyhow that you're connected with him. They're going to bring him here, see if you gives yourself away when you sees him. Thought I'd better warn you so's you don't recognise him, else you'll all be for it. They're right on my heels, best tell you quick. Shall I keep Kattrin away? *Mother Courage shakes her head.* Does she know? She mayn't have heard the drumming or know what it meant.

MOTHER COURAGE: She knows. Get her.

Yvette fetches Kattrin, who goes to her mother and stands beside her. Mother Courage takes her hand. Two lansequenets come carrying a stretcher with something lying on it covered by a sheet. The sergeant marches beside them. They set down the stretcher.

SERGEANT: Here's somebody we dunno the name of. It's got to be listed, though, so everything's shipshape. He had a meal here. Have a look, see if you know him. *He removes the sheet.* Know him? *Mother Courage shakes her head.* What, never see him before he had that meal here? *Mother Courage shakes her head.* Pick him up. Chuck him in the pit. He's got nobody knows him. *They carry him away.*

4

Mother Courage sings the Song of the Grand Capitulation

Outside an officer's tent.

Mother Courage is waiting. A clerk looks out of the tent.

THE CLERK: I know you. You had a paymaster from the Lutherans with you, what was in hiding. I'd not complain if I were you.

MOTHER COURAGE: But I got a complaint to make. I'm innocent, would look as how I'd a bad conscience if I let this pass. Slashed everything in me cart to pieces with their sabres, they did, then wanted I should pay five taler fine for nowt, I tell you, nowt.

THE CLERK: Take my tip, better shut up. We're short of canteens, so we let you go on trading, specially if you got a bad conscience and pay a fine now and then.

MOTHER COURAGE: I got a complaint.

THE CLERK: Have it your own way. Then you must wait till the captain's free. *Withdraws inside the tent.*

YOUNG SOLDIER *enters aggressively*: Bouque la Madonne! Where's that bleeding pig of a captain what's took my reward money to swig with his tarts? I'll do him.

OLDER SOLDIER *running after him*: Shut up. They'll put you in irons.

YOUNG SOLDIER: Out of there, you thief! I'll slice you into pork chops, I will. Pocketing my prize money after I'd swum the river, only one in the whole squadron, and now I can't even buy meself a beer. I'm not standing for that. Come on out there so I can cut you up!

OLDER SOLDIER: Blessed Mother of God, he's asking for trouble.

MOTHER COURAGE: Is it some reward he weren't paid?

YOUNG SOLDIER: Lemme go, I'll slash you too while I'm at it.

OLDER SOLDIER: He rescued the colonel's horse and got no reward for it. He's young yet, still wet behind the ears.

MOTHER COURAGE: Let him go, he ain't a dog you got to chain up. Wanting your reward is good sound sense. Why be a hero otherwise?

YOUNG SOLDIER: So's he can sit in there and booze. You're shit-scared, the lot of you. I done something special and I want my reward.

MOTHER COURAGE: Don't you shout at me, young fellow. Got me own worries, I have; any road you should spare your voice, be needing it when captain comes, else there he'll be and you too hoarse to make a sound, which'll make it hard for him to clap you in irons till you turn blue. People what shouts like that can't keep it up ever; half an hour, and they have to be rocked to sleep, they're so tired.

YOUNG SOLDIER: I ain't tired and to hell with sleep. I'm hungry. They make our bread from acorns and hemp-seed, and they even skimp on that. He's whoring away my reward and I'm hungry. I'll do him.

MOTHER COURAGE: Oh I see, you're hungry. Last year that general of yours ordered you all off roads and across fields so corn should be trampled flat; I could've got ten florins for a pair of boots s'pose I'd had boots and s'pose anyone'd been able to pay ten florins. Thought he'd be well away from that area this year, he did, but here he is, still there, and hunger is great. I see what you're angry about.

YOUNG SOLDIER: I won't have it, don't talk to me, it ain't fair and I'm not standing for that.

MOTHER COURAGE: And you're right; but how long? How long you not standing for unfairness? One hour, two hours? Didn't ask yourself that, did you, but it's the whole point, and why, once you're in irons it's too bad if you suddenly finds you can put up with unfairness after all.

YOUNG SOLDIER: What am I listening to you for, I'd like to know? Bouque la Madonne, where's that captain?

MOTHER COURAGE: You been listening to me because you knows it's like what I say, your anger has gone up in smoke already, it was just a short one and you needed a long one, but where you going to get it from?

YOUNG SOLDIER: Are you trying to tell me asking for my reward is wrong?

MOTHER COURAGE: Not a bit. I'm just telling you your anger ain't long enough, it's good for nowt, pity. If you'd a long one I'd be trying to prod you on. Cut him up, the swine, would be my advice to you in that case; but how about if you don't cut him up cause you feels your tail going between your legs? Then I'd look silly and captain'd take it out on me.

OLDER SOLDIER: You're perfectly right, he's just a bit crazy.

YOUNG SOLDIER: Very well, let's see if I don't cut him up. *Draws his sword.* When he arrives I'm going to cut him up.

THE CLERK *looks out*: The captain'll be here in one minute. Sit down.

The young soldier sits down.

MOTHER COURAGE: He's sitting now. See, what did I say? you're sitting now. Ah, how well they know us, no one need tell 'em how to go about it. Sit down! and, bingo, we're sitting. And sitting and sedition don't mix. Don't try to stand up, you won't stand the way you was standing before. I shouldn't worry about what I think; I'm no better, not one moment. Bought up all our fighting spirit, they have. Eh? S'pose I kick back, might be bad for business. Let me tell you a thing or two about the Grand Capitulation. *She sings the Song of the Grand Capitulation*:

Back when I was young, I was brought to realise
What a very special person I must be
(Not just any old cottager's daughter, what with my looks
    and my talents and my urge towards Higher Things)
And insisted that my soup should have no hairs in it.
No one makes a sucker out of me!
(All or nothing, only the best is good enough, each man
    for himself, nobody's telling *me* what to do.)
Then I heard a tit
Chirp: Wait a bit!

And you'll be marching with the band
In step, responding to command
And striking up your little dance:
Now we advance.
And now: parade, form square!
Then men swear God's there –
Not the faintest chance!

In no time at all anyone who looked could see
That I'd learned to take my medicine with good grace.
(Two kids on my hands and look at the price of bread, and
    things they expect of you!)
When they finally came to feel that they were through with
    me
They'd got me grovelling on my face.
(Takes all sorts to make a world, you scratch my back and
    I'll scratch yours, no good banging your head against a
    brick wall.)
Then I heard that tit
Chirp: Wait a bit!
    And you'll be marching with the band
    In step, responding to command
    And striking up you little dance:
    Now they advance.
    And now: parade, form square!
    Then men swear God's there –
    Not the faintest chance!

I've known people tried to storm the summits:
There's no star too bright or seems too far away.
(Dogged does it, where there's a will there's a way, by
    hook or by crook.)
As each peak disclosed fresh peaks to come, it's
Strange how much a plain straw hat could weigh.
(You have to cut your coat according to your cloth.)
Then I hear the tit
Chirp: Wait a bit!

And they'll be marching with the band
In step, responding to command
And striking up their little dance:
Now they advance
And now: parade, form square!
Then men swear God's there –
Not the faintest chance!

MOTHER COURAGE *to the young soldier*: That's why I reckon you should stay there with your sword drawn if you're truly set on it and your anger's big enough, because you got grounds, I agree, but if your anger's a short one best leave right away.

YOUNG SOLDIER: Oh stuff it. *He staggers off with the older soldier following.*

CLERK *sticks his head out*: Captain's here now. You can make your complaint.

MOTHER COURAGE: I changed me mind. I ain't complaining. *Exit.*

5

Two years have gone by. The war is spreading to new areas. Ceaselessly on the move, Courage's little cart crosses Poland, Moravia, Bavaria, Italy then Bavaria again. 1631. Tilly's victory at Magdeburg costs Mother Courage four officers' shirts

Mother Courage's cart has stopped in a badly shot-up village.

Thin military music in the distance. Two soldiers at the bar being served by Kattrin and Mother Courage. One of them has a lady's fur coat over his shoulders.

MOTHER COURAGE: Can't pay, that it? No money, no schnapps. They give us victory parades, but catch them giving men their pay.

SOLDIER: I want my schnapps. I missed the looting. That double-crossing general only allowed an hour's looting in the town. He ain't an inhuman monster, he said. Town must of paid him.

THE CHAPLAIN *stumbles in*: There are people still lying in that yard. The peasant's family. Somebody give me a hand. I need linen.

The second soldier goes off with him. Kattrin becomes very excited and tries to make her mother produce linen.

MOTHER COURAGE: I got none. All my bandages was sold to regiment. I ain't tearing up my officers' shirts for that lot.

THE CHAPLAIN *calling back*: I need linen, I tell you.

MOTHER COURAGE *blocking Kattrin's way into the cart by sitting on the step*: I'm giving nowt. They'll never pay, and why, nowt to pay with.

CHAPLAIN *bending over a woman he has carried in*: Why d'you stay around during the gunfire?

PEASANT WOMAN *feebly*: Farm.

MOTHER COURAGE: Catch them abandoning anything. But now I'm s'posed to foot the bill. I won't do it.

FIRST SOLDIER: Those are Protestants. What they have to be Protestants for?

MOTHER COURAGE: They ain't bothering about faith. They lost their farm.

SECOND SOLDIER: They're no Protestants. They're Catholics like us.

FIRST SOLDIER: No way of sorting 'em out in a bombardment.

A PEASANT *brought in by the chaplain*: My arm's gone.

THE CHAPLAIN: Where's that linen? *All look at Mother Courage who does not move.*

MOTHER COURAGE: I can't give nowt. What with expenses, taxes, loan interest and bribes. *Making guttural noises, Kattrin raises a plank and threatens her mother with it.* You gone plain crazy? Put that plank away or I'll paste you one, you cow. I'm giving nowt, don't want to, got to think of meself. *The chaplain lifts her off the steps and sets her on the ground, then starts pulling out shirts and tearing them into strips.* My officers' shirts! Half a florin apiece! I'm ruined. *From the house comes the cry of a child in pain.*

THE PEASANT: The baby's in there still. *Kattrin dashes in.*

THE CHAPLAIN *to the woman*: Don't move. They'll get it out.

MOTHER COURAGE: Stop her, roof may fall in.

THE CHAPLAIN: I'm not going back in there.

MOTHER COURAGE *torn both ways*: Don't waste my precious linen. *The second soldier restrains her.*

Kattrin brings a baby out of the ruins.

MOTHER COURAGE: How nice, found another baby to cart around? Give it to its ma this instant, unless you'd have me fighting for hours to get it off you, like last time, d'you hear? *To the second soldier*: Don't stand there gawping, you go back and tell them cut out that music, we can see it's a victory with our own eyes. All your victories mean to me is losses.

THE CHAPLAIN *tying a bandage*: Blood's coming through.

Kattrin is rocking the baby and making lullaby noises.

MOTHER COURAGE: Look at her, happy as a queen in all this misery; give it back at once, its mother's coming round. *She catches the first soldier, who has been attacking the drinks and is trying to make off with one of the bottles.* Psia krew! Thought you'd score another victory, you animal? Now pay.

FIRST SOLDIER: I got nowt.

MOTHER COURAGE *pulling the fur coat off his back*: Then leave that coat, it's stolen any road.

THE CHAPLAIN: There's still someone under there.

6

Outside the Bavarian town of Ingolstadt Courage participates in the funeral of the late Imperial commander Tilly. Discussions are held about war heroes and the war's duration. The chaplain complains that his talents are lying fallow, and dumb Kattrin gets the red boots. The year is 1632

Inside a canteen tent.

It has a bar towards the rear. Rain. Sound of drums and funeral music. The chaplain and the regimental clerk are playing a board game. Mother Courage and her daughter are stocktaking.

THE CHAPLAIN: Now the funeral procession will be moving off.

MOTHER COURAGE: Too bad about commander in chief — twenty-two pairs those socks — he fell by accident, they say. Mist over fields, that was the trouble. General had just been haranguing a regiment saying they must fight to last man and last round, he was riding back when mist made him lose direction so he was up front and a bullet got him in midst of battle — only four hurricane lamps left. *A whistle from the rear. She goes to the bar.* You scrimshankers, dodging your commander in chief's funeral, scandal I call it. *Pours drinks.*

THE CLERK: They should never of paid troops out before the funeral. Instead of going now they're all getting pissed.

THE CHAPLAIN *to the clerk*: Aren't you supposed to go to the funeral?

THE CLERK: Dodged it cause of the rain.

MOTHER COURAGE: It's different with you, your uniform might get wet. I heard they wanted to toll bells for funeral as usual, except it turned out all churches had been blown to smithereens by his orders, so poor old commander in chief won't be hearing no bells as they let the coffin down. They're going to let off three salvoes instead to cheer things up — seventeen belts.

SHOUTS *from the bar*: Hey, Missis, a brandy!

MOTHER COURAGE: Let's see your money. No, I ain't having you in my tent with your disgusting boots. You can drink outside, rain or no rain. *To the clerk*: I'm only letting in sergeants and up. Commander in chief had been having his worries, they say. S'posed to have been trouble with Second Regiment cause he stopped their pay, said it was a war of faith and they should do it for free. *Funeral march. All look to the rear.*

THE CHAPLAIN: Now they'll be filing past the noble corpse.

MOTHER COURAGE: Can't help feeling sorry for those generals and emperors, there they are maybe thinking they're doing something extra special what folk'll talk about in years to come, and earning a public monument, like conquering the world for instance, that's a fine ambition for a general, how's he to know any better? I mean, he plagues hisself to death, then it all breaks down on account of ordinary folk what just wants their beer and bit of a chat, nowt higher. Finest plans get bolloxed up by the pettiness of them as should be carrying them out, because emperors can't do nowt themselves, they just counts on soldiers and people to back 'em up whatever happens, am I right?

THE CHAPLAIN *laughs*: Courage, you're right, aside from the soldiers. They do their best. Give me that lot outside there, for instance, drinking their brandy in the rain, and I'd guarantee to make you one war after another for a hundred years if need be, and I'm no trained general.

MOTHER COURAGE: You don't think war might end, then?

THE CHAPLAIN: What, because the commander in chief's gone? Don't be childish. They're two a penny, no shortage of heroes.

MOTHER COURAGE: Ee, I'm not asking for fun of it, but because I'm thinking whether to stock up, prices are low now, but if war's going to end it's money down the drain.

THE CHAPLAIN: I realise it's a serious question. There've always been people going round saying 'the war can't go on for ever'. I tell you there's nothing to stop it going on for ever. Of course there can be a bit of a breathing space. The war may need to get its second wind, it may even have an accident so to speak. There's no guarantee against that; nothing's perfect on this earth of ours. A perfect war, the sort you might say couldn't be improved on, that's something we shall probably never see. It can suddenly come to a standstill for some quite unforeseen reason, you can't allow for everything. A slight case of negligence, and it's bogged down up to the axles. And then it's a matter of hauling the war out of the mud again. But emperor and kings and popes will come to its rescue. So on the whole it has nothing serious to worry about, and will live to a ripe old age.

A SOLDIER *sings at the bar*:

> A schnapps, landlord, you're late!
> A soldier cannot wait
> To do his emperor's orders.

Make it a double, this is a holiday.

MOTHER COURAGE: S'pose I went by what you say . . .

THE CHAPLAIN: Think it out for yourself. What's to compete with the war?

THE SOLDIER *at the rear*:

> Your breast, my girl, you're late!
> A soldier cannot wait
> To ride across the borders.

THE CLERK *unexpectedly*: And what about peace? I'm from Bohemia and I'd like to go home some day.

THE CHAPLAIN: Would you indeed? Ah, peace, Where is the hole once the cheese has been eaten?

THE SOLDIER *at the rear*:

> Lead trumps, my friend, you're late!
> A soldier cannot wait.
> His emperor needs him badly.

Your blessing, priest, you're late!
A soldier cannot wait.
Must lay his life down gladly.

THE CLERK: In the long run life's impossible if there's no peace.

THE CHAPLAIN: I'd say there's peace in war too; it has its peaceful moments. Because war satisfies all requirements, peaceable ones included, they're catered for, and it would simply fizzle out if they weren't. In war you can do a crap like in the depths of peacetime, then between one battle and the next you can have a beer, then even when you're moving up you can lay your head on your arms and have a bit of shuteye in the ditch, it's entirely possible. During a charge you can't play cards maybe, but nor can you in the depths of peacetime when you're ploughing, and after a victory there are various openings. You may get a leg blown off, then you start by making a lot of fuss as though it were serious, but afterwards you calm down or get given a schnapps, and you end up hopping around and the war's no worse off than before. And what's to stop you being fruitful and multiplying in the middle of all the butchery, behind a barn or something, in the long run you can't be held back from it, and then the war will have your progeny and can use them to carry on with. No, the war will always find an outlet, mark my words. Why should it ever stop?

Kattrin has ceased working and is staring at the chaplain.

MOTHER COURAGE: I'll buy fresh stock then. If you say so. *Kattrin suddenly flings a basket full of bottles to the ground and runs off.* Kattrin! *Laughs.* Damn me if she weren't waiting for peace. I promised her she'd get a husband soon as peace came. *Hurries after her.*

THE CLERK *standing up*: I won. You been talking too much. Pay up.

MOTHER COURAGE *returning with Kattrin*: Don't be silly, war'll go on a bit longer, and we'll make a bit more money, and peacetime'll be all the nicer for it. Now you go into town, that's ten minutes' walk at most, fetch things from Golden Lion, the expensive ones, we can fetch rest in cart later, it's all arranged, regimental clerk here will go with you. Nearly everybody's attending commander in chief's funeral, nowt can happen to you. Careful now, don't let them steal nowt, think of your dowry.

Kattrin puts a cloth over her head and leaves with the clerk.

THE CHAPLAIN: Is that all right to let her go with the clerk?

MOTHER COURAGE: She's not that pretty they'd want to ruin her.

THE CHAPLAIN: I admire the way you run your business and always win through. I see why they called you Courage.

MOTHER COURAGE: Poor folk got to have courage. Why, they're lost. Simply getting up in morning takes some doing in their situation. Or ploughing a field, and in a war at that. Mere fact they bring kids into world shows they got courage, cause there's no hope for them. They have to hang one another and slaughter one another, so just looking each other in face must call for courage. Being able to put up with emperor and pope shows supernatural courage, cause those two cost 'em their lives. *She sits down, takes a little pipe from her purse and smokes.* You might chop us a bit of kindling.

THE CHAPLAIN *reluctantly removing his coat and preparing to chop up sticks*: I happen to be a pastor of souls, not a wood-cutter.

MOTHER COURAGE: I got no soul, you see. Need firewood, though.

THE CHAPLAIN: Where's that stumpy pipe from?

MOTHER COURAGE: Just a pipe.

THE CHAPLAIN: What d'you mean, 'just', it's a quite particular pipe, that.

MOTHER COURAGE: Aha?

THE CHAPLAIN: That stumpy pipe belongs to the Oxenstierna Regiment's cook.

MOTHER COURAGE: If you know that already why ask, Mr Clever?

THE CHAPLAIN: Because I didn't know if you were aware what you're smoking. You might just have been rummaging around in your things, come across some old pipe or other, and used it out of sheer absence of mind.

MOTHER COURAGE: And why not?

THE CHAPLAIN: Because you didn't. You're smoking that deliberately.

MOTHER COURAGE: And why shouldn't I?

THE CHAPLAIN: Courage, I'm warning you. It's my duty. Probably you'll never clap eyes on the gentleman again, and that's no loss but your good fortune. He didn't make at all a reliable impression on me. Quite the opposite.

MOTHER COURAGE: Really? Nice fellow that.

THE CHAPLAIN: So he's what you would call a nice fellow? I wouldn't. Far be it from me to bear him the least ill-will, but nice is not what I would call him. More like one of those Don Juans, a slippery one. Have a look at that pipe if you don't believe me. You must admit it tells you a good deal about his character.

MOTHER COURAGE: Nowt that I can see. Worn out, I'd call it.

THE CHAPLAIN: Practically bitten through, you mean. A man of wrath. That is the pipe of an unscrupulous man of wrath; you must see that if you have any discrimination left.

MOTHER COURAGE: Don't chop my chopping block in two.

THE CHAPLAIN: I told you I'm not a woodcutter by trade. I studied to be a pastor of souls. My talent and abilities are being abused in this place, by manual labour. My God-given endowments are denied expression. It's a sin. You have never heard me preach. One sermon of mine can put a regiment in such a frame of mind it'll treat the enemy like a flock of sheep. Life to them is a smelly old foot-cloth which they fling away in a vision of final victory. God has given me the gift of speech. I can preach so you'll lose all sense of sight and hearing.

MOTHER COURAGE: I don't wish to lose my sense of sight and hearing. Where'd that leave me?

THE CHAPLAIN: Courage, I have often thought that your dry way of talking conceals more than just a warm heart. You too are human and need warmth.

MOTHER COURAGE: Best way for us to get this tent warm is have plenty of firewood.

THE CHAPLAIN: Don't change the subject. Seriously, Courage,

I sometimes ask myself what it would be like if our relationship were to become somewhat closer. I mean, given that the whirlwind of war has so strangely whirled us together.

MOTHER COURAGE: I'd say it was close enough. I cook meals for you and you run around and chop firewood for instance.

THE CHAPLAIN *coming closer*: You know what I mean by closer; it's not a relationship founded on meals and wood-chopping and other such base necessities. Let your heart speak, harden thyself not.

MOTHER COURAGE: Don't you come at me with that axe. That'd be too close a relationship.

THE CHAPLAIN: You shouldn't make a joke of it. I'm a serious person and I've thought about what I'm saying.

MOTHER COURAGE: Be sensible, padre. I like you. I don't want to row you. All I'm after is get myself and children through all this with my cart. I don't see it as mine, and I ain't in the mood for private affairs. Right now I'm taking a gamble, buying stores just when commander in chief's fallen and all the talk's of peace. Where d'you reckon you'd turn if I'm ruined? Don't know, do you? You chop us some kindling wood, then we can keep warm at night, that's quite something these times. What's this? *She gets up. Enter Kattrin, out of breath, with a wound above her eye. She is carrying a variety of stuff: parcels, leather goods, a drum and so on.*

MOTHER COURAGE: What happened, someone assault you? On way back? She was assaulted on her way back. Bet it was that trooper was getting drunk here. I shouldn't have let you go, love. Drop that stuff. Not too bad, just a flesh wound you got. I'll bandage it and in a week it'll be all right. Worse than wild beasts, they are. *She ties up the wound.*

THE CHAPLAIN: It's not them I blame. They never went raping back home. The fault lies with those that start wars, it brings humanity's lowest instincts to the surface.

MOTHER COURAGE: Calm down. Didn't clerk come back with you? That's because you're respectable, they don't bother. Wound ain't a deep one, won't leave no mark. There you are, all bandaged up. You'll get something, love, keep calm.

Something I put aside for you, wait till you see. *She delves into a sack and brings out Yvette's red high-heeled boots.* Made you open your eyes, eh? Something you always wanted. They're yours. Put 'em on quick, before I change me mind. Won't leave no mark, and what if it does? Ones I'm really sorry for's the ones they fancy. Drag them around till they're worn out, they do. Those they don't care for they leaves alive. I seen girls before now had pretty faces, then in no time looking fit to frighten a hyaena. Can't even go behind a bush without risking trouble, horrible life they lead. Same like with trees, straight well-shaped ones get chopped down to make beams for houses and crooked ones live happily ever after. So it's a stroke of luck for you really. Them boots'll be all right, I greased them before putting them away.

Kattrin leaves the boots where they are and crawls into the cart.

THE CHAPLAIN: Let's hope she's not disfigured.

MOTHER COURAGE: She'll have a scar. No use her waiting for peacetime now.

THE CHAPLAIN: She didn't let them steal the things.

MOTHER COURAGE: Maybe I shouldn't have dinned that into her so. Wish I knew what went on in that head of hers. Just once she stayed out all night, once in all those years. Afterwards she went around like before, except she worked harder. Couldn't get her to tell what had happened. Worried me quite a while, that did. *She collects the articles brought by Kattrin, and sorts them angrily.* That's war for you. Nice way to get a living!

Sound of cannon fire.

THE CHAPLAIN: Now they'll be burying the commander in chief. This is a historic moment.

MOTHER COURAGE: What I call a historic moment is them bashing my daughter over the eye. She's half wrecked already, won't get no husband now, and her so crazy about kids; any road she's only dumb from war, soldier stuffed something in her mouth when she was little. As for Swiss

Cheese I'll never see him again, and where Eilif is God alone knows. War be damned.

7

Mother Courage at the peak of her business career

High road.

The chaplain, Mother Courage and Kattrin are pulling the cart, which is hung with new wares. Mother Courage is wearing a necklace of silver coins.

MOTHER COURAGE: I won't have you folk spoiling my war for me. I'm told it kills off the weak, but they're write-off in peacetime too. And war gives its people a better deal.
She sings:

> And if you feel your forces fading
> You won't be there to share the fruits.
> But what is war but private trading
> That deals in blood instead of boots?

And what's the use of settling down? Them as does are first to go. *Sings*:

> Some people think to live by looting
> The goods some others haven't got.
> You think it's just a line they're shooting
> Until you hear they have been shot.

> And some I saw dig six feet under
> In haste to lie down and pass out.
> Now they're at rest perhaps they wonder
> Just what was all their haste about.

They pull it further.

8

The same year sees the death of the Swedish king Gustavus Adolphus at the battle of Lützen. Peace threatens to ruin Mother Courage's business. Courage's dashing son performs one heroic deed too many and comes to a sticky end

Camp.

A summer morning. In front of the cart stand an old woman and her son. The son carries a large sack of bedding.

MOTHER COURAGE'S VOICE *from inside the cart*: Does it need to be this ungodly hour?

THE YOUNG MAN: We walked twenty miles in the night and got to be back today.

MOTHER COURAGE'S VOICE: What am I to do with bedding? Folk've got no houses.

THE YOUNG MAN: Best have a look first.

THE OLD WOMAN: This place is no good either. Come on.

THE YOUNG MAN: What, and have them sell the roof over our head for taxes? She might pay three florins if you throw in the bracelet. *Bells start ringing.* Listen, mother.

VOICES *from the rear*: Peace! Swedish king's been killed.

MOTHER COURAGE *sticks her head out of the cart. She has not yet done her hair*: What's that bell-ringing about in mid-week?

THE CHAPLAIN *crawling out from under the cart*: What are they shouting? Peace?

MOTHER COURAGE: Don't tell me peace has broken out just after I laid in new stock.

THE CHAPLAIN *calling to the rear*: That true? Peace?

VOICES: Three weeks ago, they say, only no one told us.

THE CHAPLAIN *to Courage*: What else would they be ringing the bells for?

VOICES: A whole lot of Lutherans have driven into town, they brought the news.

THE YOUNG MAN: Mother, it's peace. What's the matter? *The old woman has collapsed.*

MOTHER COURAGE *speaking into the cart*: Holy cow! Kattrin, peace! Put your black dress on, we're going to church. Least we can do for Swiss Cheese. Is it true, though?

THE YOUNG MAN: The people here say so. They've made peace. Can you get up? *The old woman stands up dumb-founded.* I'll get the saddlery going again, I promise. It'll all work out. Father will get his bedding back. Can you walk? *To the chaplain*: She came over queer. It's the news. She never thought there'd be peace again. Father always said so. We're going straight home. *They go off.*

MOTHER COURAGE'S VOICE: Give her a schnapps.

THE CHAPLAIN: They've already gone.

MOTHER COURAGE'S VOICE: What's up in camp?

THE CHAPLAIN: They're assembling. I'll go on over. Shouldn't I put on my clerical garb?

MOTHER COURAGE'S VOICE: Best check up before parading yourself as heretic. I'm glad about peace, never mind if I'm ruined. Any road I'll have got two of me children through the war. Be seeing Eilif again now.

THE CHAPLAIN: And who's that walking down the lines? Bless me, the army commander's cook.

THE COOK *somewhat bedraggled and carrying a bundle*: What do I behold? The padre!

THE CHAPLAIN: Courage, we've got company.

Mother Courage clambers out.

THE COOK: I promised I'd drop over for a little talk soon as I had the time. I've not forgotten your brandy, Mrs Fierling.

MOTHER COURAGE: Good grief, the general's cook! After all these years! Where's my eldest boy Eilif?

THE COOK: Hasn't he got here? He left before me, he was on his way to see you too.

THE CHAPLAIN: I shall don my clerical garb, just a moment. *Goes off behind the cart.*

MOTHER COURAGE: Then he may be here any minute. *Calls*

into the cart: Kattrin, Eilif's on his way. Get cook a glass of brandy, Kattrin! *Kattrin does not appear*. Drag your hair down over it, that's all right. Mr Lamb's no stranger. *Fetches the brandy herself*. She don't like to come out, peace means nowt to her. Took too long coming, it did. They gave her a crack over one eye, you barely notice it now but she thinks folks are staring at her.

THE COOK: Ah yes. War. *He and Mother Courage sit down*.

MOTHER COURAGE: Cooky, you caught me at bad moment. I'm ruined.

THE COOK: What? That's hard.

MOTHER COURAGE: Peace'll wring my neck. I went and took Chaplain's advice, laid in fresh stocks only t'other day. And now they're going to demobilise and I'll be left sitting on me wares.

THE COOK: What d'you want to go and listen to padre for? If I hadn't been in such a hurry that time, the Catholics arriving so quickly and all, I'd warned you against that man. All piss and wind, he is. So he's the authority around here, eh?

MOTHER COURAGE: He's been doing washing-up for me and helping pull.

THE COOK: Him pull! I bet he told you some of those jokes of his too, I know him, got a very unhealthy view of women, he has, all my good influence on him went for nowt. He ain't steady.

MOTHER COURAGE: You steady then?

THE COOK: Whatever else I ain't, I'm steady. Mud in your eye!

MOTHER COURAGE: Steady, that's nowt. I only had one steady fellow, thank God. Hardest I ever had to work in me life; he flogged the kids' blankets soon as springtime came, and he called me mouth-organ an unchristian instrument. Ask me, you ain't saying much for yourself admitting you're steady.

THE COOK: Still tough as nails, I see; but that's what I like about you.

MOTHER COURAGE: Now don't tell me you been dreaming of me nails.

THE COOK: Well, well, here we are, along with armistice bells and your brandy like what nobody else ever serves, it's famous, that is.

MOTHER COURAGE: I don't give two pins for your armistice bells just now. Can't see 'em handing out all the back pay what's owing, so where does that leave me with my famous brandy? Had your pay yet?

THE COOK *hesitantly*: Not exactly. That's why we all shoved off. If that's how it is, I thought, I'll go and visit friends. So here I am sitting with you.

MOTHER COURAGE: Other words you got nowt.

THE COOK: High time they stopped that bloody clanging. Wouldn't mind getting into some sort of trade. I'm fed up being cook to that lot. I'm s'posed to rustle them up meals out of tree roots and old bootsoles, then they fling the hot soup in my face. Cook these days is a dog's life. Sooner do war service, only of course it's peacetime now. *He sees the chaplain reappearing in his old garments*. More about that later.

THE CHAPLAIN: It's still all right, only had a few moths in it.

THE COOK: Can't see why you bother. You won't get your old job back, who are you to inspire now to earn his pay honourably and lay down his life? What's more I got a bone to pick with you, cause you advised this lady to buy a lot of unnecessary goods saying war would go on for ever.

THE CHAPLAIN *heatedly*: I'd like to know what concern that is of yours.

THE COOK: Because it's unscrupulous, that sort of thing is. How dare you meddle in other folks' business arrangements with your unwanted advice?

THE CHAPLAIN: Who's meddling? *To Courage*: I never knew this gentleman was such an intimate you had to account to him for everything.

MOTHER COURAGE: Keep you hair on, cook's only giving his personal opinion and you can't deny your war was a flop.

THE CHAPLAIN: You should not blaspheme against peace, Courage. You are a hyaena of the battlefield.

MOTHER COURAGE: I'm what?

THE COOK: If you're going to insult this lady you'll have to settle with me.

THE CHAPLAIN: It's not you I'm talking to. Your intentions are only too transparent. *To Courage*: But when I see you picking up peace betwixt your finger and your thumb like some dirty old snot-rag, then my humanity feels outraged; for then I see that you don't want peace but war, because you profit from it; in which case you shouldn't forget the ancient saying that whosoever sups with the devil needs a long spoon.

MOTHER COURAGE: I got no use for war, and war ain't got much use for me. But I'm not being called no hyaena, you and me's through.

THE CHAPLAIN: Then why grumble about peace when everybody's breathing sighs of relief? Because of some old junk in your cart?

MOTHER COURAGE: My goods ain't old junk but what I lives by, and you too up to now.

THE CHAPLAIN: Off war, in other words. Aha.

THE COOK *to the chaplain*: You're old enough to know it's always a mistake offering advice. *To Courage*: Way things are, your best bet's to get rid of certain goods quick as you can before prices hit rock-bottom. Dress yourself and get moving, not a moment to lose.

MOTHER COURAGE: That ain't bad advice. I'll do that, I guess.

THE CHAPLAIN: Because cooky says it.

MOTHER COURAGE: Why couldn't you say it? He's right, I'd best go off to market. *Goes inside the cart.*

THE COOK: That's one to me, padre. You got no presence of mind. What you should of said was: what, me offer advice, all I done was discuss politics. Better not take me on. Cock-fighting don't suit that get-up.

THE CHAPLAIN: If you don't stop your gob I'll murder you, get-up or no get-up.

THE COOK *pulling off his boots and unwrapping his foot-clothes*: Pity the war made such a godless shit of you, else you'd easily get another parsonage now it's peacetime.

Cooks won't be needed, there's nowt to cook, but faith goes on just the same, nowt changed in that direction.

THE CHAPLAIN: Mr Lamb, I'm asking you not to elbow me out. Since I came down in the world I've become a better person. I couldn't preach to anyone now.

Enter Yvette Pottier in black, dressed up to the nines, carrying a cane. She is much older and fatter, and heavily powdered. She is followed by a manservant.

YVETTE: Hullo there, everybody. Is this Mother Courage's establishment?

THE CHAPLAIN: It is. And with whom have we the honour . . . ?

YVETTE: With the Countess Starhemberg, my good man. Where's Courage?

THE CHAPLAIN *calls into the cart*: The Countess Starhemberg wishes to speak to you.

MOTHER COURAGE'S VOICE: Just coming.

YVETTE: It's Yvette.

MOTHER COURAGE'S VOICE: Oh, Yvette!

YVETTE: Come to see how you are. *Sees the cook turn round aghast*: Pieter!

THE COOK: Yvette!

YVETTE: Well I never! How d'you come to be here?

THE COOK: Got a lift.

THE CHAPLAIN: You know each other then? Intimately?

YVETTE: I should think so. *She looks the cook over.* Fat.

THE COOK: Not all that skinny yourself.

YVETTE: All the same I'm glad to see you, you shit. Gives me a chance to say what I think of you.

THE CHAPLAIN: You say it, in full; but don't start till Courage is out here.

MOTHER COURAGE *coming out with all kinds of goods*: Yvette! *They embrace.* But what are you in mourning for?

YVETTE: Suits me, don't it? My husband the colonel died a few years back.

MOTHER COURAGE: That old fellow what nearly bought the cart?

YVETTE: His elder brother.

MOTHER COURAGE: Then you're sitting pretty. Nice to find somebody what's made it in this war.

YVETTE: Up and down and up again, that's the way it went.

MOTHER COURAGE: I'm not hearing a word against colonels, they make a mint of money.

THE CHAPLAIN: I would put my boots back on if I were you. *To Yvette*: You promised you would say what you think of the gentleman, your ladyship.

THE COOK: Don't kick up a stink here, Yvette.

MOTHER COURAGE: Yvette, this is a friend of mine.

YVETTE: That's old Puffing Piet.

THE COOK: Let's drop the nicknames. I'm called Lamb.

MOTHER COURAGE *laughs*: Puffing Piet! Him as made all the women crazy! Here, I been looking after your pipe for you.

THE CHAPLAIN: Smoking it too.

YVETTE: What luck I can warn you against him. Worst of the lot, he was, rampaging along the whole Flanders coast-line. Got more girls in trouble than he has fingers.

THE COOK: That's all a long while ago. 'Tain't true anyhow.

YVETTE: Stand up when a lady brings you into the conversation! How I loved this man! All the time he had a little dark girl with bandy legs, got her in trouble too of course.

THE COOK: Got you into high society more like, far as I can see.

YVETTE: Shut your trap, you pathetic remnant! Better watch out for him, though; fellows like that are still dangerous even when on their last legs.

MOTHER COURAGE *to Yvette*: Come along, got to get rid of my stuff afore prices start dropping. You might be able to put a word in for me at regiment, with your connections. *Calls into the cart*: Kattrin, church is off, I'm going to market instead. When Eilif turns up, one of you give him a drink. *Exit with Yvette.*

YVETTE *as she leaves*: Fancy a creature like that ever making me leave the straight and narrow path. Thank my lucky stars I managed to reach the top all the same. But I've cooked your goose, Puffing Piet, and that's something that'll be credited to me one day in the world to come.

THE CHAPLAIN: I would like to take as a text for our little talk 'The mills of God grind slowly'. Weren't you complaining about my jokes?

THE COOK: Dead out of luck, I am. It's like this, you see: I thought I might get a hot meal. Here am I starving, and now they'll be talking about me and she'll get quite a wrong picture. I think I'll clear out before she's back.

THE CHAPLAIN: I think so too.

THE COOK: Padre, I'm fed up already with this bloody peace. Human race has to go through fire and sword cause it's sinful from the cradle up. I wish I could be roasting a fat capon once again for the general, wherever he's got to, in mustard sauce with a carrot or two.

THE CHAPLAIN: Red cabbage. Red cabbage for a capon.

THE COOK: You're right, but carrots was what he had to have.

THE CHAPLAIN: No sense of what's fitting.

THE COOK: Not that it stopped you guzzling your share.

THE CHAPLAIN: With misgivings.

THE COOK: Anyway you must admit those were the days.

THE CHAPLAIN: I might admit it if pressed.

THE COOK: Now you've called her a hyaena your days here are finished. What you staring at?

THE CHAPLAIN: Eilif! *Eilif arrives, followed by soldiers with pikes. His hands are fettered. His face is chalky-white.* What's wrong?

EILIF: Where's mother?

THE CHAPLAIN: Gone into town.

EILIF: I heard she was around. They've allowed me to come and see her.

THE COOK *to the soldiers*: What you doing with him?

A SOLDIER: Something not nice.

THE CHAPLAIN: What's he been up to?

THE SOLDIER: Broke into a peasant's place. The wife's dead.

THE CHAPLAIN: How could you do a thing like that?

EILIF: It's what I did last time, ain't it?

THE COOK: Aye, but it's peace now.

EILIF: Shut up. All right if I sit down till she comes?

THE SOLDIER: We've no time.

THE CHAPLAIN: In wartime they recommended him for that, sat him at the general's right hand. Dashing, it was, in those days. Any chance of a word with the provost-marshal?

THE SOLDIER: Wouldn't do no good. Taking some peasant's cattle, what's dashing about that?

THE COOK: Dumb, I call it.

EILIF: If I'd been dumb you'd of starved, clever bugger.

THE COOK: But as you were clever you're going to be shot.

THE CHAPLAIN: We'd better fetch Kattrin out anyhow.

EILIF: Let her be. Sooner have a glass of schnapps.

THE SOLDIER: No time, come along.

THE CHAPLAIN: And what shall we tell your mother?

EILIF: Tell her it wasn't any different, tell her it was the same thing. Or tell her nowt. *The soldiers propel him away.*

THE CHAPLAIN: I'll accompany you on your grievous journey.

EILIF: Don't need any bloody parsons.

THE CHAPLAIN: Wait and see. *Follows him.*

THE COOK *calls after them*: I'll have to tell her, she'll want to see him.

THE CHAPLAIN: I wouldn't tell her anything. At most that he was here and will come again, maybe tomorrow. By then I'll be back and can break it to her. *Hurries off.*
The cook looks after him, shaking his head, then walks restlessly around. Finally he comes up to the cart.

THE COOK: Hoy! Don't you want to come out? I can understand you hiding away from peace. Like to do the same myself. Remember me, I'm general's cook? I was wondering if you'd a bit of something to eat while I wait for your mum. I don't half feel like a bit of pork, or bread even, just to fill the time. *Peers inside.* Head under blanket. *Sound of gunfire off.*

MOTHER COURAGE *runs in, out of breath and with all her goods still*: Cooky, peacetime's over. War's been on again three days now. Heard news before selling me stuff, thank God. They're having a shooting match with Lutherans in town. We must get cart away at once. Kattrin, pack up! What you in the dumps for? What's wrong?

THE COOK: Nowt.

MOTHER COURAGE: Something is. I see it way you look.

THE COOK: Cause war's starting up again, I s'pose. Looks as if it'll be tomorrow night before I get next hot food inside me.

MOTHER COURAGE: You're lying, cooky.

THE COOK: Eilif was here. Had to leave almost at once, though.

MOTHER COURAGE: Was he now? Then we'll be seeing him on march. I'm joining our side this time. How's he look?

THE COOK: Same as usual.

MOTHER COURAGE: Oh, he'll never change. Take more than war to steal him from me. Clever, he is. You going to help me get packed? *Begins to pack up.* What's his news? Still in general's good books? Say anything about his deeds of valour?

THE COOK *glumly*: Repeated one of them, I'm told.

MOTHER COURAGE: Tell it me later, we got to move off. *Kattrin appears.* Kattrin, peacetime's finished now. We're moving on. *To the cook*: How about you?

THE COOK: Have to join up again.

MOTHER COURAGE: Why don't you . . . Where's padre?

THE COOK: Went into town with Eilif.

MOTHER COURAGE: Then you come along with us a way, Lamb. Need somebody to help me.

THE COOK: That business with Yvette, you know . . .

MOTHER COURAGE: Done you no harm in my eyes. Opposite. Where there's smoke there's fire, they say. You coming along?

THE COOK: I won't say no.

MOTHER COURAGE: The Twelfth moved off already. Take the shaft. Here's a bit of bread. We must get round behind to Lutherans. Might even be seeing Eilif tonight. He's my favourite one. Short peace, wasn't it? Now we're off again. *She sings as the cook and Kattrin harness themselves up*:

> From Ulm to Metz, from Metz to Munich
> Courage will see the war gets fed.
> The war will show a well-filled tunic
> Given its daily shot of lead.
> But lead alone can hardly nourish

It must have soldiers to subsist.
It's you it needs to make it flourish.
The war's still hungry. So enlist!

9

It is the seventeenth year of the great war of faith.
Germany has lost more than half her inhabitants.
Those who survive the bloodbath are killed off by
terrible epidemics. Once fertile areas are ravaged
by famine, wolves roam the burnt-out towns. In
autumn 1634 we find Courage in the Fichtelge-
birge, off the main axis of the Swedish armies.
The winter this year is early and harsh. Business is
bad, so that there is nothing to do but beg. The
cook gets a letter from Utrecht and is sent packing

Outside a semi-dilapidated parsonage.

*Grey morning in early winter. Gusts of wind. Mother Courage
and the cook in shabby sheepskins, drawing the cart.*

THE COOK: It's all dark, nobody up yet.

MOTHER COURAGE: Except it's parson's house. Have to crawl
out of bed to ring bells. Then he'll have hot soup.

THE COOK: What from when whole village is burnt, we seen it.

MOTHER COURAGE: It's lived in, though, dog was barking.

THE COOK: S'pose parson's got, he'll give nowt.

MOTHER COURAGE: Maybe if we sing. . . .

THE COOK: I've had enough. *Abruptly:* Got a letter from
Utrecht saying mother died of cholera and inn's mine. Here's
letter if you don't believe me. No business of yours the way
aunty goes on about my mode of existence, but have a look.

MOTHER COURAGE *reads the letter:* Lamb, I'm tired too of

always being on the go. I feel like butcher's dog, dragging meat round customers and getting nowt off it. I got nowt left to sell, and folk got nowt left to buy nowt with. Saxony a fellow in rags tried landing me a stack of old books for two eggs, Württemberg they wanted to swap their plough for a titchy bag of salt. What's to plough for? Nowt growing no more, just brambles. In Pomerania villages are s'posed to have started in eating the younger kids, and nuns have been caught sticking folk up.

THE COOK: World's dying out.

MOTHER COURAGE: Sometimes I sees meself driving through hell with me cart selling brimstone, or across heaven with packed lunches for hungry souls. Give me my kids what's left, let's find some place they ain't shooting, and I'd like a few more years undisturbed.

THE COOK: You and me could get that inn going, Courage, think it over. Made up me mind in the night, I did: back to Utrecht with or without you, and starting today.

MOTHER COURAGE: Have to talk to Kattrin. That's a bit quick for me; I'm against making decisions all freezing cold and nowt inside you. Kattrin! *Kattrin climbs out of the cart.* Kattrin, got something to tell you. Cook and I want to go to Utrecht. He's been left an inn there. That'd be a settled place for you, let you meet a few people. Lots of 'em respect somebody mature, looks ain't everything. I'd like it too. I get on with cook. Say one thing for him, got a head for business. We'd have our meals for sure, not bad, eh? And your own bed too; like that, wouldn't you? Road's no life really. God knows how you might finish up. Lousy already, you are. Have to make up our minds, see, we could move with the Swedes, up north, they're somewhere up that way. *She points to the left.* Reckon that's fixed, Kattrin.

THE COOK: Anna, I got something private to say to you.

MOTHER COURAGE: Get back in cart, Kattrin.

Kattrin climbs back.

THE COOK: I had to interrupt, cause you don't understand, far as I can see. I didn't think there was need to say it, sticks out a mile. But if it don't, then let me tell you straight, no question of taking her along, not on your life. You get me, eh.

Kattrin sticks her head out of the cart behind them and listens.

MOTHER COURAGE: You mean I'm to leave Kattrin back here?

THE COOK: Use your imagination. Inn's got no room. It ain't one of the sort got three bar parlours. Put our backs in it we two'll get a living, but not three, no chance of that. She can keep cart.

MOTHER COURAGE: Thought she might find husband in Utrecht.

THE COOK: Go on, make me laugh. Find a husband, how? Dumb and that scar on top of it. And at her age?

MOTHER COURAGE: Don't talk so loud.

THE COOK: Loud or soft, no getting over facts. And that's another reason why I can't have her in the inn. Customers don't want to be looking at that all the time. Can't blame them.

MOTHER COURAGE: Shut your big mouth. I said not so loud.

THE COOK: Light's on in parson's house. We can try singing.

MOTHER COURAGE: Cooky, how's she to pull the cart on her own? War scares her. She'll never stand it. The dreams she must have . . . I hear her nights groaning. Mostly after a battle. What's she seeing in those dreams, I'd like to know. She's got a soft heart. Lately I found she'd got another hedgehog tucked away what we'd run over.

THE COOK: Inn's too small. *Calls out:* Ladies and gentlemen, domestic staff and other residents! We are now going to give you a song concerning Solomon, Julius Caesar and other famous personages what had bad luck. So's you can see we're respectable folk, which makes it difficult to carry on, particularly in winter.

They sing:

You saw sagacious Solomon
You know what came of him.
To him complexities seemed plain.
He cursed the hour that gave birth to him

And saw that everything was vain.
How great and wise was Solomon!
The world however didn't wait
But soon observed what followed on.
It's wisdom that had brought him to this state –
How fortunate the man with none!

Yes, the virtues are dangerous stuff in this world, as this fine song proves, better not to have them and have a pleasant life and breakfast instead, hot soup for instance. Look at me: I haven't any but I'd like some. I'm a serving soldier but what good did my courage do me in all them battles, nowt, here I am starving and better have been shit-scared and stayed at home. For why?

You saw courageous Caesar next
You know what he became.
They deified him in his life
Then had him murdered just the same.
And as they raised the fatal knife
How loud he cried: You too, my son!
The world however didn't wait
But soon observed what followed on.
It's courage that had brought him to that state.
How fortunate the man with none!

Sotto voce: Don't even look out. *Aloud*: Ladies and gentlemen, domestic staff and other inmates! All right, you may say, gallantry never cooked a man's dinner, what about trying honesty? You can eat all you want then, or anyhow not stay sober. How about it?

You heard of honest Socrates
The man who never lied:
They weren't so grateful as you'd think
Instead the rulers fixed to have him tried
And handed him the poisoned drink.
How honest was the people's noble son!
The world however didn't wait
But soon observed what followed on.

It's honesty that brought him to that state.
How fortunate the man with none!

Ah yes, they say, be unselfish and share what you've got, but how about if you got nowt? It's all very well to say the do-gooders have a hard time, but you still got to have something. Aye, unselfishness is a rare virtue, cause it just don't pay.

Saint Martin couldn't bear to see
His fellows in distress.
He met a poor man in the snow
And shared his cloak with him, we know.
Both of them therefore froze to death.
His place in Heaven was surely won!
The world however didn't wait
But soon observed what followed on.
Unselfishness had brought him to that state.
How fortunate the man with none!

That's how it is with us. We're respectable folk, stick together, don't steal, don't murder, don't burn places down. And all the time you might say we're sinking lower and lower, and it's true what the song says, and soup is few and far between, and if we weren't like this but thieves and murderers I dare say we'd be eating our fill. For virtues aren't their own reward, only wickednesses are, that's how the world goes and it didn't ought to.

Here you can see respectable folk
Keeping to God's own laws.
So far he hasn't taken heed.
You who sit safe and warm indoors
Help to relieve our bitter need!
How virtuously we had begun!
The world however didn't wait
But soon observed what followed on.
It's fear of God that brought us to that state.
How fortunate the man with none!

VOICE *from above*: Hey, you there! Come on up! There's hot soup if you want.

MOTHER COURAGE: Lamb, me stomach won't stand nowt. 'Tain't that it ain't sensible, what you say, but is that your last word? We got on all right.

THE COOK: Last word. Think it over.

MOTHER COURAGE: I've nowt to think. I'm not leaving her here.

THE COOK: That's proper senseless, nothing I can do about it though. I'm not a brute, just the inn's a small one. So now we better get on up, or there'll be nowt here either and wasted time singing in the cold.

MOTHER COURAGE: I'll get Kattrin.

THE COOK: Better bring a bit back for her. Scare them if they sees three of us coming. *Exeunt both.*

Kattrin climbs out of the cart with a bundle. She looks around to see if the other two have gone. Then she takes an old pair of trousers of the cook's and a skirt of her mother's, and lays them side by side on one of the wheels, so that they are easily seen. She has finished and is picking up her bundle to go, when Mother Courage comes back from the house.

MOTHER COURAGE *with a plate of soup*: Kattrin! Will you stop there? Kattrin! Where you off to with that bundle? Has devil himself taken you over? *She examines the bundle.* She's packed her things. You been listening? I told him nowt doing, Utrecht, his rotten inn, what'd we be up to there? You and me, inn's no place for us. Still plenty to be got out of war. *She sees the trousers and the skirt.* You're plain stupid. S'pose I'd seen that, and you gone away? *She holds Kattrin back as she tries to break away.* Don't you start thinking it's on your account I given him the push. It was cart, that's it. Catch me leaving my cart I'm used to, it ain't you, it's for cart. We'll go off in t'other direction, and we'll throw cook's stuff out so he finds it, silly man. *She climbs in and throws out a few other articles in the direction of the trousers.* There, he's out of our business now, and I ain't having nobody else in, ever. You and me'll carry on now. This

winter will pass, same as all the others. Get hitched up, it
looks like snow.
They both harness themselves to the cart, then wheel it
round and drag it off. When the cook arrives he looks
blankly at his kit.

10

During the whole of 1635 Mother Courage and
her daughter Kattrin travel over the high roads of
central Germany, in the wake of the increasingly
bedraggled armies

High road.

Mother Courage and Kattrin are pulling the cart. They pass a
peasant's house inside which there is a voice singing.

THE VOICE:
    The roses in our arbour
    Delight us with their show:
    They have such lovely flowers
    Repaying all our labour
    After the summer showers.
    Happy are those with gardens now:
    They have such lovely flowers.

    When winter winds are freezing
    As through the woods they blow
    Our home is warm and pleasing.
    We fixed the thatch above it
    With straw and moss we wove it.
    Happy are those with shelter now
    When winter winds are freezing.

Mother Courage and Kattrin pause to listen, then continue pulling.

11

January 1636. The emperor's troops are threatening the Protestant town of Halle. The stone begins to speak. Mother Courage loses her daughter and trudges on alone. The war is a long way from being over

The cart is standing, much the worse for wear, alongside a peasant's house with a huge thatched roof, backing on a wall of rock. It is night.

An ensign and three soldiers in heavy armour step out of the wood.

THE ENSIGN: I want no noise now. Anyone shouts, shove your pike into him.

FIRST SOLDIER: Have to knock them up, though, if we're to find a guide.

THE ENSIGN: Knocking sounds natural. Could be a cow bumping the stable wall.

The soldiers knock on the door of the house. A peasant woman opens it. They stop her mouth. Two soldiers go in.

MAN'S VOICE *within*: What is it?

The soldiers bring out a peasant and his son.

THE ENSIGN *pointing at the cart, where Kattrin's head has appeared*: There's another one. *A soldier drags her out.* Anyone else live here beside you lot?

THE PEASANTS: This is our son. And she's dumb. Her mother's gone into town to buy stuff. For their business, cause so many people's getting out and selling things cheap. They're just passing through. Canteen folk.

THE ENSIGN: I'm warning you, keep quiet, or if there's the least noise you get a pike across your nut. Now I want someone to come with us and show us the path to the town. *Points to the young peasant.* Here, you.

THE YOUNG PEASANT: I don't know no path.

SECOND SOLDIER *grinning*: He don't know no path.

THE YOUNG PEASANT: I ain't helping Catholics.

THE ENSIGN *to the second soldier*: Stick your pike in his ribs.

THE YOUNG PEASANT *forced to his knees, with the pike threatening him*: I won't do it, not to save my life.

FIRST SOLDIER: I know what'll change his mind. *Goes towards the stable.* Two cows and an ox. Listen, you: if you're not reasonable I'll chop up your cattle.

THE YOUNG PEASANT: No, not that!

THE PEASANT'S WIFE *weeps*: Please spare our cattle, captain, it'd be starving us to death.

THE ENSIGN: They're dead if he goes on being obstinate.

FIRST SOLDIER: I'm taking the ox first.

THE YOUNG PEASANT *to his father*: Have I got to? *The wife nods.* Right.

THE PEASANT'S WIFE: And thank you kindly, captain, for sparing us, for ever and ever, Amen.

The peasant stops his wife from further expressions of gratitude.

FIRST SOLDIER: I knew the ox was what they minded about most, was I right?

Guided by the young peasant, the ensign and his men continue on their way.

THE PEASANT: What are they up to, I'd like to know. Nowt good.

THE PEASANT'S WIFE: Perhaps they're just scouting. What you doing?

THE PEASANT *putting a ladder against the roof and climbing up it*: Seeing if they're on their own. *From the top*: Something moving in the wood. Can see something down by the quarry. And there are men in armour in the clearing. And a gun. That's at least a regiment. God's mercy on the town and everyone in it!

THE PEASANT'S WIFE: Any lights in the town?

THE PEASANT: No. They'll all be asleep. *Climbs down*. If those people get in they'll butcher the lot.

THE PEASANT'S WIFE: Sentries're bound to spot them first.

THE PEASANT: Sentry in the tower up the hill must have been killed, or he'd have blown his bugle.

THE PEASANT'S WIFE: If only there were more of us.

THE PEASANT: Just you and me and that cripple.

THE PEASANT'S WIFE: Nowt we can do, you'd say. . . .

THE PEASANT: Nowt.

THE PEASANT'S WIFE: Can't possibly run down there in the blackness.

THE PEASANT: Whole hillside's crawling with 'em. We can't even give a signal.

THE PEASANT'S WIFE: What, and have them butcher us too?

THE PEASANT: You're right, nowt we can do.

THE PEASANT'S WIFE *to Kattrin*: Pray, poor creature, pray! Nowt we can do to stop bloodshed. You can't talk, maybe, but at least you can pray. He'll hear you if no one else can. I'll help you. *All kneel, Kattrin behind the two peasants*. Our Father, which art in Heaven, hear Thou our prayer, let not the town be destroyed with all what's in it sound asleep and suspecting nowt. Arouse Thou them that they may get up and go to the walls and see how the enemy approacheth with pikes and guns in the blackness across fields below the slope. *Turning to Kattrin*: Guard Thou our mother and ensure that the watchman sleepeth not but wakes up, or it will be too late. Succour our brother-in-law also, he is inside there with his four children, spare Thou them, they are innocent and know nowt. *To Kattrin, who gives a groan*: One of them's not two yet, the eldest's seven. *Kattrin stands up distractedly*. Our Father, hear us, for only Thou canst help; we look to be doomed, for why, we are weak and have no pike and nowt and can risk nowt and are in Thy hand along with our cattle and all the farm, and same with the town, it too is in Thy hand and the enemy is before the walls in great strength.

Unobserved, Kattrin has slipped away to the cart and taken from it something which she hides beneath her apron; then she climbs up the ladder on to the stable roof.

THE PEASANT'S WIFE: Forget not the children, what are in danger, the littlest ones especially, the old folk what can't move, and every living creature.

THE PEASANT: And forgive us our trespasses as we forgive them that trespass against us. Amen.

Sitting on the roof, Kattrin begins to beat the drum which she has pulled out from under her apron.

THE PEASANT'S WIFE: Jesus Christ, what's she doing?

THE PEASANT: She's out of her mind.

THE PEASANT'S WIFE: Quick, get her down.

The peasant hurries to the ladder, but Kattrin pulls it up on to the roof.

THE PEASANT'S WIFE: She'll do us in.

THE PEASANT: Stop drumming at once, you cripple!

THE PEASANT'S WIFE: Bringing the Catholics down on us!

THE PEASANT *looking for stones to throw*: I'll stone you.

THE PEASANT'S WIFE: Where's your feelings? Where's your heart? We're done for if they come down on us. Slit our throats, they will. *Kattrin stares into the distance towards the town and carries on drumming.*

THE PEASANT'S WIFE *to her husband*: I told you we shouldn't have allowed those vagabonds on to farm. What do they care if our last cows are taken?

THE ENSIGN *runs in with his soldiers and the young peasant*: I'll cut you to ribbons, all of you!

THE PEASANT'S WIFE: Please, sir, it's not our fault, we couldn't help it. It was her sneaked up there. A foreigner.

THE ENSIGN: Where's the ladder?

THE PEASANT: There.

THE ENSIGN *calls up*: I order you, throw that drum down. *Kattrin goes on drumming.*

THE ENSIGN: You're all in this together. It'll be the end of you.

THE PEASANT: They been cutting pine trees in that wood. How about if we got one of the trunks and poked her off. . . .

FIRST SOLDIER *to the ensign*: Permission to make a suggestion, sir! *He whispers something in the ensign's ear.* Listen, we got a suggestion could help you. Get down off there and come into town with us right away. Show us which your mother is and we'll see she ain't harmed.

Kattrin goes on drumming.

THE ENSIGN *pushes him roughly aside*: She doesn't trust you; with a mug like yours it's not surprising. *Calls up*: Suppose I gave you my word? I can give my word of honour as an officer.

Kattrin drums harder.

THE ENSIGN: Is nothing sacred to her?

THE YOUNG PEASANT: There's more than her mother involved, sir.

FIRST SOLDIER: This can't go on much longer. They're bound to hear in the town.

THE ENSIGN: We'll have somehow to make a noise that's louder than her drumming. What can we make a noise with?

FIRST SOLDIER: Thought we weren't s'posed to make no noise.

THE ENSIGN: A harmless one, you fool. A peaceful one.

THE PEASANT: I could chop wood with my axe.

THE ENSIGN: Good: you chop. *The peasant fetches his axe and attacks a tree-trunk.* Chop harder! Harder! You're chopping for your life. *Kattrin has been listening, drumming less loudly the while. She now looks wildly round, and goes on drumming.*

THE ENSIGN: Not loud enough. *To the first soldier*: You chop too.

THE PEASANT: Only got the one axe. *Stops chopping.*

THE ENSIGN: We'll have to set the farm on fire. Smoke her out, that's it.

THE PEASANT: It wouldn't help, captain. If the townspeople see a fire here they'll know what's up.

Kattrin has again been listening as she drums. At this point she laughs.

THE ENSIGN: Look at her laughing at us. I'm not having that.

I'll shoot her down, and damn the consequences. Fetch the harquebus.

Three soldiers hurry off. Kattrin goes on drumming.

THE PEASANT'S WIFE: I got it, captain. That's their cart. If we smash it up she'll stop. Cart's all they got.

THE ENSIGN *to the young peasant*: Smash it up. *Calls up*: We're going to smash up your cart if you don't stop drumming. *The young peasant gives the cart a few feeble blows.*

THE PEASANT'S WIFE: Stop it, you animal!

Desperately looking towards the cart, Kattrin emits pitiful noises. But she goes on drumming.

THE ENSIGN: Where are those clodhoppers with the harquebus?

FIRST SOLDIER: Can't have heard nowt in town yet, else we'd be hearing their guns.

THE ENSIGN *calls up*: They can't hear you at all. And now we're going to shoot you down. For the last time: throw down that drum!

THE YOUNG PEASANT *suddenly flings away his plank*: Go on drumming! Or they'll all be killed! Go on, go on. . . .

The soldier knocks him down and beats him with his pike. Kattrin starts to cry, but she goes on drumming.

THE PEASANT'S WIFE: Don't strike his back! For God's sake, you're beating him to death!

The soldiers hurry in with the harquebus.

SECOND SOLDIER: Colonel's frothing at the mouth, sir. We're all for court-martial.

THE ENSIGN: Set it up! Set it up! *Calls up while the gun is being erected*: For the very last time: stop drumming! *Kattrin, in tears, drums as loud as she can.* Fire! *The soldiers fire. Kattrin is hit, gives a few more drumbeats and then slowly crumples.*

THE ENSIGN: That's the end of that.

But Kattrin's last drumbeats are taken up by the town's cannon. In the distance can be heard a confused noise of tocsins and gunfire.

FIRST SOLDIER: She's made it.

12

Before first light. Sound of the fifes and drums of troops marching off into the distance

In front of the cart Mother Courage is squatting by her daughter. The peasant family are standing near her.

THE PEASANT *with hostility*: You must go, missis. There's only one more regiment behind that one. You can't go on your own.

MOTHER COURAGE: I think she's going to sleep. *She sings*:

> Lullaby baby
> What's that in the hay?
> Neighbours' kids grizzle
> But my kids are gay.
> Neighbours' are in tatters
> And you're dressed in lawn
> Cut down from the raiment an
> Angel has worn.
> Neighbours' kids go hungry
> And you shall eat cake
> Suppose it's too crumbly
> You've only to speak.
> Lullaby baby
> What's that in the hay?
> The one lies in Poland
> The other – who can say?

Better if you'd not told her nowt about your brother-in-law's kids.

THE PEASANT: If you'd not gone into town to get your cut it might never of happened.

MOTHER COURAGE: Now she's asleep.

THE PEASANT'S WIFE: She ain't asleep. Can't you see she's passed over?

THE PEASANT: And it's high time you got away yourself. There are wolves around and, what's worse, marauders.

MOTHER COURAGE: Aye.

She goes and gets a tarpaulin to cover the dead girl with.

THE PEASANT'S WIFE: Ain't you got nobody else? What you could go to?

MOTHER COURAGE: Aye, one left. Eilif.

THE PEASANT *as Mother Courage covers the dead girl*: Best look for him, then. We'll mind her, see she gets proper burial. Don't you worry about that.

MOTHER COURAGE: Here's money for expenses.

She counts out coins into the peasant's hands.

The peasant and his son shake hands with her and carry Kattrin away.

THE PEASANT'S WIFE *as she leaves*: I'd hurry.

MOTHER COURAGE *harnessing herself to the cart*: Hope I can pull cart all right by meself. Be all right, nowt much inside it. Got to get back in business again.

Another regiment with its fifes and drums marches past in the background.

MOTHER COURAGE *tugging the cart*: Take me along!

Singing is heard from offstage:

> With all its luck and all its danger
> The war is dragging on a bit
> Another hundred years or longer
> The common man won't benefit.
> Filthy his food, no soap to shave him
> The regiment steals half his pay.
> But still a miracle may save him:
> Tomorrow is another day!
>> The new year's come. The watchmen shout.
>> The thaw sets in. The dead remain.
>> Wherever life has not died out
>> It staggers to its feet again.

Notes and Variants

LIFE OF GALILEO

Texts by Brecht

FOREWORD

It is well known how beneficially people can be influenced by the conviction that they are poised on the threshold of a new age. At such a moment their environment appears to be still entirely unfinished, capable of the happiest improvements, full of dreamt-of and undreamt-of possibilities, like malleable raw material in their hands. They themselves feel as if they have awakened to a new day, rested, strong, resourceful. Old beliefs are dismissed as superstitions, what yesterday seemed a matter of course is today subject to fresh examination. We have been ruled, says mankind, but now we shall be the rulers.

Around the turn of this century no other line from a song so powerfully inspired the workers as the line: 'Now a new age is dawning'; old and young marched to it, the poorest, the down-and-outs and those who had already won something of civilisation for themselves – all felt young. Under a house painter the unprecedented seductive power of these selfsame words was also tried and proved; for he too promised a new age. Here the words revealed their emptiness and vagueness. Their strength lay in their very indefiniteness, which was now being exploited in demoralising the masses. The new age – that was something and is something that affects everything, leaves nothing unchanged, but is also still only unfolding its character gradually; something in which all imagination has scope to flower, and which is only restricted by too precise description. Glorious is the feeling of beginning, of pioneering; the fact of being a beginner inspires enthusiasm. Glorious is the feeling of happiness in those who oil a new machine before it is to display its strength, in those who fill in a blank space on an old map, in those who dig the foundation of a new house, their house.

This feeling comes to the researcher who makes a discovery that will change everything, to the orator who prepares a speech that will create an entirely new situation. Terrible is the disappointment when men discover, or think they discover, that they have fallen victims to an illusion, that the old is stronger than the new, that the 'facts' are against them and not for them, that their age – the new age – has not yet arrived. Then things are not merely as bad as before, but much worse because people have made immense sacrifices for their schemes and have lost everything; they have ventured and are now defeated; the old is taking its revenge on them. The researcher or the discoverer – an unknown but also unpersecuted man before he has published his discovery – when once his discovery has been disproved or discredited is a swindler and a charlatan, and all too well known; the victim of oppression and exploitation, when once his insurrection has been crushed, is a rebel who is subject to special repression and punishment. Exertion is followed by exhaustion, possibly exaggerated hope by possibly exaggerated hopelessness. Those who do not relapse into indifference and apathy fall into worse; those who have not sacrificed their energies for their ideals now turn those selfsame energies against those very ideals. There is no more remorseless reactionary than a frustrated innovator, no crueller enemy of the wild elephant than the tame elephant.

And yet these disappointed men may still go on existing in a new age, an age of great upheaval. Only, they know nothing of new ages.

In these days the conception of the new is itself falsified. The Old and the Very Old, now re-entering the arena, proclaim themselves as new, or else it is held to be new when the Old or the Very Old are put over in a new way. But the really New, having been deposed today, is declared old-fashioned, degraded to being a transitory phase whose day is done. 'New' for example is the system of waging wars, whereas 'old', so they say, is a system of economy, proposed but never put into practice, which makes wars superfluous. In the new system, society is being entrenched in classes; while old, so they say, is the desire to abolish classes. The hopes of mankind do not so much become discouraged in these times; rather, they become diverted. Men had hoped that one day there would be bread to eat. Now they may hope that one day there will be stones.

Amid the darkness gathering fast over a fevered world, a world surrounded by bloody deeds and no less bloody thoughts, by increasing barbarism which seems to be leading irresistibly to perhaps the greatest and most terrible war of all time, it is difficult to adopt an attitude appropriate to people on the threshold of a new and happier age. Does not everything point to night's arrival and nothing to the dawning of a new age? So shouldn't one, therefore, assume an attitude appropriate to people heading towards the night?

What is this talk of a 'new age'? Is not this expression itself obsolete? When it is shouted at us, it is bellowed from hoarse throats. Now indeed, it is mere barbarism which impersonates the new age. It says of itself that it hopes it will last a thousand years.

So should one hold fast to the old times? Should one discuss sunken Atlantis?

Am I already lying down for the night and thinking, when I think of the morning, of the one that has passed, in order to avoid thinking of the one to come? Is that why I occupy myself with that epoch of the flowering of the arts and sciences three hundred years ago? I hope not.

These images of the morning and the night are misleading. Happy times do not come in the same way as a morning follows a night's sleep.

[Dated 1939; not revised by Brecht. From Werner Hecht (ed.): *Materialien zu Brechts 'Leben des Galilei'*, Frankfurt, Suhrkamp, 1968, pp. 7 ff.]

THE *Life of Galileo* IS NOT A TRAGEDY

So, from the point of view of the theatre, the question will arise whether the *Life of Galileo* is to be presented as a tragedy or as an optimistic play. Is the keynote to be found in Galileo's 'Salutation to the New Age' in scene 1 or in certain parts of scene 14? According to the prevailing rules of play construction, the end of a drama must carry the greater weight. But this play is not constructed according to these rules. The play shows the dawn of a new age and tries to correct some of the prejudices about the dawn of a new age.

[Dated 1939. From Werner Hecht (ed.), *ibid*., p. 13.]

PORTRAYAL OF THE CHURCH

For the theatre it is important to understand that this play must lose a great part of its effect if its performance is directed chiefly against the Roman Catholic Church.

Of the dramatis personae, many wear the church's garb. Actors who, because of that, try to portray these characters as odious would be doing wrong. But neither, on the other hand, has the church the right to have the human weaknesses of its members glossed over. It has all too often encouraged these weaknesses and suppressed their exposure. But in this play there is also no question of the church being admonished: 'Hands off science!' Modern science is a legitimate daughter of the church, a daughter who has emancipated herself and turned against the mother.

In the present play the church functions, even when it opposes free investigation, simply as authority.

Since science was a branch of theology, the church is the intellectual authority, the ultimate scientific court of appeal. The play shows the temporary victory of authority, not the victory of the priesthood. It corresponds to the historical truth in that the Galileo of the play never turns directly against the church. There is not a sentence uttered by Galileo in that sense. If there had been, such a thorough commission of investigation as the Inquisition would undoubtedly have brought it to light. And it equally corresponds to the historical truth that the greatest astronomer of the Papal Roman College, Christopher Clavius, confirmed Galileo's discoveries (scene 6). It is also true that clerics were among his pupils (scenes 8, 9 and 13).

To take satirical aim at the worldly interests of high dignitaries seems to me cheap (it would be in scene 7). But the casual way in which these high officials treat the physicist is only meant to show that, by reason of their past experiences, they think they can count on ready complaisance from Galileo. They are not mistaken.

When one looks at our bourgeois politicians, one cannot but extol the spiritual (and scientific) interests of those politicians of old.

The play, therefore, ignores the falsifications made to the protocol of 1616 by the Inquisition of 1633, falsifications established by recent historical studies under the direction of the German scholar Emil Wohlwill. Doubtless the judgment and sentence of 1633 were thereby made juridically possible. Anybody who understands the point of view outlined above will appreciate that the author was not concerned with this legal side of the trial.

There is no doubt that Urban VIII was personally incensed at Galileo and, in the most detestable manner, played a personal part in the proceedings against him. The play passes this over.

Anyone who understands the standpoint of the author will realise that this attitude implies no reverence for the church of the seventeenth, let alone of the twentieth century.

Casting the church as the embodiment of authority in this theatrical trial of the persecutors of the champions of free research certainly does not help to get the church acquitted. But it would be highly dangerous, particularly nowadays, to treat a matter like Galileo's fight for freedom of research as a religious one; for thereby attention would be most unhappily deflected from present-day reactionary authorities of a totally unecclesiastical kind.

[Dated 1939. From Werner Hecht (ed.), *ibid.*, pp. 14 f.]

THREE NOTES ON THE CHARACTER OF GALILEO

1. [*The new type of physicist*]

[. . .] It's important that you shouldn't idealise Galileo: You know the kind of thing – the stargazer, the pallid intellectualised idealist. I know you wouldn't if left to yourself, but the pictures you'll see in the books are already idealised. My Galileo is a powerful physicist with a tummy on him, a face like Socrates, a vociferous, full-blooded man with a sense of humour, the new type of physicist, earthly, a great teacher. Favourite attitude: stomach thrust forward, both hands on the buttocks, head back, using one meaty hand all the time to gesticulate with, but with precision; comfortable trousers for working in, shirtsleeves or (particularly at the end) a long whitish-yellow robe with broad sleeves, tied with a cord round his stomach. You get the idea – preferably an etching of this figure or some kind of steel engraving or wood engraving to maintain its historical flavour: in other words, realistic. Or for that matter one could have pen drawings standing freely on the page. Don't be scared of a bit of humour. History without humour is a ghastly thing . . .

N.B. As far as I know, Galileo's telescope was about two and a half feet long and the thickness of a man's arm. You can stand it on an ordinary tripod. The model of the Ptolemaic system (in scene 1) is of wood, some twenty inches in diameter. You could probably get a rough idea from the keeper of the planetarium.

2. *The Sensual Element in Galileo*

Galileo of course is not a Falstaff: He insists on his physical pleasures because of his materialist convictions. He wouldn't, for instance, drink at his work; the point is that he *works* in a sensual way. He gets pleasure from handling his instruments with elegance. A great part of his sensuality is of an intellectual kind: for instance, the 'beauty' of an experiment, the little theatrical performance with which he gives shape to each of his lessons, the often abrupt way in which he will confront somebody with the truth, not to mention those passages in his speeches (in 1, 7, 13) where he picks good words and tests them like a spice. (This has nothing to do with that bel canto of the actor who may produce his arias as if he enjoyed them, but fails to show the enjoyment of the character he is playing.)

3. *About the Part of Galileo*

What gives this new historical character his quality of strangeness, novelty, strikingness, is the fact that he, Galileo, looks at the world of 1600 around him as if he himself were a stranger. He studies this world and finds it remarkable, outdated, in need of explanation. He studies:

in scene 1, Ludovico Marsili and Priuli
in scene 2, the way in which the senators look though the telescope
    (When am I going to be able to buy one of these things?)
in scene 3, Sagredo (the prince being a child of nine)
in scene 4, the court scholars
in scene 5, the monks
in scene 7, the young monk
in scene 8, Federzoni and Ludovico
in scene [11], (for just one second) Virginia
in scene [13], his pupils
in scene [14], Andrea and Virginia.

[From Werner Hecht (ed.), *ibid*. pp. 27 f. The first section comes from a letter from Brecht to the painter Hans Tombrock in March 1941, and refers to the first version of the play, which Tombrock illustrated for a proposed publication in the USSR which never materialised. The second and third are undated, but appear to refer to the second, American version.]

ENTRIES FROM BRECHT'S JOURNAL 1944-5

10 Sept 45

the atom bomb, in which atomic energy makes a timely first appearance, strikes 'normal folk' as simply awful. to those impatiently awaiting their sons and husbands, the victory in japan seems to have a bitter taste. this superfart is louder than all the victory bells.

(for a moment LAUGHTON fears quite naively that science might be so utterly discredited by it, that the birth of science – in GALILEO – could lose all sympathy. '*the wrong kind of publicity, old man.*')

20 Sept 45

most of the time we are still working on GALILEO, which laughton's audience in the military hospital listen to with quite extraordinary interest. the atom bomb has, in fact, made the relationship between society and science into a life-and-death-problem.

in between times i am making a COPY OF MACBETH for a film with lorre and reyher. the great shakespearian motif, the fallibility of instinct (the lack of clarity in the inner voice) cannot be renewed. from it i take the little people's defencelessness against the ruling moral code, which limits the criminal potential of their contribution.

10 Oct 45

driven on by his theatrical instinct, LAUGHTON plugs away relentlessly at the political elements in GALILEI too. at his behest i have worked in the new 'ludovico-line', and the same goes for the reordering of the last galileo scene (handing over the book first, then the lesson that the book must in no way alter the social condemnation of the author). laughton is fully prepared to throw his character to the wolves. he has a kind of lucifer in mind, in whom self-contempt has turned into a kind of hollow pride – pride in the *magnitude* of his crime etc. he insists on a full presentation of the degradation that results from the crime which has unleashed all g[alileo]'s negative features. all that is left is the excellent brain, functioning in the void independently of the control of its owner who is happy to let himself sink.

he brings this conception out most clearly one evening when they had shouted '*scab*' at him as he went through a picket line in front of the studio. this wounded him deeply – no applause for him here.

[From the Methuen edition of the *Journals*, translated by Ralph Manheim and edited by John Willett, 1993. The first of these refers to the prewar version of the play, which had had its première seven months previously in Zurich (where Wilder had seen it). 'I am given to understand' – presumably by the accounts of that production. The collaboration with Laughton began at the end of 1944. The atom bombs were dropped on Japan on 6 and 9 August; the war ended five days later.]

DRAFTS FOR A FOREWORD TO *Life of Galileo*

The *Life of Galileo* was written in those last dark months of 1938, when many people felt fascism's advance to be irresistible and the final collapse of Western civilisation to have arrived. And indeed we were approaching the end of that great age to which the world owes the development of the natural sciences, together with such new arts as music and the theatre. There was a more or less general expectation of a barbaric age 'outside history'. Only a minority saw the evolution of new forces and sensed the vitality of the new ideas. Even the significance of expressions like 'old' and 'new' had been obscured. The doctrines of the socialist classics had lost the appeal of novelty, and seemed to belong to a vanished day.

The bourgeois single out science from the scientist's consciousness, setting it up as an island of independence so as to be able in practice to interweave it with *their* politics, *their* economics, *their* ideology. The research scientist's object is 'pure' research; the product of that research is not so pure. The formula $E = mc^2$ is conceived of as eternal, not tied to anything. Hence other people can do the tying: suddenly the city of Hiroshima became very short-lived. The scientists are claiming the irresponsibility of machines.

Let us think back to the founding father of experimental science, Francis Bacon, whose phrase that one must obey nature in order to command her was not written in vain. His contemporaries obeyed his nature by bribing him with money, and so thoroughly commanded him when he was Lord Chief Justice that in the end Parliament had to lock him up. Macaulay, the puritan, drew a distinction between Bacon the scientist, whom he admired, and Bacon the politician, of whom he disapproved. Should we be doing the same thing with the German doctors of Nazi times?

Among other things, war promotes the sciences. What an opportunity! It creates discoverers as well as thieves. A higher responsibility (that of the higher ranks) replaces the lower (that for the lowly). Obedience is the midwife of arbitrariness. Disorder is perfectly in order. Those doctors who combatted yellow fever had to use themselves as guinea pigs; the fascist doctors had material supplied them. Justice played a part too; they had to freeze only 'criminals', in other words those who did not share their opinions. For their experiments in using 'animal warmth' as a means of thawing they were given prostitutes, women who had transgressed the rule of chastity. They had served sin; now they were being allowed to serve science. It incidentally emerged that hot water restores life better than a woman's body; in its small way it can do more for the fatherland. (Ethics must never be overlooked in war.) Progress all round. At the beginning of this century politicians of the lower classes were forced to treat the prisons as their universities. Now the prisons became universities for the warders (and doctors). Their experiments would of course have been perfectly in order – 'from a scientific point of view', that is – even if the state had been forced to exceed the ethical bounds. None the less the bourgeois world still has a certain right to be outraged. Even if it is only a matter of degrees it is a matter of degrees. When Generals von Mackensen and Maltzer were being tried in Rome for shooting hostages, the English prosecutor, a certain Colonel Halse, admitted that 'reprisal killings' in war were not illegal so long as the victims were taken from the scene of the incident in question, some attempt was made to find the persons responsible for it, and there were not too many executions. The German generals however had gone too far. They took ten Italians for every German soldier killed (not twenty, though, as demanded by Hitler), and dispatched the whole lot too quickly, within some twenty-four hours. The Italian police, by an oversight, handed over several Italians too many, and by another oversight the Germans shot them too, out of a misplaced reliance on the Italians. But here again they had ransacked the prisons for hostages, taking criminals or suspects awaiting trial, and filling the gaps with Jews. So a certain humanity asserted itself, and not merely in the errors of arithmetic. All the same, bounds were exceeded in this case, and something had to be done to punish the excess.

It can none the less be shown that, in this period when the bourgeoisie has gone completely to pieces, those pieces are still made of the same stuff as the original polished article.

And so in the end the scientists get what they want: state resources, large-scale planning, authority over industry; their Golden Age has come. And their great production starts as the production of weapons of destruction; their planning leads to extreme anarchy, for they are arming the state against other states. As soon as he represents such a threat to the world, the people's traditional contempt for the unworldly professor turns into naked fear. And just when he has wholly cut himself off from the people as the complete specialist, he is appalled to see himself once again as one of the people, because the threat applies to him too; he has reason to fear for his own life, and the best reason of anybody to know just how much. His protests, of which we have heard quite a number, refer not only to the attacks on his science, which is to be hampered, sterilised, and perverted, but also to the threat which his knowledge represents to the world, and also to the threat to himself.

The Germans have just undergone one of those experiences that are so difficult to convert into usable conclusions. The leadership of the state had fallen to an ignorant person who associated himself with a gang of violent and 'uneducated' politicians to proclaim a vast war and utterly ruin the country. Shortly before the catastrophic end, and for some time after it, the blame was attributed to these people. They had conducted an almost total mobilisation of the intellectuals, providing every branch with trained manpower, and although they made a number of clumsy attempts to interfere, the catastrophe cannot be ascribed to clumsy interference alone. Not even the military and political strategy appears to have been all that wrong, while the courage of the army and of the civil population is beyond dispute. What won in the end was the enemy's superiority in men and technology, something that had been brought into play by a series of almost unpredictable events.

Many of those who see, or at any rate suspect, capitalism's short-comings are prepared to put up with them for the sake of the personal freedom which capitalism appears to guarantee. They believe in this freedom mainly because they scarcely ever make use of it. Under the scourge of Hitler they saw this freedom more or less abrogated; it was like a little nest-egg in the savings bank which could normally be drawn on at any time, though it was clearly more sensible not to touch it, but had now, as it were, been frozen – i.e., could not be drawn on, although it was still there. They regarded the Hitler period as abnormal; it was a matter of some warts on capitalism, or even of an anticapitalist movement. The latter was something that one could only believe if one accepted the Nazis' own definition of capitalism, while as for the wart theory one was after all dealing with a system where warts flourished, and there was no question of the intellectuals being able to prevent them or make them go away. In either case freedom could only be restored by a catastrophe. And when the catastrophe came, not even that was able to restore freedom, not even that.

Among the various descriptions of the poverty prevailing in denazified Germany was that of spiritual poverty. 'What they want, what they're waiting for, is a message,' people said. 'Didn't they have one?' I asked. 'Look at the poverty,' they said, 'and at the lack of leadership.' 'Didn't they have leadership enough?' I asked, pointing to the poverty. 'But they must have something to look forward to,' they said. 'Aren't they tired of looking forward to such things?' I asked. 'I understand they lived quite a while on looking forward either to getting rid of their leader or to having him lay the world at their feet for them to pillage.'

The hardest time to get along without knowledge is the time when knowledge is hardest to get. It is the condition of bottom-most poverty, where it seems possible to get along without knowledge. Nothing is calculable any longer, the measures went up in the fire, short-range objectives hide those in the distance, at that point chance decides.

[From Werner Hecht (ed.), *ibid.*, pp. 16 ff. These different items are given in the same order as there, though they appear to date from after the end of the Second World War and not, as there suggested, mainly from 1938–1939.]

UNVARNISHED PICTURE OF A NEW AGE

Preamble to the American Version

When, during my first years in exile in Denmark, I wrote the play *Life of Galileo*, I was helped in the reconstruction of the Ptolemaic cosmology by assistants of Niels Bohr who were working on the problem of splitting the atom. My intention was, among others, to give an unvarnished picture of a new age – a strenuous undertaking since all those around me were convinced that our own era lacked every attribute of a new age. Nothing of this aspect had changed when, years later, I began together with Charles Laughton to prepare an American version of the play. The 'atomic' age made its debut at Hiroshima in the middle of our work. Overnight the biography of the founder of the new system of physics read differently. The infernal effect of the great bomb placed the conflict between Galileo and the authorities of his day in a new, sharper light. We had to make only a few alterations – not a single one to the structure of the play. Already in the original version the church was portrayed as a secular authority, its ideology as fundamentally interchangeable with many others. From the first, the keystone of the gigantic figure of Galileo was his conception of a science for the people. For hundreds of years and throughout the whole of Europe people had paid him the honour, in the Galileo legend, of not believing in his recantation, just as they had for long derided scientists as biased, unpractical and eunuch-like old fogeys. [. . .]

[Dated 1946. From Werner Hecht (ed.), *ibid.*, pp. 10 ff. The rest of the note, here omitted, was incorporated in the Model Book.]

SHOULD GALILEO BE LIKEABLE?

I think you are right in saying that I should have defined Galileo's progressiveness more closely. But he is not 'for the peasants' when he contradicts the physicist-monk and the landowner, he is against the subhuman conditions to which they are reduced. (In the last – I hope – version I have secured the end of the eighth scene against misinterpretations). Actually G does not simply advocate the free practice of his profession (which he recognises as a link in the ideological chain which holds down the peasants and the bourgeoisie, and which it is up to him to saw through). He saws rather cautiously. First, in Padua, he doesn't so much as mention Copernicus; then he finds proofs and decides to make a career with them, goes to Florence, grovels before the prince and submits his proofs to the papal astronomer. His proofs are acknowledged but he is forbidden to draw inferences from them. For almost ten years he complies and is again silent. Then he relies on the liberal Pope (not on the people or the bourgeoisie) and when the Pope leaves him in the lurch he submits totally and publicly. While imprisoned, he collaborates shamelessly (in the play) and allows his main work to be stolen from him – meanwhile suffering violent stomach cramps. I really believe that the 'attractive' quality which irritates you is his vitality.

[From Letter 528, to Stefan S. Brecht, translated by Ralph Manheim in Brecht: *Letters 1913–1956* (Methuen, 1990). Brecht's son had written to say that he found Galileo's sympathy for the peasants historically improbable. He should not be presented as likeable. The letter dates from September or October 1946.]

PRAISE OR CONDEMNATION OF GALILEO?

It would be a great weakness in this work if those physicists were right who said to me – in a tone of approval – that Galileo's recantation of his teachings was, despite one or two 'waverings', portrayed as being sensible, on the principle that this recantation enabled him to carry on with his scientific work and to hand it down to posterity. The fact is that Galileo enriched astronomy and physics by simultaneously robbing these sciences of a greater part of their social importance. By discrediting the Bible and the church, these sciences stood for a while at the barricades on behalf of all progress. It is true that a forward movement took place in the following centuries, and these sciences were involved in it, but it was a slow movement, not a revolution; the scandal, so to speak, degenerated into a dispute between experts. The church, and with it all the forces of reaction, was able to bring off an organised retreat and more or less reassert its power. As far as these particular sciences were concerned, they never again regained their high position in society, neither did they ever again come into such close contact with the people.

Galileo's crime can be regarded as the 'original sin' of modern natural sciences. From the new astronomy, which deeply interested a new class – the bourgeoisie – since it gave an impetus to the revolutionary social current of the time, he made a sharply defined special science which – admittedly through its very 'purity', i.e., its indifference to modes of production – was able to develop comparatively undisturbed.

The atom bomb is, both as a technical and as a social phenomenon, the classical end-product of his contribution to science and his failure to contribute to society.

Thus the 'hero' of this work is not Galileo but the people, as Walter Benjamin has said. This seems to me to be rather too briefly expressed. I hope this work shows how society extorts from its individuals what it needs from them. The urge to research, a social phenomenon no less delightful or compulsive than the urge to reproduce, steers Galileo into that most dangerous territory, drives him into agonising conflict with his violent desires for other pleasures. He raises his telescope to the stars and delivers himself to the rack. In the end he indulges his science like a vice, secretly, and probably with pangs of conscience. Confronted with such a situation, one can scarcely wish only to praise or only to condemn Galileo.

[Dated 1947. From Werner Hecht (ed.), *ibid.*, pp. 12 f.]

PROLOGUE TO THE AMERICAN PRODUCTION

Respected public of the way called Broad-
Tonight we invite you to step on board
A world of curves and measurements, where you'll descry
The newborn physics in their infancy.

Here you will see the life of the great Galileo Galilei,
The law of falling bodies versus the GRATIAS DEI
Science's fight versus the rulers, which we stage
At the beginning of a brand-new age.
Here you'll see science in its blooming youth
Also its first compromises with the truth.
It too must eat, and quickly gets prostrated
Takes the wrong road, is violated –
Once Nature's master, now it is no more
Than just another cheap commercial whore.
The Good, so far, has not been turned to goods
But already there's something nasty in the woods
Which cuts it off from reaching the majority
So it won't relieve, but aggravate their poverty.
We think such sights are relevant today
The new age is so quick to pass away.
We hope you'll lend a charitable ear
To what we say, since otherwise we fear
If you won't learn from Galileo's experience
The Bomb might make a personal appearance.

[From Brecht's *Arbeitsjournal*, entry for 1 December 1945.]

EPILOGUE OF THE SCIENTISTS

And the lamp his work ignited
We have tried to keep alight
Stooping low, and yet high-minded
Unrestrained, yet laced up tight.
Making moon and stars obey us
Grovelling at our rulers' feet
We sell our brains for what they'll pay us
To satisfy our bodies' need.
So, despised by those above us
Ridiculed by those below
We have found out the laws that move us
Keep this planet on the go.
Knowledge grows too large for nitwits
Servitude expands as well
Truth becomes so many titbits

Liberators give us hell.
Riding in new railway coaches
To the new ships on the waves
Who is it that now approaches?
Only slave-owners and slaves.
Only slaves and slave-owners
Leave the trains
Taking new aeroplanes
Through the heaven's age-old blueness.
Till the last device arrives
Astronomic
White, atomic
Obliterating all our lives.

[From Werner Hecht (ed.), *ibid*., pp. 38 f.]

NOTES ON INDIVIDUAL SCENES

[*Scene 11*]

Could Galileo have acted any differently?

This scene gives ample reasons for Galileo's hesitation about escaping from Florence and seeking asylum in the North Italian cities. None the less the audience can imagine him putting himself in the hands of Matti the ironfounder, and discover various tendencies in his character and situation which would support this.

The actor Laughton showed Galileo in a state of great inner agitation during his talk with the ironfounder. He played it as a moment of decision – the wrong one. (Connoisseurs of dialectics will find Galileo's possibilities further clarified in the ensuing scene 'The Pope', where the inquisitor insists that Galileo must be forced to recant his theory because the Italian maritime cities need his star charts, which derive from it and of which it would not be possible to deprive them.)

An objectivist approach is not permissible here.*

*Objectivists who prove the necessity of a given sequence of facts are always in danger of slipping into the position of justifying those facts (Lenin).

[*Scene 14*]

Galileo after his recantation

His crime has made a criminal of him. When he reflects on the *scale* of his crime he is pleased with himself. He defends himself against the outside world's impertinent expectations of its geniuses. What has Andrea done to oppose the Inquisition? Galileo applies his intellect to solving the problems of the clergy, which these blockheads have overlooked. His mind functions automatically, like a motor in neutral. His appetite for knowledge feels to him like the impetus that makes him twitch. Scholarly activity, for him, is a sin: mortally dangerous, but impossible to do without. He has a fanatical hatred for humanity. Andrea's readiness to revise his damning verdict as soon as he sees the book means that he has been corrupted. As to a lame and starving wolf, Galileo tosses him a crust, the logical scientific analysis of the Galileo phenomenon. Behind this lies his rejection of the moral demands of a humanity which does nothing to relieve the deadliness of that morality and those demands.

[. . .]

Once Galileo knows that his book has set out on its journey towards publication he changes his attitude again. He proposes that the book should be prefaced by an introduction sharply condemning the author's treachery. Andrea passionately refuses to pass on such a request, pointing out that everything is different now; that Galileo's recantation gave him the chance to finish this immensely significant work. What needs to be altered is the popular concept of heroism, ethical precepts and so on. The one thing that counts is one's contribution to science, and so forth.

At first Galileo listens in silence to Andrea's speech, which builds a golden bridge for his return to the esteem of his fellow scientists, then contemptuously and cuttingly contradicts him, accusing Andrea of squalidly recanting every principle of science. Starting with a denunciation of 'bad thinking' which seems designed as a brilliant demonstration of how the trained scientist ought to analyse a case like his own, he proves to Andrea that no achievement is valuable enough to make up for the damage caused by a betrayal of mankind.

Galileo's portrayal in scene 14

The fact that the author is known to all and sundry as an opponent of the church might lead a theatre to give the play's performance a primarily anticlerical slant. The church, however, is mainly being treated here as a secular establishment. Its specific ideology is being looked at in the light of its function as a prop to practical rule. The old cardinal (in scene 6) can be turned into a Tory or a Louisiana Democrat without much adjustment. Galileo's illusions concerning a 'scientist in the chair of St. Peter' have more than one parallel in contemporary history, and these are scarcely related to the church. In scene 13 Galileo is not returning 'to the bosom of the church'; as we know, he never left it. He is simply trying to make his peace with those in power. One can judge his demoralisation by his social attitude; he buys his comfort (even his scientific activity having degenerated to the status of a comfort) by means of hackwork, unashamedly prostituting his intellect. (His use of clerical quotations is thus sheer blasphemy.) On no account should the actor make use of his self-analysis to endear the hero to the audience by his self-reproaches. All it does is to show that his brain is unimpaired, never mind what area he directs it to. Andrea Sarti's final remark in no sense represents the playwright's own view of Galileo, merely his opinion of Andrea Sarti. The playwright was not out to have the last word.

Galileo is a measure of the standard of Italian intellectuals in the first third of the seventeenth century, when they were defeated by the feudal nobility. Northern countries like Holland and England developed productive forces further by means of what is called the Industrial Revolution. In a sense Galileo was responsible both for its technical creation and for its social betrayal.

[*Crime and Cunning*]

The first version of the play ended differently. Galileo had written the *Discorsi* in the utmost secrecy. He uses the visit of his favourite pupil Andrea to get him to smuggle the book across the frontier. His recantation had given him the chance to create a seminal work. He had been wise.

In the Californian version [. . .] Galileo interrupts his pupil's hymns of praise to prove to him that his recantation had been a crime, and was not to be compensated by this work, important as it might be.

In case anybody is interested, this is also the opinion of the playwright.

[Shortened from Werner Hecht (ed.), *ibid.*, pp. 32–37. These notes were written at various times, those on scene 14 mainly during Brecht's work on the Berliner Ensemble production. The reference to a new critical introduction to the *Discorsi* must relate to a proposed change which Brecht never made; it is not to be found in our text.]

BUILDING UP A PART: LAUGHTON'S GALILEO*

Preface

In describing Laughton's Galileo Galilei the playwright is setting out not so much to try and give a little more permanence to one of those fleeting works of art that actors create, as to pay tribute to the pains a great actor is prepared to take over a fleeting work of this sort. This is no longer at all common. It is not just that the under-rehearsing in our hopelessly commercialised theatre is to blame for lifeless and stereotyped portraits – give the average actor more time, and he would hardly do better. Nor is it simply that this century has very few outstanding individualists with rich characteristics and rounded contours – if that were all, care could be devoted to the portrayal of lesser figures. Above all it is that we seem to have lost any understanding and appreciation of what we may call a *theatrical conception*: what Garrick did when, as Hamlet, he met his father's ghost; Sorel when, as Phèdre, she knew that she was going to die; Bassermann when, as Philip, he had finished listening to Posa. It is a question of inventiveness.

The spectator could isolate and detach such theatrical conceptions, but they combined to form a single rich texture. Odd insights into men's nature, glimpses of their particular way of living together, were brought about by the ingenious contrivance of the actors.

With works of art, even more than with philosophical systems, it is impossible to find out how they are made. Those who make them work hard to give the impression that everything just happens, as it were of its own accord, as though an image were forming in a clear mirror that is itself inert. Of course this is a deception, and apparently the idea is that if it comes off it will increase the spectator's pleasure. In fact it does not. What the spectator – anyway the experienced spectator – enjoys about art is the making of art, the active creative element. In art we view nature herself as if she were an artist.

The ensuing account deals with this aspect, with the process of manufacture rather than with the result. It is less a matter of the artist's

*[The text referred to throughout this essay is that of the Brecht–Laughton translation, for which see p. 333 ff.]

temperament than of the notion of reality which he has *and communicates*; less a matter of his vitality than of the observations which underlie his portraits and can be derived from them. This means neglecting much that seemed to us to be 'inimitable' in Laughton's achievement, and going on rather to what can be learned from it. For we cannot create talent; we can only set it tasks.

It is unnecessary here to examine how the artists of the past used to astonish their public. Asked why he acted, L. answered: 'Because people don't know what they are like, and I think I can show them.' His collaboration in the rewriting of the play showed that he had all sorts of ideas which were begging to be disseminated, about how people *really* live together, about the motive forces that need to be taken into account here. L.'s attitude seemed to the playwright to be that of a realistic artist of our time. For whereas in relatively stationary ('quiet') periods artists may find it possible to merge wholly with their public and to be a faithful 'embodiment' of the general conception, our profoundly unsettled time forces them to take special measures to penetrate to the truth. Our society will not admit of its own accord what makes it move. It can even be said to exist purely through the secrecy with which it surrounds itself. What attracted L. about *Life of Galileo* was not only one or two formal points but also the subject matter; he thought this might become what he called a contribution. And so great was his anxiety to show things as they really are that despite all his indifference (indeed timidity) in political matters he suggested and even demanded that not a few of the play's points should be made sharper, on the simple ground that such passages seemed 'somehow weak' to him, by which he meant that they did not do justice to things as they are.

We usually met in L.'s big house above the Pacific, as the dictionaries of synonyms were too bulky to lug about. He had continual and inexhaustibly patient recourse to these tomes, and used in addition to fish out the most varied literary texts in order to examine this or that gest, or some particular mode of speech: Aesop, the Bible, Molière, Shakespeare. In my house he gave readings of Shakespeare's works to which he would devote perhaps a fortnight's preparation. In this way he read *The Tempest* and *King Lear*, simply for me and one or two guests who happened to have dropped in. Afterward we would briefly discuss what seemed relevant, an 'aria' perhaps or an effective scene opening. These were exercises and he would pursue them in various directions, assimilating them in the rest of his work. If he had to give a reading on the radio he would get me to hammer out the syncopated rhythms of Whitman's poems (which he found somewhat strange) on a table with my fists, and once he hired a studio where we recorded half a dozen ways of telling the story of the creation, in which he was an African planter telling the Negroes how he had created the world, or an English butler ascribing it to His Lordship. We needed such broadly ramified studies, because he spoke no German whatever and we had to decide the gest of dialogue by my acting it all in bad English or even in German and his then acting it back in proper English in a variety of ways until I could say: That's it. The result he would write down sentence by sentence in longhand. Some sentences, indeed many, he carried around for days, changing them continually. This system of performance-and-repetition had one immense advantage in that psychological discussions were almost entirely avoided. Even the most fundamental gests, such as Galileo's way of observing, or his showmanship, or his craze for pleasure, were established in three dimensions by actual performance. Our first concern throughout was for the smallest fragments, for sentences, even for exclamations – each treated separately, each needing to be given the simplest, freshly fitted form, giving so much away, hiding so much or leaving it more. More radical changes in the structure of entire scenes or of the work itself were meant to help the story to move and to bring our fairly general conclusions about people's attitudes to the great physicist. But this reluctance to tinker with the psychological aspect remained with L. all through our long period of collaboration, even when a rough draft of the play was ready and he was giving various readings in order to test reactions, and even during the rehearsals.

The awkward circumstance that one translator knew no German and the other scarcely any English compelled us, as can be seen, from the outset to use acting as our means of translation. We were forced to do what better-equipped translators should do too: to translate gests. For language is theatrical in so far as it primarily expresses the mutual attitude of the speakers. (For the 'arias', as has been described, we brought in the playwright's own gest, by observing the bel canto of Shakespeare or the writers of the Bible.)

In a most striking and occasionally brutal way L. showed his lack of interest in the 'book', to an extent the playwright could not always share. What we were making was just a text; the performance was all that counted. Impossible to lure him to translate passages which the playwright was willing to cut for the proposed performance but wanted to keep in the book. The theatrical occasion was what mattered, the text was only there to make it possible: it would be expended in the production, would be consumed in it like gunpowder in a firework. Although L.'s theatrical experience had been in a London which had become thoroughly indifferent to the theatre, the old Elizabethan London still lived in him, the London where theatre was such a passion that it could swallow immortal works of art greedily and barefacedly as so many 'texts'. These works which have survived the centuries were in fact like improvisations thrown off for an all-important moment. Printing them at all was a matter of little interest, and probably only took place so that the spectators – in other words, those who were present at the actual event, the performance – might have a souvenir of their enjoyment. And the theatre seems in those days to have been so potent that the cuts and interpolations made at rehearsal can have done little harm to the text.

We used to work in L.'s small library, in the mornings. But often L. would come and meet me in the garden, running barefoot in shirt and trousers over the damp grass, and would show me some changes in his flowerbeds, for his garden always occupied him, providing many problems and subtleties. The gaiety and the beautiful proportions of this world of flowers overlapped in a most pleasant way into our work. For quite a while our work embraced everything we could lay our hands on. If we discussed gardening it was only a digression from one of the scenes in *Galileo*; if we combed a New York museum for technical drawings by Leonardo to use as background pictures in the performance we would digress to Hokusai's graphic work. L., I could see, would make only marginal use of such material. The parcels of books or photocopies from books, which he persistently ordered, never turned him into a bookworm. He obstinately sought for the external: not for physics but for the physicists' behaviour. It was a matter of putting together a bit of theatre, something slight and superficial. As the material piled up, L. became set on the idea of getting a good draughtsman to produce entertaining sketches in the manner of Caspar Neher, to expose the anatomy of the action. 'Before you amuse others you have to amuse yourself,' he said.

For this no trouble was too great. As soon as L. heard of Caspar Neher's delicate stage sketches, which allow the actors to group themselves according to a great artist's compositions and to take up attitudes that are both precise and realistic, he asked an excellent draughtsman from the Walt Disney Studios to make similar sketches. They were a little malicious; L. used them, but with caution.

What pains he took over the costumes, not only his own, but those of all the actors! And how much time we spent on the casting of the many parts!

First we had to look through works on costume and old pictures in order to find costumes that were free of any element of fancy dress. We sighed with relief when we found a small sixteenth-century panel that showed long trousers. Then we had to distinguish the classes. There the elder Brueghel was of great service. Finally we had to work out the colour scheme. Each scene had to have its basic tone: the first, e.g., a delicate morning of white, yellow, and grey. But the entire sequence of scenes had to have its development in terms of colour. In the first scene a deep and distinguished blue made its entrance with Ludovico Marsili, and this deep blue remained, set apart, in the second scene with the upper bourgeoisie in their blackish-green coats made of felt and leather. Galileo's social ascent could be followed by means of colour. The silver and pearl-grey of the fourth (court) scene led into a nocturne in brown and black (where Galileo is jeered by the monks of the Collegium Romanum), then on to the seventh, the cardinals' ball, with delicate and fantastic individual masks (ladies and gentlemen) moving about the cardinals' crimson figures. That was a burst of colour, but it still had to be fully unleashed, and this occurred in the tenth scene, the carnival. After the nobility and the cardinals the poor people too had their masquerade. Then came the descent into dull and sombre colours. The difficulty of such a plan of course lies in the fact that the costumes and their wearers wander through several scenes; they have always to fit in and contribute to the colour scheme of the new scene.

We filled the parts mainly with young actors. The speeches presented certain problems. The American stage shuns speeches except in (maybe because of) its frightful Shakespearean productions. Speeches just mean a break in the story; and, as commonly delivered, that is what they are. L. worked with the young actors in a masterly and conscientious manner, and the playwright was impressed by the freedom he allowed them, by the way in which he avoided anything Laughtonish and simply taught them the structure. To those actors who were too easily influenced by his own personality he read passages from Shakespeare, without rehearsing the actual text at all; to none did he read the text itself. The actors were incidentally asked on no account to prove their suitability for the part by putting something 'impressive' into it.

We jointly agreed on the following points:

1. The decorations should not be of a kind to suggest to the spectators that they are in a medieval Italian room or the Vatican. The audience should be conscious of being in a theatre.

2. The background should show more than the scene directly

surrounding Galileo; in an imaginative and artistically pleasing way, it should show the historical setting, but still remain background. (This can be achieved when the decoration itself is not independently colourful, but helps the actors' costumes and enhances the roundedness of the figures by remaining two-dimensional even when it contains three-dimensional elements, etc.)

3. Furniture and props (including doors) should be realistic and above all be of social and historical interest. Costumes must be individualised and show signs of having been worn. Social differences were to be underlined since we find it difficult to distinguish them in ancient fashions. The colours of the various costumes should harmonise.

4. The characters' groupings must have the quality of historical paintings (but not to bring out the historical aspect as an aesthetic attraction; this is a directive which is equally valid for contemporary plays). The director can achieve this by inventing historical titles for the episodes. (In the first scene such titles might be *Galileo the physicist explains the new Copernican theory to his subsequent collaborator Andrea Sarti and predicts the great historical importance of astronomy – To make a living the great Galileo teaches rich pupils – Galileo who has requested support for his continued investigations is admonished by the university officials to invent profitable instruments – Galileo constructs his first telescope based on information from a traveller.*)

5. The action must be presented calmly and in a large sweep. Frequent changes of position involving irrelevant movements of the characters must be avoided. The director must not for a moment forget that many of the actions and speeches are hard to understand and that it is therefore necessary to express the underlying idea of an episode by the positioning. The audience must be assured that when someone walks, or gets up, or makes a gesture it has meaning and deserves attention. But groupings and movements must always remain realistic.

6. In casting the ecclesiastical dignitaries realism is of more than ordinary importance. No caricature of the church is intended, but the refined manner of speech and the 'breeding' of the seventeenth-century hierarchy must not mislead the director into picking spiritual types. In this play, the church mainly represents authority; as types the dignitaries should resemble our present-day bankers and senators.

7. The portrayal of Galileo should not aim at rousing the audience to sympathy or empathy; they should rather be encouraged to adopt a deliberate attitude of wonder and criticism. Galileo should be por-

trayed as a phenomenon of the order of Richard III; the audience's emotions will be engaged by the vitality of this strange figure.

8. The more profoundly the historical seriousness of a production is established, the more scope can be given to humour. The more sweeping the overall plan, the more intimately individual scenes can be played.

9. There is no reason why *Life of Galileo* cannot be performed without drastically changing the present-day style of production, as a historical 'war-horse', for instance, with a star part. Any conventional performance, however (which need not seem at all conventional to the actors, especially if it contained interesting inventions), would weaken the play's real strength considerably without making it any easier for the audience. The play's main effects will be missed unless the theatre changes its attitude. The stock reply, 'Won't work here,' is familiar to the author; he heard it at home too. Most directors treat such plays as a coachman would have treated an automobile when it was first invented. On the arrival of the machine, mistrusting the practical instructions accompanying it, this coachman would have harnessed horses in front – more horses, of course, than to a carriage, since the new car was heavier – and then, his attention being drawn to the engine, he would have said, 'Won't work here.'*

The performance took place in a small theatre in Beverly Hills, and L.'s chief worry was the prevailing heat. He asked that trucks full of ice be parked against the theatre walls and fans be set in motion 'so that the audience can think'.

Notes on individual scenes

I

The Scholar, a Human Being

The first thing L. did when he set to work was to rid the figure of Galileo of the pallid, spiritual, stargazing aura of the text books. Above all, the scholar must be made into a man. The very term 'scholar' [Gelehrter] sounds somewhat ridiculous when used by simple people; there is an implication of having been prepared and fitted, of something passive. In Bavaria people used to speak of the

*[Brecht added Note 9 at a later date for inclusion in his Notes to the Play.]

Nuremberg Funnel by which simpletons were more or less forcibly fed undue quantities of knowledge, a kind of enema for the brain. When someone had 'crammed himself with learning', that too was considered unnatural. The educated – again one of those hopelessly passive words – talked of the revenge of the 'uneducated', of their innate hatred for the mind; and it is true that their contempt was often mixed with hatred; in villages and working-class districts, the mind was considered something alien, even hostile. The same contempt, however, could also be found among the 'better classes'. A scholar was an impotent, bloodless, quaint figure, conceited and barely fit to live. He was an easy prey for romantic treatment. L.'s Galileo never strayed far from the engineer at the great arsenal in Venice. His eyes were there to see with, not to flash, his hands to work with, not to gesticulate. Everything worth seeing or feeling L. derived from Galileo's profession, his pursuit of physics and his teaching, the teaching, that is, of something very concrete with its concomitant real difficulties. And he portrayed the external side not just for the sake of the inner man – that is to say, research and everything connected with it, not just for the sake of the resulting psychological reactions – these reactions, rather, were never separated from the everyday business and conflicts, they never became 'universally human', even though they never lost their universal appeal. In the case of the Richard III of Shakespeare's theatre, the spectator can easily change himself along with the actor, since the king's politics and warfare play only a very vague role; there is hardly more of it than a dreaming man would understand. But with Galileo it is a continual handicap to the spectator that he knows much less about science than does Galileo. It is a piquant fact that in representing the history of Galileo, both playwright and actor had to undo the notion which Galileo's betrayal had helped to create, the notion that schoolteachers and scientists are by nature absent-minded, hybrid, castrated. (Only in our own day when, in the shape of ruling-class hirelings remote from the people, they delivered the latest product of Galileo's laws of motion, did popular contempt change to fear.) As for Galileo himself, for many centuries, all over Europe, the people honoured him for his belief in a popularly based science by refusing to believe in his recantation.

Subdivisions and Line

We divided the first scene into several parts:

We had the advantage that the beginning of the story was also a beginning for Galileo, that is, his encounter with the telescope, and since the significance of this encounter is hidden from him for the time being, our solution was to derive the joy of beginning from the early morning: having him wash with cold water – L., with bare torso, lifted a copper pitcher with a quick sweeping motion to let the jet of water fall into the basin – find his open books on the high desk, have his first sip of milk, and give his first lesson, as it happens, to a young boy. As the scene unfolds, Galileo keeps coming back to his reading at the high desk, annoyed at being interrupted by the returning student with his shallow preference for new-fangled inventions such as this spyglass, and by the procurator of the university who denies him a grant; finally reaching the last obstacle that keeps him from his work, the testing of the lenses which, however, would not have been possible without the two prior interruptions, and makes an entirely new field of work accessible.

Interest in Interest and Thinking as Expression of Physical Contentment

Two elements in the action with the child may be mentioned:

Washing himself in the background, Galileo observes the boy's interest in the astrolabe as little Andrea circles around the strange instrument. L. emphasised what was novel in G. at that time by letting him look at the world around him as if he were a stranger and as if it needed explanation. His chuckling observation made fossils out of the monks at the Collegium Romanum. In that scene he also showed amusement at their primitive method of proof.

Some people objected to L.'s delivering his speech about the new astronomy in the first scene with a bare torso, claiming that it would confuse the audience if it were to hear such intellectual utterances from a half-naked man. But it was just this mixture of the physical and the intellectual that attracted L. 'Galileo's physical contentment' at having his back rubbed by the boy is transformed into intellectual production. Again, in the ninth scene, L. brought out the fact that Galileo recovers his taste for wine on hearing of the reactionary pope's expected demise. His sensual walking, the play of his hands in his pockets while he is planning new researches, came close to being offensive. Whenever Galileo is creative, L. displayed a mixture of aggressiveness and defenceless softness and vulnerability.

Rotation of the Earth and Rotation of the Brain

L. arranges a little demonstration of the earth's rotation to be quick and offhand, leaving his high desk where he has begun to read and returning to it. He avoids anything emphatic, seems to pay no attention to the child's intellectual capacity, and at the end leaves him sitting there alone with his thoughts.

This casual manner, in keeping with his limited time, simultaneously admits the boy to the community of scholars. Thus L. demonstrated how for Galileo learning and teaching are one and the same – which makes his subsequent betrayal all the more horrible.

Balanced Acting

During this demonstration of the earth's rotation Galileo is surprised by Andrea's mother. Questioned about the nonsensical notions he is teaching the child he answers: 'Apparently we are on the threshold of a new era, Mrs Sarti.' The way in which L. caressingly emptied his glass of milk while he said it was enchanting.

Response to a Good Answer

A small detail: the housekeeper has gone to let the new student in. Galileo feels constrained to make a confession to Andrea. His science is in no very good state, its most important concerns must be concealed from the authorities, and for the moment they are only hypotheses. 'I want to become an astronomer,' Andrea says quickly. At this answer Galileo looks at him with an almost tender smile. Usually actors do not rehearse such details separately, or often, enough to render them quickly in the performance.

[Dismissal of Andrea]

The dismissal of Andrea during the conversation with Ludovico is a piece of stage business for which time must be allowed. Galileo now drinks his milk as if it were the only pleasure to be had, and one which will not last very long. He is fully aware of Andrea's presence. Ill-humouredly he sends him away. One of those unavoidable everyday compromises!

Galileo Underestimates the New Invention

Ludovico Marsili describes a new spyglass which he has seen in Holland and cannot understand. Galileo asks for detailed information and makes a sketch which solves the problem. He holds the cardboard with the sketch without showing it to his pupil, who expected to have a look. (L. insisted that the actor playing Ludovico should expect this.) The sketch itself he drew casually, just to solve a problem that offered some relief from the conversation. Then, his way of asking the housekeeper to send Andrea for lenses and borrowing a scudo from the entering procurator – all that had an automatic and routine quality. The whole incident seemed only to demonstrate that Galileo too was capable of ploughing water.

A New Commodity

The birth of the telescope as a commodity took a long time to emerge clearly in the rehearsals. We found out why: L. had reacted too quickly and arrogantly to the university's refusal of a grant. All was well as soon as he accepted the blow in hurt silence and then went on, almost sadly, to speak like a poor man. As a natural result, Galileo's 'Mr Priuli, I may have something for you,' came out in a way to make Galileo's dismissal of the new spyglass as 'bosh' perfectly clear.

[Interruption of Work]

When Andrea returns with the lenses he finds Galileo deep in his work. (L. has shown, during a by no means brief interval, how the scholar handles his books.) He has already forgotten the lenses, he lets the boy wait, then proceeds, almost guiltily because he has no desire to take up the lucrative bosh, to arrange the two lenses on a piece of cardboard. Finally he takes the 'thing' away, not without a little demonstration of his showmanship.

The senators surround and congratulate Galileo and draw him to the rear, but the tiny exchange with Ludovico Marsili, with its imputation of plagiarism, must as it were still hover in the air; for when the half-curtain closes behind them [Ludovico and Virginia] and in front of Galileo and the others, they continue and conclude the conversation while exiting along the footlights. And Ludovico's cynical remark, 'I am beginning to understand science,' serves as a springboard for the ensuing third scene – that of the great discoveries.

3

[Confidence in Objective Judgment]

Galileo lets his friend Sagredo look through the telescope at the moon and Jupiter. L. sat down, his back to the instrument, relaxed, as though his work was done and he only wanted his friend to pass impartial judgment on what he saw, and that this was all he needed to do since his friend was now seeing for himself. By this means he established that the new possibilities of observation must bring all controversy about the Copernican system to an end.

This attitude explains at the very beginning of the scene the boldness of his application for the lucrative position at the court of Florence.

The Historical Moment

L. conducted the exchange with his friend at the telescope without any emphasis. The more casually he acted, the more clearly one could sense the historic night; the more soberly he spoke, the more solemn the moment appeared.

An Embarrassment

When the procurator of the university comes in to complain about the fraud of the telescope, L.'s Galileo shows noticeable embarrassment by studiously looking through the telescope, obviously less to observe the sky than to avoid looking the procurator in the eye. Shamelessly he exploits the 'higher' function of the instrument which the Venetians have found not to be very profitable.

It is true that he also shows his behind to the angry man who has trusted him. But, far from trying to put him off with the discoveries of 'pure' science, he at once offers him another profitable item, the astronomical clock for ships. When the procurator has left, he sits glumly before the telescope, scratching his neck and telling Sagredo about his physical and intellectual needs which must be satisfied in one way or another. Science is a milch cow for all to milk, he himself of course included. While at this point in time Galileo's attitude is still helpful to science, later on, in his fight with Rome, it is going to push science to the brink of the abyss, in other words, deliver it into the hands of the rulers.

The Wish Is Father to the Thought

Looking up from their calculations of the movements of Jupiter's moons, Sagredo voices his concern for the man about to publish a discovery so embarrassisng to the church. Galileo mentions the seductive power of evidence. He fishes a pebble from his pocket and lets it fall from palm to palm, following gravity: 'Sooner or later everybody must succumb to it' [the evidence]. As he argued along these lines, L. never forgot for a moment to do it in such a way that the audience would remember it later when he announced his decision to hand over his dangerous discoveries to the Catholic court of Florence.

[Rejection of Virginia]

L.'s Galileo used the little scene with his daughter Virginia to indicate how far he might be blamed for Virginia's subsequent behaviour as a spy for the Inquisition. He does not take her interest in the telescope seriously and sends her off to matins. L. scrutinised his daughter after her question, 'May I look through it?' before replying, 'What for? It's not a toy.'

The Fun in Contradictions

Saying, 'I am going to Florence,' Galileo carefully signs his letter of application. In this hasty capitalisation of his discoveries as well as in his discourse on the seductive power of evidence and the representative value of great discoveries, L. left the spectator completely at liberty to study, criticise, admire Galileo's contradictory personality.

4

The Acting of Anger

Vis-à-vis the court scholars who refuse to look through the telescope, because to do so would either confirm Aristotle's doctrine or show up Galileo as a swindler, what L. acted was not so much anger as the attempt to dominate anger.

Servility

After Galileo, erupting at last, has threatened to take his new science to the dockyards, he sees the court depart abruptly. Deeply alarmed and disturbed, he follows the departing prince in cringing servility, stumbling, all dignity gone. In such a case an actor's greatness can be seen in the degree to which he can make the character's behaviour incomprehensible or at least objectionable.

4 and 6*

The Fight and the Particular Manner of Fighting

L. insisted that throughout the following scenes, 4 and 6, the sketch of Jupiter's moons from Galileo's original report should remain projected on the backdrop screen. It was a reminder of the fight. To show one of its aspects, the heel-cooling for the sake of truth, L., at the end of scene 4, when the chamberlain stays behind after the hasty departure of the court to inform him of the appeal to Rome, let himself be driven out of the space that stood for his house and stood in front of the half-curtain. He stood there between scenes 4 and 6 and again between scenes 6 and 7, waiting, and occasionally verifying that the pebble from his pocket continued to fall from one raised hand to the other stretched out below.

6

[Observation of the Clergy]

Galileo is not entirely devoid of appreciation when he observes the jeering monks at the Collegium Romanum – after all, by pretending to stand on a rolling globe they are trying to *prove* the absurdity of his propositions. The very old cardinal fills him with pity.

After the astronomer Clavius has confirmed Galileo's findings, Galileo shows his pebble to the hostile cardinal who retreats in dismay; L. did this by no means triumphantly, rather as if he wanted to offer his adversary a last chance to convince himself.

Fame

Invited to the masked ball of Cardinals Bellarmin and Barberini, Galileo lingers for a moment in the anteroom alone with the clerical secretaries who later turn out to be secret agents. He has been greeted on his arrival by distinguished masked guests with great respect: obviously he stands in high favour. From the halls a boys' choir is heard, and Galileo listens to one of these melancholic stanzas which

*Scene 5 was not played in this production.

are sung amid the joy of life. L. needed no more than this brief listening and the word 'Rome!' to express the pride of the conqueror who has the capital of the world at his feet.

The Duel of Quotations

In the brief duel of Bible quotations with Cardinal Barberini, L.'s Galileo shows, beside the fun he has with such intellectual sport, that the possibility of an unfavourable outcome to his affairs is dawning on him. For the rest, the effectiveness of the scene depends on the elegance of its performance; L. made full use of his heavy body.

Two Things at Once

The brief argument about the capacity of the human brain (which the playwright was delighted to have heard formulated by Albert Einstein) furnished L. the opportunity to show two traits: 1) a certain arrogance of the professional when his field is invaded by laymen, and 2) an awareness of the difficulty of such a problem.

[Disarmed by Lack of Logic]

When the decree is read out forbidding the guest to teach a theory acknowledged to have been proven, L.'s Galileo reacts by twice turning abruptly from the reading secretaries to the liberal Barberini. Thunderstruck, he lets the two cardinals drag him to the ball as if he were a steer stunned by the axe. L. was able, in a manner the playwright cannot describe, to give the impression that what mainly disarmed Galileo was the lack of logic.

8

[Indomitable Urge to Research]

If in the seventh scene Galileo experiences the No of the church, in the eighth he is confronted with the No of the people. It comes from the lips of the little monk, himself a physicist. Galileo is disturbed, then recognises the situation: in the fight against science it is not the church that defends the peasant, but the peasant who defends the church. It was L.'s theatrical conception to let Galileo be so profoundly upset that he delivers his counter-arguments in a spirit of defence, even of angry self-defence, and makes the throwing down of the manuscript into a gesture of helplessness. He blamed his indomitable urge to research like a sex offender blaming his glands.

Laughton Does Not Forget to Tell the Story

In the eighth scene one of Galileo's lines contains a sentence which continues the story: 'Should I condone this decree . . .' L. distilled this small but important detail with great care.

9

[The Impatience of Galileo the Scientist]

Whereas L. insisted he must be allowed to give Galileo's character a markedly criminal evolution after the recantation in scene 13, he did not feel a similar need at the beginning of scene 9. Here too, to oblige the church, Galileo has for many years abstained from publicising his discoveries, but this cannot be considered a betrayal like the later one. At this point the people know very little about the new science, the cause of the new astronomy has not yet been taken up by the North Italian bourgeoisie, the battle fronts are not yet political. There may not be an open declaration on his part, but there is no recantation either. In this scene therefore it is still the scientist's personal impatience and dissatisfaction which must be portrayed.

When Does Galileo Become Antisocial?

The issue in Galileo's case is not that a man must stand up for his opinion as long as he holds it to be true; that would entitle him to be called a 'character'. The man who started it all, Copernicus, did not stand up for his opinion; it would be truer to say that he lay down for it inasmuch as he had it published only after his death; and yet, quite rightly, no one has ever reproached him for this. Something had been laid down to be picked up by anybody.

The man who had laid it down had gone, out of range of blame or thanks. Here was a scientific achievement which allowed simpler, shorter and more elegant calculations of celestial motions; so let humanity make use of it. Galileo's life's work is on the whole of the same order, and humanity used it. But unlike Copernicus who had avoided a battle, Galileo fought it and betrayed it. If Giordano Bruno, of Nola, who did not avoid the battle and had been burned twenty years earlier, had recanted, no great harm might have come of it; it could even be argued that his martyrdom deterred scientists more than it aroused them. In Bruno's time the battle was still a feeble one. But time did not stand still: a new class, the bourgeoisie with its new industries, had assertively entered the scene; no longer was it only scientific achievements that were at stake, but battles for their large-scale general exploitation. This exploitation had many aspects because the new class, in order to pursue its interests, had to come to power and smash the prevailing ideology that obstructed it. The church, which defended the privileges of princes and landowners as God-given and therefore natural, did not rule by means of astronomy, but it ruled within astronomy, as in everything else. And in no field could it allow its rule to be smashed. The new class, clearly, could exploit a victory in any field including that of astronomy. But once it had singled out a particular field and concentrated the battle in it, the new class became broadly vulnerable there. The maxim, 'A chain is as strong as its weakest link,' applies to chains that bind (such as the ideology of the church) as well as to transmission chains (such as the new class's new ideas about property, law, science, etc.). Galileo became antisocial when he led his science into this battle and then abandoned the fight.

Teaching

Words cannot do justice to the lightness and elegance with which L. conducted the little experiment with the pieces of ice in the copper basin. A fairly long reading from books was followed by the rapid demonstration. Galileo's relationship with his pupils is like a duel in which the fencing master uses all his feints – using them against the pupil to serve the pupil. Catching Andrea out in a hasty conclusion, Galileo crosses out his wrong entry in the record book with the same matter-of-fact patience as he displays in correcting the ice's position in the submersion experiment.

Silence

With his pupils he uses his tricks mainly to quell their dissatisfaction with him. They are offended by his keeping silent in the European controversy about sunspots, where his views are constantly being solicited as those of the greatest authority in the field. He knows he owes his authority to the church, and hence owes the clamour for his views to his silence. His authority was given him on condition that he should not use it. L. shows how Galileo suffers by the episode of the

book on sunspots, which has been brought along and is discussed by
his pupils. He pretends complete indifference, but how badly he does
it! He is not allowed to leaf through the book, probably full of errors
and thus twice as attractive. In little things he supports their revolt,
though not himself revolting. When the lens grinder Federzoni angrily
drops the scales on the floor because he cannot read Latin, Galileo
himself picks them up – casually, like a man who would pick up
anything that fell down.

Resumption of Research – a Sensual Pleasure

L. used the arrival of Ludovico Marsili, Virginia's fiancé, to show his
disgust at the routine nature of his work. He organised the reception of
his guest in such a way that it interrupted the work and made his
pupils shake their heads. On being told that the reactionary pope was
on his deathbed Galileo visibly began to enjoy his wine. His bearing
changed completely. Sitting at the table, his back to the audience, he
experienced a rebirth; he put his hands in his pockets, placed one leg
on the bench in a delicious sprawl. Then he rose slowly and walked up
and down with his glass of wine. At the same time he let it be seen how
his future son-in-law, the landowner and reactionary, displeased him
more with every sip. His instructions to the pupils for the new
experiment were so many challenges to Ludovico. With all this, L. still
took care to make it plain that he was seizing the opportunity for new
research not by the forelock, but just by a single little hair.

The Gest of Work

The speech about the need for caution with which Galileo resumes a
scientific activity that defies all caution shows L. in a rare gest of
creative, very vulnerable softness.

Even Virginia's fainting spell on finding her fiancé gone barely
interests Galileo. As the pupils hover over her, he says painfully: 'I've
got to know.' And in saying it he did not seem hard.

10

Political Attitude on Dramatic Grounds

L. took the greatest interest in the tenth (carnival) scene, where the
Italian people are shown relating Galileo's revolutionary doctrine to

their own revolutionary demands. He helped sharpen it by suggesting that representatives of the guilds, wearing masks, should toss a rag doll representing a cardinal in the air. It was so important to him to demonstrate that property relationships were being threatened by the doctrine of the earth's rotation that he declined a New York production where this scene was to be omitted.

11

Decomposition

The eleventh scene is the decomposition scene. L. begins it with the same authoritative attitude as in the ninth scene. He does not permit his increasing blindness to detract one iota from his virility. (Throughout, L. strictly refused to exploit this ailment which Galileo had contracted in the pursuit of his profession, and which of course could easily have won him the sympathy of the audience. L. did not want Galileo's surrender to be ascribable to his age or physical defects. Even in his last scene he was a man who was spiritually, not physically broken.)

The playwright would sooner have Galileo's recantation in this scene, rather than let it take place before the Inquisition. Galileo executes it when he rejects the offer of the progressive bourgeoisie, in the person of the iron founder Vanni, to support him in his fight against the church, and insists that what he has written is an unpolitical scientific work. L. acted this rejection with the utmost abruptness and strength.

Two Versions

In the New York production L. changed his gest for the meeting with the cardinal inquisitor as he emerges from the inner chambers. In the California production he remained seated, not recognising the cardinal, while his daughter bowed. This created the impression of something ominous passing through, unrecognisable but bowing. In New York L. rose and himself acknowledged the cardinal's bow. The playwright finds no merit in the change, since it establishes a relationship between Galileo and the cardinal inquisitor which is irrelevant, and turns Galileo's ensuing remark, 'His attitude was respectful, I think,' into a statement rather than a question.

The Arrest

As soon as the chamberlain appears at the head of the stairs, Galileo hastily puts the book under his arm and runs upstairs, passing the startled chamberlain. Stopped short by the chamberlain's words, he leafs through the book as though its quality was all that mattered. Left standing on the lower part of the staircase, he must now retrace his steps. He stumbles. Almost at the footlights – his daughter has to run to meet him – he completely pulls himself together and gives his instructions firmly and to the point. It becomes clear that he has taken certain precautions. Holding his daughter close and supporting her, he sets out to leave the hall at a rapid, energetic pace. When he reaches the wings the chamberlain calls him back. He receives the fateful decision with great composure. Acting thus, L. shows that this is neither a helpless nor an ignorant man who is being caught, but one who has made great mistakes.

13

A Difficulty for the Actor: Some Effects become Apparent only when the Play is seen a Second Time

In preparing for the recantation scene L. never neglected in the preceding scenes to exhibit in all their fine shades the compliance and non-compliance in Galileo's conduct vis-à-vis the authorities, even those instances which would only mean anything to a spectator who had already seen the entire play once. Both he and the playwright recognised that in this type of play certain details unavoidably depend on a knowledge of the whole.

The Traitor

In the book there is a stage direction for Galileo when he returns to his pupils after he recanted to the Inquisition: 'He is changed, almost unrecognisable.' The change in L. was not of a physical nature as the playwright had intended. There was something infantile, bed-wetting in his loose gait, his grin, indicating a self-release of the lowest order, as if restraints had been thrown off that had been very necessary.

This, like what follows, can best be seen in photographs of the California production.

Andrea Sarti is feeling sick; Galileo has asked for a glass of water for him, and now the little monk passes by him, his face averted. Galileo's gaze is answered by Federzoni, the artisan-scholar, and for some time the two stare at each other until the monk returns with the water. This is Galileo's punishment: it will be the Federzonis of future centuries who will have to pay for his betrayal at the very inception of their great career.

'Unhappy the Land'

The pupils have abandoned the fallen man. Sarti's last word had been: 'Unhappy is the land that breeds no hero.' Galileo has to think of an answer, then calls after them, too late for them to hear: 'Unhappy is the land that needs a hero.' L. says it soberly, as a statement by the physicist who wants to take away nature's privilege to ordain tragedies and mankind's need to produce heroes.

14

The Goose

Galileo spends the last years of his life on an estate near Florence as a prisoner of the Inquisition. His daughter Virginia, whom he has neglected to instruct, has become a spy for the Inquisition. He dictates his *Discorsi* to her, in which he lays down his main teaching. But to conceal the fact that he is making a copy of the book he exaggerates the extent of his failing eyesight. Now he pretends not to recognise a goose which she shows him, the gift of a traveller. His wisdom has been degraded to cunning. But his zest for food is undiminished: he instructs his daughter carefully how he wants the liver prepared. His daughter conceals neither her disbelief in his inability to see nor her contempt for his gluttony. And Galileo, aware that she defends him vis-à-vis the Inquisition's guards, sharpens the conflicts of her troubled conscience by hinting that he may be deceiving the Inquisition. Thus in the basest manner he experiments with her filial love and her devotion to the church. Nonetheless L. succeeded brilliantly in eliciting from the spectator not only a measure of contempt but also a measure of horror at degradations that debase. And for all this he had only a few sentences and pauses at his disposal.

Collaboration

Anxious to show that crime makes the criminal more criminal, L. insisted, during the adaptation of the original version, on a scene in which Galileo collaborates with the authorities in full view of the audience. There was another reason for this: during the scene Galileo makes the most dignified use of his well-preserved intellectual powers by analysing his betrayal for the benefit of his former pupil. So he now dictates to his daughter, to whom he had for many weeks been dictating his main work, the *Discorsi*, an abject letter to the archbishop in which he advises him how the Bible may be used for the suppression of starving artisans. In this he quite frankly shows his daughter his cynicism without being entirely able to conceal the effort this ignominious exercise costs him. L. was fully aware of the recklessness with which he swam against the stream by thus throwing away his character – no audience can stand a thing like that.

The Voice of the Visitor

Virginia has laid down the manuscript of the letter to the archbishop and gone out to receive a belated visitor. Galileo hears the voice of Andrea Sarti, formerly his favourite pupil, who had broken with him after the recantation. To those readers of the play who complained that it gave no description of the spiritual agonies to which our nuclear physicists were subject by the authorities ordering the bombs, L. could show that no first-rate actor needs more than a fleeting moment to indicate such spiritual discomfort. It is of course right to compare Galileo's submissiveness towards his authorities with that of our physicists towards rulers whom they distrust, but it would be wrong to go all the way into their stomach pains. What would be gained by that? L. was simply making this the moment to display his bad conscience, which could not have been shown later in the scene when his betrayal is analysed, without getting in his way.

The Laughter

The laughter in the picture [in the Model Book] was not suggested by the text, and it was frightening. Sarti, the former favourite pupil, calls and Virginia overhears the strained conversation. When Galileo inquires about his former collaborators, Sarti answers with utter frankness calculated to hurt his master. They get to Federzoni, a lens grinder whom Galileo had made his scientific collaborator even though he had no Latin. When Sarti reports he is back in a shop grinding lenses Galileo answers: 'He can't read the books': Then L. makes him laugh. The laugh however does not contain bitterness about a society that treats science as something secret reserved for the well-to-do, but a disgraceful mocking of Federzoni's inadequacies together with a brazen complicity in his degradation, though this is simply (and completely) explained by his being inadequate. L. thus intended to make the fallen man a provocateur. Sarti, naturally, responds with indignation and seizes the opportunity to inflict a blow on the shameless recanter when Galileo cautiously inquires about Descartes's further work. Sarti coldly reports that Descartes shelved his investigations into the nature of light when he heard that Galileo had recanted. And Galileo once had exclaimed that he would willingly be 'imprisoned a thousand feet beneath the earth, if in exchange he could find out what light is'. L. inserted a long pause after this unpleasant information.

The Right to Submit

During the first sentences of his exchange with Sarti he listens inconspicuously for the footsteps of the Inquisition's official in the anteroom, who stops every now and then, presumably in order to eavesdrop. Galileo's inconspicuous listening is difficult to act since it must remain concealed from Sarti but not from the audience; concealed from Sarti because otherwise he would not take the prisoner's repentant remarks at face value. But Galileo must convey them to him at face value so that his visitor can cash them when he reaches foreign parts; it would not do at all if it were rumoured abroad that the prisoner was recalcitrant. Then the conversation reaches a point where Galileo abandons this way of speaking for the benefit of hostile ears, and proclaims, authoritatively and forcefully, that it is his right to submit. Society's command to its members to produce is but vague and accompanied by no manner of guarantee; a producer produces at his own risk; and Galileo can prove any time that being productive endangers his comfort.

Handing over the Book

L. made the disclosure about the existence of the *Discorsi* quickly and with exaggerated indifference; but in a way suggesting that the old man was only trying to get rid of the fruits of a regrettable lapse, with yet another implication beneath this: anxiety lest the visitor reject the imposition together with the risk involved in taking the book with him. As he was protesting ill-humouredly that he wrote the book only as a slave of habit – the thoroughly vicious habit of thinking – the spectator could see that he was also listening. (Having made his eyesight worse by secretly copying the book which is endangered by the Inquisition, when he wants to gauge Sarti's reaction he is wholly dependent on his ears.) Toward the end of his appeal he virtually abandons his attitude of 'condescending grandeur' and comes close to begging. The remark about having continued his scientific work simply to kill time, uttered when Sarti's exclamation 'The *Discorsi!*' had made him aware of his visitor's enthusiasm, came so falsely from L.'s lips that it could deceive no one.

It is furthermore important to realise that when Galileo so strongly emphasises his own condemnation of the teaching activities which are now forbidden to him he is mainly trying to deceive himself. Since working, let alone sharing the results with the outside world, would threaten whatever was left of his comfort, he himself is passionately against this 'weakness' which makes him like a cat that cannot stop catching mice. Indeed the audience is witnessing his defeat when it sees him yield so reluctantly yet helplessly to an urge fostered in him by society. He must consider the risks to be larger than ever because now he is wholly in the hands of the Inquisition; his punishment would no longer be a public one; and the body of people who formerly would have protested has dispersed – thanks to his own fault. And not only has the danger increased, but he would be too late now with any contribution anyway, since astronomy has become apolitical, the exclusive concern of scientists.

Watchfulness

After the young physicist has found the book for which the scientific community no longer dares to hope, he at once changes his opinion about his former teacher and launches, with great passion, into a rationalisation of Galileo's motives for the betrayal; motives, he finds, which exonerate him completely. Galileo has recanted so that he can go on with his work and find more evidence for the truth. Galileo listens for a while, interjecting monosyllables. What he is hearing now may well be all that he can expect posterity to say in recognition of his difficult and dangerous endeavour. First he seems to be testing his pupil's improvised theory, just in the same way as any other theory must be tested for its validity. But presently he discovers that it is not tenable. At this point, immersed in the world of his scientific concerns, he forgets his watchfulness vis-à-vis a possible eavesdropper: he stops listening for steps.

The Analysis

Galileo's great counterattack against the golden bridge opens with a scornful outburst that abandons all grandeur: 'Welcome to my gutter, dear colleague in science and brother in treason! I sold out, you are a buyer.' This is one of the few passages which gave L. trouble. He doubted whether the spectator would get the meaning of the words, apart from the fact that the words are not taken from Galileo's usual, purely logical vocabulary. L. could not accept the playwright's argument that there must be some gest simply showing how the opportunist damns himself by damning all who accept the rewards of opportunism; what he understood even less was that the playwright would be quite satisfied with the exhibition of a state of mind that defies rational analysis. The omission of a spiteful and strained grin at this point robbed the opening of the great instructional speech of its malice. It was not fully brought out that deriding the ignorant is the lowest form of instruction and that it is an ugly light that is shed solely for the purpose of letting one's own light shine. Because the lowest starting point was missing some spectators were unable to gauge the full height which L. undoubtedly reached in the course of the great speech, nor was it entirely possible to see the collapse of Galileo's vain and violently authoritarian attitude that coloured even his scientific statements. The theatrical content of the speech, in fact, is not directly concerned with the ruthless demonstration of bourgeois science's fall from grace at the beginning of its rise – its surrender of scientific knowledge to the rulers who are authorised 'to use it, not use it, abuse it, as it suits their ends'. The theatrical content derives from the whole course of the action, and the speech should show how well this perfect brain functions when it has to judge its owner. That man, the spectator should be able to conclude, is sitting in a hell more terrible than Dante's, where the true function of intellect has been gambled away.

Background of the Performance

It is important to realise that our performance took place at the time and in the country of the atom bomb's recent production and military application: a country where nuclear physics was then shrouded in deepest secrecy. The day the bomb was dropped will not easily be forgotten by anyone who spent it in the United States.

The Japanese war had cost the United States real sacrifices. The troop ships left from the west coast, and the wounded and the victims of tropical diseases returned there. When the news reached Los

Angeles it was at once clear that this was the end of the hateful war, that sons and brothers would soon come home. But the great city rose to an astonishing display of mourning. The playwright heard bus drivers and saleswomen in fruit markets express nothing but horror. It was victory, but it was the shame of defeat. Next came the suppression of the tremendous energy source by the military and politicians, and this upset the intellectuals. Freedom of investigation, the exchange of scientific discoveries, the international community of scholars: all were jettisoned by authorities that were strongly distrusted. Great physicists left the service of their bellicose government in headlong flight; one of the best known took an academic position where he was forced to waste his working time in teaching rudimentary essentials soley to escape working for the government. It had become ignominious to make new discoveries.

[From *Aufbau einer Rolle/Laughtons Galilei*, East Berlin, Henschel, 1956.]

Appendices to 'Building up a part'

Sense and sensuality

The demonstrative style of acting, which depicts life in such a way that it is laid open to intervention by the human reason, and which strikes Germans as thoroughly doctrinaire, presented no special difficulty to the Englishman L. What makes the sense seem so striking and insistent once it is 'lugged in' is our particular lack of sensuality. To lack sensuality in art is certainly senseless, nor can any sense remain healthy if it is not sensual. Reason, for us, immediately implies something cold, arbitrary, mechanical, presenting us with such pairs of alternatives as ideas and life, passion and thinking, pleasure and utility. Hence when we stage a performance of our *Faust* – a regular occurrence for educational reasons – we strip it of all sensuality and thus transport the audience into an indefinite atmosphere where they feel themselves confronted with all sorts of thoughts, no single one of which they can grasp clearly. L. didn't even need any kind of theoretical information about the required 'style'. He had enough taste not to make any distinction between the supposedly lofty and the supposedly base, and he detested preaching. And so he was able to unfold the great physicist's contradictory personality in a wholly corporeal form, without either suppressing his own thoughts about the subject or forcing them on us.

Beard or no beard

In the California production L. acted without a beard, in the New York with one. This order has no significance, nor were there any fundamental discussions about it. It is the sort of case where the desire for a change can be the deciding factor. At the same time it does of course lead to modifications in the character. People who had seen the New York production confirmed what can be seen from the pictures [in the Model Book], namely that L. acted rather differently. But everything essential was still there, and the experiment can be taken as evidence to show how much room is left for the 'personal' element.

The leavetaking

Certainly nothing could have been more horrible than the moment when L. has finished his big speech and hastens to the table saying 'I must eat now', as though in delivering his insights Galileo has done everything that can be expected of him. His leavetaking from Sarti is cold. Standing absorbed in the sight of the goose he is about to eat, he replies to Sarti's repeated attempt to express his regard for him with a formal 'Thank you, sir'. Then, relieved of all further responsibility, he sits down pleasurably to his food.

Concluding remark

Though it resulted from several years of preparation and was brought about by sacrifices on the part of all concerned, the production of *Galileo* was seen by a bare ten thousand people. It was put on in two small theatres, a dozen times in each: first in Beverly Hills, Los Angeles, and then with a completely new cast in New York. Though all the performances were sold out the notices in the main papers were bad. Against that could be set the favourable remarks of such people as Charles Chaplin and Erwin Piscator, as well as the interest of the public, which looked like being enough to fill the theatre for some considerable time. But the size of the cast meant that the potential earnings were low even if business was really good, and when an artistically interested producer made an offer it had to be rejected because L., having already turned down a number of film engagements and made considerable sacrifices, could not afford to turn down another. So the whole thing remained a private operation by a great artist who, while earning his keep outside the theatre, indulged himself by displaying a splendid piece of work to a (not very large) number of interested parties. Though this is something that needed to be said, it does not however convey the complete picture. Given the way the American theatre was organised in those years, it was impossible that such plays and such productions should reach their audience. Productions like this one, therefore, should be treated as examples of a kind of theatre that might become possible under other political and economic conditions. Their achievements, like their mistakes, make them object lessons for anyone who is looking for a theatre of great themes and rewarding acting.

[From Werner Hecht (ed.), *Materialien zu Brechts 'Leben des Galilei'*, pp. 78–80. In the last of these notes Brecht is perhaps being undeservedly kind to Laughton, since the actor's wariness of Communist associations, at a time when Brecht and Hanns Eisler were being heard by the Un-American Activities Committee, appears to have been another strong factor in deciding him to close the play.]

NOTE OF TWO CONVERSATIONS WITH CASPAR NEHER ABOUT
Life of Galileo

After the Italian fashion, a lightly built stage that is recognisable as having been lightly built. Nothing stony, weighty, massive. No interior decoration.

Colour to emerge from the costumes, i.e. in movement.

The stage shows Galileo's background, making use of contemporary evidence (Leonardo's technical drawings, Romulus and Remus with the she-wolf, a man of war from the Venice arsenal and so on).

No projections, since this would prevent the full illumination of the stage. Giant photographs, maybe, nobly suspended. A flagged floor.

[Dated October 3 and 5, 1955. From Werner Hecht (ed.), *ibid.*, p. 88. The eventual stage set for the Berliner Ensemble's production, completed by Erich Engel after Brecht's death and first performed on January 15, 1957, was somewhat different from this.]

Editorial Notes

Much of the information that follows, including some of the quotations from Brecht, is derived from Ernst Schumacher's *Drama und Geschichte. Bertolt Brecht's 'Leben des Galilei' und andere Stücke*, Henschel, East Berlin, 1965, whose usefulness is gratefully acknowledged.

I. GENERAL

Judging by the proportion of Brecht's papers devoted to it in the Brecht Archive in Berlin, *Galileo* is much the most heavily worked-over of all his plays. None of the others went through such stages, for not only did *Galileo* occupy him during the last nineteen years of his life, but its linguistic, theatrical, and thematic bases all changed drastically during that period, as did the dramatist's own circumstances. Thus it was written in German, then entirely rewritten in English (with Brecht himself contributing in a mixture of English and German), then rewritten in German once more largely on the basis of the English-language version. Again, it was first written with no clear prospect of production, then rewritten for a specific actor, Laughton, and a specific production before an American audience, then rewritten once more for Brecht's own Berliner Ensemble to play in East Berlin. During Brecht's work on the first version, it became known that Niels Bohr had split the uranium atom; then while he and Laughton were preparing the second, the first atom bomb dropped on Hiroshima, on August 6, 1945. Finally, Brecht himself was at first living as an exile, close to Germany, on the eve of an impending war; he rewrote the play once in the aura of Hollywood, when an allied victory was at last certain, then the second time after his own successful reestablishment in his country, within a bitterly divided world.

There are thus three principal versions of the play whose differences will be described in what follows. The first is the German version whose earliest typescript was entitled *The Earth Moves* and which was originally written in November 1938. What appear to be early sketches lay down a structure as follows:

Life of Galileo

It did not take long to complete. On November 17 his secretary-collaborator Margarete Steffin wrote to Walter Benjamin:

> Ten days ago Brecht began getting *Galileo* down in dramatic form, after it had been plaguing his mind for some while. He has already finished nine of the fourteen scenes, and very fine they are.

A mere six days after that, according to his diary, he had completed it, commenting that

> The only scene to present difficulties was the last one. As in *St. Joan* [*of the Stockyards*] I needed some sort of twist at the end to make absolutely certain of the necessary detachment on the part of the audience. At any rate, now even a man subject to unthinking empathy must experience the A-effect in the course of identifying

himself with Galileo. A legitimate degree of empathy occurs, given strictly epic presentation.

On January 6, 1939, the *Berlingske Tidende* published an interview in which he said that the play was 'really written for New York'; this referred no doubt to his discussions with Ferdinand Reyher. A few weeks later he carefully revised it under the title *Life of Galileo* and had a number of duplicated copies run off, of which Walter Benjamin and Fritz Sternberg each appear to have been given one. This was also to all intents and purposes the version sent to Zurich and staged there on 9 September 1943.

But already Brecht was dissatisfied with it:

Technically, *Life of Galileo* is a great step backwards, far too opportunistic, like *Señora Carrar's Rifles*. The play would need to be completely rewritten to convey that 'breath of wind that cometh from new shores', that rosy dawn of science. It would all have to be more direct, without the interiors, the atmospherics, the empathy. And all switched to planetary demonstration. The division into scenes can be kept, Galileo's characterisation likewise, but work, the pleasures of work, would need to be realised in practical form, through contact with a theatre. The first thing would be to study the *Fatzer* and *Breadshop* fragments [two unfinished plays dating from before 1933]. Technically those represent the highest standard.

So he noted on February 25. On the 27th he heard a Danish radio interview with three of Niels Bohr's assistants, one of whom, Professor C. Møller, knew Brecht and later recalled discussing Galileo and the *Discorsi* with him early the previous year. This interview described the splitting of the uranium atom, which (so Ernst Schumacher suggests) may have prompted the passage in the revised text about 'the greatest discoveries . . . being made at one or two places'. The revision, however, certainly did nothing to change the play 'technically'. Though an early but undated note speaks of a *Life of Galileo* version for workers, there appears to be no indication that a start was ever made on this.

The second or American version dates from April 1944, when Brecht took up the play again as a result of a meeting with Jed Harris, the producer of Thornton Wilder's *Our Town*. A translation of the first version had already been made by Desmond Vesey; in addition Brecht now got a rough interlinear translation made by one of his own collaborators, followed by a new acting version by two of Orson

Welles's associates, Brainerd Duffield and Emerson Crocker. The two last-named had been recommended to him by Charles Laughton, who seems to have become interested in the play some time that autumn and to have used their version for his own work with Brecht on the adaptation. 'Now working systematically with Laughton on the translation and stage version of *The Life of the Physicist Galileo*' said a diary note of December 10. In the course of this activity, which lasted off and on until December 1945, Brecht redrafted many passages in a remarkable mixture of German and English; thus his sketch for the beginning of scene 4 runs:

Rede des Mathematikers

Das Universum des göttlichen Aristoteles mit seinen

mystisch musizierenden Sphären und Kristallnen Gewöl-

circles   heavenly bodies
ben sowie den Kreisläufen seiner Himmelskörper,

obliquity of the ecliptic
seinem Schiefenwinkel der Sonnenbahn/den Geheimnissen

Sternen
der Table of Cords, dem/Reichtum des Catalogue

inspirierten
for the southern hemisphere/der/construction of a

celestial globe is ein Gebäude von grosser Ordnung

und Schönheit.

The Universe of divine Classics.

For the New York production, which took place after Brecht's return to Europe, there were, according to its director Joseph Losey, 'Different words, thanks in part to the collaboration of George Tabori in rewriting with Laughton and me from notes left behind in New York by Brecht.'

The text as we reproduce it in the appendix (p. 333 ff.) was published by Indiana University Press in 1953 in *From the Modern Repertoire, Series Two*, edited by Eric Bentley, then in *Seven Plays by Bertolt Brecht*, Grove Press, New York, 1961, and separately by Grove Press again in 1966. The play still struck Brecht himself as formally conventional, to judge from a note of January 1945 which found that with its interiors and atmospheric effects the construction of the scenes, derived from the epic theatre, makes a singularly theatrical impact.

He also told an interviewer somewhat apologetically that summer that 'Galileo is anyway interesting as a contrast to my parables. Where they embody ideas, it extracts ideas from a subject'. And on July 30 he noted that 'I wouldn't go to the stake for the formal aspects of this play'.

In 1953, he got Elisabeth Hauptmann and Benno Besson of the Berliner Ensemble, with some advice from Ruth Berlau to draft a third version in German, using the best parts of the previous texts. This he himself revised to form the play which was given its German première at Cologne in April 1955, published as *Versuche 14* and subsequently rehearsed by him for some three months with his own company. With minor amendments it is the text of the *Gesammelte Werke* on which our edition is based. It differs substantially from the second version, not least by being very much longer.

2. THE FIRST VERSION, 1938–1943

From Brecht's first completed typescript, dating presumably from 23 November 1938, to the text used for the Zurich production of 1943, the play remained essentially the same, the only changes of real substance being those in the last scene but one, which define the nature of Galileo's crime. The general structure of this first version was already very similar to that of the text which we have followed, and certain scenes, or large parts of them, were taken into the latter without drastic rewriting, for instance the first half of scene 1, scene 3, the start of scene 4, scene 5b (Plague), scene 6 (Collegium Romanum), much of scene 8, scene 11 (The Pope) and the last (Smuggling) scene. Even the carnival scene (10) had the same place, gist and purpose, though the ballad round which it centres was later rewritten. There were, however, some striking differences among the characters. To sum these up briefly:

Mrs Sarti originally died of the plague in scene 5b. The character in 9 was 'the housekeeper'. This was altered after the first typescript.

Ludovico, Virginia's fiancé, did not appear till scene 7 (The Ball). He was then called Sitti, and was not a member of the landowning aristocracy; indeed in scene 9 (Sunspots) he lamented that he had no fortune of his own. His function of introducing Galileo to the principle of the telescope (scenes 1 and 2) was performed by a silly-ass character called Doppone, son of a wool merchant, whose only other appearance was, briefly, as a papal chamberlain in the ball scene.

Virginia was much less contemptuously treated by her father. Her relations with Andrea were friendlier, though her role in the penultimate scene was the same.

Federzoni the lens grinder did not figure in the play at all. Some of his lines were spoken by an 'elderly scholar'.

Vanni the iron founder did not figure in the play either.

A stove-fitter and a doctor appeared in the penultimate scene.

In the first typescript the play was called *The Earth Moves* (Die Erde bewegt sich) and the scenes bore no titles. The title *Life of Galileo*, together with the individual scene titles, more or less in their final form, are to be found in the revised scripts of early 1939. The verses before each scene are absent from this version.

The following is a scene-by-scene account of it.

1

Galileo Galilei, teacher of mathematics in Padua, sets out to demonstrate the new Copernican system

Galileo's long speech about the 'new age' (pp. 6–8) was about ten lines shorter, omitting inter alia the passages about the ships previously hugging the shores and about the masons in Siena, but taking in the lines about 'those old constructions that people have believed in for the last thousand years' which come at the close of the scene in the final text (p. 17). Andrea's age was not originally specified, but the revised versions make him thirteen (as opposed to eleven in the final text).

The whole episode with Ludovico is absent. Instead Galileo

explains to Andrea the nature of a hypothesis. Copernicus, he says, knows that the earth rotates

> only because he has worked it out. Actually he doesn't know it at all. He's assuming it. It's simply what is called a hypothesis. No facts. No proofs. They're being looked for. A few people in Prague and in England are looking for the proofs. It's the greatest hypothesis there has ever been, but it's no more than that. Hence the great flaw in the new system is that nobody who isn't a mathematician *can* understand why it's like that and can't be any other way. All I've showed you is that it can be that way. There's no reason why not, if you see what I mean.

ANDREA: Can't I become a mathematician and find out the reason why it should?

GALILEO: And how am I going to pay the butcher and the milkman and the bookseller if I start giving you lessons for nothing? Off you go, now; I must get on with my work.

In the revised versions Andrea asks 'What's a hypothesis?' and gets the answer which the final text puts at the end of the scene, down to 'that can hardly see at all' (p. 17), concluding 'Copernicus's hypothesis is the greatest hypothesis there has ever been, but it's no more than that.'

ANDREA: Then what about what the church is saying? What's that?

GALILEO: Oh, that's a hypothesis too, but not such a good one. Lots of flaws that don't explain very much. But the great flaw of the new system . . .

– and so on, as above.

The episode with the procurator of the university, which follows, is close to the final text, though the reference to the scientific implications of 'the cry for better looms' is lacking. Doppone appears *after* this, and is taken on as a private pupil for thirty scudi a month; his father wants him to become a theologian, since he likes arguing. Before leaving, he tells Galileo about the telescope, which Galileo then constructs from two lenses bought for him by Andrea. The scene ends with them looking through it.

GALILEO: You didn't eat the apple – which shows you've got the makings of a mathematician. A taste for unrewarding art. I'll teach you. It won't break me. This flimflam is worth five hundred scudi.

ANDREA (*after Galileo has allowed him another look*): How clearly one sees. Here's Signor Gambione the bailiff coming up to our house.

GALILEO: Quick, shove those forty-five scudi in your pocket!

2

Galileo presents a new invention to the Republic of Venice

Federzoni and Ludovico do not figure in this scene, which is dated August 24, 1609. Nor does Virginia. The telescope is handed over by Andrea, who however has nothing to say. The scene starts with Galileo's telling Sagredo that he has used it to look at the moon. Then his presentation speech is read for him by the procurator, including as Galileo's own the emphasis on the instrument's military usefulness; he adds a comment that Galileo hopes to continue serving the Venetians. During this speech Doppone appears and tries to catch the eye of Galileo, who is annoyed and embarrassed: 'It's one of my pupils, an unbelievable idiot. I can't imagine what he wants.' As the city fathers try the instrument Galileo goes on talking to Sagredo about its relevance to Copernican theory.

> GALILEO (*without looking at him*): How about this? Flecks of light on the dark portion of the disk, dark patches on the bright sickle. It fits almost too well. Of course, I'm very sceptical, extremely sceptical.

The scene ends with Doppone breaking through the Doge's guards and saying breathlessly:

> Signor Galilei, why wouldn't you listen to me before the presentation? It's all wrong. The cover ought to be green. It was green; trust Doppone.

3

January 10, 1610: By means of the telescope Galileo discovers celestial phenomena which prove the Copernican system. Warned by his friend of the possible consequences of his investigations, Galileo affirms his faith in reason

Up to Mrs Sarti's exit two-thirds of the way through (p. 28) this scene is very close to the final text, the main differences being the omission of

Galileo's six lines on the value of star charts for navigation (p. 25); the fact that Sarti appears 'in night attire'; and the doubling of Galileo's eventual salary (one thousand scudi in this version, as against the final five hundred). The episode with Virginia is then shifted to the end of the scene, after Sagredo's second 'Don't go to Florence, Galileo' (p. 31), which leads to a cross-fade, thus:

GALILEO: You'd do better helping me write my letter to the Florentines.

SAGREDO: You really mean to go there?

GALILEO: Certainly. And with the tube. And with the truth. And with my belief in human reason.

SAGREDO: Then there's nothing more to say, is there? *He leaves hurriedly without speaking.*

GALILEO *laughs as he sits down at the telescope and starts making notes. It gets dark. When the lights come on again it is morning. Galileo is still sitting at his table writing by two candles. He has his coat on, as the fire has evidently gone out. A bell is ringing for early mass. Enter Galileo's very young daughter Virginia, warmly dressed.*

As in the final text she announces that she is going to matins, though without mention of Ludovico. In her dialogue with her father, which is rather differently phrased here, he does not snub her with such words as 'It's not a toy' (p. 29) and 'Nothing in your line', though she complains of never being allowed to look through the telescope. He then tells her to read his letter to Duke Cosimo to see if it is humble enough, and she reads out the text which is now at the end of the scene. They discuss it, and in conclusion he sleepily comments:

The only way an unpopular and embarrassing man can get a job that gives him enough free time is by crawling on his belly.

VIRGINIA *hugging him*: Shall we have a big house there?

GALILEO: Time, that's the main thing, my dear, time!

Virginia expresses no particular joy about going to court.

4

Galileo has exchanged the Venetian republic for the court of Florence. The discoveries he has made with the help of the telescope are met with disbelief by the court scholars

The first part, up to the quarrel between the two boys, is close to the final text, apart from the substitution of the court chamberlain for Cosimo's tutor and the fact that in the earliest typescript Mrs Sarti's opening speech was about a third of its subsequent length. After that, however, the scene was, in the main, differently written (again, without Federzoni) and incorporated scene 5a, thus reducing the plague scene to 5b only. In this version the reason given for Cosimo's sudden departure was not the court ball but 'a particularly important message', leading the three representatives of orthodox physics to continue the speculations with which they made their original appearance.

> I wonder what sort of message His Highness got? I don't like those cases of illness in the old town – The message couldn't possibly have anything to do with that! The medical faculty is quite certain that . . . *There is a knock on the door downstairs. Mrs Sarti opens it. Virginia comes in with a travelling bag* (p. 41).

And so into 5a.

The preceding argument between Galileo and the three scholars (who in the typescript were simply Professors A, B, and C, before being distinguished in the revised versions as astronomer, mathematician and theologian) is the same in substance, but largely different in form. There is no formal dispute, no attempt to use Latin, no accompanying court ladies, the dialogue is slacker and more repetitive. Galileo's references to his work with the employees of the Venice arsenal and to the sailors are not yet included (p. 40). On the other hand, he begins his immediately preceding speech with:

> You must realise that it is up to you to set an example and trust your reason. That the meanest stableboy is waiting to be encouraged and challenged to trust his reason.

The next lines about 'doctrines believed to be unshakeable are beginning to totter' were already there in the first typescript.

The cannibalised 5a is somewhat differently arranged, since Galileo appears at the top of the stairs, chuckling at the scholars' panicky departure, sees Virginia and asks what she is doing here (when she should be at her convent school). Virginia's presence in this scene was in fact an amendment to the first typescript, which originally gave her lines to the neighbour's wife. Mrs Sarti then announced that the neighbour had arranged a carriage to take them all away, but Brecht changed this to 'The court is sending a carriage' and added the lackey's speech which in this version finished with a friendly message from Cosimo to Andrea.

> After Mrs Sarti's 'But it's not exactly sensible' (p. 42) Galileo adds:
> And I can tell you another reason. In times like these nobody can say how long he's going to remain alive. *He smiles.* So let's go and paint more stars on the lens. *Goes into his study.*

The first two of these sentences were added in pen to the original typescript.

5b [5]

Undeterred even by the plague, Galileo carries on with his researches

Originally, after the old women's 'Your mother may be there', Andrea replies 'No, she's dead'. Brecht, however, amended this on the typescript to read as now. Otherwise the differences from the final text are insignificant. Conceivably this scene was a last-minute addition to the first typescript. The numbering and typing seem to suggest it.

6 [*5 on first typescript, 6 in revised versions*]

1616: The Vatican research institute, the Collegium Romanum, confirms Galileo's findings

Virtually the same as the final text, apart from the ending, which in the first typescript (later reworded) read:
> *The astronomer escorts him in.*

THE ASTRONOMER: That was him, Your Eminence.
THE INQUISITOR *very politely*: May I look through the tube? I find
this tube extremely interesting.

7 [6 *in first typescript only*]

But the Inquisition places Copernicus's teachings on the Index (March 5, 1616)

Though the structure and general gist of this, the ball scene, are the
same as in the final version, there are considerable differences in the
dialogue. Partly this is due to the fact that Ludovico, who makes his
first appearance here, is not specifically identified with the aristocracy
or even, in the first typescript, given a surname; hence the absence of
the First Secretary's reference to 'All the great families of Italy', with
their resounding names. Doppone also makes a last brief entry,
speaking jerkily like Mr Jingle:

GALILEO: I've concluded my business here.

DOPPONE: Yes, I know – known to one and all – brilliant triumph –
    sat at your feet myself – epicircle and all that.

Neither Galileo's verse ('Fret not, daughter') nor the Lorenzo de'
Medici madrigal are included. The old cardinal does not appear, and
Bellarmin and Barberini are in different disguises, the former as a fox,
the latter as a donkey.

In Galileo's argument with these two cardinals some of the key
phrases are already there, such as Barberini's reference to astronomy
as 'the itch', Galileo's pronouncement 'I believe in men's reason' (only
uttered once however), Bellarmin's account of the Campagna peasants
whose situation can only be justified by positing a Higher Being, and
his objection that Galileo is accusing God of 'the most elementary
errors in astronomy' (p. 55). Bellarmin's reference to star charts and
navigation, however, is once again missing, as is the subsequent
bandying of Biblical texts and Barberini's 'Welcome to Rome . . .'
(p. 54) to which it leads. Instead the dialogue runs (after 'the itch'):

BELLARMIN: Unfortunately not only have the new theories dis-
    placed our good earth, which the Almighty designated as our
    dwelling place, from the centre of the cosmos, in an almost
    contemptuous way, but the assumption of utterly incredible

distances in the cosmos makes the world seem so tiny that the interest which God evidently takes in the human race becomes almost impossible to understand.

GALILEO: As the Collegium Romanum has at last admitted . . .

BELLARMIN: What we feel is, that to say it's easier to explain phenomena by positing that the earth moves and the sun stands still, than by accepting the Ptolemaic cycles and epicycles, is a wholly admirable thing, risks nothing and is all right for mathematicians. But suppose one tried to suggest that the sun is really at the centre of our world and rotates only round itself without moving across from east to west while the earth circles round the sun at immense speed, then that would be a very risky affair, don't you think, because it would upset philosophy and the theologians, who are awkward customers and what's more it would make the scriptures untrue.

BARBERINI: But don't you see, Bellarmin, the scriptures don't satisfy his reason? Whereas Copernicus does . . .

After Barberini, leading Bellarmin aside, has asked Galileo about the possibility of God giving the stars irregular movements, Galileo makes much the same reply as in the final text, but forgets himself and calls the future pope 'my dear man'. Then the instruction to the secretaries not to take the discussion down comes some two dozen lines later than in the final text, just before Bellarmin formally tells Galileo of the Holy Office's decision. This is not repeated by the secretary, but in the revised versions Bellarmin on leaving instructs the secretaries to 'Make a note of the fact that I have today informed Signor Galileo of the decree of the Holy Office concerning the Copernican doctrine'.

The remainder of the scene, with the inquisitor, is almost as in the final text, except that he enters with two ladies, saying:

Oh, truly I don't know half what you do. You're so much crueller than I ever could be.

and in asking Virginia about her engagement omits the words 'your future husband comes from a distinguished family' (p. 57).

8 [*Transformation scene*]

This conversation with the little monk has no title, and is presumably intended to be played before the curtain. Its general direction, and much of its dialogue, have remained constant since the first typescript, though Brecht continually added to it. Notable differences in the first version are:

(1) The start:

THE LITTLE MONK: You're right.

GALILEO: Haven't you read the Index Congregation's decree?

THE LITTLE MONK: I have read it.

GALILEO After that you can't go on saying I'm right, wearing the habit you wear.

THE LITTLE MONK: I have been unable to sleep for four nights (etc.).

(2) In the first typescript Galileo's next speech ran:

See that man down there hiding behind the oleanders and peeping up now and again? Since the cardinal inquisitor looked through my tube I've never lacked for company. They're very interested in criminals in Rome. I'll give him one of my tubes to help him observe me better.

THE LITTLE MONK: Please believe me when I say that I have nothing to do with that man and the people who sent him. I'm a mathematician.

GALILEO: And I'm a criminal.

This was removed in revision. Then after the little monk's long speech about his peasant family, ending 'a vast goodness of soul?' (p. 61), Galileo originally went straight to the speech about the Priapus (p. 62). The first part of his comment on the situation of the peasants (p. 62) was added on the first typescript, but not the passage about the oyster and the pearls. The important exchange about whether the truth will out ('The only truth that gets through will be what we force through', p. 63) was added in the process of revision. The ensuing sentence about 'divine patience' is not in this version.

9 [8 or 7 in first typescript]

After keeping silent for eight years Galileo is encouraged by the accession of a new pope, who is himself a scientist, to resume his researches into the forbidden area. The sunspots

Apart from the penultimate scene, this is the most heavily amended of them all. In place of Federzoni there is the 'elderly scholar', while, in the first typescript only, 'the housekeeper' figured instead of Mrs Sarti. The exchanges with Ludovico are entirely different, as well as shorter; again Ludovico is no aristocrat, and his nervousness about his prospective father-in-law's theories seem to stem from hints dropped at the university where he is a student without private means. The order of events also underwent subsequent changes.

Thus the scene opens with Galileo demonstrating the behaviour of floating bodies. He begins with an extended version of the remarks later put after the experiment with the needle (p. 69):

GALILEO: The aim of science is not to open the door to everlasting wisdom, but to set a limit to everlasting error. Philosophy for the most part is limitless, wild and indefinite, but truth is restricted and contained in small examples. A main cause of poverty in the sciences is the illusion of wealth. We only conquer nature by obeying her. Whatever counts as a cause when we are observing counts as a rule when we are putting something into effect. By observing the small errors on which the great philosophies are erected we arrived in the course of the summer at all kinds of concepts which have been obstructing the advance of science ever since Aristotle's time. Such as cold and thinness, dampness and length, from which some people think they can construct a whole world if they put the words together the right way.

Andrea then puts the Aristotelian case, about the ice and the needle, going on to describe Galileo's disproof of it while Galileo demonstrates. When he succeeds they all laugh, leading the women to make their remarks about laughter (p. 69) up to Sarti's 'I don't know'.

Mucius then appears, and is dealt with very much as in the final text. Then after Galileo has gone into his study Virginia and Mrs Sarti have their chat about horoscopes (p. 66), in its final form – an episode which was not, however, in the first typescript – before Andrea starts asking Galileo about sunspots, saying he has read Fabricius's book. The dialogue here is largely different. Thus when the elderly scholar asks Galileo 'Is it really right to keep one's mouth shut?' Galileo replies with the Keuner story about the man who was asked if he would serve his enemy, served him for seven years till he died, and then bundled up his corpse, scrubbed out the room, breathed deeply and replied 'No'. Only Galileo tells it, in the first typescript, of 'Mr Sarrone, a philosopher in Modena', amended to 'the Cretan philosopher Keunos, who was much loved by the Cretans for his libertarian views'. As the others laugh Andrea shakes his head and (in the revised versions) says he doesn't care for the story.

Gaffone the rector makes his brief appearance, as on p. 67, followed by some twenty lines of dialogue between the two women, including Virginia's remark about 'a very high church person' (p. 65), some references to signs of official surveillance, and an inquiry to Andrea about his fiancée:

VIRGINIA: How's Jessica? Are you still quarrelling?

ANDREA *laughing*: No. I've found out now why she didn't want to marry me. Pangs of conscience. Because astronomers are unholy people, you know. Of course that wasn't a very serious obstacle. We're together again. *Goes upstairs.*

MRS SARTI [in the revised versions]: She knows she's doing well for herself. Her father's just an ordinary artisan . . .

Ludovico enters in travelling clothes, followed by a servant, saying he has got to speak to Galileo, about a rumour. Is he writing a book on sunspots? Galileo says what nonsense; did Ludovico come all the way to ask that?

LUDOVICO: I hope you understand. They're all talking about Copernicus again in connection with these sunspots. And I was hoping you weren't getting involved. I've already had hints dropped at the university.

GALILEO: Oh, so you're frightened?

Like the final Ludovico, this one brings the news that Barberini may soon be pope. Much of Galileo's speech in the first typescript about what his election might mean for science – e.g.

This means nothing less than the start of a new century of the arts and sciences. No more fear. Knowledge will be a passion and research a self-indulgence. What a dreadful age, where saying what is, is considered a crime. But now people will say, what a dreadful age it was. Who's scared of discoveries now, they'll ask. Who's got reason to be?

– was shifted to immediately in front of his 'Put a grid of squares on the screen' (p. 72), so that his order to focus the telescope on the sun follows instantly on the news, without any of the teasing of Ludovico which is found in the final text. Ludovico begs him not to join in the sunspot controversy, to which Galileo answers:

> . . . Are they to say Galileo hasn't got the courage to open his mouth? People are looking at me, man. The earth rotates – it's I who say that, do you get me? If I keep silent it'll stop!

> LUDOVICO: Virginia, I know I love you. But I can't marry you if this is how things are. I haven't any money of my own.

Andrea suggests Galileo should help them. 'My Jessica has come to terms with her conscience, but after all she's only risking hell. I don't know what she'd do if the city clergy stopped getting their communion vessels from her father the silversmith. A threat of that sort is far worse.' But Galileo turns away to his collaborators.

> LUDOVICO: Virginia, I love you, and I love your father the way he is. But his concerns are not mine; I don't understand them and I haven't got the courage.

And because Galileo remains silent, Virginia gives Ludovico back his ring.

Thus virtually everything in the final text from Mrs Sarti's 'Almost!' (p. 72) to Andrea's interruption (p. 75) is missing in this version. Galileo goes straight on to his big speech (p. 75), including already such key phrases as 'My object is not to establish that I have been right all along but to find out if I am' and 'And whatever we wish to find we shall regard, once found, with particular mistrust.' As Ludovico embraces Virginia and leaves, Galileo continues (from 'go on talking all the same')

> Then we'll crush this stupidity underfoot, eh, my boy? We'll peel off its skin to carry as our banner. And we'll write on it in blood: look out! Or, rather, in ink – which is more dangerous. At last we're going to bang those narrow-minded heads together till they burst like eggshells. Yes, we're going to make cruel use of our arguments. Perhaps it'll be the first time in history that cruelty has been directed against ignorance. A historic date!

> ANDREA: And are you going to write the book on the world systems?

> GALILEO: Yes, and not in Latin for the few but in Tuscan for the many. Because this book has got to be understood by everybody.

For that I need people who work with their hands. Who else is going to want to know the causes of everything? [Then, in the revised versions, as on p. 74 to 'will probably laugh'.] And the peasants who force their plough into the earth, and the weavers at their looms, the people now stirring in every street, are all going to point at the sun and say: it's not a golden coat of arms but a motor. We move it, because it moves us.

Virginia repacks her trousseau, and Andrea closes the scene with his four-line epigram from p. 71.

10 [9, *or 8 in first typescript*]

The Copernican doctrine circulates among the common people

The setting is a street, with a street singer and his wife singing to a hurdy-gurdy and the populace listening from windows. The ballad differs, above all structurally, from that in the final text, and goes roughly as follows:

Great Galileo told the sun
(Or so the story says)
To give up turning around the earth
On which it casts its rays.
What a to-do!
The sun has started turning around itself
Not around me and you.

And immediately the sun had ceased
Reserving all its light for us
The verger gave up following after the priest
The apprentice after his boss.
No doubt you've guessed:
They all want to turn around themselves
And do what suits them best.

The bricklayer who was building the house
Is now its occupier.
The woodcutter who chops down trees
Puts the wood on his own fire.
What a to-do!

The woodcutter was telling his wife
His feet were frozen through.

I saw two housewives shopping for fish
The clock was striking twelve.
The fishwife took out a piece of bread
And ate the fish herself.
What a to-do!
The fishwife thought she'd have fish for once
Very nutritious too.

The master appears, the maids don't get up
The footmen omit to bow.
The master observes to his great surprise
Nothing turns around him now.
No doubt you've guessed:
The footmen have their hands too full
The maids give them no rest.

THE WOMAN

I too had been dancing out of line
And said to my husband, 'My dear
What you do for me might well be done
By any other star.'

THE MAN

What a to-do!
My wife ought to turn around no one but me —
That's always been my view

The princes clean their boots with their own hands.
The emperor bakes his own bread.
The soldiers no longer obey commands
But stroll in the streets instead.
No doubt you've guessed:
There was too much work for too many to do.
In the end they had to protest.

(*In a confidential undertone*)

The cardinals all stood in St. Peter's Square
When the pope showed himself to the crowd

The cardinals acted as if he weren't there.
And went on talking too loud.
What a to-do!
Their eminences have taken to kissing their own feet –
You know who that's due to.

Three archangels came down to earth, to complain
It should praise God more audibly.
But the earth said: 'There are so many worlds in space
Why do they have to pick on me?'
No doubt you've guessed:
If our earth is just one of a whole lot of worlds
It can share such chores with the rest.

At the end of the ballad '*a Jesuit crosses the square. He crouches when he hears the song, and goes off like a drenched poodle. The people laugh and throw down coins.*'

A note then says that the scene can develop into a ballet. '*A popular carnival celebration can be shown in the style of Brueghel's The Battle Between Carnival and Lent. Following the first verse of the ballad a carnival procession can move across the square, including a man dressed as a BIBLE with a hole in it, and a cart with a monk stretching out, trying with both hands to hold back a collapsing ST. PETER'S THRONE. Then after the last verse the MOON, SUN, EARTH and PLANETS can appear and demonstrate the new system of motion in a dance, to a severe musical setting.*'

11 [*10, or 9 in first typescript*]

1633. The Inquisition summons the world-famous scientist to Rome

This short scene in the Medici palace is close to the final text, except that the episode with Vanni the iron founder from Virginia's 'Here's Mr Vanni' on p. 80 to Galileo's 'you risk losing your arm' on p. 82 is not in this version. Instead a man passes to whom Galileo vainly calls out 'Galliardo! Galliardo!', commenting:

That was the director of artillery equipment. He must have seen me. He usually eats out of my hand. Today he's running away as if he thought I was infectious.

Then a student passes, who wants to stop and talk to Galileo but is called away by his tutor. Just before Cosimo's entrance Galileo comments:

> After all, we're not here to get polite attentions paid us. I crawled into this position years ago on all fours, since anybody wanting to introduce the truth – or even a morsel of it – into a place like this can only enter through the lowest hole of all, the one for dogs. But it was a good thing to do, as now they'll have to protect me. There's something in the air. If I hadn't got the pope's imprimatur for it I'd think it was the book. But they know the book has passed the censors. The pope would flatly reject any attempt to make a trap for me out of it. And after all the grand duke is my pupil. I shall complain to him.

The passage about Sagredo's invitation (p. 83) and the appearance of the cardinal inquisitor were added before this in revision. Galileo's resolve to escape in Volpi's wine cart is not in this version; nor is the last sentence of the final text.

12 [11, or 10 *in first typescript*]

The pope

This scene is divided by a 'transformation' into two halves, of which the second is not in the later versions and is given in full below. The first half, in the pope's own room, is a slightly shorter version of the final text. It excludes notably the reference to Galileo's star charts and the maritime cities' need for them, the mention of his powerful friends, leading to the pope's order 'Hands off him!' (p. 86) with the inquisitor's cynical reply and the pope's comment that 'His thinking springs from sensuality.' This half accordingly ends with 'Not the whole of it, but its best part.' Then, after the transformation:

> *Another room. At the window, Galileo, waiting. Here too the stamping and shuffling of many feet of the gathering congregation is heard. In the foreground two officials of the Inquisition.*

> OFFICIAL *sotto voce to his companion*: He's got good nerves. He's having a look at all his enemies.

> GALILEO: I hope the interview with His Holiness will take place before the session. It's important for me, as I want to ask for my evidence and proofs to be investigated before any decision is come to. It is of course quite impossible for me to make any kind

of statement in a matter of such importance for the world of science without my evidence and proofs first getting a most scrupulous hearing and examination. I'd be glad of a little water. *The first official pours him some water from a carafe on the table. Galileo reaches for it uncertainly and spills some.*

SECOND OFFICIAL *when the firsts returns*: Having a look at his enemies, but at nothing else. Had you forgotten he's half blind?

GALILEO: I suppose His Holiness really does want to see me?

FIRST OFFICIAL: Definitely.

GALILEO: Then I'd prefer to wait in another room if that's possible.

SECOND OFFICIAL: It's not possible. You wouldn't like His Holiness to arrive and find you weren't here, because you couldn't stand the shuffling.

GALILEO *looks at him blankly.*

SECOND OFFICIAL: Yes, you must be beginning to realise it isn't just a handful of people gathering there to testify against you. It's the most distinguished minds in Italy, the most learned scholars, the stars of all the universities, in short it's everybody.

GALILEO: Yes. *He turns to his window again.*

FIRST OFFICIAL: He must feel rather like someone before the flood who was expecting a spring shower, then the real rain came, then came an endless downpour and that turned into the flood, don't you think?

A high official appears. Galileo turns to face him and makes a deep bow. He thinks it is the pope.

THE HIGH OFFICIAL: Has this person eaten?

FIRST OFFICIAL: He was served a substantial meal.

THE HIGH OFFICIAL: The session later may go on a long time. *Goes out.*

GALILEO *has risen to his feet in confusion*: Gentlemen, I know His Holiness personally, having met him once at Cardinal Bellarmin's. But my eyesight is not what it was, and I must beg you to tell me when he is coming.

FIRST OFFICIAL: Shall be done, even though you wouldn't oblige us by making a proper meal.

GALILEO: The fact that the gentleman who just left used the word 'later' when speaking about the Inquisition's session today is surely a definite sign that His Holiness wants to speak to me first?

FIRST OFFICIAL *shrugs his shoulders.*

GALILEO: Did you say something?

FIRST OFFICIAL: I shrugged my shoulders.

13 [12 or 11 *in first typescript*]

Apart from the fact that Federzoni's subsequent lines are given to the elderly scholar, that the end of the scene (after the blackout) was at first conceived as a short scene on its own, and that Andrea's insults ('Wine-pump!' etc., p. 91) are missing, this version is not much different from the final one. In the first typescript a speech for the elderly scholar was written in; it appears to belong after Andrea's 'He couldn't write his book there' (p. 88) but was omitted in revision.

> Clearly he didn't pay enough attention to that part. It's true that he said: it's not enough to know something, you have to be able to prove it. And he held his tongue till he was forty-six years old, and only spoke when he was able to prove his knowledge. But then he talked about his proofs to people with bunged-up ears, not to those who were dissatisfied with what had been believed in up to then but to those who were content with it. His mistake was to think that the choice between speaking in a republic and speaking in a grand duchy wasn't an astronomical problem.

14 [13, or 12 *in first typescript*]

1633–1642. A prisoner of the Inquisition, Galileo continues his scientific studies up to his death. He manages to smuggle his principal work out of Italy

Like 9, this is a heavily altered scene with substantial differences from the final text. To sum them up briefly: (a) Galileo has conspired with a stove-fitter to conceal and smuggle out his writings; (b) Virginia reads him aphorisms by Montaigne, not scribbled texts provided by the archbishop; (c) his big speech (pp. 100–101) is differently conceived, though containing one or two phrases that recur in its final form; it omits all but the most general references to science's social implications, accuses himself only of failure to speak up for reason, and includes neither the warning of a 'universal cry of horror', nor the proposal for a scientists' Hippocratic oath; (d) it is only *after* this speech that Virginia leaves the room and Galileo admits to having written the *Discorsi*; (e) Andrea's enthusiastic reaction in praise of the 'new ethics' is missing, as also is Galileo's counter-speech of self-abasement ('Welcome to the gutter', p. 99); thus there are no dramatic reversals of feeling between the handing-over of the *Discorsi* and the end of the scene.

In the opening stage direction Galileo is described as '*old and ill, and moves like a blind man*'. Virginia solicitously serves him his supper ('Now let's eat up our good soup, and try not to spill a drop of it'). He then complains that the stove isn't working properly, and asks when the stove-fitter is coming. The official in the antechamber (the monk of the final text) complains to Virginia that manuscripts have been leaking out:

> Don't forget that the *Dialogue Concerning the Two Chief World Systems* was smuggled to Holland from here. And now they've intercepted a letter to Strasbourg, saying a manuscript will be coming. It must already have got out. Who took it? *Enter a big, broad-shouldered man, the stove-fitter. He has his tools with him.*

The stove-fitter is indeed the agent responsible, but this time he has brought the manuscript back because 'They are after us. Villagio has been arrested'. The doctor then appears, to check on Galileo's eyesight.

THE OFFICIAL: Can he or can he not see?

THE DOCTOR *shrugs his shoulders*: I don't know; very little, I'd say. I'll be making my report.

Virginia then comes in again to read to her father. The following passage was published in 1957 in *Versuche 15* as an addendum to the play:

VIRGINIA: Shall I read to you?

GALILEO: Yes, those inscriptions on the beams of M. de Montaigne's library. But only the ones I've marked.

VIRGINIA *gets the book and reads*: 54th Inscription: Without leaning.

GALILEO: Is that all?

VIRGINIA: Yes.

GALILEO: But that depends on at least three things: the force of the thrust applied to one, the visibility of the objective and the solidity of the base. Some advice! Go on.

VIRGINIA: 52nd inscription: I do not understand.

GALILEO: That's good. It's a starting point.

VIRGINIA: 13: It is possible and it is not possible.[1]

GALILEO: Good, so long as he gives reasons.

VIRGINIA: 5: It's no more like this than like that or like neither.[2]

GALILEO: Provided one goes on looking.

VIRGINIA: 21: He who knows that he knows doesn't know how he knows.[3]

GALILEO: Again, that's very good. But it all tastes of defeatism.

VIRGINIA: 10: What are heaven and earth and sea, with all they embrace, against the sum of sums of the immeasurable whole?[4]

GALILEO: One has to start, though. Make a note.

VIRGINIA: 2: He gave them curiosity, that he might torment them.[5]

GALILEO: Rubbish.

VIRGINIA: 15: Man is too fragile.[6]

GALILEO: Not fragile enough.

VIRGINIA: 20: Be wise in moderation, that you may not grow stupid.[7]

GALILEO: Go on.

VIRGINIA: 42: Men are not confused by things but by opinions about things.[8]

GALILEO: That could be wrong too. Who confuses the opinions?

VIRGINIA: Should I make a note of that?

GALILEO: No.

VIRGINIA: 19: I am a human; nothing human is alien to me.[9]

GALILEO: Good.

(1) Sextus Empiricus, *Hypotyposes*, 1, 21.

(2) Ibid., 1, 19, cited Montaigne *Essays* 2, 12.

(3) 1 Corinthians 8:2. The A.V. quotation is 'And if any man think that he knoweth anything, he knoweth nothing yet as he ought to know.'

(4) Lucretius, *De Rerum Natura*, 6, cited Montaigne *Essays* 2, 12.

(5) Ecclesiastes 1, of which verse 13 in A.V. reads 'And I gave my heart to seek and search out by wisdom concerning all things that are done under heaven: this sore travail hath God given to the sons of man to be exercised therewith' (*Essays* 2, 17).

(6) Keramos anthropos. Wrongly attributed to Romans 9.

(7) Ecclesiastes 7: '. . . neither make thyself over wise: why shouldest thou destroy thyself?'

(8) Epictetus, cited by Stobaeus. (*Essays* 1, 14.)

(9) Terence, *Heautontimoroumenos* Act 1 (*Essays* 2, 2). This was Karl Marx's favourite saying.

VIRGINIA: 37: God has created man like a shadow. Who can judge him once the sun has set?[10]
Galileo is silent.

VIRGINIA: 17: You should neither fear your last day nor yearn for it.[11]

GALILEO: I used to find the first point difficult: now it's the second.

VIRGINIA: 14: A wondrous thing is goodness.[12]

GALILEO: Louder!

VIRGINIA *louder*: A wondrous thing is goodness.

A much shorter alternative to the whole passage, which is also given in the first typescript, with Galileo and Virginia going over proofs, replaces it in the revised versions. In this Virginia reads Galileo the extract from the *Discorsi* which appears at the end of the previous scene in the final text.

At this point Andrea enters, and the dialogue is fairly close to the final text, up to where Galileo asks about his scientific friends 'Did they learn anything from my recantation?' (p. 96). Andrea hardly answers the question; he says nothing about Fulganzio, or, of course, Federzoni; the immediately preceding exchange about Descartes is also missing. Instead the text continues:

ANDREA: For a time there was a considerable difference of opinion about you. Some of your former friends insisted that you had recanted because of services you still hoped to render physics by remaining alive. Because of such works as only you could write.

GALILEO *brusquely*: There are no such works.

ANDREA: How do you mean? If you hadn't written the *Dialogue* . . .

GALILEO: Then someone else would have written it.

ANDREA: So that wasn't your motive?

GALILEO: Shortly after my trial various people who had known me earlier were good enough to credit me with all kinds of noble intentions. I wouldn't have this. To me it simply signified a decline of the critical faculties, brought about by the fact that they found drastic physical changes in me.

After carefully considering all the circumstances, extenuating

(10) Ecclesiastes 7. Or more probably 6:12, which reads 'For who knoweth what is good for man in this life, all the days of his vain life which he spendeth as a shadow? For who can tell a man what shall be after him under the sun?' (*Essays* 2, 12).

(11) *Essays* 2, 37, after Martial, 10.

(12) Plato, *Cratylus*.

and otherwise, it is impossible to conclude that a man could arrive at this state of – call it obedience, from any other motive than an undue fear of death. *Pause.* That is not to deny *addressing Virginia* the profound regret which I, as a son of the church, felt when my superiors induced me, by the most weighty of all arguments, to see the error of my ways. As a rule nothing less than threatening a man with death will serve to dissuade him from something of which his reason, that most dangerous of all God's gifts, has persuaded him. I fully understood that I could now only expect that hell which, so the poet tells, is inhabited by people who have gambled away the gifts of the mind and are accordingly without hope.

He tells Andrea that science should be able to get along without authority (including his own). 'Authority and absence of truth doubtless go together, and so do truth and absence of authority.' Andrea then sums up the case against him, as it emerges in this version:

> . . . a lot of people everywhere were hanging on your words and actions because they felt what you stood for was not a particular theory about the movements of the stars but the freedom to theorise in any field. Not just for any particular thoughts, in other words, but the right to think in the first place, which was now being threatened. So as soon as these people heard you recanting all you had said they concluded that it was not merely certain thoughts about celestial motions that were being discredited but thinking itself that was being regarded as unholy, since it operates by means of causes and proofs.

Virginia replies that the church has not forbidden science, but has even absorbed Galileo's main discoveries. 'Only he mustn't attack the opinions of theology, which is an entirely different science.' The big speech follows, starting very much as it does in the final text (p. 100):

GALILEO: In my free time, and I've got plenty of that, I have asked myself how the world of science, of which I no longer consider myself a member, even if I still know a thing or two about its pursuits, will judge my conduct. *In lecture style, hands folded over his paunch.* It will have to take into account whether it is good enough for its members to provide it with a given number of principles, for instance about the tendencies of falling bodies or the motions of certain stars. I have, as I said, excluded myself from the scientific way of thinking; however, I take it that when faced with the threat of destruction that world will be in no position to lay down more far-reaching duties for its members, e.g., that of collaborating in its own maintenance as science. Even a wool merchant, in addition to buying cheap and providing good wool, has to worry about his trade being permitted at all without restriction. On that principle no member of the scientific world is logically entitled to point to his own possible contributions to research if he has failed to honour his profession as such and to defend it against any use of force. This, however, is a business of vast scope. For science consists, not in a licence to subordinate facts to opinions, but in an obligation to subordinate opinions to facts. It is not in any position to permit restriction of these principles or to establish them only for 'certain views' and 'those particular facts'. In order to make sure that it can apply these principles unrestrictedly at any one time, science has to fight to be respected in every sphere. For science and humanity as a whole happen to be in the same boat. So it can't say 'What business is it of mine if the boat springs a leak at the other end?' [A passage cut from the original typescript here is repeated between two asterisks on p. 262 below.] Science has no use for people who fail to stick up for reason. It must expel them in ignominy, because, however many truths science knows, it could have no future in a world of lies. If the hand that feeds it occasionally seizes it unpredictably by the throat then humanity will have to chop it off. That is why science cannot tolerate a person like me in its ranks.

VIRGINIA *with passion*: But you are accepted in the ranks of the faithful (cf. p. 101)

GALILEO: That is the position. In my view I have wrecked every experiment that might have been injurious to blind faith. Only my ingrained habit of making allowances for improbabilities would lead me to say 'nearly every experiment'. Plainly nothing but the irresistible arguments put forward by the Inquisition could have convinced me of the harmfulness of my researches.

ANDREA *in a strangled voice*: Yes.

Virginia leaves the room, and Galileo at once slyly admits that he has had relapses (p. 97). The dialogue then roughly anticipates that in the final text, up to where Andrea takes up the manuscript of the *Discorsi*, with the difference that Andrea never assumes that the work has been irrevocably handed over to 'the monks' as occurs, with consequently heightened tension, in the final text. Nor does Galileo simply tell him to 'Stuff it under your coat' (p. 98), but makes more elaborate and self-protective hints as to how he might take it away. Then as Andrea leaves, there is a significantly different exchange, to which the section in square brackets was added in the course of revision:

ANDREA *who has concealed the manuscript on him*: Yes, I'm going now. [I realise it's as if a tower had collapsed which was enormously tall and thought to be unshakeable. The noise it made collapsing was louder than the noise of the builders and their machines during the whole period of its construction, and the column of dust which its collapse caused was even higher than it had been. But conceivably when the dust disperses it may turn out that although the top twelve stories fell down the bottom thirty are still standing. In which case the building could be developed further. Is that what you mean? It would be supported by the fact that the inconsistencies in our science are still all in evidence and have been sifted. The difficulty seems to have increased, but at the same time the necessity has become greater.] I'm glad I came. *He holds out his hand to him.*

GALILEO *does not take it; hesitantly*: My eyesight is bad, Andrea. I can't see any more, I only stare. You had better go. *He walks slowly to [the globe and sees if it is shut.* I'm not unresponsive to the kindnesses I'm always being shown. Travellers passing through remember me, and so on. I don't misinterpret such things.] I'm glad too to have talked to you, and to have found you as you are. You have had experiences which could have given you a quite wrong view of what we've always termed the future of reason. But of course, no single man could either bring it to pass or discredit it. *It is too big an affair ever to be contained inside a single head. Reason is something people can be divided into. It can be described as the egoism of all humanity.* Such egoism is not strong enough. But even a person like myself can still see that reason is not coming to an end but beginning. And I still believe that this is a new age. It may look like a bloodstained old harridan, but if so that must be the way new ages look. When light breaks in it does so in the uttermost darkness. While a few places are the scene of the most immense discoveries, which must contribute immeasurably to humanity's resources for happiness, great areas of this world still lie entirely in the dark. In fact the blackness has actually deepened there. Look out for yourself when you travel through Germany with the truth under your coat.

Andrea goes out.

Andrea says nothing about a 'devastating analysis' (p. 102). The scene quickly closes, somewhat as in the final text, though not on the word 'Clear' but on Galileo's ensuing comment: 'That's good. Then he'll be able to see his way.'

15 [*14*]

1637. Galileo's book the *Discorsi* crosses the Italian frontier

Very close to the final text.

3. THE AMERICAN VERSION, 1944–1947

This English-language version, which Brecht and Laughton worked on from the end of 1944 up to the Hollywood production of July 1947, maintains the general structure of the play, but shortens and very largely rewrites it. The main structural changes are the omission of the first half of scene 4; the cutting of scene 5a off the end of scene 4 and the elimination of it and 5b (the plague scenes); also the cutting of the second half of scene 12 (pp. 254–5 above), with Galileo waiting for the pope. An element of social interest was introduced by making Ludovico an aristocrat and creating two new characters: Federzoni the lens grinder, who helps bring out the point of Galileo's use of the vernacular language, and the iron founder here called Matti, whose function is to appear in scenes 1 and 11 and show that the embryo bourgeoisie is on Galileo's side. Ludovico takes over Doppone's role in scenes 1 and 2; not surprisingly he becomes a little unconvincing. Federzoni too gets some of the elderly scholar's lines in scene 9. In this scene Mucius is cut, in scene 14 the stove-fitter and the doctor. According to Brecht it was Laughton who insisted on transposing the handing-over of the *Discorsi* in this scene so that Galileo's big self-accusatory speech should come after it.

The carnival scene (10) was rewritten entirely, with a new English-language ballad, though the gist of this remained much the same. The actions of the masqueraders and the crowd, while not exactly amounting to the 'ballet' proposed in the first version, were described in some detail, finishing with the appearance of the enormous dummy figure of 'Galileo, the Bible-buster'.

Finally there are no scene titles in the text as published, but short English verses were put at the beginning of each scene, and at the end of the play, which now finished with the warning:

> May you now guard science' light,
> Kindle it and use it right,

Lest it be a flame to fall
Downward to consume us all.

The full text of this version is given on page 333 ff. After the first plan for an American publication of the plays had fallen through, it was included in Eric Bentley's anthology *From the Modern Repertoire 2* and published by University of Denver Press in 1952. Scene 15, which had been available in 1946 but was not played in the Los Angeles and New York production, was now added, and the resulting version seems closer to what Brecht wanted published for readers than any other.

The following is a brief scene-by-scene commentary on its changes from the first version. Scene numbers are those of the final text, with the American version's numbering in square brackets.

1.

The scene begins with the arrival of the Ptolemaic model which was previously already there. Galileo's speech on the 'new age' is shorter and simpler and more sloppily worded ('A new age was coming. I was on to it years ago'), but includes the ships and the Sienese masons. His second demonstration to Andrea, with the apple (which is in both the first and the final versions), is cut from Andrea's 'But it isn't true' (p. 10) to Galileo's 'Ha' on p. 11. Ludovico then appears, the gist of the dialogue being much the same as in the final text, but very much shortened. Galileo's discussion with Andrea about hypotheses is cut. The procurator, who follows Ludovico's exit, is for some reason a museum curator; again the dialogue is shortened and simplified, even vulgarised:

CURATOR: You've never let me down yet, Galilei.

GALILEO: You are always an inspiration to me, Priuli.

The ending of the scene is likewise shorter.

2.

The form of the scene is as in the final text, except that Virginia makes the presentation, that Matti the (Florentine) ironfounder appears, and that the Doge has nothing to say. Note the curator's '*best chamber-of-commerce manner*' and the allusion to him as a businessman, also the new silliness of Virginia as exemplified in the closing exchanges.

3.

This is the same scene as in the final version, but shortened. It introduces Galileo's remarks about star charts, but cuts the episode with Mrs Sarti (p. 28) who does not appear at all. Virginia enters earlier – there is no cross-fade as before – and stays long enough to hear Sagredo read out the end of the letter to the grand duke. The scene now ends approximately as in the final text, though rather more abruptly.

4.

The first half of the scene has been cut: Mrs Sarti's speech, the grand duke's arrival and the episode with the two boys, also Galileo's opening speech and the beginning of the scientific argument up to where Cosimo's three professors are invited to look through the telescope for themselves (p. 36 in the final version). Instead it begins with the philosopher talking Latin and the exchange (p. 36) about the need to use the vernacular for Federzoni's sake. The argument which follows, now interrupted by the court ladies with jarringly improbable comments, follows the same pattern as the final version, though again in shortened form. It introduces notably Galileo's remark, 'Why defend shaky teaching? You should be doing the shaking,' and the speech that follows about the arsenal workers and the sailors. The professors leave without speculating about Cosimo's hurried departure, now attributed to the state ball.

5.

[is cut]

6. [5]

Apart from the ending, this is a shortened form of the Collegium Romanum scene as we have it. The episode with the two astronomers is cut (from their entry p. 47 to their exit p. 49), apart from the very thin (or in this version infuriated) monk's first remark. His ensuing speech (starting 'They degrade humanity's dwelling place') is likewise cut. The scene ends on the little monk's remark about Galileo's having won. Galileo's answer and the appearance of the cardinal inquisitor are omitted. The inscription about astronomical charts which is lowered after the curtain is not found in the other versions.

7. [6]

Again, this is a slightly shortened form of the final text. The great families attending the ball are named, Doppone is omitted, the two cardinals are now lamb and dove, the reference to star charts is new, Barberini swaps Biblical texts with Galileo and welcomes him to Rome, Bellarmin's speech about the Campagna peasants and the 'great plan' is cut, the inquisitor greets Virginia with the comment that her fiancé comes 'from a fine family'. The Lorenzo de' Medici madrigal is still missing.

8. [7]

The scene with the little monk is virtually as in the final version. Most of Galileo's speech about the Priapus is cut, but the beginning is as we now have it, and the phrases about the oyster and the pearl, and the peasants' 'divine patience' are included.

9. [8]

The order of events is as in the final text, though the episode with Mucius has been cut. The scene thus starts with Virginia's dialogue with Mrs Sarti, including the talk about horoscopes. The Keunos story has gone, as have all allusions to Andrea's Jessica. Instead there is the dialogue between the collaborators as the experiment is prepared, including the little monk's remark about 'happiness in doubting' but omitting Andrea's account of how he has been observing the sun's rays in the attic. The whole episode with Ludovico corresponds closely to the final text, from his entrance on p. 69 to his exit on p. 74, apart from the omission of Mrs Sarti's long speech (pp. 72–3) and the little monk's immediately preceding remark about God and physics. The end of the scene too is the same, except that it stops at the end of Galileo's important speech.

10. [9]

The rewriting of this scene has already been mentioned (p. 238).

11. [10]

Close to the final text. Half the Vanni episode is here, though he is called Matti (as in scene 2) and it ends at the equivalent of 'please remember you've friends in every branch of business' (p. 81). (The rest appears to have been written at the same time, but not included in the published text.) Galliardo and the student do not appear. The passages about Sagredo's invitation and the possibility of escape were not in the earlier version.

12. [11]

The inquisitor's long speech is shortened by half, notably by the references to papal politics and the abolition of top and bottom, with the ensuing quotation from Aristotle. The exchange about Galileo's self-indulgence is new. That about the conclusion of his book is omitted. The ending, after 'but its best part' (p. 87) is new; the final stage instruction (which does not read like Brecht) being found only in this version. Otherwise this part of the scene is as we now have it. As already noted, the second part of the scene is cut.

13. [12]

From Andrea's cry 'someone who doesn't know the truth' (p. 88) to his imitation of Galileo is cut. The rest is as in the final version except for Federzoni's remark about Andrea not getting paid, and the shifting of Andrea's 'Unhappy is the land that breeds no hero' to immediately before Galileo's answer.

14. [13]

The order of events has been shifted, and is the same as in the final text. There is now nothing about the Inquisition's suspicions that manuscripts are being smuggled out, and the episodes with the doctor and the stove-fitter are cut. The 'weekly letter to the archbishop', whose discussion replaces that of the Montaigne inscriptions, is about half as long as in the final text. Andrea's ensuing dialogue with Galileo is as in the final text up to the point where Virginia leaves the room (which now comes very much earlier), that is to say it discusses what has happened to his former collaborators. The revelation of the *Discorsi* then comes before the analysis of Galileo's motives and conduct, which is now without the passages quoted on pp. 259 ff., but introduces Andrea's gradually waning praise of Galileo's behaviour, from Andrea's 'Two new branches of science' (p. 97) to Galileo's 'It was not' (p. 99). The 'welcome to the gutter' speech which follows is new, though shorter than its final version. The big speech is likewise about one-third shorter than in the final text, omitting notably the phrases 'But can we deny ourselves to the crowd and still remain scientists?' and 'Science, Sarti, is involved in both these battles', as well as the suggestion of a Hippocratic oath and the picture of scientists as 'inventive dwarfs'. The shift of emphasis from intellectual to social betrayal, the stressing of the liberating popular effects of the new science, finally the introduction of allusions to the horrors of the atom bomb, can all best be seen by comparing the actual text with that of the earlier version (pp. 260–261).

Galileo's view of 'the new age', in the final exchanges, is expressed in the same terms as in the previous version. Again he ignores Andrea's hand, without comment. There is no mention of Andrea's journey through Germany, and the scene ends with Virginia's final remark.

15. [14]

The scene is broadly similar to its earlier version, but has been wholly rewritten, including the song. Among other things, the witch's house is shown, and the children steal her milk jug and kick it over.

4. THE BERLIN VERSION, 1953–1956

We can now summarise what happened when Brecht decided to make a new German version of the play after his return to Berlin. Two principal texts are involved: that published in his *Versuche 14* in 1955, and the final revised text of the collected *Stücke* (1957), which incorporates minor changes made in the course of Brecht's rehearsals and as a result of the Cologne production in the former year. This version follows the general structure of the American version, giving more or less the same account of characters, incidents, motivations and social substructure. However, it brings back important stretches of dialogue (from the first version, eliminating many of the crudities of the American text and giving more elbow-room to the arguments) at the cost, of course, of making a considerably longer play.

The characters remain the same as in the American version, apart from the bringing back of Mucius at the beginning of scene 9, and the renaming of Vanni, who no longer figures in scene 2. So do their social roles. The plague scene is restored in a new form by running together 5a and 5b; this, presumably, being something that Brecht had wished to have 'in the book' even though, like Laughton, he was excluding it from the acting version. Scene 4 is restored to its full length, scene 15 put back into its old form. The original German text of the ballad in scene 10 has not been restored; instead it has been (freely) re-translated from the English, so as to fit Eisler's setting, though with the addition of the singer's remarks to the crowd. The same applies to the between-scene verses, which were not done in time for the *Versuche* edition. The Lorenzo de' Medici madrigal in scene 7 (which appears to derive from the sixtieth and last stanzas of his Eclogue 'La Ritrozia') now makes its appearance for the first time.

The play again begins as in the first version, though Galileo's speech on the 'new age' has been slightly expanded; the second demonstration with Andrea and the full conversation with the procurator are restored. In scene 3 the episode with Mrs Sarti is brought back, leading to the (shortened) conclusion, 'They grab at it' (p. 28), while immediately before her entry Galileo's speech is given a new last sentence: 'Thinking is one of the greatest pleasures of the human race' (p. 27). Virginia is now made to leave before the reading of the letter to the grand duke. In scene 4 some of the fatuous remarks of the court ladies (e.g. 'Perfect poise!' and 'What diction!') are eliminated; the professors' proposal for a formal disputation is new, as is Federzoni's call for new textbooks.

In the plague scene the second half (b) is virtually as in the (revised) first version, but the first half has been revised, notably cutting Galileo's last remarks, with their reference to the uncertainty of remaining alive 'in times like these'. In the ball scene (7) a new poem for Galileo, which could be a quasi-Horatian variant on Herrick's 'Delight in Disorder', replaces the English one which we give, and Bellarmin's remarks about the Campagna peasants and the (social) need to attribute all the world's horrors to a 'great plan' are restored. In the sunspot scene (9) the episode with Mucius now comes near the start of the scene, which has been correspondingly rewritten; Mrs Sarti's speech (p. 72) has also been restored, as has Galileo's call for 'people who work with their hands' (p. 74), in lieu of the American version's too simple view that scientific work is not worth doing 'for less than the population at large'. The end of this scene ('I've got to know') is quite new.

In the carnival scene (10) the procession is now described briefly in a single stage direction at the end. In scene 11 the episode with Vanni is extended to emphasise Galileo's sense of security (and of his own comforts). Scene 12 restores the inquisitor's comments on papal politics and introduces the graffito about the Barberinis' love of art, as well as the exchange about condemning the doctrine and keeping its practical applications. For the slight changes in scenes 13 and 14 see pp. 267–268 above. There is in the Brecht Archive a sketch for the notion of a Hippocratic oath for scientists which was evidently noted down in America (in Brecht's homemade English) but for some reason not then worked into the play. (See Introduction, p. xv.) It goes thus:

ingenious dwarfs
Hypocratic
hypocrades Oath

Had I resisted, the natural sciences might have
something like the   of the physicians.
develloped their own Hypöcratic oath
mankind

Now, the most we can hope for will be a race of ingenious dwarfs who can be hired for any purpose who will, as on islands, produce whatever their masters demand.

means
what's the use of progress, if it is a
leaving behind of mankind? There even
a state of things could develop, when our
inventions

[Spelling and spacing as on Brecht's typescript, but not showing his corrections and deletions. From BBA 609/91, reproduced in Schumacher: *Drama und Geschichte*, 1965, p. 208.]

MOTHER COURAGE AND HER CHILDREN

Texts by Brecht

NOTE

The effect of the première of *Mother Courage and Her Children*, given in Zurich during the Second World War with the exceptional Therese Giehse in the title part, was to allow the bourgeois press to talk about a Niobe-like tragedy and the heart-rending vitality of all maternal creatures. This despite the pacifist and anti-fascist convictions of the Zurich Schauspielhaus and its predominantly émigré German actors. Thus forewarned, the playwright made certain changes for the Berlin production. What follows is the original text.

Scene 1, p. 117, line 14:

MOTHER COURAGE: . . . Look out for yourselves, you'll need to. And now up we get and on we go.
THE SERGEANT: I don't feel very well.
THE RECRUITER: Perhaps you caught a chill taking your helmet off in that wind.
The sergeant snatches back his helmet.
MOTHER COURAGE: Hey, gimme my papers, you. Someone else might ask to see them, and there'd I be with no papers.
She puts them all in her pewter box.
THE RECRUITER *to Eilif*: Have a look at them boots anyway. And then we men'll have one together. And come round behind the cart. I'll show you I got the bounty money on me.
THE SERGEANT: I don't get it, I'm always at the rear. Sergeant's safest job there is. You can send the others up front, cover themselves with glory. Me dinner hour's properly spoiled. Shan't be able to hold nowt down, I know.
MOTHER COURAGE *addressing him*: Mustn't let it prey on you so's you can't eat. Just stay at the rear. Here, take a swig of brandy, man. *Gives him a drink from the cart.*
THE RECRUITER *has taken Eilif by the arm and is leading him away up*

stage: If a bullet's got your name on there's nowt you can do about it. You drew a cross, that's all. Ten florins bounty money, then you're a gallant fellow fighting for the king and women'll be after you like flies. And you can clobber me free for insulting you. *Exeunt both.*

Dumb Kattrin, having watched this seduction, makes hoarse noises.

MOTHER COURAGE: All right, Kattrin, all right. Sergeant's not feeling well, he's superstitious, I hadn't realised. And now let's get moving. Where's Eilif gone?

SWISS CHEESE: Must have gone off with the recruiter. They was talking together the whole time.

Scene 5, p. 151, line 1:

MOTHER COURAGE *to the other*: Can't pay, that it? No money, no schnapps. They give us military marches, but catch them giving men their pay.

SOLDIER: I want my schnapps. I missed the looting. That double-crossing general only allowed an hour's looting in the town. He ain't an inhuman monster, he said. Town must of paid him.

THE CHAPLAIN *stumbles in*: There are people still lying in that yard. The peasant's family. Somebody give me a hand. I need linen.

The second soldier goes off with him.

MOTHER COURAGE: I got none. All my bandages was sold to regiment. I ain't tearing up my officers' shirts for that lot.

CHAPLAIN *calling back*: I need linen, I tell you.

MOTHER COURAGE *rummages in her cart*: I'm giving nowt. They'll never pay, and why, nowt to pay with.

CHAPLAIN *bending over a woman he has carried in*: Why d'you stay around during the gunfire?

PEASANT WOMAN *feebly*: Farm.

MOTHER COURAGE: Catch them abandoning anything. My lovely shirts! Tomorrow officers'll be around and I'll have nowt for 'em. *She throws down one which Kattrin gives to the peasant woman.* What's got into me, giving stuff away? Wasn't me started this war.

FIRST SOLDIER: Those are Protestants. What they have to be Protestants for?

MOTHER COURAGE: They ain't bothering about faith. They lost their farm.

SECOND SOLDIER: They're no Protestants. They're Catholics like us.

FIRST SOLDIER: No way of sorting 'em out in a bombardment.

A PEASANT *brought in by the chaplain*: My arm's gone.

The painful screams of a child are heard from the house.

THE CHAPLAIN *to the peasant woman*: Lie where you are.

MOTHER COURAGE: Get that child out of there!

Kattrin dashes in.

MOTHER COURAGE *tearing up shirts*: A hundred florins apiece. I'm ruined. Don't shift her as you're doing her bandage, it might be her back. *To Kattrin, who has rescued a baby from the ruins and is cradling it as she walks*: How nice, found another baby to cart around? Give it to its ma this instant, unless you'd have me fighting for hours to get it off you, like last time, d'you hear? *Kattrin pays no attention.* All your victories mean to me is losses. That's enough, padre, come on, easy with my linen for Christ sake.

THE CHAPLAIN: I need more, blood's coming through.

MOTHER COURAGE *referring to Kattrin*: Look at her, happy as a queen in all this misery; give it back at once, its mother's coming round. *As Kattrin reluctantly hands the baby back to its mother, Mother Courage tears up another shirt.* I can't give nowt, catch me, got to think of meself. *To the second soldier*: Don't stand there gawping, you go back and tell them cut out that music, we can see it's a victory with our own eyes. Help yourself to a glass of schnapps, padre, don't argue, I've enough troubles. *She has to climb down off the cart to pull her daughter away from the first soldier, who is drunk.* Thought you'd score another victory, you animal? You're not getting away like that till you've paid. *To the peasant*: Your kid won't go short. *Indicating the woman*: Help yourself to something for her. *To the first soldier*: Then leave that coat, it's stolen any road. *The first soldier goes lurching away. Mother Courage tears up further shirts.*

THE CHAPLAIN: There's still someone under there.

MOTHER COURAGE: Don't worry, I'm tearing up the lot.

Scene 7, p. 161, line 5:

High road. The chaplain, Mother Courage and Kattrin are pulling the cart. It is filthy and neglected, but hung with new wares none the less.

MOTHER COURAGE *sings*:

Some people think to live by looting [etc. with one or two small variations not affecting the meaning] . . .

The refrain 'The new year's come' is played by her on her mouth-organ.

Scene 12, p. 185, line 5:

THE PEASANTS: You must go, missis. There's only one more regiment behind that one. You can't go on your own.
MOTHER COURAGE: She's still breathing. Maybe she's falling asleep.

The effect of the peasant wars, the greatest disaster in German history, was to draw the teeth of the Reformation. That left business and cynicism. Along with her friends and guests and almost everyone else, Courage – and I say this as an aid to theatrical production – recognises the purely commercial nature of the war; indeed this is what attracts her to it. She believes in the war right to the end. It never even strikes her that in a war you need a big pair of scissors if you are to get your cut. Observers of catastrophes are wrong to imagine that the victims will learn from them. So long as the masses remain the passive *object* of politics they will never be able to view what happens to them as an experiment, merely as a fate; they learn no more from the catastrophe than a guinea pig learns about biology. It is not the playwright's job to open Courage's eyes at the end – she catches a glimpse of something around the middle of the play, at the end of scene 6, then loses sight of it once more – his concern is with the eyes of the audience.

['Anmerkung' from *Versuche* 9, Suhrkamp, Frankfurt, 1949, reprinted in GW *Stücke* 4.]

THE STORY

Curve of the dramaturgy

I

This scene emphasises that things are at the beginning. Courage's canteen business and the new war as new undertakings of a familiar sort. (They begin and they continue; they begin by continuing.) Needed: energy, enterprise, the prospect of new times, arrival of new business, together with new dangers. She longs for war and at the same time fears it. She wants to join in, but as a peaceable business woman, not in a warlike way. She wants to maintain her family during the war and by means of it. She wants to serve the army and also to keep out of its clutches.

Her children: With her eldest son she is afraid of his bravery, but counts on his cleverness. With the second she is afraid of his stupidity but counts on his honesty. With her daughter she is afraid of her pity but counts on her dumbness. Only her fears prove to be justified.

She is anticipating business; she is going to go bankrupt.

The play begins with the entrance (i.e. hanging about) of the men of war. The vast disorder of war begins with order, the vast disorganisation with organisation.

The peaceful landscape and the men of iron. Courage arrives four strong, goes away three strong.

2

War as a business idyll. Courage swindles peasants out of a capon; her elder son robs peasants of their oxen. He wins fame and possessions; she profits. She pillages the army somewhat too. The danger for her son becomes more real.

3

Being taken prisoner need be no disadvantage to her business. It seems that she had nothing to say against her younger son's joining the army as a paymaster. All she thinks necessary in his case is honesty. This is the finish of him. If he had not been connected with the army he would not have been killed. Her stubborn bargaining over her cart costs her son his life. She stops her daughter from becoming a whore – the only career open to her in wartime, and one which brings good fortune to Yvette. In any case she is no Antigone.

4

Courage stifles her human reactions (any kind of outrage, rebellion or criticism) for the sake of her business. She thinks capitulation will do something for her.

5

All the same, human reactions sometimes override her business principles. The general's victory leads to financial losses.

6

Business, meant to earn her daughter's (peacetime) dowry, leads to her wartime disfigurement. Courage counts on the length of the war, which is helpful to her finances but means spinsterhood for her daughter. Finally for the first time she curses the war which, from a business standpoint, she must needs want.

7

Peacetime is pleasant, if also ruinous. Thanks to the peace she does not get her son back, but loses him for good. In her daughter's case peace arrives too late. The son falls because he has applied the principles of war in peacetime. The former camp prostitute Yvette Pottier has prospered as a result of the war and married a colonel. The war starts up again. Will business start up again too?

8

Business is on the downgrade. The war is too long. Disorganisation and disorder on every side. In a song Courage (quâ beggar) curses all the human virtues as not only uncommercial but positively dangerous. For her daughter's sake she must give up the cook, who could have provided her with a roof over her head. She is bound to the war by pity for her daughter.

9

The daughter perishes because of her pity for other people's children. Courage goes on dragging her empty cart, alone, in the wake of the tattered army.

[From Werner Hecht (ed.): *Materialien zu Brechts 'Mutter Courage'*, Frankfurt, Suhrkamp, 1967, pp. 7–9.]

THREE DIARY NOTES

(i)

Going over *Mother Courage* I am quite pleased to see how war emerges as a vast field akin to the fields of modern physics, in which bodies experience peculiar deviations from their courses. Any calculation about the individual based on peacetime experience proves to be unreliable, bravery is no help, nor is caution, nor honesty, nor crookedness, nor brutality, nor pity: all are equally fatal. We are left with those same forces that turn peace into war, the ones that can't be named.

(ii)

Why is *Courage* a realist work?

It adopts a realist point of view on behalf of the people *vis-à-vis* all ideologies. To the people war is neither an uprising nor a business operation, merely a disaster.

Its point of view is not a moral one: that is to say, it is ethical, but without being derived from the currently prevailing morality.

The actions of the characters are given motives that can be recognised and allowed for and will facilitate dealing with real people.

The work functions in terms of the present state of consciousness of the majority of mankind.

(iii)

Rehearsing the new production of *Courage* (with Busch, Geschonneck and Lutz). Paying particular attention to the dialectical elements. Cook and chaplain in scene 8, where peace brings them both to the edge of the precipice, are fighting for their quarters: their respective setbacks make them better people. The two enemies meet amicably on the plane of reminiscent nostalgia for the war.

Working on Ruth's Model book is a grind; but it has to be done if only to show how many things have to be taken into account for a production.

[From Brecht's *Arbeitsjournal*, Suhrkamp, 1973, entries for 5 January 1941, 22 April 1941 and 4 June 1951. The new production by the Berliner Ensemble had its première in September 1951 and was then seen at the Paris International Theatre Festival in 1954. Ruth Berlau was a collaborator.]

THE MOTHER COURAGE MODEL

Now, after the great war, life goes on in our ruined cities, but it is a different life, the life of different or differently composed groups, guided or thwarted by new surroundings, new because so much has been destroyed. The great heaps of rubble are piled on the city's invaluable substructure, the water and drainage pipes, the gas mains and electric cables. Even those large buildings that have remained intact are affected by the damage and rubble around them, and may become an obstacle to planning. Temporary structures must be built and there is always a danger of their becoming permanent. All this is reflected in art, for our way of thinking is part of our way of living. In the theatre we set up models to fill the gap. They immediately meet with strong opposition from all supporters of the old ways, of the routine that masquerades as experience and of the conventionality that calls itself creative freedom. And they are endangered by those who take them up without having learned to use them. While meant to simplify matters, they are not simple to handle. They were designed not to make thought unnecessary, but to provoke it; not to replace but to compel artistic creation.

First of all we must imagine that the information which the printed text provides about certain events – in this case the adventures of Mother Courage and the losses she incurs – has to some extent been complemented; it has now been established that when the woman's dead son was brought to her she was sitting beside her mute daughter, and so on – the kind of information which an artist painting some historic incident can arrive at by questioning eye-witnesses. Later he can still change certain details as for one reason or another he may think advisable. Until one has learned to copy (and construct) models in a living and intelligent way, one had better not copy too much. Such things as the cook's makeup or Mother Courage's costume should not be imitated. The models should not be used to excess.

Pictures and descriptions of a performance are not enough. One does not learn much by reading that a character moves in a particular direction after a given sentence, even if the tone of the sentence, the way of walking, and a convincing motive can be supplied – which is very difficult. The persons available for the imitation are not the same as those of the pattern; with them it would not have come into being. Anyone who deserves the name of artist is unique; he represents something universal, but in his own individual way. He can neither be perfectly imitated nor give a perfect imitation. Nor is it so important for artists to imitate art as to imitate life. The use of models is a particular kind of art, and there is a limit to what can be learned from it. The aim must be neither to copy the pattern exactly nor to break away from it too quickly.

In studying what follows – a number of explanations and discoveries emerging from the rehearsal of a play – one should above all be led by the solutions of certain problems to consider the problems themselves.

Music

Paul Dessau's music for *Mother Courage* is not meant to be particularly easy; like the stage set, it left something to be supplied by the audience; in the act of listening they had to link the voices with the melody. Art is not a land of Cockaigne. In order to make the transition to the musical items, to let the music have its say, we lowered a musical emblem from the grid whenever there was a song which did not spring directly from the action, or which did spring from it but remained clearly apart. This consisted of a trumpet, a drum, a flag, and electric globes that lit up; a slight and delicate thing, pleasant to look at, even if scene 9 found it badly damaged. Some people regarded this as sheer playfulness, as an unrealistic element. But on the one hand playfulness in the theatre should not be condemned out of hand as long as it is kept within bounds, and on the other it was not wholly unrealistic, for it served to set the music apart from the reality of the action. We made use of it as a visible sign of the shift to another artistic level – that of music – and in order to give the right impression that these were musical insertions, rather than to lead people to think quite mistakenly that the songs 'sprang from the action'. People who object to this are quite simply opposed to anything intermittent, inorganic, pieced-together – this chiefly because they object to any shattering of illusion. What they ought to have objected to was not the tangible symbol of music, but the manner of fitting the musical numbers into the play: i.e. as insertions.

The musicians were placed so that they could be seen, in a box beside the stage – thus their performances became little concerts, independent contributions made at suitable points in the play. The box communicated with the stage, so that a musician or two could occasionally go backstage for trumpet calls or when music occurred as part of the action.

We began with the overture. It was a bit thin, for it was performed by only four musicians; still, it was a reasonably ceremonious preparation for the confusions of war.

Stage Design

For the production we are describing, at the Deutsches Theater in Berlin, we used the well-known model devised by Teo Otto during the war for the Zurich Schauspielhaus. There was a permanent framework of huge screens, making use of such materials as one would expect to find in the military encampments of the seventeenth century: tenting, wooden posts lashed together with ropes, etc. Three-dimensional structures, realistic both as to construction and as to material, were placed on the stage to represent such buildings as the parsonage and the peasants' house, but in artistic abbreviation, only so much being shown as was necessary for the action. Coloured projections were thrown on the cyclorama, and the revolving stage was used to give the impression of travel – we varied the size and position of the screens and used them only for the camp scenes, so as to distinguish these from the scenes on the highway. The Berlin stage designer made his own versions of the buildings (in scenes 2, 4, 5, 9, 10 and 11), but on the same principle. We dispensed with the background projections used in Zurich and hung the names of the various countries over the stage in large black letters. We used an even, white light, as much of it as our equipment permitted. In this way we eliminated any vestige of 'atmosphere' that could easily have given the incidents a romantic tinge. We retained almost everything else down to the smallest details (chopping block, hearth, etc.), particularly the admirable positionings of the cart. This last was very important because it determined much of the grouping and movement from the outset.

Surprisingly little is lost by the sacrifice of complete freedom of 'artistic creation'. You have to start somewhere, with something, and it may as well be with something that has already been fully thought out. Freedom will be acquired through the principle of contradiction, which is continually active and vocal in all of us.

Realistic Theatre and Illusion

Writing in 1826, Goethe spoke of the 'inadequacy of the English wooden stage' of Shakespeare's day. He says: 'There is no trace here of the aids to naturalness to which we have gradually become accustomed through the improvement in machinery, in the art of perspective and in costuming.' 'Who?' he asks, 'would tolerate such a thing today? Under those conditions Shakespeare's plays would become highly interesting fairy tales, narrated by a number of persons who tried to increase their effectiveness somewhat by making up as the characters, by coming and going and carrying out the movements necessary to the story, but left it to the audience to imagine as many paradises and palaces as they pleased on the empty stage.'

Since he wrote these words, the mechanical equipment of our theatres has been improving for a hundred years, and 'aids to naturalness' have led to such emphasis on illusion that we late-comers would be more inclined to put up with Shakespeare on an empty stage than with a Shakespeare who had ceased to require or provoke any use of the imagination.

In Goethe's day such improvement as had been made in the mechanics of illusion was relatively harmless, since the machinery was so imperfect, so much 'in the childhood of its beginnings', that theatre itself was still a reality and both imagination and ingenuity could still be employed to turn nature into art. The sets were still theatrical displays, in which the stage designer gave an artistic and poetic interpretation of the places concerned.

The bourgeois classical theatre occupied a happy halfway point on the road to naturalistic illusionism. Stage machinery provided enough elements of illusion to improve the representation of some aspects of reality, but not so much as to make the audience feel that they were no longer in a theatre; art had not yet come to signify the obliteration of all indications that art is at work. Since there was no electricity, lighting effects were still primitive; where poor taste decreed sunset effects, poor equipment prevented total enchantment. The Meiningers' authentic costumes came later; they were usually magnificent, though not always beautiful, and they were after all compensated by an inauthentic manner of speaking. In short, theatre remained the theatre, at least where it failed in its business of deception. Today the restoration of the theatre's reality as theatre is a precondition for any realistic representation of human relations. Too much heightening of the illusion in the setting, along with a 'magnetic' manner of acting which gives the spectator the illusion of being present at a fleeting, fortuitous 'real' event, create such an impression of naturalness that one can no longer interpose one's judgment, imagination or reactions, and must simply conform by sharing in the experience and becoming one of 'nature's' objects. The illusion created by the theatre must be a partial one, so that it can always be recognised as illusion. Reality, however completely represented, must be changed by art, in order that it may be seen to be subject to change and treated as such.

That is why we are demanding naturalness today – because we want to change the nature of our human relations.

Elements of Illusion

No doubt the sight of the cyclorama behind a completely empty stage (in the prologue and in the seventh and last scenes) creates the illusion of a flat landscape with the sky above it. There is no objection to this, because there must be some stirring of poetry in the soul of the spectator if such an illusion is to come about. Thanks to the ease with which it is created, the actors are able to suggest by their manner of playing, at the beginning that a wide horizon lies open to the business enterprise of the little family of provisioners, then at the end that the exhausted seeker after fortune is faced by boundless devastation. And we can always hope that this substantial impression of the play will combine with a formal one: that when the spectator sees the empty stage, soon to be inhabited, he will be able to share in the initial void from which everything arises. On this tabula rasa, he knows, the actors have been working for weeks, testing first one detail, then another, coming to know the incidents of the chronicle by portraying them, and portraying them by judging them. And now the play is starting and Mother Courage's cart comes rolling on to the stage.

If in big matters such a thing as a beautiful approximation is possible, in matters of detail it is not. A realistic portrayal requires carefully worked-out detail in costumes and props, for here the imagination of the audience can add nothing. All implements connected with working and eating must have been most lovingly made. And the costumes, of course, cannot be as for a folklore festival; they must show signs of individuality and social class. They have been worn for a longer or shorter time, are made of cheaper or more expensive material, are well or not so well taken care of, etc.

The costumes for this production of *Mother Courage* were by [Kurt] Palm.

What is a performance of Mother Courage and Her Children *primarily meant to show?*

That in wartime the big profits are not made by little people. That war, which is a continuation of business by other means, makes the human virtues fatal even to their possessors. That no sacrifice is too great for the struggle against war.

Prologue

By way of a prologue, Mother Courage and her little family were shown on their way to the war zone. Mother Courage sang her business song from scene 1 (so that in scene 1 her answer 'In business' is followed immediately by the sergeant's question: 'Halt! Who are you lot with?'). After the overture, to spare the performer the exertion of singing against the rumbling of the revolve, the first stanza was played on a record, the house being darkened. Then the prologue began.

The Long Road to War

The linen half-curtain, on which in the following the titles of the scenes are projected, opens and Mother Courage's cart is rolled forward against the movement of the revolve.

The cart is a cross between a military vehicle and a general store. A sign affixed to the side of it says: 'Second Finnish Regiment' and another 'Mother Courage, Groceries'. On the canvas Swedish pork sausages are displayed next to a flag with a price tag indicating 'Four Florins'. The cart will undergo several changes in the course of the chronicle. There will be sometimes more, sometimes less merchandise hanging on it, the canvas will be dirtier or cleaner, the letters on the signs will be faded and then again freshly painted, depending on the state of business. Now, at the start, it is clean and richly covered with wares.

The cart is pulled by the two sons. They sing the second stanza of Mother Courage's Business Song: 'Captains, how can you make them face it – / March off to death without a brew?' On the box sit dumb Kattrin, playing the jew's harp, and Mother Courage. Courage is sitting in lazy comfort, swaying with the cart and yawning. Everything, including her one backward glance, indicates that the cart has come a long way.

We had conceived of the song as a dramatic entrance, lusty and cocky – we had the last scene of the play in mind. But Weigel saw it as a realistic business song and suggested that it be used to picture the long journey to the war. Such are the ideas of great actors.

Once this was settled, it seemed to us that by showing the business woman's long journey to the war zone we would be showing clearly enough that she was an active and voluntary participant in the war. But certain reviews and many discussions with persons who had seen the play showed that a good many people regarded Mother Courage merely as a representative of the 'little people' who 'become involved in the war in spite of themselves', who are 'helpless victims of the war', and so on. A deeply engrained habit leads the theatregoer to pick out the more emotional utterances of the characters and overlook everything else. Like descriptions of landscapes in novels, references to business are received with boredom. The 'business atmosphere' is simply the air one breathes and as such requires no special mention. And so, regardless of all our efforts to represent the war as an aggregate of business deals, the discussions showed time and time again that people regarded it as a timeless abstraction.

Too Short can be Too Long

The two stanzas of the opening song plus the pause between them during which the cart rolls silently along, take up a certain amount of time, too much time it seemed to us at first in rehearsal. But when we cut the second stanza, the prologue seemed longer, and when we prolonged the pause between the stanzas, it seemed shorter.
[. . .]

I

The business woman Anna Fierling, known as Mother Courage, encounters the Swedish army

Recruiters are going about the country looking for cannon fodder. Mother Courage introduces her mixed family, acquired in various theatres of war, to a sergeant. The canteen woman defends her sons against the recruiters with a knife. She sees that her sons are listening to the recruiters and predicts that the sergeant will meet an early death. To make her children afraid of the war, she has them draw black crosses as well. Thanks to a small business deal, she nevertheless loses her brave son. And the sergeant leaves her with a prophecy:

'Like the war to nourish you?
Have to feed it something too.'

Overall arrangement

Recruiters are going about the country looking for cannon fodder. On the empty stage the sergeant and the recruiter are standing right front on the lookout, complaining in muffled voices of the difficulty of finding cannon fodder for their general. The city of which the sergeant speaks is assumed to be in the orchestra. Mother Courage's cart appears and the recruiters' mouths water at the sight of the young men. The sergeant cries 'Halt!' and the cart stops.

Mother Courage introduces her mixed family, acquired in various theatres of war, to a sergeant. The professionals of commerce and of war meet, the war can start. At the sight of the military, the Fierlings may hesitate for a moment as though afraid: the soldiers of their own side are also enemies; the army gives, but it also takes. Mother

Courage's 'Morning, sergeant' is spoken in the same curt, military monotone as his 'Morning, all.' Climbing down from her cart, she makes it clear that she regards showing her papers as a formality, superfluous among professionals ('All right, we'll run through the whole routine'). She introduces her little family, acquired in various theatres of war, in a jocular tone: she puts on a bit of a 'Mother Courage' act.

The cart and the children are on the left, the recruiters on the right. Mother Courage crosses over with her tin box full of papers. She has been summoned, but she is also sallying forth to scout and do business. She describes her children from the other side of the stage, as though better able to take them in from a distance. The recruiter makes forays behind her back, stalking the sons, tempting them. The pivotal point is in the lines: 'I bet you could use a good pistol, or a belt buckle?' and 'I could use something else.'

The canteen woman defends her sons against the recruiters with a knife. The sergeant leaves her standing there and goes over to the sons, followed by the recruiter. He thumps their chests, feels their calves. He goes back and stands before Mother Courage: 'Why aren't they in the army?' The recruiter has stayed with the sons: 'Let's see if you're a chicken.' Mother Courage runs over, thrusts herself between the recruiter and her son: 'He's a chicken.' The recruiter goes over to the sergeant (on the right) and complains: 'He was crudely offensive'; Mother Courage snatches her Eilif away. The sergeant tries to reason, but Mother Courage pulls a knife and stands there in a rage, guarding her sons.

Mother Courage sees that her sons are listening to the recruiter and predicts that the sergeant will meet an early death. Again she goes over to the sergeant ('Give me your helmet'). Her children follow her and look on, gaping. The recruiter makes a flank movement, comes up to Eilif from behind and speaks to him.

When after some hesitation the sergeant has drawn his black cross, the children, satisfied, go back to the cart, but the recruiter follows them. And when Mother Courage turns ('I've got to take advantage'), she sees the recruiter between her sons; he has his arms around their shoulders.

To make her children afraid of the war, Mother Courage has them draw black crosses as well. The rebellion in her own ranks is in full swing. She runs angrily behind her cart to paint black crosses for her children. When she returns to the cart's shaft with the helmet, the recruiter, grinning, leaves the children to her and goes back (right) to the sergeant. When the sombre ceremony is over, Mother Courage goes to the sergeant, returns his helmet, and with fluttering skirts climbs up on the seat of the cart. The sons have harnessed themselves, the cart starts moving. Mother Courage has mastered the situation.

Because of a small business deal, she nevertheless loses her brave son. But the sergeant has only been half defeated; on the recruiter's advice, he offers to make a purchase. Electrified, Mother Courage climbs down from the cart and the sergeant draws her off left behind the cart. While the deal is in progress, the recruiter takes the harness off Eilif and leads him away. Kattrin sees this, climbs down from the cart and tries in vain to call her mother's attention to Eilif's disappearance. But Mother Courage is deep in her bargaining. Only after she has snapped her moneybag shut does she notice his absence. For a moment she has to sit down on the cart shaft, still holding her buckles. Then she angrily flings them into the cart, and the family, with one less member, moves gloomily off.

And the sergeant leaves her with a prophecy. Laughing, he predicts that if she wants to live off the war, she will also have to give the war its due.

[. . .]

The recruiters

The empty stage of the prologue was transformed into a specific locality by means of a few clumps of wintry grass marking the edge of a highway. Here the military men stand waiting, freezing in their armour.

The great disorder of war begins with order, disorganisation with organisation. The troublemakers have troubles of their own. We hear complaints to the effect that it takes intelligence to get a war started. The military are businessmen. The sergeant has a little book that he consults, the recruiter has a map to help him fight with geography. The fusion of war and business cannot be established too soon.

Grouping

There will be some difficulty in persuading the actors playing the sergeant and the recruiter to stay together and in one place until Mother Courage's cart appears. In our theatre, groups always show a strong tendency to break up, partly because each actor believes he can heighten audience interest by moving about and changing his position, and partly because he wants to be alone, so as to divert the attention of the audience from the group to himself. But there is no reason not to leave the military men together; on the contrary, both the image and the argument would be impaired by a change of position.

Changes of position

Positions should be retained as long as there is no compelling reason for changing them – and a desire for variety is not a compelling reason. If one gives in to a desire for variety, the consequence is a devaluation of all movement on the stage; the spectator ceases to look for a specific meaning behind each movement, he stops taking movement seriously. But, especially at the crucial points in the action, the full impact of a change of position must not be weakened. Legitimate variety is obtained by ascertaining the crucial points and planning the arrangement around them. For example, the recruiters have been listening to Mother Courage; she has succeeded in diverting and entertaining them with her talk and so putting them in a good humour; so far there has been only one ominous circumstance: the sergeant has asked for her papers; but he has not examined them – his only purpose was to prolong their stay. She takes the next step (physically too: she goes up to the sergeant, takes hold of his belt buckle, and says: 'I bet you could use a belt-buckle?'), she tries to sell them something, and that is when the recruiters spring into action. The sergeant says ominously: 'I could use something else' and along with the recruiter goes over to the sons at the cart's shaft. The recruiters look the sons over as they would horses. The crucial point is accented when the sergeant goes back to Mother Courage, comes to a standstill before her, and asks: 'Why are they dodging their military service?' (The effect of such movements should not be weakened by having the actors speak during them.) If changes of position are needed to make certain developments clear to the audience, the movement must be utilised to express something significant for the action and for this particular moment; if nothing of the sort can be found, it is advisable to review the whole arrangement up to this point; it will probably be seen to be at fault, because the sole purpose of an arrangement is to express the action, and the action (it is to be hoped) involves a logical development of incidents, which the arrangement need only present.

On details

On the brightly lighted stage every detail, even the smallest, must of course be acted out to the full. This is especially true of actions which on our stage are glossed over almost as a matter of principle, such as payment on conclusion of a sale. Here Weigel devised (for the sale of the buckle in 1, the sale of the capon in 2, the sale of drinks in 5 and 6, the handing out of the burial money in 12, etc.) a little gesture of her own: she audibly snaps shut the leather moneybag that she wears slung from her neck. It is indeed difficult in rehearsals to resist the impatience of actors who are in the habit of trying to sweep an audience off its feet, and to work out the details painstakingly and inventively in accordance with the principle of epic theatre: *one thing after another*. Even minute details are very revealing, e.g. the fact that when the recruiters step up to her sons and feel their muscles as if they were horses, Mother Courage displays maternal pride for a moment, until the sergeant's question ('Why are they dodging their military service?') shows her the danger their qualities put them in: then she rushes between her sons and the recruiters. The pace at rehearsals should be slow, if only to make it possible to work out details; determining the pace of the performance is another matter and comes later.

A detail

In pulling a knife, Mother Courage shows no savagery. She is merely showing how far she will go in defending her children. The performer must show that Mother Courage is familiar with such situations and knows how to handle them.

Mother Courage has her children draw lots. Only by a mild tirade and by eloquently averting her face when Swiss Cheese draws his slip from the helmet – in other words by a slightly exaggerated display of impartiality (see for yourself, no sleight-of-hand, no tricks) does the actress show that Mother Courage knows she has been tampering with fate – otherwise she fully believes what she says, namely, that in certain situations certain of her children's qualities and defects could be fatal.

Mother Courage predicts that the sergeant will meet an early death. We discovered that Mother Courage had to turn around towards Eilif before stepping up to the sergeant to let him draw his lot. Otherwise it would not have been understood that she does this in order to frighten her warlike son away from the war.

The belt-buckle deal. Mother Courage loses her son to the recruiter because she can't resist the temptation to sell a belt buckle. After climbing down from the cart to bring the sergeant the buckle, she must at first show a certain amount of distrust by looking around anxiously for the recruiter. Once the sergeant, seizing the string of buckles, has drawn her behind the cart, her distrust shifts to the area of business. When she goes to get schnapps for the sergeant, she takes the buckle, which has not yet been paid for, out of his hands; and she bites into the coin. The sergeant is dismayed at her distrust.

If the distrust at the beginning were omitted, we should have a stupid, utterly uninteresting woman, or a person with a passion for business but no experience. The distrust must not be absent, it must merely be too weak to do any good.

Pantomime

The recruiter must act out the scene where he removes the harness from Eilif ('women'll be after you like flies'). He is freeing him from his yoke.

He has forced a florin on him; holding out his fist with the florin in it in front of him, Eilif goes off as if in a trance.

Proportion

Weigel showed a masterful sense of proportion in playing Mother Courage's reaction to the abduction of her brave son. She showed dismay rather than horror. In becoming a soldier, her son has not been lost, he is merely in danger. And she will lose other children. To show that she knows very well why Eilif is no longer with her, Weigel let her string of belt buckles drag on the ground and threw it angrily into the cart after holding it between her legs while sitting on the shaft for a few moments to rest. And she does not look her daughter in the face as she puts her into Eilif's harness.

2

Before the fortress of Wallhof Mother Courage meets her brave son again

Mother Courage sells provisions at exorbitant prices in the Swedish camp; while driving a hard bargain over a capon, she makes the acquaintance of an army cook who is to play an important part in her life. The Swedish general brings a young soldier into his tent and honours him for his bravery. Mother Courage recognises her lost son in the young soldier; taking advantage of the meal in Eilif's honour, she gets a steep price for her capon. Eilif relates his heroic deed and Mother Courage, while plucking her capon in the kitchen adjoining the tent, expresses opinions about rotten generals. Eilif does a sword dance and his mother answers with a song. Eilif hugs his mother and gets a slap in the face for putting himself in danger with his heroism.

Overall arrangement

Mother Courage sells provisions at exorbitant prices in the Swedish camp before the fortress of Wallhof; while driving a hard bargain over a capon she makes the acquaintance of an army cook who is to play an important part in her life. In this scene the movement occurs at the pivotal point ('You know what I'm going to do?'). The cook stops peeling his carrots, fishes a piece of rotten meat out of the garbage barrel and takes it over to the butcher's block. Courage's attempt at blackmail has failed.

The Swedish general brings a young soldier into his tent and makes a short speech commending him for his bravery. A drumroll outside the tent announces the arrival of highly placed persons. It need not be clear whether the general drinks in order to honour the soldier or honours the soldier in order to drink. Meanwhile in the kitchen adjoining the tent the cook is preparing the meal. Courage stays right there with her capon.

Mother Courage recognises her lost son in the young soldier; taking advantage of the meal in Eilif's honour, she get a steep price for her capon. Mother Courage is overcome with joy at seeing her son, but not too overcome to turn Eilif's reappearance to her business advantage. Meanwhile, the general gets the chaplain to bring him a spill to light his clay pipe.

Eilif relates his heroic deed and Mother Courage, while plucking her capon in the kitchen, expresses opinions about rotten generals. At first the mother beams as she listens to the story, then her face clouds over, and in the end she throws her capon angrily into the tub in front of her. Resuming her work, she lets it be known what she thinks of the general; at the same time the general in the tent shows her son on the map what new deeds of heroism he needs him for.

Eilif does a sword dance and his mother answers with a song. Eilif does his sword dance front stage near the partition between tent and kitchen. Mother Courage creeps up to the partition to finish the song. Then she goes back to her tub but remains standing.

Eilif hugs his mother and gets a slap in the face for putting himself in danger with his heroism.

The capon deal

The bargaining over the capon between Courage and the cook served among other things to establish the beginning of their tender relationship. Both showed pleasure in the bargaining, and the cook expressed his admiration not only for her ready tongue but also for the shrewdness with which she exploited the honouring of her son for business purposes. Courage in turn was amused at the way the cook fished the chunk of rotten beef out of the garbage barrel with the tip of his long meat knife and carried it, carefully as though it were a precious object – though to be kept at a safe distance from one's nose – over to his kitchen table. The actor Bildt played the scene brilliantly, making the cook, a Don Juan fired by budding passion, prepare the capon with theatrical elegance. This dumb show, it should be observed, was performed with restraint, so that it did not distract from the scene in the tent.

Bildt even took the trouble to acquire a Dutch accent with the help of a Dutchman.

[. . .]

The general

The general was made into something of a cliché. Too much gruff bluster, and the peformance showed too little about the ruling class. It would have been better to make him an effete Swedish aristocrat, who honours the brave soldier as a matter of routine action, almost absently. If this had been done, his very entrance – he is drunk, supports himself on the guest of honour, and heads straight for the wine jug – would have been more instructive. As it was, one saw little more than rowdy drunkenness.

[. . .]

The war of religion

The general's treatment of the chaplain is meant to show the role of religion in a war of religion. This was played rather crudely. The general has him bring the burning spill for his pipe and contemptuously pours wine over his coat; with his eyes on Eilif, the chaplain wipes the hem of his cassock, half protesting, half taking it as a joke. He is not invited to sit down to table like the young murderer, nor is he given anything to drink. But what shows his position most clearly is the undignified way, resulting from the indignity of his position, with which he sits down at table and pours himself wine when the general leads the young soldier, in whose presence all this is enacted, to the map on the tent wall, thereby leaving the table unoccupied. This position is the source of the chaplain's cynicism.

Eilif's dance

The brave son's short sword dance must be executed with passion as well as ease. The young man is imitating a dance he has seen somewhere. It is not easy to make such things evident.

Costume: Eilif has a cheap, dented breastplate and is still wearing his frayed trousers. Not until scene 8 (the outbreak of peace) does he wear expensive clothing and gear; he dies rich.

A detail

During her angry speech about rotten generals Courage plucks her capon violently, giving the plucking a kind of symbolic significance. Brief bursts of laughter from the amused cook interrupt her blasphemies.

[. . .]

3

Mother Courage switches from the Lutheran to the Catholic camp and loses her honest son Swiss Cheese

Black-marketing in ammunition. Mother Courage serves a camp whore and warns her daughter not to take up with soldiers. While Courage flirts with the cook and the chaplain, dumb Kattrin tries on the whore's hat and shoes. Surprise attack. First meal in the Catholic camp. Conversation between brother and sister and arrest of Swiss Cheese. Mother Courage mortgages her cart to the camp whore in order to ransom Swiss Cheese. Courage haggles over the amount of the bribe. She haggles too long and hears the volley that lays Swiss Cheese low. Dumb Kattrin stands beside her mother to wait for the dead Swiss Cheese. For fear of giving herself away, Courage denies her dead son.

Overall arrangement

During the whole scene the cart stands left with its shaft pointed towards the audience, so that those to the left of it are not seen by those on the right. Centre rear there is a flagpole, right front a barrel serving as a dining table. The scene is divided into four parts: *The surprise attack, The arrest of the honest son, The bargaining, The denial*. After the first two parts the half-curtain is drawn; after the third part the stage is darkened.

Black-marketing in ammunition. Mother Courage enters from the left, followed by an ordnance officer who is trying to talk her into something. For a moment she stands front stage with him; after 'Not at that price', she turns away from him and sits down on a box near the cart, where Swiss Cheese is already sitting. The business is conducted in an undertone. Kattrin is called away from taking down the washing and goes behind the cart left with the ordnance officer. Courage has started mending Swiss Cheese's pants; while working, she admonishes him to be honest. Returning from the other side of the cart, the ordnance officer takes him away with him. This and the following scenes have the tone of an idyll.

Mother Courage serves a camp whore and warns her daughter not to take up with soldiers. Taking her sewing, Courage sits down with the Pottier woman. Kattrin listens to their conversation as she takes the washing off the line. After her song, Pottier, with a conspicuously whorish gait, goes behind the cart.

While Courage flirts with the cook and the chaplain, dumb Kattrin tries on the whore's hat and shoes. After some brief banter, Mother Courage leads her guests behind the cart for a glass of wine and they strike up a political conversation. After the inserted sentence 'This is a war of faith', the cook ironically starts singing the hymn 'A stronghold sure'. This gives Kattrin time to try on Yvette's hat and shoes.

Surprise attack. The fixed point amid all the running and shouting of the surprise attack is the chaplain, who stands still and gets in everybody's way. The rest of the arrangement follows from the printed text.

First meal in the Catholic camp. The chaplain, now Mother

Courage's potboy, joins the little family around the cooking pot; Swiss Cheese keeps slightly to one side; he wants to get away.

Conversation between brother and sister and arrest of Swiss Cheese. The conversation between brother and sister takes place at the improvised dining table. When Kattrin sees the spy behind the cart, she tries to stop her brother from climbing into it. When Courage comes back with the chaplain, Kattrin runs towards her as far as the centre of the stage. Courage, the chaplain and Kattrin group themselves around the table, waiting for the Catholics.

Mother Courage tries to mortgage her wagon to the camp whore in order to ransom Swiss Cheese. The chaplain runs to meet Courage; she is exhausted and he catches her in his arms in front of the cart. She quickly frees herself from his embrace, which has restored her strength a little, and starts thinking. Her plan is all ready when Pottier comes along with the colonel. Pottier leaves the colonel standing there, runs over to Courage, gives her the kiss of Judas, runs back to her cavalier, and then crawls avidly into the cart. Courage pulls her out, curses her, and sends her off with a push to negotiate over Swiss Cheese.

Mother Courage haggles over the amount of the bribe. Courage has set Kattrin and the chaplain to washing glasses and scouring knives, thus creating a certain atmosphere of siege. Standing centre stage between her family and the whore, she refuses to give up her cart entirely – she has fought too hard for it. She sits down again to scour knives and does not stand up when Pottier comes back with the news that the soldiers are asking two hundred florins. Now she is willing to pay.

Mother Courage hears the volley that lays Swiss Cheese low. No sooner has Courage sent Pottier away than she suddenly stands up and says: 'I think I bargained too long.' The volley rings out, the chaplain leaves her and goes behind the wagon. It grows dark.

For fear of giving herself away, Courage denies her dead son. Yvette walks slowly out from behind the wagon. She scolds Courage, warns her not to give herself away, and brings Kattrin out from behind the wagon. Her face averted, Kattrin goes to her mother and stands behind her. Swiss Cheese is brought in. His mother goes over to him and denies him.

Movements and groupings

The arrangement of the movements and groupings must follow the rhythm of the story and give pictorial expression to the action.

In scene 3 a camp idyll is disrupted by the enemy's surprise attack.

The idyll should be composed from the start in such a way as to make it possible to show a maximum of disruption. It must leave room for people to run to and fro in clearly laid-out confusion; the parts of the stage must be able to change their functions.

At the beginning of the scene Kattrin is hanging out washing on a clothes-line stretched between the cart and the cannon right rear so that Courage can hurriedly take it down at the end of the scene. In order to rescue her washing, Courage must go diagonally right across the stage. Kattrin sits huddled by the barrel right front, where at the beginning Yvette was being served as a customer; Courage takes soot from the cart and brings it to the barrel to rub on her daughter's face. The same place which up until then had been devoted exclusively to business is now the scene of a private incident. Carrying the cash-box, Swiss Cheese enters diagonally from right rear to the cart left front in such a way that his path crosses that of Courage hurrying to her daughter. First she runs a few steps past him, but she has seen the cash box and turns round towards him just as he is about to enter the cart. She stands for a moment like a hen between two endangered chicks, undecided which to save first. While she is smearing her daughter's face, her son hides the cash box in the cart; she cannot reprove him until she has finished with her daughter and comes back out of the cart. She is still standing beside him when the chaplain rushes out from behind the cart and points to the Swedish flag. Courage runs to it centre rear and takes it down.

The camp idyll that is disrupted by the attack must be divided into distinct parts. After the shady little deal in black-market ammunition has been completed by the cart steps, Swiss Cheese followed by the ordnance officer goes out right. The ordnance officer recognises the camp whore who is sitting by the barrel, sewing her hat; he looks away in disgust. Yvette shouts something after him, and then, when the centre of gravity has shifted to the right side of the stage, Courage also comes slowly over to the barrel. (A little later Kattrin follows, coming out from behind the cart and starting once more to hang up the washing.) The two women talk and Kattrin listens as she hangs up the washing. Yvette sings her song. With a provocative gait, she goes out from right front to left rear. Kattrin watches her and is admonished by her mother. The cook and the chaplain come in from the right rear. After a brief bit of banter during which they attract the attention of the audience to Kattrin by the attention they pay to her, Mother Courage leads them behind the wagon. The political discussion and Kattrin's pantomine follow. She imitates Yvette, walking over the same ground. The alarm begins with the ordnance officer and soldiers running in from right rear. The cook goes out in that direction after Courage has run to the cannon to rescue her washing and Kattrin to the barrel to hide her feet.

Important

Courage's unflagging readiness to work is important. She is hardly ever seen not working. It is her energy and competence that make her lack of success so shattering.

A tiny scene

The tiny scene at the beginning of 3, in which army property is black-marketed, shows the general and matter-of-fact corruption in army camps during the great war of religion. The honest son listens with half an ear, as to something quite usual, his mother does not conceal the crooked business from him, but admonishes him to be honest because he is not bright. His heeding of this advice is going to cost him his life.

Yvette Pottier

Kattrin has the example of Yvette before her. She herself must work hard; the whore drinks and lolls about. For Kattrin too the only form of love available in the midst of the war would be prostitution. Yvette sings a song showing that other forms of love lead to grave trouble. At times the whore becomes powerful by selling herself at a high price. Mother Courage, who only sells boots, must struggle desperately to defend her cart against her. Mother Courage of course makes no moral condemnation of Yvette and her special type of business.

The colonel

The colonel whom Yvette lugs in to buy Courage's cart for her is difficult to play, because he is a purely negative quantity. His only function is to show the price the whore must pay for her rise in life; consequently he must be repellent. [Georg-Peter] Pilz portrayed the aged colonel subtly, making him mime an ardent passion of which he was not for one moment capable. The old man's lechery erupted as though in response to a cue, and he seemed to forget his surroundings. An instant later he forgot his lechery and stared absently into the void.

The actor produced a striking effect with his stick. In his passionate moments he pressed it to the ground so hard that it bent; an instant later it snapped straight – this suggested loathsome aggressive impotence and produced an irresistibly comic effect. Considerable elegance is required to keep such a performance within the bounds of good taste.

A detail

Having finished hanging up the washing, Kattrin stares open-mouthed at the visitors from the general's tent. The cook honours her with special attention as he follows Courage behind the cart. This is probably what gives her the idea of stealing Yvette's weapons.

The two sides

While on one side of the cart the war is being discussed with frank mockery, Kattrin is appropriating some of the tools of the whore's trade and practising Yvette's swaying gait, which she has just seen. Here [Angelika] Hurwicz's facial expression was strained and deeply serious.

'A stronghold sure'

The first part of Kattrin's pantomime occurs after 'I wasn't mistaken in your face.' (The cook added: 'This is a war of faith.') At this point Courage, the cook and the chaplain placed themselves to one side of the cart in such a way that they could not see Kattrin, and struck up 'A stronghold sure'. They sang it with feeling, casting anxious glances around them as though such a song were illegal in the Swedish camp.

The surprise attack

It must be brought out that Courage is used to such surprises and knows how to handle them. Before she thinks about saving the cannon, she rescues her washing. She helps the chaplain to disguise himself, she smears her daughter's face, she tells her son to throw the cash box away, she takes down the Swedish flag. All this she does as a matter of routine, but by no means calmly.

[. . .]

The meal

Courage has prepared it. Enlarged by the new employee who was a chaplain only that morning, the little family still seem somewhat flurried; in talking they look around like prisoners, but the mother is making jokes again; the Catholics, she says, need trousers as much as the Protestants. They have not learned that honesty is just as mortally dangerous among Catholics as among Lutherans.

The chaplain

The chaplain has found a refuge. He has his own bowl to eat from and he makes himself awkwardly useful, hauls buckets of water, scours knives, and so on. Otherwise he is still an outsider. For this reason or because of his phlegmatic disposition he shows no exaggerated involvement in the tragedy of the honest son. While Courage is engaged in her unduly prolonged bargaining, he looks upon her simply as his source of support.

Swiss Cheese

It seems to be hard for an actor to repress his pity for the character he is playing and not to reveal his knowledge of his impending death. In speaking to his sister Swiss Cheese shows no forebodings; this is what makes him so moving when he is taken.

Brother and sister

The short conversation between dumb Kattrin and Swiss Cheese is quiet and not without tenderness. Shortly before the destruction we are shown for the last time what is to be destroyed.

The scene goes back to an old Japanese play in which two boys conclude a friendship pact. Their way of doing this is that one shows the other a flying bird, while the second shows the first a cloud.

A detail

Kattrin gesticulates too wildly in telling her mother about the arrest of Swiss Cheese. Consequently Courage does not understand her and says: 'Use your hands, I don't like it when you howl like a dog, what'll his reverence say? Makes him uncomfortable.' Hurwicz made Kattrin pull herself together and nod She understands this argument, it is a strong one.

A detail

While the sergeant was questioning her in the presence of Swiss Cheese, Courage rummaged in a basket – a busy business woman with no time for formalities. But after the sentence: 'And don't you twist his shoulder' she ran after the soldiers who were leading him away.

Yvette's three trips

Yvette runs back and forth three times for the sake of Courage's son and her cart. Her anger changes from mere anger at Courage's attempt to swindle her by paying her out of the regimental cash box to anger at Courage's betrayal of her son.

Kattrin and the bargaining over Swiss Cheese

The portrayal of dumb Kattrin is not realistic if her goodness is stressed to the point of making her oppose her mother's attempt to get the amount of the bribe reduced. She runs off from scouring the knives when she begins to see that the bargaining has been going on too long. When after the execution Yvette sends her ahead and she goes to her mother with her face averted, there may be a reproach in this – but above all she cannot look her in the face.

The denial

Courage is sitting, holding the hand of her daughter who is standing. When the soldiers come in with the dead boy and she is asked to look at him, she stands up, goes over, looks at him, shakes her head, goes back and sits down. During all this she has an obstinate expression, her lower lip thrust forward. Here Weigel's recklessness in throwing away her rôle reached its highest point.

(The actor playing the sergeant can command the spectator's

astonishment by looking around at his men in astonishment at such hardness.)

Observation

Her look of extreme suffering after she has heard the shots, her unscreaming open mouth and backward-bent head probably derived from a press photograph of an Indian woman crouched over the body of her dead son during the shelling of Singapore. Weigel must have seen it years before, though when questioned she did not remember it. That is how observations are stored up by actors. — Actually it was only in the later performances that Weigel assumed this attitude. [. . .]

4

The Song of the Grand Capitulation

Mother Courage is sitting outside the captain's tent; she has come to put in a complaint about damage to her cart; a clerk advises her in vain to let well alone. A young soldier appears, also to make a complaint; she dissuades him. The bitter 'Song of the Grand Capitulation'. Courage herself learns from the lesson she has given the young soldier and leaves without having put in her complaint.

Overall arrangement

Mother Courage is sitting outside the captain's tent; she has come to put in a complaint about damage to her cart; a clerk advises her in vain to let well alone. The clerk comes up to the bench where Courage is sitting and speaks to her kindly. She remains obstinate.

A young soldier appears, also to make a complaint; she dissuades him, arguing that his anger is too short. Two soldiers enter. The younger wants to rush into the captain's tent and the older is holding him back by main force. Courage intervenes and involves the young man in a conversation about the danger of short attacks of anger.

The bitter 'Song of the Grand Capitulation'. The young soldier, whose anger has evaporated, goes off cursing.

Courage herself learns from the lesson she has given the young soldier, and leaves without putting in her complaint.

Courage's state of mind at the beginning of the scene

In the first rehearsals Weigel opened this scene in an attitude of dejection. This was not right.

Courage learns by teaching. She teaches capitulation and learns it.

The scene calls for bitterness at the start and dejection at the end.

Courage's depravity

In no other scene is Courage so depraved as in this one, where she instructs the young man in capitulation to the higher-ups and then puts her own teaching into effect. Nevertheless Weigel's face in this scene shows a glimmer of wisdom and even of nobility, and that is good. Because the depravity is not so much that of her person as that of her class, and because she herself at least rises above it somewhat by showing that she understands this weakness and that it even makes her angry.

[. . .]

The scene played without alienation

Such a scene is socially disastrous if by hypnotic action the actress playing Mother Courage invites the audience to identify with her. This will only increase the spectator's own tendencies to resignation and capitulation – besides giving him the pleasure of being superior to himself. It will not put him in a position to feel the beauty and attraction of a social problem.

5

Mother Courage loses four officers' shirts and dumb Kattrin finds a baby

After a battle. Courage refuses to give the chaplain her officers' shirts to bandage wounded peasants. Kattrin threatens her mother. At the risk of her life Kattrin saves an infant. Courage laments the loss of her shirts and snatches a stolen coat away from a soldier who has stolen some schnapps, while Kattrin rocks the baby in her arms.

Overall arrangement

After a battle. Courage is standing with two soldiers outside her cart; its sideboard is lowered for use as a bar. Kattrin, sitting on the steps, is uneasy. Courage gulps down two glasses of schnapps; she needs them to harden her to the sight of misery.

Courage refuses to give the chaplain her officers' shirts to bandage wounded peasants. From inside a peasant's wrecked house the chaplain shouts for linen. Kattrin is prevented by her mother from taking officers' shirts from the cart. Courage obstinately blocks the steps, letting no one in.

Kattrin threatens her mother. With the help of one soldier the chaplain has carried a wounded woman out of the house, then an old peasant whose arm is dangling. Again he calls for linen and all look at Courage who lapses into silence. Angrily Kattrin seizes a plank and threatens her mother. The chaplain has to take it away from her. He picks Courage up, sets her down on a chest, and takes some officers' shirts.

At the risk of her life Kattrin saves an infant. Still stuggling with the chaplain, Courage sees her daughter rush into the house that is threatening to cave in, to save a baby. Tugged both ways, between Kattrin and the officers' shirts, she runs about until the shirts are torn into bandages and Kattrin comes out of the house with the infant. Now she runs after Kattrin to make her get rid of the baby. (Movements: Kattrin with the baby runs counter-clockwise around the wounded, then clockwise around the cart.) Her mother stops in the middle of the stage because the chaplain is coming out of the cart with the shirts. Kattrin sits down on the chest right.

Courage laments the loss of her shirts and snatches a stolen coat away from a soldier who has stolen some schnapps, while Kattrin rocks the baby in her arms. After springing like a tigress at the soldier who has failed to pay, Mother Courage stuffs his fur coat into the cart.

A new Courage

A change has taken place in Courage. She has sacrificed her son to the cart and now she defends the cart like a tigress. She has been hardened by the hard bargains she drives.

A detail

At the beginning of the scene (after 'They give us victory marches all right, but catch them giving men their pay') Weigel's Courage tossed off two glasses of schnapps. Apart from this extenuating circumstance, she provided no justification for Courage's haggling, scolding and raging throughout the scene.

A detail

There was a kind of by-play between the soldier who gets no schnapps from Courage and the soldier drinking schnapps at the bar. It expressed the hostility between the haves and the have-nots. The drinker grins scornfully and drains his glass with ostentatious enjoyment, the have-not gives him a long hostile stare before turning around in disgust and going defeated to the rear – to wait for a chance to lay hands on the schnapps. Later the drinker will show more sympathy than the thirsty man for the wounded peasant woman.

The contradictions must not disappear

The character of the chaplain is based on a contradiction. He is part scoundrel, part superior intelligence. The actor [Werner] Hinz gave him a wooden, awkward, comical quality, which he retained in his rôle of good Samaritan. His manner was stiff and cold, as though it were only his clergyman's past that impelled him to turn against his present employer. But something else shone through: his former high position gives him the leadership on the battlefield where he acts in a spirit deriving from the realisation that in the last analysis he himself is one of the oppressed. When he helps the injured, it becomes clear that he too is to be pitied.

The scene is dependent on mime

The effect of the battlefield scene depends entirely on the scrupulously detailed mime with which Kattrin shows her mounting anger at her mother's inhumanity. Angelika Hurwicz ran back and forth like an alarmed hen between the wounded peasants and Mother Courage. Up to the point when she began to argue, in gestures, with her mother, she made no attempt to repress the voluptuous curiosity that horror

inspires in infantile persons. She carried the baby out of the house like
a thief; at the end of the scene she lifted the baby up in the air,
prodding it with both hands as though to make it laugh. If her
mother's share in the spoils is the fur coat, hers is the baby.

Kattrin

In the battlefield scene Kattrin threatens to kill her mother because she
refuses the wounded peasants the linen. It is necessary to show an
intelligent Kattrin from the start. (Her infirmity misleads actors into
representing her as dull.) At the beginning she is fresh, gay and even-
tempered – Hurwicz gave her a kind of awkward charm even in the
conversation with her brother in scene 3. True, the helplessness of her
tongue communicates itself to her body; but it is the war that breaks
her, not her infirmity; in technical terms, the war must find something
that remains to be broken.

The whole point is missed if her love of children is depreciated as
mindless animal instinct. Her saving of the city of Halle is an
intelligent act. How else would it be possible to bring out what must be
brought out, namely, that here the most helpless creature of all is ready
to help?

A detail

At the end of the scene Kattrin lifted the baby into the air, while
Courage rolled up the fur coat and threw it into the cart: both women
had their share of the spoils.

Music and pauses

Music played an essential part in the fifth (battlefield) scene.
   Victory march: from the start to 'Somebody give me a hand'.
   From after 'My arm's gone' to 'I can't give nowt'.
   From after '. . . happy as a queen in all this misery' to the end of the
scene.

Pauses after:
   'Town must of paid him something.'
   'Where's that linen?'

'Blood's coming through.' [This line spoken by the chaplain is deleted from the final text. It followed 'All your victories mean to me is losses'.]

6

Prosperity has set in, but Kattrin is disfigured

Mother Courage, grown prosperous, is stocktaking; funeral oration for the fallen field marshal Tilly. Conversation about the duration of the war; the chaplain proves that the war is going to go on for a long time. Kattrin is sent to buy merchandise. Mother Courage declines a proposal of marriage and insists on firewood. Kattrin is permanently disfigured by some soldiers and rejects Yvette's red shoes. Mother Courage curses the war.

Overall arrangements

Mother Courage, grown prosperous, is stocktaking; funeral oration for the fallen field marshal Tilly. Courage interrupts her counting of merchandise to serve brandy to some soldiers who are playing hooky from the funeral. She virtuously reproves them, declaring that she feels sorry for generals because the common people don't give their grandiose plans proper support. Meanwhile she is looking for worms in a tin box. The regimental clerk listens in vain, hoping to catch her in a subversive utterance.

Conversation about the duration of the war; the chaplain proves that the war will go on for a long time. The right section of the stage is the private quarters. To the left are the bar and the guest table at which the clerk and the chaplain are sitting. There is by-play between right and left when the drinking soldier sings for Kattrin and she smiles at him, while Courage, with a bundle of belt buckles which she is counting, comes over to the table to ask the chaplain-potboy how long he thinks the war will go on. All through his cynical comments she stands deep in thought. Should she lay in new supplies?

Kattrin is sent to buy merchandise. When the chaplain-potboy says the war will go on for a long time, Kattrin runs angrily behind the cart.

Courage laughs, brings her back and sends her to the camp with a big basket to buy merchandise. 'Don't let them take nowt, think of your dowry.'

Mother Courage declines a proposal of marriage and insists on firewood. Courage has sat down on a stool beside her cart; she fills a pipe and tells the potboy to chop some firewood. He chops clumsily, complaining that his talents are lying fallow, and, probably with a view to avoiding physical labour, asks her to marry him. She hints that she doesn't want to take anybody into her business, and leads him gently back to the chopping block.

Kattrin is permanently disfigured by some soldiers and rejects Yvette's red shoes. Kattrin staggers in with a basket full of merchandise. She collapses at the entrance to the tent and Courage has to drag her over to her stool and dress her wound. Kattrin rejects the red shoes that her mother brings out to comfort her; they are now useless. With silent reproach she crawls into the cart.

Mother Courage curses the war. Slowly Courage brings forward the new supplies, which Kattrin has defended at such cost, and gets down on her knees to look them over in the place where she was stocktaking at the beginning of the scene. She recognises that war is a miserable source of income and for the first and last time curses the war.

Inventory

Again Courage has changed. Increasing prosperity has made her softer and more human. Both qualities attract the chaplain and he proposes to her. For the first time we see her sitting briefly at rest, not working.

Funeral oration for Tilly

In the course of many performances it was found that Courage's funeral oration for the field marshal is more effective if during the pause, when all are looking to the rear and the funeral march has grown loud and solemn, the clerk, who is slightly tipsy, rises from his chair and watches Courage closely, suspecting that in this oration she is ridiculing the field marshal. He sits down again in disappointment, because Courage has not said anything demonstrably incriminating.

(The pause during the funeral march must be long; otherwise the funeral scene will not produce the right effect.)

A detail

In the funeral oration for field marshal Tilly ('Can't help feeling sorry for those generals and emperors') Weigel added – after 'how's he to know any better?' – 'Jesus Christ, the worms have got into my biscuits.' While saying this she laughed. Here Mother Courage releases the merriment which, with the clerk looking on, she was unable to express in her evasively subversive speech.

Mime

The chaplain's remarks on the longevity of the war must not take on an independent existence. They are the answer to Courage's anxious question as to whether she can risk taking in new merchandise. While the chaplain was talking, Weigel mimed Courage's anxiety and calculations.

A detail

The drunken soldier addresses his song to Kattrin. She smiles at him. For the last time before she is disfigured the spectator is reminded that she is capable of love.

A point to consider

Violent occupations lead actors to shout. The actor playing the chaplain shouted occasionally while chopping wood. The scene suffered.

[. . .]

Kattrin

Again sitting huddled on the chest as during the drunken soldier's song, the injured girl merely touches her forehead gingerly once or twice to make sure where the wound is; otherwise, except for the willingness with which she lets herself be bandaged, she gives no indication of knowing what the scar will mean to her. Protest is expressed by her lack of interest in Yvette's red shoes and by the way she crawls into the cart: she blames her mother for what has happened to her.

Contradiction

Courage has cursed the war while gathering up the supplies in defence of which her daughter has been disfigured.

Resuming the stocktaking begun at the start of the scene, she now counts the new articles.

7

Mother Courage at the peak of her business career

Mother Courage has corrected her opinion of the war and sings its praises as a good provider.

Overall arrangement

Mother Courage has corrected her opinion of the war and sings its praises as a good provider. Pulled by Kattrin and the chaplain-potboy, the cart comes in from the rear and rolls along the footlights. Courage walks beside them, arguing with them; then, while singing, she turns to the audience. Pause.

Signs of prosperity

After some forty performances it seemed to us that in scene 6, for the stocktaking, Courage should have rings on her fingers and a chain of silver talers round her neck as a sign of the relative prosperity she had achieved. But after a few more performances one of us discovered that this weakened her speech about the courage of the poor, and we decided to put the signs of prosperity in scene 7. Here, where she retracts her condemnation of war, her recently acquired signs of prosperity show her up for what she is: bribed.

In this short scene Weigel showed Courage in the full possession of her vitality, as previously only in scene 5 (the battlefield scene); in scene 5, however, she was gloomy; here she was cheerful.
[. . .]

8

Peace threatens to ruin Mother Courage's business. Her dashing son performs one heroic deed too many and comes to a sticky end

Courage and the chaplain hear a rumour that peace has broken out. The cook reappears. The fight for the feedbag. An old friend who has made a good thing of the war; Puffing Piet is unmasked. The downfall of Eilif, Mother Courage's dashing son; he is executed for one of the misdeeds that had brought him rewards during the war. The peace comes to an end; Courage leaves the chaplain and goes on with the cook in the wake of the Swedish army.

Overall arrangement

Courage and the chaplain hear a rumour that peace has broken out. On the right stand an old woman and her son who have come from the city with all sorts of household goods to sell. It is early in the morning, and Courage, still half asleep, answers sulkily from the cart left. Then bells are heard from the right, the chaplain crawls out from under the cart where he has been sleeping and Courage sticks her head out of the cart. The bells seem to have made the old woman happy – not so Mother Courage.

The cook reappears. The bells of peace bring all sorts of visitors. First comes – from the right like the rest – the cook, ragged, with all his possessions in a bundle. The chaplain is not pleased to see him, but Courage, who is braiding her hair, runs out to meet him and shakes his hand heartily. She invites him over to a wooden bench in front of the cart, while the chaplain goes behind the cart to put on his clerical garb. Amid the ringing of the bells they sit there almost like lovers, telling each other about the bankruptcy that peace has brought them.

The fight for the feedbag. When the chaplain comes back – he stands in the middle of the stage like a last incisor in a toothless mouth – the cook begins to demolish him. Courage climbs into her cart to get her pack ready; she is going to sell the merchandise she bought when the chaplain promised her a long war. The cook starts unwrapping his feet because he means to stay, and the chaplain is obliged to beg him humbly not to drive him out. The cook merely shrugs his shoulders.

An old friend who has made a good thing of the war; Puffing Piet is unmasked. Another visitor. Fat and asthmatic, walking with the help of a cane, the Countess Starhemberg, the former camp whore, enters, clothed in black silk and followed by a servant. She has dismounted from her carriage to call on Mother Courage. She catches sight of the cook, known to her as Puffing Piet, and angrily denounces him to Courage, who has difficulty in preventing her from attacking him with her cane.

The downfall of Eilif, Mother Courage's dashing son; he is executed for one of the misdeeds that brought him rewards during the war. When the women have left, the cook gloomily puts his foot wrappings on again and the chaplain relishes his triumph. Their conversation turns to melancholy recollections of the good old war days. Blown in by the bells of peace, soldiers with arquebuses bring in a richly dressed lieutenant – Eilif. His courage deserts him when he hears that his mother is not there. The chaplain gives him a swallow of brandy and, a clergyman once again, accompanies him to the place of execution.

The peace comes to an end; Courage goes on with the cook, in the wake of the Swedish army. The cook tries to get Kattrin to come out of the cart so he can beg some bread from her. Courage comes running in, overjoyed. The peace is over. The cook does not mention Eilif's death. With the cook's help she packs her belongings into the cart and they go on without the chaplain.

Advance preparation

In her conversation with the chaplain in scene 6 Weigel very carefully laid the groundwork for her conversation with the cook in scene 8. She said 'Nice fellow that' a little more warmly and thoughtfully than required by her good-natured rebuff of the chaplain. Consequently in scene 8 she had an audience who knew what was what. This enabled her to take a dry, matter-of-fact tone with the cook. Knowing what it knew, the audience could be touched as well as amused that the subject of their love dialogue should be the fact that they were both ruined.

The dignity of misery

In the cockfight between the chaplain and the cook, Hinz as the chaplain obtained a powerful and natural effect when, suddenly throwing all arrogance to the winds, he begged the cook not to squeeze him out of his place with Courage because, having become a better man, he could no longer practise the clergyman's profession. His fear of losing his job lent him a new dignity.

Humiliations

The cook too is capable of enduring humiliations. At the end of the dialogue in which he triumphs over the chaplain, he removes his shoes and foot wrappings like a man who has come to the end and goal of a long peregrination. Yvette finds him barefooted, which embarrasses the ageing Don Juan. After he has been unmasked and the chaplain has lectured him, he sorrowfully puts his footwear back on. The episode in which he begs Kattrin for food was played brilliantly by Bildt. His bundle slung over his shoulder, ready to hit the road, he first tapped his stick nonchalantly on the drum hanging from the cart. Talking into the cart, he uttered the words 'pork' and 'bread' in the tone of a gourmet and connoisseur: the starving cook.

Good business

Yvette Pottier is the only character in the play who strikes it rich; she has sold herself for a good price. She has been as badly disfigured by good food as Kattrin by her scar; she is so fat one has the impression that eating has become her only passion. She speaks with the accent of the Austrian aristocracy.

[. . .]

War the provider

Courage comes back from the village exhausted from running but overjoyed that the war has started up again. In high spirits she lets the cook relieve her of her pack. The prospect of good business will enable her to take the cook in. She speaks light-heartedly of the possibility of seeing her son again. 'Now there's war again, everything will work out all right' [not in the final text]. She is going to ride over his grave.

A detail

While they are packing, Kattrin appears. She sees the cook staring at her scar, covers it with her hand and turns away. She has come to fear the light.

Again in scene 11, when the soldiers drag her out of the cart, she holds her hand over her eye.

9

Times are hard, the war is going badly. On account of her daughter, she refuses the offer of a home

The cook has inherited a tavern in Utrecht. Kattrin hears the cook refuse to take her along there. The 'Song of the Temptations of the Great'. Kattrin decides to spare her mother the need to make a decision, packs her bundle and leaves a message. Mother Courage stops Kattrin from running away and goes on alone with her. The cook goes to Utrecht.

Overall arrangement

Times are hard. The cook has inherited a tavern in Utrecht. In the early dawn of a stormy winter day Courage and the cook, both in rags, bring the cart to a stop outside a parsonage. The cook morosely unharnesses himself and admits to Courage that he means to go to Utrecht where he has inherited a tavern. He asks her to go with him. Sitting shivering on the shaft, Courage complains of the bad business situation: the war is no longer finding much to feed on.

Kattrin hears the cook refuse to take her along there. The cook interrupts the conversation between mother and daughter about the peaceful life in Utrecht, and motions Courage to step to one side with him (to the right, in front of the parsonage). Hidden beside the cart, Kattrin hears the cook refuse to take her along.

The cook and Courage sing the 'Song of the Temptations of the Great'. While they sing their begging song, Courage desperately thinks over the cook's offer, presumably her last hope of settling down.

Kattrin decides to spare her mother the need to make a decision, packs her bundle and leaves a message. By the end of the begging song, Courage has made up her mind to decline the offer. She still goes into the parsonage with the cook for the sake of the soup. Kattrin comes in with a bundle and deposits her mother's skirt with the cook's trousers over it on the cart's shaft.

Mother Courage stops Kattrin from running away and goes on alone with her. Courage catches Kattrin just as she is about to steal away. She has brought a dish of soup. Feeding her as one would a child, she assures her that it has never occurred to her to desert the cart. She throws the cook's bundle and trousers out of the cart, puts herself and Kattrin in harness and starts off with her (behind the house, to the right).

The cook goes to Utrecht. The cook sees that the women and cart are gone. He silently picks up his bundle and sets out on his way, right rear, to settle down in Utrecht.

The cook

In this scene the cook must not under any circumstances be represented as brutal. The tavern he has inherited is too small to keep three people, and the customers cannot be expected to put up with the sight of the disfigured Kattrin. That's all there is to it. Courage does not find his arguments unreasonable. Weigel showed plainly that Courage thought the proposition over – she thinks every proposition over. This she did by looking over towards the cart during the first stanza of the begging song with an expression compounded of indecision, fear and pity.

[. . .]

A detail

In this scene, in which her arguments are rather thin, Courage spoke to her daughter as one speaks to a person who is hard of hearing. Her loud, slow delivery also gives the impression that she is speaking in the name of the cook as well, but without being at all sure of herself in this.

Kattrin's demonstration

In laying out the trousers and skirt Kattrin tries to leave her mother a message explaining why she has gone away. But Hurwicz also indicated a note of resentment by glancing at the parsonage where her mother and the cook were presumably eating soup, then looking at her composition and stifling an uncanny, malignant giggle by raising her hand to her mouth before sneaking away.

A detail

While saying the words 'Don't you go thinking it's on your account I gave him the push,' Courage put a spoonful of soup into Kattrin's mouth.

[. . .]

The cook sets out for Utrecht

Scenes of this kind must be fully acted out: Courage and Kattrin harness themselves to the cart, push it back a few feet so as to be able to circle the parsonage, and then move off to the right. The cook comes out, still chewing a piece of bread, sees his belongings, picks them up and goes off to the rear with long steps. We see him disappear. Thus the parting of the ways is made visible.

10

Still on the road

Mother and daughter hear someone in a peasant house singing the 'Song of Home'.

The song in the Munich production

A fine variation used in the Munich production: the song was sung with unfeeling, provocative self-assurance. The arrogant pride of possession expressed in the singing turned the listeners on the road into damned souls.

Expression not wanted

The two women enter, pulling the cart. They hear the voice from the peasant house, stop, listen, and start off again. What goes on in their minds should not be shown; the audience can imagine.

A detail

In one of the later performances Weigel, when starting off again, tossed her head and shook it like a tired cart horse getting back to work. It is doubtful whether this gesture can be imitated.

11

Dumb Kattrin saves the city of Halle

A surprise attack is planned on the city of Halle; soldiers force a young peasant to show them the way. The peasant and his wife tell Kattrin to join them in praying for the city. Kattrin climbs up on the barn roof and beats the drum to awaken the city. Neither the offer to spare her mother in the city nor the threat to smash the cart can make her stop drumming. Death of dumb Kattrin.

Overall arrangement

A surprise attack is planned on the city of Halle; soldiers force a young peasant to show them the way. An ensign and two soldiers come to a farm at night. They drag the peasants, still half asleep, out of the house and Kattrin out of her cart. By threatening to kill the peasants' only ox they force the young peasant to serve as their guide. (They lead him to the rear; the party go out right.)

The peasant and his wife tell Kattrin to join them in praying for the city. The peasant moves a ladder over to the barn (right), climbs up and sees that the woods are swarming with armed men. He comes down, he and his wife talk it over and decide not to endanger themselves by trying to warn the city. The peasant woman goes over to Kattrin (right front) and tells her to pray God to help the city. The three of them kneel down and pray.

Kattrin climbs up on the barn roof and beats the drum to awaken the city. From the peasant woman's prayer Kattrin learns that the children in Halle are in danger. Stealthily she takes the drum from the cart, the same drum she had brought back when she was disfigured. With it she climbs up on the barn roof. She starts drumming. The peasants try in vain to make her stop.

Neither the offer to spare her mother in the city nor the threat to smash the cart can make her stop drumming. At the sound of the drum the ensign and the soldiers come back with the young peasant. The soldiers take up a position by the cart and the ensign threatens the peasants with his sword. First one of the soldiers, then the ensign moves to the centre to make promises to Kattrin. The peasant goes over to a log (left front) and chops at it with an axe to drown out the sound of the drum. Kattrin is victorious in the noise contest, the ensign starts to go into the house to set it on fire, the peasant woman indicates the cart. One of the soldiers kicks the young peasant and forces him to batter the cart with a plank, the other soldier is sent off for an arquebus. He sets up the arquebus, the ensign orders him to fire.

Kattrin's death. Kattrin falls forward, the drumsticks in her dropping hands strike one full beat followed by a feeble beat; for a moment the ensign is triumphant, then the cannon of Halle respond, taking up the rhythm of Kattrin's drumbeats.

Bad comedians are always laughing
Bad tragedians are always weeping

In sad scenes just as in comic ones precision must be combined with ease; the hand that guides the arrangement must be both firm and relaxed. The actors take their positions and form their groups in very much the same way as the marbles tossed into a wooden bowl in certain roulette-like children's games fall into hollows, with the difference that in the games it is not decided in advance which marbles will fall into which hollows, whereas in theatrical arrangements there only *seems* to be no advance decision. And indeed the reason for the stiffness or heaviness that is so characteristic of sad scenes in the German theatre is that in tragedy the human body is unjustifiably neglected and so seems to be afflicted with muscular cramp. Which is deplorable.

Kattrin's two fears

Kattrin's dumbness does not save her. The war gives her a drum. With this unsold drum she must climb up on the barn roof and save the children of Halle.

Conventional heroism must be avoided. Kattrin is ridden by two fears: her fear for the city of Halle and her fear for herself.

'The dramatic scene'

Audiences were especially stirred by the drum scene. Some explained this by saying that it is the most dramatic scene in the play and that the public likes its theatre dramatic rather than epic. In reality the epic theatre, while capable of portraying other things than stirring incidents, clashes, conspiracies, psychological torments and so on, is also capable of portraying these. Spectators may identify themselves with

Kattrin in this scene; empathy may give them the happy feeling that they too possess such strength. But they are not likely to have experienced such empathy throughout the play – in the first scenes, for example.

Alienation

If the scene is to be saved from a wild excitement amid which everything worth noticing is lost, close attention must be given to alienation.

For example: if the conversation of the peasants is swallowed up by a general hubbub, the audience will be in danger of being 'carried away'; then they will fail to take note how the peasants justify their failure to act, how they fortify each other in the belief that there is nothing they can do, so that the only remaining possibility of 'action' becomes prayer.

In view of this, the actors in rehearsal were made to add 'said the man' or 'said the woman' after each speech. For example:

' "Sentries are bound to spot them first," said the woman.'
' "Sentry must have been killed," said the man.'
' "If only there were more of us," said the woman.'
' "Just you and me and that cripple," said the man.'
' "Nowt we can do, you'd say . . ." said the woman.'
' "Nowt," said the man,' and so on.

Kattrin's drumming

Kattrin keeps watching what is going on down below. Consequently her drumming breaks off after the following sentences,

'Jesus Christ, what's she doing?'
'I'll cut you all to ribbons!'
'We got a suggestion could do you some good.'
'With a mug like yours it's not surprising.'
'We must set the farm on fire.'

Detail in tempestuous scenes

Such scenes as the one where the peasant tries to drown the noise of Kattrin's drumming by chopping wood must be fully acted out. As she drums, Kattrin must look down at the peasant and accept the challenge. In tempestuous scenes the director needs a certain amount of stubbornness to make miming of this sort last long enough.

A detail

Hurwicz showed increasing exhaustion while drumming.

The ritual character of despair

The lamentations of the peasant woman, whose son the soldiers have taken away and whose farm they threaten when Kattrin starts her drumming to wake the townspeople, must have a certain routine quality about it; it must suggest a 'set behaviour pattern'. The war has been going on too long. Begging, lamenting, and informing have frozen into fixed forms: they are the things you do when the soldiery arrive.

It is worth forgoing the 'immediate impression' of a particular, seemingly unique episode of horror so as to penetrate a deeper stratum of horror and to show how repeated, constantly recurring misfortune has driven people to ritualise their gestures of self-defence – though of course these ritual gestures can never free them from the reality of fear, which on the stage must permeate the ritual.

[. . .]

12

Mother Courage moves on

The peasants have to convince Courage that Kattrin is dead. The lullaby for Kattrin. Mother Courage pays for Kattrin's burial and receives the condolences of the peasants. Alone, Mother Courage harnesses herself to the empty cart; still hoping to get back into business, she follows the ragged army.

Overall arrangement

The peasants have to convince Courage that Kattrin is dead. The cart is standing on the empty stage. Mother Courage is sitting with the dead Kattrin's head in her lap. The peasants are standing in a hostile knot at the dead girl's feet. Courage speaks as if her daughter were only sleeping, deliberately disregarding the reproaches of the peasants who are saying that she is to blame for Kattrin's death.

The lullaby for Kattrin. The mother's face is bent low over her daughter's face. Her song fails to pacify the peasants.

Mother Courage pays for Kattrin's burial and receives the condolences of the peasants. When she realises that her last child is dead, she rises painfully to her feet and hobbles around the corpse (on the right) and along the footlights to behind the cart. She comes back with a sheet of canvas. The peasants ask her if she has no one else; she answers over her shoulder: 'Aye, one left. Eilif.' And with her back to the audience she lays the canvas over the body. Then at the head end of the body she pulls it up over the face and stands behind the body, facing the audience. The peasant and his son give her their hands and bow ceremoniously before carrying the body away (to the right). The woman also gives Courage her hand, goes to the right and stops again in indecision. The women exchange a few words, then the peasant woman goes away.

Alone, Mother Courage harnesses heself to her empty cart; still hoping to get back into business, she follows the ragged army. Slowly the old woman goes to the cart, unrolls the cord which Kattrin had until then been pulling, takes a stick, examines it, pulls the loop of the second cord through, wedges the stick under her arm and moves off. The last stanza of the 'Mother Courage Song' has begun as she is bending down over the shaft. The revolve begins to turn and Mother Courage circles the stage once. The curtain falls as she turns right rear for the second time.

The peasants

The peasants' attitude towards Courage is hostile. She has caused them great difficulties and they will have her on their hands if she cannot catch up with the departing army. As they see it, she is to blame for what has happened. Besides, she is an unsedentary element, and now in wartime belongs with the incendiaries, cut-throats and looters who follow in the wake of armies. In condoling with her by giving her their hands, they are only doing what is customary.

The bow

During the whole scene Weigel showed an almost bestial stupor. All the more beautiful was her deep bow when the body was carried away.

The lullaby

The lullaby must be sung without any sentimentality or desire to provoke sentimentality. Otherwise its significance is lost. The idea underlying this song is murderous: this mother's child must fare better than other children of other mothers. By slight emphasis on the 'you', Weigel portrayed Courage's treacherous hope of bringing her child, and perhaps hers alone, through the war. To this child who had lacked even the most ordinary things, she promised the most extraordinary.

Paying for the burial

Even in paying for the burial, Weigel gave one last hint of Courage's character. She fished a few coins out of her leather bag, put one back and gave the peasants the rest. This did not in the least detract from the overpowering effect of desolation.

The last stanza

The last stanza of the 'Mother Courage Song' was struck up by the musicians in the box while Courage was slowly harnessing herself to the cart. It gives powerful expression to her still unshattered hope of getting her cut from the war. It gains in power if the illusion that the song is being sung by marching armies in the distance is dropped.
[. . .]

Timing

At the end as at the beginning the cart must be seen rolling along. Of course the audience would understand if it were simply pulled away. When it goes on rolling there is a moment of irritation ('this has been going on long enough'). But when it goes on still longer, a deeper understanding sets in.

The pulling of the cart in the last scene

For scene 12 the peasants' house and the barn with roof (from scene 11) were removed from the stage; only the cart and Kattrin's body remained. The word 'Saxony' in big letters is hoisted into the flies when the music starts. Thus the cart was hauled off a completely empty stage recalling scene 1. Mother Courage described a complete circle with it on the revolving stage, passing the footlights for the last time. As usual, the stage was brilliantly lit.

Realist discoveries

In giving the peasants the money for Kattrin's burial, Weigel quite mechanically puts back one of the coins she has taken out of her purse. What does this gesture accomplish? It shows that in all her grief the business woman has not wholly forgotten how to reckon – money is hard to come by. This little gesture has the power and suddenness of a discovery – a discovery concerning human nature, which is moulded by conditions. To dig out the truth from the rubble of the self-evident, to link the particular strikingly with the universal, to capture the particular that characterises a general process, that is the art of the realist.

A change in the text

After 'I'll manage, there isn't much in it,' Courage added, first in the Munich, then in the Berlin production: 'I've got to get back into business.'

Mother Courage learns nothing

In the last scene Weigel's Courage seemed to be eighty years old. And she understands nothing. She reacts only to remarks connected with the war, such as that she mustn't be left behind, and takes no notice when the peasants brutally accuse her of being to blame for Kattrin's death.

In 1938, when the play was written, Courage's inability to learn from war's unprofitable character was a prophecy. At the time of the 1948 Berlin production the wish was expressed that at least in the play Courage would understand.

In order that the realism of this play should benefit the spectator, that is, in order that the spectator should learn something, the theatre must work out a way of playing it which does not lead to audience identification with the principal character (heroine).

To judge by press reviews and statements of spectators, the original production in Zurich, for example, though artistically on a high level, merely pictured war as a natural catastrophe and ineluctable fate, confirming the belief of the petit-bourgeois members of the audience in their own indestructibility and power to survive. But even for the equally petit-bourgeois Mother Courage the decision whether or not to join in was left open throughout the play. It follows that the production must have represented Courage's business activity, her desire to get her cut and her willingness to take risks, as perfectly natural and 'eternally human' phenomena, so that there was no way out. Today the petit-bourgeois can no longer in fact keep out of the war, as Courage could have done. And probably no performance of the play can give a petit-bourgeois anything more than a real horror of war and a certain insight into the fact that the big business deals which constitute war are not made by the little people. A play is more instructive than reality, because in it the war situation is set up experimentally for the purpose of giving insight; that is, the spectator assumes the attitude of a student – provided the production is right. The proletarians in the audience, the members of a class which really can take action against war and eliminate it, must be given an insight – which of course is possible only if the play is performed in the right way – into the connection between war and commerce: the proletariat as a class can do away with war by doing away with capitalism. Here, of course, a good deal depends on the growth of self-awareness among the proletariat, a process that is going on both inside and outside the theatre.

The epic element

As for the epic element in the Deutsches Theater production, indications of it could be seen in the arrangement, in the delineation of the characters, in the accurate execution of detail, and in the spirited rhythm of the entire performance. Moreover, the contradictions that pervade the play were not taken over ready-made, but worked out, and the parts, visible as such, fitted well into the whole. Nonetheless, the central aim of the epic theatre was not achieved. Much was shown, but the element of showing was absent. Only in a few rehearsals devoted to recasting was it brought out clearly. Here the actors 'marked', that is, they merely showed the new members of the cast certain positions and tones, and the whole took on the wonderfully relaxed, effortless, and unobtrusive quality that stimulates the spectator to think and feel for himself.

No one missed this fundamental epic element; and this is probably why the actors did not dare to provide it.

Concerning these notes

It is to be hoped that the present notes, indicating a few of the ideas and devices of various kinds that are necessary for the performance of a play, will not make an impression of misplaced seriousness. It is difficult in writing about these things to convey the carefree lightness that is essential to the theatre. Even in their instructive aspect, the arts belong to the realm of entertainment.

[From *Mutter Courage und ihre Kinder. Text/Aufführung/Anmerkungen.* Henschel-Verlag, East Berlin, 1956.]

TWO WAYS OF PLAYING MOTHER COURAGE

When the title rôle is played in the usual way, so as to communicate empathy, the spectator (according to numerous witnesses) experiences an extraordinary pleasure: the indestructible vitality of this woman beset by the hardships of war leaves him with a sense of triumph. Mother Courage's active participation in the war is not taken seriously; the war is a source, perhaps her only source, of livelihood. Apart from this element of participation, in spite of it, the effect is very much as in *Schweyk*, where – in a comic perspective, to be sure – the audience triumphs with Schweyk over the plans of the belligerent powers to sacrifice him. But in the case of Mother Courage such an effect has far less social value, precisely because her participation, however indirect it may seem, is not taken into consideration. The effect is indeed negative. Courage is represented chiefly as a mother, and like Niobe she is unable to protect her children against fate – in this case, war. At most, her merchant's trade and the way she plies it give her a 'realistic, un-ideal' quality; they do not prevent the war from being seen as fate. It remains, of course, wholly evil, but after all she comes through it alive, though deformed. By contrast Weigel, employing a technique which prevents complete empathy, treated the merchant's trade not as a natural but as a historical one – that is, belonging to a historical, *transient* period – and war as the best time for it. Here too the war was a self-evident source of livelihood, but this spring from which Mother Courage drank death was a polluted one. The merchant-mother became a great living contradiction, and it was this contradiction which utterly disfigured and deformed her. In the battlefield scene, which is cut in most productions, she really was a hyaena; she parted with the shirts because she saw her daughter's hatred and feared violence; she cursed at the soldier with the coat and pounced on him like a tigress. When her daughter was disfigured, she cursed the war with the same profound sincerity that characterised her praise of it in the scene immediately following. Thus she played the contradictions in all their irreconcilable sharpness. Her daughter's rebellion against her (when the city of Halle is saved) stunned her completely and taught her nothing. The tragedy of Mother Courage and of her life, which the audience was made to feel deeply, lay in a terrible contradiction which destroyed a human being, a contradiction which has been transcended, but only by society itself in long and terrible struggles. What made this way of playing the part morally superior was that human beings – even the strongest of them – were shown to be destructible.

[Written 1951. From GW *Schriften zum Theater*, p. 895. First published in *Theaterarbeit*, 1952.]

[MISFORTUNE IN ITSELF IS A POOR TEACHER]

The audience gave off the acrid smell of clothing that had not been properly cleaned, but this did not detract from the festive atmosphere. Those who had come to see the play had come from ruins and would be going back to ruins. There was more light on the stage than on any square or in any house.

The wise old stage manager from the days of Max Reinhardt had received me like a king, but what gave the production its hard realism was a bitter experience shared by all. The dressmakers in the workshops realised that the costumes had to be richer at the beginning of the play than at the end. The stage hands knew how the canvas over Mother Courage's cart had to be: white and new at the beginning, then dirty and patched, then somewhat cleaner, but never again really white, and at the end a rag.

Weigel's way of playing Mother Courage was hard and angry; that is, her Mother Courage was not angry; she herself, the actress, was angry. She showed a merchant, a strong crafty woman who loses her children to the war one after another and still goes on believing in the profit to be derived from war.

A number of people remarked at the time that Mother Courage learns nothing from her misery, that even at the end she does not *understand*. Few realised that just this was the bitterest and most meaningful lesson of the play.

Undoubtedly the play was a great success; that is, it made a big impression. People pointed out Weigel on the street and said: 'Mother

Courage!' But I do not believe, and I did not believe at the time, that the people of Berlin – or of any other city where the play was shown – understood the play. They were all convinced that they had learned something from the war; what they failed to grasp was that, in the playwright's view, Mother Courage was meant to have learned nothing from her war. They did not see what the playwright was driving at: that war teaches people nothing.

Misfortune in itself is a poor teacher. Its pupils learn hunger and thirst, but seldom hunger for truth or thirst for knowledge. Suffering does not transform a sick man into a physician. Neither what he sees from a distance nor what he sees face to face is enough to turn an eyewitness into an expert.

The audiences of 1949 and the ensuing years did not see Mother Courage's crimes, her participation, her desire to share in the profits of the war business; they saw only her failure, her sufferings. And that was their view of Hitler's war in which they had participated: it had been a bad war and now they were suffering. In short, it was exactly as the playwright had prophesied. War would bring them not only suffering, but also the inability to learn from it.

The production of *Mother Courage and Her Children* is now in its sixth year. It is certainly a brilliant production, with great actors. Undoubtedly something has changed. The play is no longer a play that came too late, that is, *after* a war. Today a new war is threatening with all its horrors. No one speaks of it, but everyone knows. The masses are not in favour of war. But life is so full of hardships. Mightn't war do away with these? Didn't people make a very good living in the last war, at any rate till just before the end? And aren't there such things as successful wars?

I am curious to know how many of those who see *Mother Courage and Her Children* today understand its warning.

[Written 1954. From GW *Schriften zum Theater*, p. 1147.]

Editorial Note

The first typescript of *Mother Courage*, in Brecht's own typing with its characteristic absence of capital letters, was made in 1939, though there is also what may be a slightly earlier draft of the first few pages in verse. Amended by Brecht and by his collaborator Margarete Steffin, who died in 1941, it was then duplicated for the Zurich production and again in 1946 by the Kurt Reiss agency in Basel. This seems to have been the text which Brecht circulated to some of his friends, and of which one scene was accordingly published in the Moscow *Internationale Literatur* before the première, while a copy served as the basis for H. R. Hays's first American translation. Brecht made a few further additions and alterations to the 1946 version, which was once again duplicated for the Deutsches Theater production of 1949. Brecht's own copies of this Deutsches Theater script bear yet more notes and small amendments, as well as cuts which were disregarded in the published version. This appeared as *Versuche* 9 in 1949, continuing the grey paperbound series of Brecht's writings which had been interrupted in 1933.

The main shifts of emphasis in the play were indicated by Brecht in his own notes which followed the first publication of the play in the *Versuche* (1949) and have been reprinted in subsequent editions (pp. 271–274 above). The final versions of these passages, with the exception of the last (which concludes the play) are to be found in the additions to the Deutsches Theater typescript. The change in scene 1, says Brecht's diary, was proposed by his assistant Kuckhahn. In the case of the last scene, the major change took place subsequently, between the *Versuche* edition of 1949 and the reprint of 1950. It consisted in the insertion of the stage directions showing Mother Courage first covering her daughter's body, then handing over money to the peasants who carry it away, and of the last sentence 'Got to get back in business again'. In previous versions, too, she was made to join in the refrain of the final song. Now, presumably, she was too old and exhausted to do more than pull her cart.

These changes were, as Brecht said, calculated to bring out Courage's short-sighted concentration on business and alienate the audience's sympathies. Thus in scene 1 she now became distracted by the chance of selling a belt buckle; in scene 5 she no longer helped the others to make bandages of her expensive shirts; while in scene 7 she was shown prospering (her lines up to 'Them as does are the first to go' were new, while the scene title 'Mother Courage at the peak of her business career' and the silver necklace of the stage direction were added after the 1949 edition). Besides these, however, Brecht made earlier alterations to two of the main characters – the cook and the camp prostitute Yvette – and to virtually all the songs, whose independent role in the play became considerably strengthened as a result. Scene 8 seems to have called for repeated amendment, thanks partly to Brecht's uncertainty about the Yvette–cook relationship, which in turn depended on the choice of song for scene 3, where it is first expressed. Another confusion which has perhaps left its mark on the final text concerns religion: the first typescript gave the chaplain the Catholic title of 'Kaplan' throughout, putting Courage initially in the Catholic camp, which the Lutherans then overran in scene 3. Though Brecht corrected this on the script, to conform with the rest of the story, the religious antagonism emerges none too clearly even in the final version.

Brecht's first typescript also numbered the scenes rather differently, so as to run from 1 to 11, omitting the present scenes 7 to 10. He altered this to make 9 scenes, a division which he retained in the 1946 script, writing the original scene titles, to correspond with it, very nearly in their present form. 'The Story' (pp. 274–276 above) refers to this numbering, as also does a note attached to the typescript:

The minor parts can easily be divided among a small number of actors. For instance the sergeant in scene 1 can also play the wounded peasant in scene 5 and the young man in scene 7 [8]; the general in scene 2 can be the clerk in scene 4 and the old peasant in scene 9 [11], and so on. Moreover the soldier in scene 3, the young soldier in scene 4 and the ensign in scene 9 [11] can be performed by the same actor without alteration of make-up.

Settings and costumes

High road with a Swedish city in the background/Inside the general's tent/Camp/Outside an officer's tent/In a bombarded village/In a canteen tent during rain/In the woods outside a city/ Outside a parsonage in the winter/Near a thatched peasant dwelling.

The chief item of scenery consists in Courage's cart, from which one must be able to deduce her current financial situation. The brief scenes on the high road which are appended to scenes 6 and 8 [now scenes 7 and 10] can be played in front of the curtain.

So far as the costumes are concerned, care must be taken to avoid the brand-new elegance common in historical plays. They must show the poverty involved in a long war.

The following scene-by-scene résumé of the changes follows the same numbering, the present scene numbers being given in square brackets.

1. [1]

In Brecht's first typescript the family arrive to the sound of a piano-accordion, not a jew's harp, and there are some minor differences in the Mother Courage song.

2. [2]

The cook's original name 'Feilinger' is amended to 'Lamb' on the first typescript. The general's reference to the king and Eilif's reply were added to this; the general's following 'You've got something in common already' was an afterthought added on the Deutsches Theater script (according to Manfred Wekwerth it was meant to refer to the enthusiasm with which Eilif drank). Eilif's 'dancing a war dance with his sabre' was penned by Brecht on the 1946 script.

The song itself is taken over from Brecht's first collection of poems, Die Hauspostille (1927), and derives originally from the verse at the end of Kipling's short story Love o' Women, itself taken from the song of the Girl and the Soldier in the story My Great and Only.

3. [3]

The three sub-scenes (divided by the passage of time) are numbered 3, 3a and 3b, of which only the first has a title. Yvette originally was Jessie Potter, amended on the first typescript to Jeannetté Pottier; she had become Yvette by 1946. The scene started with Mother Courage's remark to Swiss Cheese 'Here's your woollies', everything to do with the armourer being added to the first typescript (p. 126).

Instead of the 'Song of Fraternisation', Jessie 'sings the song of Surabaya-Johnny' (from Happy End), immediately after the words 'Then I'll tell you, get it off my chest', Courage having just said 'Just don't start in on your Johnny'. The text of this song is not reproduced in the typescript, but a first version of Johnny's description is inserted, with Jeannette 'growing up on Batavia' and the man being a 'ship's cook, blond, a Swede, but skinny'. In pen, Batavia is changed to Flanders, ship's cook to army cook and Swede to Dutchman. A 'Song of Pipe-and-Drum Henny' is added, which is a slightly adapted version of 'Surabaya-Johnny' in three verses (the refrain appears only in the 1946 script). In the text of this song, which still fits the Weill music, Burma is amended to Utrecht and the fish market (in 'You were something to do with the fish market / And nothing to do with the army') to a tulip market. Besides the beginning ('When I was only sixteen') the second quatrain of the second verse was absorbed in the 'Song of Fraternisation', which is substituted in Brecht's amended copy of the 1946 script. This also adds that the cook was called 'Pipe-Henny' because he never took his pipe out of his mouth when he was on the job.

Some light on the camp prostitute's varying age is cast by her ensuing remark about her failure to run him to earth. In the first typescript it happened 'twenty years ago', in the 1946 and Deutsches Theater scripts 'ten years ago', before being reduced to the present 'five' some time between 1949 and 1953.

The chaplain's 'Song of the Hours' is adapted from a seventeenth-century hymn by Michael Weisse. It occurs for the first time in the Deutsches Theater script, where it consists of seven verses only and is sung before the curtain to introduce sub-scene 3b; it was cut before the première. In Mother Courage's subsequent speech on corruptibility (p. 143) there is a section which was cut in this script but is of interest for its anticipation of *The Caucasian Chalk Circle*:

I used to know a judge in Franconia who was so out for money, even small sums from poor people, that he was universally regarded as a good man right up into Saxony, and that's some way. People talked about him as if he were a saint, he'd listen to everybody, he was tough about the amount – wouldn't let anyone say they were penniless if they had anything – widow or profiteer, he treated them all alike, all of them had to give.

4. [4]

The young soldier was originally complaining about the delay in getting his basic pay. Brecht's amendments to his typescript introduced the idea of a special reward, as well as giving Mother Courage more to say. The song was called 'The Song of Waiting' in this typescript and was amended at every stage, first and foremost by adding the (spoken) parentheses.

5. [5]

See p. 272 above. The cry 'Pshagreff!' – Polish Psia Krew (blood of a dog) – near the end was simply 'Stop!' until after the 1949 edition.

6. [6]

This scene appeared in the Moscow monthly *Internationale Literatur* (then edited by J. R. Becher), No. 12, 1940. Courage's speech beginning 'Let's see your money!' was very much longer there, as also in the first two scripts. The drunken soldier and his song were additions to the first typescript; Courage's suggestion that he may have been responsible for the attack on Kattrin being an addition to the 1946 script. In *Internationale Literatur* and prior to the Deutsches Theater version Kattrin accepts the red shoes at the end of the scene and 'sets about her work; she has calmed down'.

6a. [7]

See p. 273 above.

7. [8]

This scene (Eilif's death) is the most heavily amended, partly in order to get the confrontation of the cook and Yvette straight. Originally, on the first typescript, she denounces him as 'That's Surabaya-Johnny', which prompts Courage to hum the refrain of the song. Courage previously has a song of her own, following the chaplain's 'Off war, in other words. Aha!' (p. 166), which she introduces by the lines:

> If the Emperor's on top now, what with King of Sweden being dead, all it'll mean is that taxes go to the Emperor. Ever seen a water wheel? Mills have them. I'm going to sing you a song about one of them water wheels, a parable featuring the great. (*She sings the Song of the Water Wheel*)

– a song to Eisler's music which is to be found in Brecht's *The Round Heads and the Pointed Heads*. It was omitted from the 1946 script.

8. [*9*]

The fourth (St. Martin) verse of the 'Solomon Song' (itself of course partly taken over from the *Threepenny Opera*) made its appearance in the 1946 script. The cook's tavern was originally in Uppsala, amended when he became a Dutchman.

8a. [*10*]

The scene was originally un-numbered. The title was added between the 1949 and 1953 *Versuche* editions.

9. [*11*]

The date of the title was at first March 1635 and the threatened town Havelberg. The only change of any substance took place after the peasant's 'Suppose we got one of the trunks and poked her off . . .', where in all three scripts the soldiers proceeded to fetch one and actually tried to dislodge Kattrin with it. This was deleted on Brecht's Deutsches Theater script, which incidentally bears marks showing exactly where the drumbeats should fall.

9a. [*12*]

See p. 274. On the first typescript lines 5–7 of the song originally read

> He gets his uniform and rations
> The regiment gives him his pay.
> The rest defeats our comprehension
> Tomorrow is another day.

before Brecht amended them to read as now.

APPENDIX

Galileo

BY BERTOLT BRECHT

Translated by Charles Laughton

It is my opinion that the earth is very noble and admirable by reason of so many and so different alterations and generations which are incessantly made therein.

— GALILEO GALILEI

CHARACTERS

GALILEO GALILEI
ANDREA SARTI (*two actors: boy and man*)
MRS. SARTI
LUDOVICO MARSILI
PRIULI, THE CURATOR
SAGREDO, *Galileo's friend*
VIRGINIA GALILEI
TWO SENATORS
MATTI, *an iron founder*
PHILOSOPHER (*later, Rector of the University*)
ELDERLY LADY
YOUNG LADY
FEDERZONI, *assistant to Galileo*
MATHEMATICIAN
LORD CHAMBERLAIN
FAT PRELATE
TWO SCHOLARS
TWO MONKS
INFURIATED MONK
OLD CARDINAL

ATTENDANT MONK
CHRISTOPHER CLAVIUS
LITTLE MONK
TWO SECRETARIES
CARDINAL BELLARMIN
CARDINAL BARBERINI
CARDINAL INQUISITOR
YOUNG GIRL
HER FRIEND
GIUSEPPE
STREET SINGER
HIS WIFE
REVELLER
A LOUD VOICE
INFORMER
TOWN CRIER
OFFICIAL
PEASANT
CUSTOMS OFFICER
BOY
SENATORS, OFFICIALS, PROFESSORS, LADIES, GUESTS, CHILDREN

There are two wordless roles: the DOGE *in Scene Two and* PRINCE COSMO DI MEDICI *in Scene Four. The ballad of Scene Nine is filled out by a pantomime: among the individuals in the pantomimic crowd are three extras (including the* "KING OF HUNGARY"), COBBLER'S BOY, THREE CHILDREN, PEASANT WOMAN, MONK, RICH COUPLE, DWARF, BEGGAR, *and* GIRL.

Scene One

In the year sixteen hundred and nine
Science' light began to shine.
At Padua City, in a modest house
Galileo Galilei set out to prove
The sun is still, the earth is on the move.

Galileo's scantily furnished study. Morning. Galileo is washing himself. A bare-footed boy, Andrea, son of his housekeeper, Mrs. Sarti, enters with a big astronomical model.

GALILEO Where did you get that thing?

ANDREA The coachman brought it.

GALILEO Who sent it?

ANDREA It said "From the Court of Naples" on the box.

GALILEO I don't want their stupid presents. Illuminated manuscripts, a statue of Hercules the size of an elephant – they never send money.

ANDREA But isn't this an astronomical instrument, Mr. Galilei?

GALILEO That is an antique too. An expensive toy.

ANDREA What's it for?

GALILEO It's a map of the sky according to the wise men of ancient Greece. Bosh! We'll try and sell it to the university. They still teach it there.

ANDREA How does it work, Mr. Galilei?

GALILEO It's complicated.

ANDREA I think I could understand it.

GALILEO (*interested*) Maybe. Let's begin at the beginning. Description!

ANDREA There are metal rings, a lot of them.

GALILEO How many?

ANDREA Eight.

GALILEO Correct. And?

ANDREA There are words painted on the bands.

GALILEO What words?

ANDREA The names of stars.

GALILEO Such as?

ANDREA   Here is a band with the sun on it and on the inside band is the moon.

GALILEO   Those metal bands represent crystal globes, eight of them.

ANDREA   Crystal?

GALILEO   Like huge soap bubbles one inside the other and the stars are supposed to be tacked on to them. Spin the band with the sun on it. (*Andrea does*) You see the fixed ball in the middle?

ANDREA   Yes.

GALILEO   That's the earth. For two thousand years man has chosen to believe that the sun and all the host of stars revolve about him. Well. The Pope, the Cardinals, the princes, the scholars, captains, merchants, housewives, have pictured themselves squatting in the middle of an affair like that.

ANDREA   Locked up inside?

GALILEO   (*triumphant*) Ah!

ANDREA   It's like a cage.

GALILEO   So you sensed that. (*Against the model*) I like to think the ships began it.

ANDREA   Why?

GALILEO   They used to hug the coasts and then all of a sudden they left the coasts and spread over the oceans. A new age was coming. I was on to it years ago. I was a young man, in Siena. There was a group of masons arguing. They had to raise a block of granite. It was hot. To help matters, one of them wanted to try a new arrangement of ropes. After five minutes' discussion, out went a method which had been employed for a thousand years. The millenium of faith is ended, said I, this is the millenium of doubt. And we are pulling out of that contraption. The sayings of the wise men won't wash anymore. Everybody, at last, is getting nosey. I predict that in our time astronomy will become the gossip of the market place and the sons of fishwives will pack the schools.

ANDREA   You're off again, Mr. Galilei. Give me the towel. (*He wipes some soap from Galileo's back*)

GALILEO   By that time, with any luck, they will be learning that the earth rolls round the sun, and that their mothers, the captains, the scholars, the princes and the Pope are rolling with it.

ANDREA   That turning-round-business is no good. I can see with my own eyes that the sun comes up in one place in the morning and goes down in a different place in the evening. It doesn't stand still, I can see it move.

GALILEO   You see nothing, all you do is gawk. Gawking is not seeing. (*He puts the iron washstand in the middle of the room*)

Now: that's the sun. Sit down. (*Andrea sits on a chair. Galileo stands behind him*) Where is the sun, on your right or on your left?

ANDREA   Left.

GALILEO   And how will it get to the right?

ANDREA   By your putting it there, of course.

GALILEO   Of course? (*He picks Andrea up, chair and all, and carries him round to the other side of the washstand*) Now where is the sun?

ANDREA   On the right.

GALILEO   And did it move?

ANDREA   I did.

GALILEO   Wrong. Stupid! The chair moved.

ANDREA   But I was on it.

GALILEO   Of course. The chair is the earth, and you're sitting on it. (*Mrs. Sarti, who has come in with a glass of milk and a roll, has been watching*)

MRS. SARTI   What are you doing with my son, Mr. Galilei?

ANDREA   Now, mother, you don't understand.

MRS. SARTI   You understand, don't you? Last night he tried to tell me that the earth goes round the sun. You'll soon have him saying that two times two is five.

GALILEO (*eating his breakfast*)   Apparently we are on the threshold of a new era, Mrs. Sarti.

MRS. SARTI   Well, I hope we can pay the milkman in this new era. A young gentleman is here to take private lessons and he is well-dressed and don't you frighten him away like you did the others. Wasting your time with Andrea! (*To Andrea*) How many times have I told you not to wheedle free lessons out of Mr. Galilei? (*Mrs. Sarti goes*)

GALILEO   So you thought enough of the turning-round-business to tell your mother about it.

ANDREA   Just to surprise her.

GALILEO   Andrea, I wouldn't talk about our ideas outside.

ANDREA   Why not?

GALILEO   Certain of the authorities won't like it.

ANDREA   Why not, if it's the truth?

GALILEO (*laughs*)   Because we are like the worms who are little and have dim eyes and can hardly see the stars at all, and the new astronomy is a framework of guesses or very little more – yet. (*Mrs. Sarti shows in Ludovico Marsili, a presentable young man*)

GALILEO   This house is like a marketplace (*Pointing to the model*) Move that out of the way! Put it down there!

(Ludovico does)

LUDOVICO   Good morning, sir. My name is Ludovico Marsili.

GALILEO *(reading a letter of recommendation he has brought)*   You came by way of Holland and your family lives in the Campagna? Private lessons, thirty scudi a month.

LUDOVICO   That's all right, of course, sir.

GALILEO   What is your subject?

LUDOVICO   Horses.

GALILEO   Aha.

LUDOVICO   I don't understand science, sir.

GALILEO   Aha.

LUDOVICO   They showed me an instrument like that in Amsterdam. You'll pardon me, sir, but it didn't make sense to me at all.

GALILEO   It's out of date now.

(Andrea goes)

LUDOVICO   You'll have to be patient with me, sir. Nothing in science makes sense to me.

GALILEO   Aha.

LUDOVICO   I saw a brand new instrument in Amsterdam. A tube affair. "See things five times as large as life!" It had two lenses, one at each end, one lens bulged and the other was like that. *(Gesture)* Any normal person would think that different lenses cancel each other out. They didn't! I just stood and looked a fool.

GALILEO   I don't quite follow you. What does one see enlarged?

LUDOVICO   Church steeples, pigeons, boats. Anything at a distance.

GALILEO   Did you yourself – see things enlarged?

LUDOVICO   Yes, sir.

GALILEO   And the tube had two lenses? Was it like this? *(He has been making a sketch)*

(Ludovico nods)

GALILEO   A recent invention?

LUDOVICO   It must be. They only started peddling it on the streets a few days before I left Holland.

GALILEO *(starts to scribble calculations on the sketch; almost friendly)*   Why do you bother your head with science? Why don't you just breed horses?

(Enter Mrs. Sarti. Galileo doesn't see her. She listens to the following)

LUDOVICO   My mother is set on the idea that science is necessary nowadays for conversation.

GALILEO   Aha. You'll find Latin or philosophy easier. *(Mrs. Sarti catches his eye)* I'll see you on Tuesday afternoon.

LUDOVICO   I shall look forward to it, sir.

GALILEO   Good morning. (*He goes to the window and shouts into the street*) Andrea! Hey, Redhead, Redhead!

MRS. SARTI   The curator of the museum is here to see you.

GALILEO   Don't look at me like that. I took him, didn't I?

MRS. SARTI   I caught your eye in time.

GALILEO   Show the curator in.

(*She goes. He scribbles something on a new sheet of paper. The Curator comes in*)

CURATOR   Good morning, Mr. Galilei.

GALILEO   Lend me a scudo. (*He takes it and goes to the window, wrapping the coin in the paper on which he has been scribbling*) Redhead, run to the spectacle-maker and bring me two lenses; here are the measurements. (*He throws the paper out of the window. During the following scene Galileo studies his sketch of the lenses*)

CURATOR   Mr. Galilei, I have come to return your petition for an honorarium. Unfortunately I am unable to recommend your request.

GALILEO   My good sir, how can I make ends meet on five hundred scudi?

CURATOR   What about your private students?

GALILEO   If I spend all my time with students, when am I to study? My particular science is on the threshold of important discoveries. (*He throws a manuscript on the table*) Here are my findings on the laws of falling bodies. That should be worth 200 scudi.

CURATOR   I am sure that any paper of yours is of infinite worth, Mr. Galilei. . . .

GALILEO   I was limiting it to 200 scudi.

CURATOR (*cool*)   Mr. Galilei, if you want money and leisure, go to Florence. I have no doubt Prince Cosmo de Medici will be glad to subsidize you, but eventually you will be forbidden to think – in the name of the Inquisition. (*Galileo says nothing*) Now let us not make a mountain out of a molehill. You are happy here in the Republic of Venice but you need money. Well, that's human, Mr. Galilei, may I suggest a simple solution? You remember that chart you made for the army to extract cube roots without any knowledge of mathematics? Now that was practical!

GALILEO   Bosh!

CURATOR   Don't say bosh about something that astounded the Chamber of Commerce. Our city elders are businessmen. Why don't you invent something useful that will bring them a little profit?

GALILEO (*playing with the sketch of the lenses; suddenly*)　I see. Mr.
　Priuli, I may have something for you.

CURATOR　You don't say so.

GALILEO　It's not quite there yet, but . . .

CURATOR　You've never let me down yet, Galilei.

GALILEO　You are always an inspiration to me, Priuli.

CURATOR　You are a great man: a discontented man, but I've always
　said you are a great man.

GALILEO (*tartly*)　My discontent, Priuli, is for the most part with
　myself. I am forty-six years of age and have achieved nothing which
　satisfies me.

CURATOR　I won't disturb you any further.

GALILEO　Thank you. Good morning.

CURATOR　Good morning. And thank you.
　(*He goes. Galileo sighs. Andrea returns, bringing lenses*)

ANDREA　One scudo was not enough. I had to leave my cap with him
　before he'd let me take them away.

GALILEO　We'll get it back some day. Give them to me. (*He takes the
　lenses over to the window, holding them in the relation they would
　have in a telescope*)

ANDREA　What are those for?

GALILEO　Something for the senate. With any luck, they will rake in
　200 scudi. Take a look!

ANDREA　My, things look close! I can read the copper letters on the
　bell in the Campanile. And the washerwomen by the river, I can see
　their washboards!

GALILEO　Get out of the way. (*Looking through the lenses himself*)
　Aha!

Scene Two

> No one's virtue is complete:
> Great Galileo liked to eat.
> You will not resent, we hope,
> The truth about his telescope.

*The great arsenal of Venice, overlooking the harbor full of ships.
Senators and Officials on one side, Galileo, his daughter Virginia and*

his friend Sagredo, on the other side. They are dressed in formal, festive clothes. Virginia is fourteen and charming. She carries a velvet cushion on which lies a brand new telescope. Behind Galileo are some Artisans from the arsenal. There are onlookers, Ludovico amongst them.

CURATOR (*announcing*) Senators, Artisans of the Great Arsenal of Venice; Mr. Galileo Galilei, professor of mathematics at your University of Padua.

(*Galileo steps forward and starts to speak*)

GALILEO Members of the High Senate! Gentlemen: I have great pleasure, as director of this institute, in presenting for your approval and acceptance an entirely new instrument originating from this our great arsenal of the Republic of Venice. As professor of mathematics at your University of Padua, your obedient servant has always counted it his privilege to offer you such discoveries and inventions as might prove lucrative to the manufacturers and merchants of our Venetian Republic. Thus, in all humility, I tender you this, my optical tube, or telescope, constructed, I assure you, on the most scientific and Christian principles, the product of seventeen years patient research at your University of Padua.

(*Galileo steps back. The senators applaud*)

SAGREDO (*aside to Galileo*) Now you will be able to pay your bills.

GALILEO Yes. It will make money for them. But you realize that it is more than a money-making gadget? – I turned it on the moon last night . . .

CURATOR (*in his best chamber-of-commerce manner*) Gentlemen: Our Republic is to be congratulated not only because this new acquisition will be one more feather in the cap of Venetian culture . . . (*Polite applause*) . . . not only because our own Mr. Galilei has generously handed this fresh product of his teeming brain entirely over to you, allowing you to manufacture as many of these highly saleable articles as you please. . . . (*Considerable applause*) But Gentlemen of the Senate, has it occurred to you that – with the help of this remarkable new instrument – the battlefleet of the enemy will be visible to us a full two hours before we are visible to him?

(*Tremendous applause*)

GALILEO (*aside to Sagredo*) We have been held up three generations for lack of a thing like this. I want to go home.

SAGREDO What about the moon?

GALILEO Well, for one thing, it doesn't give off its own light.

CURATOR (*continuing his oration*)   And now, Your Excellency, and Members of the Senate, Mr. Galilei entreats you to accept the instrument from the hands of his charming daughter Virginia.
(*Polite applause. He beckons to Virginia who steps forward and presents the telescope to the Doge*)

CURATOR (*during this*)   Mr. Galilei gives his invention entirely into your hands, Gentlemen, enjoining you to construct as many of these instruments as you may please.
(*More applause. The Senators gather round the telescope, examining it, and looking through it*)

GALILEO (*aside to Sagredo*)   Do you know what the Milky Way is made of?

SAGREDO   No.

GALILEO   I do.

CURATOR (*interrupting*)   Congratulations, Mr. Galilei. Your extra five hundred scudi a year are safe.

GALILEO   Pardon? What? Of course, the five hundred scudi! Yes! (*A prosperous man is standing beside the Curator*)

CURATOR   Mr. Galilei, Mr. Matti of Florence.

MATTI   You're opening new fields, Mr. Galilei. We could do with you at Florence.

CURATOR   Now, Mr. Matti, leave something to us poor Venetians.

MATTI   It is a pity that a great republic has to seek an excuse to pay its great men their right and proper dues.

CURATOR   Even a great man has to have an incentive. (*He joins the Senators at the telescope*)

MATTI   I am an iron founder.

GALILEO   Iron founder!

MATTI   With factories at Pisa and Florence. I wanted to talk to you about a machine you designed for a friend of mine in Padua.

GALILEO   I'll put you on to someone to copy it for you, I am not going to have the time. – How are things in Florence? (*They wander away*)

FIRST SENATOR (*peering*)   Extraordinary! They're having their lunch on that frigate. Lobsters! I'm hungry!
(*Laughter*)

SECOND SENATOR   Oh, good heavens, look at her! I must tell my wife to stop bathing on the roof. When can I buy one of these things?
(*Laughter. Virginia has spotted Ludovico among the onlookers and drags him to Galileo*)

VIRGINIA (*to Ludovico*)   Did I do it nicely?

LUDOVICO   I thought so.
VIRGINIA   Here's Ludovico to congratulate you, father.
LUDOVICO (*embarrassed*)   Congratulations, sir.
GALILEO   I improved it.
LUDOVICO   Yes, sir. I am beginning to understand science.
  (*Galileo is surrounded*)
VIRGINIA   Isn't father a great man?
LUDOVICO   Yes.
VIRGINIA   Isn't the new thing father made pretty?
LUDOVICO   Yes, a pretty red. Where I saw it first it was covered in green.
VIRGINIA   What was?
LUDOVICO   Never mind. (*A short pause*) Have you ever been to Holland?
  (*They go. All Venice is congratulating Galileo, who wants to go home*)

Scene Three

> *January ten, sixteen ten:*
> *Galileo Galilei abolishes heaven.*

Galileo's study at Padua. It is night. Galileo and Sagredo at a telescope.

SAGREDO (*softly*)   The edge of the crescent is jagged. All along the dark part, near the shiny crescent, bright particles of light keep coming up, one after the other and growing larger and merging with the bright crescent.
GALILEO   How do you explain those spots of light?
SAGREDO   It can't be true . . .
GALILEO   It *is* true: they are high mountains.
SAGREDO   On a star?
GALILEO   Yes. The shining particles are mountain peaks catching the first rays of the rising sun while the slopes of the mountains are still dark, and what you see is the sunlight moving down the peaks into the valleys.

SAGREDO   But this gives the lie to all the astronomy that's been taught for the last two thousand years.

GALILEO   Yes. What you are seeing now has been seen by no other man beside myself.

SAGREDO   But the moon can't be an earth with mountains and valleys like our own any more than the earth can be a star.

GALILEO   The moon *is* an earth with mountains and valleys, – and the earth *is* a star. As the moon appears to us, so we appear to the moon. From the moon, the earth looks something like a crescent, sometimes like a half-globe, sometimes a full-globe, and sometimes it is not visible at all.

SAGREDO   Galileo, this is frightening.

(*An urgent knocking on the door*)

GALILEO   I've discovered something else, something even more astonishing.

(*More knocking. Galileo opens the door and the Curator comes in*)

CURATOR   There it is – your "miraculous optical tube." Do you know that this invention he so picturesquely termed "the fruit of seventeen years research" will be on sale tomorrow for two scudi apiece at every street corner in Venice? A shipload of them has just arrived from Holland.

SAGREDO   Oh, dear!

(*Galileo turns his back and adjusts the telescope*)

CURATOR   When I think of the poor gentlemen of the senate who believed they were getting an invention they could monopolize for their own profit. . . . Why, when they took their first look through the glass, it was only by the merest chance that they didn't see a peddler, seven times enlarged, selling tubes exactly like it at the corner of the street.

SAGREDO   Mr. Priuli, with the help of this instrument, Mr. Galileo has made discoveries that will revolutionize our concept of the universe.

CURATOR   Mr. Galileo provided the city with a first rate water pump and the irrigation works he designed function splendidly. How was I to expect this?

GALILEO (*still at the telescope*)   Not so fast, Priuli. I may be on the track of a very large gadget. Certain of the stars appear to have regular movements. If there were a clock in the sky, it could be seen from anywhere. That might be useful for your shipowners.

CURATOR   I won't listen to you. I listened to you before, and as a reward for my friendship you have made me the laughing-stock of the town. You can laugh – you got your money. But let me tell you this: you've destroyed my faith in a lot of things, Mr. Galilei. I'm disgusted with the world. That's all I have to say. (*He storms out*)

GALILEO (*embarrassed*)   Businessmen bore me, they suffer so. Did you see the frightened look in his eyes when he caught sight of a world not created solely for the purpose of doing business?

SAGREDO   Did you know that telescopes had been made in Holland?

GALILEO   I'd heard about it. But the one I made for the Senators was twice as good as any Dutchman's. Besides, I needed the money. How can I work, with the tax collector on the doorstep? And my poor daughter will never acquire a husband unless she has a dowry, she's not too bright. And I like to buy books – all kinds of books. Why not? And what about my appetite? I don't think well unless I eat well. Can I help it if I get my best ideas over a good meal and a bottle of wine? They don't pay me as much as they pay the butcher's boy. If only I could have five years to do nothing but research! Come on. I am going to show you something else.

SAGREDO   I don't know that I want to look again.

GALILEO   This is one of the brighter nebulae of the Milky Way. What do you see?

SAGREDO   But it's made up of stars – countless stars.

GALILEO   Countless worlds.

SAGREDO (*hesitating*)   What about the theory that the earth revolves round the sun? Have you run across anything about that?

GALILEO   No. But I noticed something on Tuesday that might prove a step towards even that. Where's Jupiter? There are four lesser stars near Jupiter. I happened on them on Monday but didn't take any particular note of their position. On Tuesday I looked again. I could have sworn they had moved. They have changed again. Tell me what you see.

SAGREDO   I only see three.

GALILEO   Where's the fourth? Let's get the charts and settle down to work.

(*They work and the lights dim. The lights go up again. It is near dawn*)

GALILEO   The only place the fourth can be is round at the back of the larger star where we cannot see it. This means there are small stars revolving around a big star. Where are the crystal shells now that the stars are supposed to be fixed to?

SAGREDO   Jupiter can't be attached to anything: there are other stars revolving round it.

GALILEO   There is no support in the heavens. (*Sagredo laughs awkwardly*) Don't stand there looking at me as if it weren't true.

SAGREDO   I suppose it is true. I'm afraid.

GALILEO   Why?

SAGREDO   What do you think is going to happen to you for saying that there is another sun around which other earths revolve? And that there are only stars and no difference between earth and heaven? Where is God then?

GALILEO   What do you mean?

SAGREDO   God? Where is God?

GALILEO   (*angrily*)   Not there! Any more than he'd be here — if creatures from the moon came down to look for him!

SAGREDO   Then where is He?

GALILEO   I'm not a theologian: I'm a mathematician.

SAGREDO   You are a human being! (*Almost shouting*) Where is God in your system of the universe?

GALILEO   Within ourselves. Or — nowhere.

SAGREDO   Ten years ago a man was burned at the stake for saying that.

GALILEO   Giordano Bruno was an idiot: he spoke too soon. He would never have been condemned if he could have backed up what he said with proof.

SAGREDO   (*incredulously*)   Do you really believe proof will make any difference?

GALILEO   I believe in the human race. The only people that can't be reasoned with are the dead. Human beings are intelligent.

SAGREDO   Intelligent — or merely shrewd?

GALILEO   I know they call a donkey a horse when they want to sell it, and a horse a donkey when they want to buy it. But is that the whole story? Aren't they susceptible to truth as well? (*He fishes a small pebble out of his pocket*) If anybody were to drop a stone . . . (*Drops the pebble*) . . . and tell them that it didn't fall, do you think they would keep quiet? The evidence of your own eyes is a very seductive thing. Sooner or later everybody must succumb to it.

SAGREDO   Galileo, I am helpless when you talk.

(*A church bell has been ringing for some time, calling people to mass. Enter Virginia, muffled up for mass, carrying a candle, protected from the wind by a globe*)

VIRGINIA   Oh, father, you promised to go to bed tonight, and it's five o'clock again.

GALILEO   Why are you up at this hour?

VIRGINIA   I'm going to mass with Mrs. Sarti. Ludovico is going too. How was the night, father?

GALILEO   Bright.

VIRGINIA   What did you find through the tube?

GALILEO   Only some little specks by the side of a star. I must draw attention to them somehow. I think I'll name them after the Prince of Florence. Why not call them the Medicean planets? By the way, we may move to Florence. I've written to His Highness, asking if he can use me as Court Mathematician.

VIRGINIA   Oh, father, we'll be at the court!

SAGREDO (*amazed*)   Galileo!

GALILEO   My dear Sagredo, I must have leisure. My only worry is that His Highness after all may not take me. I'm not accustomed to writing formal letters to great personages. Here, do you think this is the right sort of thing?

SAGREDO (*reads and quotes*)   "Whose sole desire is to reside in Your Highness' presence – the rising sun of our great age." Cosmo di Medici is a boy of nine.

GALILEO   The only way a man like me can land a good job is by crawling on his stomach. Your father, my dear, is going to take his share of the pleasures of life in exchange for all his hard work, and about time too. I have no patience, Sagredo, with a man who doesn't use his brains to fill his belly. Run along to mass now.

(*Virginia goes*)

SAGREDO   Galileo, do not go to Florence.

GALILEO   Why not?

SAGREDO   The monks are in power there.

GALILEO   Going to mass is a small price to pay for a full belly. And there are many famous scholars at the court of Florence.

SAGREDO   Court monkeys.

GALILEO   I shall enjoy taking them by the scruff of the neck and making them look through the telescope.

SAGREDO   Galileo, you are traveling the road to disaster. You are suspicious and skeptical in science, but in politics you are as naive as your daughter! How can people in power leave a man at large who tells the truth, even if it be the truth about the distant stars? Can you see the Pope scribbling a note in his diary: "10th of January, 1610, Heaven abolished?" A moment ago, when you were at the telescope, I saw you tied to the stake, and when you said you believed in proof, I smelt burning flesh!

GALILEO   I am going to Florence.

(*Before the next scene a curtain with the following legend on it is lowered*)

By setting the name of Medici in the sky, I am bestowing immortality upon the stars. I commend myself to you as your most faithful and devoted servant, whose sole desire is to reside in Your Highness' presence, the rising sun of our great age.

– GALILEO GALILEI

Scene Four

Galileo's house at Florence. Well-appointed. Galileo is demonstrating his telescope to Prince Cosmo di Medici, a boy of nine, accompanied by his Lord Chamberlain, Ladies and Gentlemen of the Court and an assortment of university Professors. With Galileo are Andrea and Federzoni, the new assistant (an old man). Mrs. Sarti stands by. Before the scene opens the voice of the Philosopher can be heard.

VOICE OF THE PHILOSOPHER Quaedam miracula universi. Orbes mystice canorae, arcus crystallini, circulatio corporum coelestium. Cyclorum epicyclorumque intoxicatio, integritas tabulae chordarum et architectura elata globorum coelestrium.

GALILEO Shall we speak in everyday language? My colleague Mr. Federzoni does not understand Latin.

PHILOSOPHER Is it necessary that he should?

GALILEO Yes.

PHILOSOPHER Forgive me. I thought he was your mechanic.

ANDREA Mr. Federzoni is a mechanic and a scholar.

PHILOSOPHER Thank you, young man. If Mr. Federzoni insists . . .

GALILEO I insist.

PHILOSOPHER It will not be as clear, but it's your house. Your Highness . . . (*The Prince is ineffectually trying to establish contact with Andrea*) I was about to recall to Mr. Galilei some of the wonders of the universe as they are set down for us in the Divine Classics. (*The Ladies "ah"*) Remind him of the "mystically musical spheres, the crystal arches, the circulation of the heavenly bodies –"

ELDERLY LADY Perfect poise!

PHILOSOPHER "– the intoxication of the cycles and epicycles, the integrity of the tables of chords and the enraptured architecture of the celestial globes."

ELDERLY LADY What diction!

PHILOSOPHER May I pose the question: Why should we go out of our way to look for things that can only strike a discord in this ineffable harmony?

(*The Ladies applaud*)

FEDERZONI   Take a look through here – you'll be interested.

ANDREA   Sit down here, please.

(*The Professors laugh*)

MATHEMATICIAN   Mr. Galilei, nobody doubts that your brain child – or is it your adopted brain child?– is brilliantly contrived.

GALILEO   Your Highness, one can see the four stars as large as life, you know.

(*The Prince looks to the Elderly Lady for guidance*)

MATHEMATICIAN   Ah. But has it occurred to you that an eyeglass through which one sees such phenomena might not be a too reliable eyeglass?

GALILEO   How is that?

MATHEMATICIAN   If one could be sure you would keep your temper, Mr. Galilei, I could suggest that what one sees in the eyeglass and what is in the heavens are two entirely different things.

GALILEO (*quietly*)   You are suggesting fraud?

MATHEMATICIAN   No! How could I, in the presence of His Highness?

ELDERLY LADY   The gentlemen are just wondering if Your Highness' stars are really, really there!

(*Pause*)

YOUNG LADY (*trying to be helpful*)   Can one see the claws on the Great Bear?

GALILEO   And everything on Taurus the Bull.

FEDERZONI   Are you going to look through it or not?

MATHEMATICIAN   With the greatest of pleasure.

(*Pause. Nobody goes near the telescope. All of a sudden the boy Andrea turns and marches pale and erect past them through the whole length of the room. The Guests follow with their eyes*)

MRS. SARTI (*as he passes her*)   What is the matter with you?

ANDREA (*shocked*)   They are wicked.

PHILOSOPHER   Your Highness, it is a delicate matter and I had no intention of bringing it up, but Mr. Galilei was about to demonstrate the impossible. His new stars would have broken the outer crystal sphere – which we know of on the authority of Aristotle. I am sorry.

MATHEMATICIAN   The last word.

FEDERZONI   He had no telescope.

MATHEMATICIAN   Quite.

GALILEO (*keeping his temper*) "Truth is the daughter of Time, not of Authority." Gentlemen, the sum of our knowledge is pitiful. It has been my singular good fortune to find a new instrument which brings a small patch of the universe a little bit closer. It is at your disposal.

PHILOSOPHER Where is all this leading?

GALILEO Are we, as scholars, concerned with where the truth might lead us?

PHILOSOPHER Mr. Galilei, the truth might lead us anywhere!

GALILEO I can only beg you to look through my eyeglass.

MATHEMATICIAN (*wild*) If I understand Mr. Galilei correctly, he is asking us to discard the teachings of two thousand years.

GALILEO For two thousand years we have been looking at the sky and didn't see the four moons of Jupiter, and there they were all the time. Why defend shaken teachings? You should be doing the shaking. (*The Prince is sleepy*) Your Highness! My work in the Great Arsenal of Venice brought me in daily contact with sailors, carpenters, and so on. These men are unread. They depend on the evidence of their senses. But they taught me many new ways of doing things. The question is whether these gentlemen here want to be found out as fools by men who might not have had the advantage of a classical education but who are not afraid to use their eyes. I tell you that our dockyards are stirring with that same high curiosity which was the true glory of Ancient Greece.
(*Pause*)

PHILOSOPHER I have no doubt Mr. Galilei's theories will arouse the enthusiasm of the dockyards.

CHAMBERLAIN Your Highness, I find to my amazement that this highly informative discussion has exceeded the time we had allowed for it. May I remind Your Highness that the State Ball begins in three-quarters of an hour?
(*The Court bows low*)

ELDERLY LADY We would really have liked to look through your eyeglass, Mr. Galilei, wouldn't we, Your Highness?
(*The Prince bows politely and is led to the door. Galileo follows the Prince, Chamberlain and Ladies towards the exit. The Professors remain at the telescope*)

GALILEO (*almost servile*) All anybody has to do is look through the telescope, Your Highness.
(*Mrs. Sarti takes a plate with candies to the Prince as he is walking out*)

MRS. SARTI A piece of homemade candy, Your Highness?

ELDERLY LADY Not now. Thank you. It is too soon before His Highness' supper.

PHILOSOPHER Wouldn't I like to take that thing to pieces.

MATHEMATICIAN Ingenious contraption. It must be quite difficult to keep clean. (*He rubs the lens with his handkerchief and looks at the handkerchief*)

FEDERZONI We did not paint the Medicean stars on the lens.

ELDERLY LADY (*to the Prince, who has whispered something to her*) No, no, no, there is nothing the matter with your stars!

CHAMBERLAIN (*across the stage to Galileo*) His Highness will of course seek the opinion of the greatest living authority: Christopher Clavius, Chief Astonomer to the Papal College in Rome.

Scene Five

Things take indeed a wondrous turn
When learned men do stoop to learn.
Clavius, we are pleased to say,
Upheld Galileo Galilei.

A burst of laughter is heard and the curtains reveal a ball in the Collegium Romanum. High Churchmen, monks and Scholars standing about talking and laughing. Galileo by himself in a corner.

FAT PRELATE (*shaking with laughter*) Hopeless! Hopeless? Hopeless! Will you tell me something people won't believe?

A SCHOLAR Yes, that you don't love your stomach!

FAT PRELATE They'd believe that. They only do not believe what's good for them. They doubt the devil, but fill them up with some fiddle-de-dee about the earth rolling like a marble in the gutter and they swallow it hook, line, and sinker. Sancta simplicitas!
(*He laughs until the tears run down his cheeks. The others laugh with him. A group has formed whose members boisterously begin to pretend they are standing on a rolling globe*)

A MONK It's rolling fast. I'm dizzy. May I hold on to you, Professor?
(*He sways dizzily and clings to one of the scholars for support*)

THE SCHOLAR Old Mother Earth's been at the bottle again. Whoa!

MONK Hey! Hey! We're slipping off! Help!

SECOND SCHOLAR   Look! There's Venus! Hold me lads. Whee!

SECOND MONK   Don't, don't hurl us off on to the moon. There are nasty sharp mountain peaks on the moon, brethren!

VARIOUSLY   Hold tight! Hold tight! Don't look down! Hold tight! It'll make you giddy!

FAT PRELATE   And we cannot have giddy people in Holy Rome.
(*They rock with laughter. An infuriated Monk comes out from a large door at the rear holding a Bible in his hand and pointing out a page with his finger*)

INFURIATED MONK   What does the Bible say – "Sun, stand thou still on Gideon and thou, moon, in the valley of Ajalon." Can the sun come to a standstill if it doesn't ever move? Does the Bible lie?

FAT PRELATE   How did Christopher Clavius, the greatest astronomer we have, get mixed up in an investigation of this kind?

INFURIATED MONK   He's in there with his eye glued to that diabolical instrument.

FAT PRELATE (*to Galileo, who has been playing with his pebble and has dropped it*)   Mr. Galilei, something dropped down.

GALILEO   Monsignor, are you sure it didn't drop up?

INFURIATED MONK   As astronomers we are aware that there are phenomena which are beyond us, but man can't expect to understand everything!
(*Enter a very old Cardinal leaning on a Monk for support. Others move aside*)

OLD CARDINAL   Aren't they out yet? Can't they reach a decision on that paltry matter? Christopher Clavius ought to know his astronomy after all these years. I am informed that Mr. Galilei transfers mankind from the center of the universe to somewhere on the outskirts. Mr. Galilei is therefore an enemy of mankind and must be dealt with as such. Is it conceivable that God would trust this most precious fruit of His labor to a minor frolicking star? Would He have sent His Son to such a place? How can there be people with such twisted minds that they believe what they're told by the slave of a multiplication table?

FAT PRELATE (*quietly to Cardinal*)   The gentleman is over there.

OLD CARDINAL   So you are the man. You know my eyes are not what they were, but I can see you bear a striking resemblance to the man we burned. What was his name?

MONK   Your Eminence must avoid excitement, the doctor said . . .

OLD CARDINAL (*disregarding him*)   So you have degraded the earth despite the fact that you live by her and receive everything from her. I won't have it! I won't have it! I won't be a nobody on an inconsequential star briefly twirling hither and thither. I tread the earth, and the earth is firm beneath my feet, and there is no motion to the earth, and the earth is the center of all things, and I am the center of the earth, and the eye of the creator is upon me. About me revolve, affixed to their crystal shells, the lesser lights of the stars and the great light of the sun, created to give light upon me that God might see me – Man, God's greatest effort, the center of creation. "In the image of God created He him." Immortal . . . (*His strength fails him and he catches for the Monk for support*)

MONK   You mustn't overtax your strength, Your Eminence.

(*At this moment the door at the rear opens and Christopher Clavius enters followed by his Astronomers. He strides hastily across the hall, looking neither to right nor left. As he goes by we hear him say –*)

CLAVIUS   He is right.

(*Deadly silence. All turn to Galileo*)

OLD CARDINAL   What is it? Have they reached a decision?

(*No one speaks*)

MONK   It is time that Your Eminence went home.

(*The hall is emptying fast. One little Monk who had entered with Clavius speaks to Galileo*)

LITTLE MONK   Mr. Galilei, I heard Father Clavius say: "Now it's for the theologians to set the heavens right again." You have won.

(*Before the next scene a curtain with the following legend on it is lowered*)

     . . . . . As these new astronomical charts enable us to determine longitudes at sea and so make it possible to reach the new continents by the shortest routes, we would beseech Your Excellency to aid us in reaching Mr. Galilei, mathematician to the Court of Florence, who is now in Rome . . . . .

> – From a letter written by a member
> of the Genoa Chamber of Commerce
> and Navigation to the Papal Legation.

Scene Six

> When Galileo was in Rome
> A Cardinal asked him to his home
> He wined and dined him as his guest
> And only made one small request.

Cardinal Bellarmin's house in Rome. Music is heard and the chatter of many guests. Two Secretaries are at the rear of the stage at a desk. Galileo, his daughter Virginia, now 21, and Ludovico Marsili, who has become her fiancé, are just arriving. A few Guests, standing near the entrance with masks in their hands, nudge each other and are suddenly silent. Galileo looks at them. They applaud him politely and bow.

VIRGINIA   O father! I'm so happy. I won't dance with anyone but you, Ludovico.

GALILEO (*to a Secretary*)   I was to wait here for His Eminence.

FIRST SECRETARY   His Eminence will be with you in a few minutes.

VIRGINIA   Do I look proper?

LUDOVICO   You are showing some lace.

(*Galileo puts his arms around their shoulders*)

GALILEO (*quoting mischievously*)

> Fret not, daughter, if perchance
> You attract a wanton glance.
> The eyes that catch a trembling lace
> Will guess the heartbeat's quickened pace.
> Lovely woman still may be
> Careless with felicity.

VIRGINIA (*to Galileo*)   Feel my heart.

GALILEO (*to Ludovico*)   It's thumping.

VIRGINIA   I hope I always say the right thing.

LUDOVICO   She's afraid she's going to let us down.

VIRGINIA   Oh, I want to look beautiful.

GALILEO   You'd better. If you don't they'll start saying all over again that the earth doesn't turn.

LUDOVICO (*laughing*)   It *doesn't* turn, sir.

(*Galileo laughs*)

GALILEO Go and enjoy yourselves. (*He speaks to one of the Secretaries*) A large fête?

FIRST SECRETARY Two hundred and fifty guests, Mr. Galilei. We have represented here this evening most of the great families of Italy, the Orsinis, the Villanis, the Nuccolis, the Soldanieris, the Canes, the Lecchis, the Estensis, the Colombinis, the . . .
(*Virginia comes running back*)

VIRGINIA Oh father, I didn't tell you: you're famous.

GALILEO Why?

VIRGINIA The hairdresser in the Via Vittorio kept four other ladies waiting and took me first. (*Exit*)

GALILEO (*at the stairway, leaning over the well*) Rome!
(*Enter Cardinal Bellarmin, wearing the mask of a lamb, and Cardinal Barberini, wearing the mask of a dove*)

SECRETARIES Their Eminences, Cardinals Bellarmin and Barberini.
(*The Cardinals lower their masks*)

GALILEO (*to Bellarmin*) Your Eminence.

BELLARMIN Mr. Galilei, Cardinal Barberini.

GALILEO Your Eminence

BARBERINI So you are the father of that lovely child!

BELLARMIN Who is inordinately proud of being her father's daughter.
(*They laugh*)

BARBERINI (*points his finger at Galileo*) "The sun riseth and setteth and returneth to its place," saith the Bible. What saith Galilei?

GALILEO Appearances are notoriously deceptive, Your Eminence. Once when I was so high, I was standing on a ship that was pulling away from the shore and I shouted, "The shore is moving!" I know now that it was the ship which was moving.

BARBERINI (*laughs*) You can't catch that man. I tell you, Bellarmin, his moons around Jupiter are hard nuts to crack. Unfortunately for me I happened to glance at a few papers on astronomy once. It is harder to get rid of than the itch.

BELLARMIN Let's move with the times. If it makes navigation easier for sailors to use new charts based on a new hypothesis let them have them. We only have to scotch doctrines that contradict Holy Writ.
(*He leans over the balustrade of the well and acknowledges various Guests*)

BARBERINI But Bellarmin, you haven't caught on to this fellow. The scriptures don't satisfy him. Copernicus does.

GALILEO Copernicus? "He that withholdeth corn the people shall curse him." Book of Proverbs.

BARBERINI "A prudent man concealeth knowledge." Also Book of Proverbs.

GALILEO "Where no oxen are, the stable is clean, but much increase is by the strength of the ox."

BARBERINI "He that ruleth his spirit is better than he that taketh a city."

GALILEO "But a broken spirit drieth up the bones." (*Pause*) "Doth not wisdom cry?"

BARBERINI "Can one walk on hot coals and his feet not be scorched?" – Welcome to Rome, Friend Galileo. You recall the legend of our city's origin? Two small boys found sustenance and refuge with a she-wolf and from that day we have paid the price for the she-wolf's milk. But the place is not bad. We have everything for your pleasure – from a scholarly dispute with Bellarmin to ladies of high degree. Look at that woman flaunting herself. No? He wants a weighty discussion! All right! (*To Galileo*) You people speak in terms of circles and ellipses and regular velocities – simple movements that the human mind can grasp – very convenient – but suppose Almighty God had taken it into his head to make the stars move like that ... (*He describes an irregular motion with his fingers through the air*) ... then where would you be?

GALILEO My good man – the Almighty would have endowed us with brains like that ... (*Repeats the movement*) ... so that we could grasp the movements ... (*Repeats the movement*) ... like that. I believe in the brain.

BARBERINI I consider the brain inadequate. He doesn't answer. He is too polite to tell me he considers *my* brain inadequate. What is one to do with him? Butter wouldn't melt in his mouth. All he wants to do is to prove that God made a few boners in astronomy. God didn't study his astronomy hard enough before he composed Holy Writ. (*To the Secretaries*) Don't take anything down. This is a scientific discussion among friends.

BELLARMIN (*to Galileo*) Does it not appear more probable – even to you – that the Creator knows more about his work than the created?

GALILEO In his blindness man is liable to misread not only the sky but also the Bible.

BELLARMIN The interpretation of the Bible is a matter for the ministers of God. (*Galileo remains silent*) At last you are quiet. (*He gestures to the Secretaries. They start writing*) Tonight the Holy

Office has decided that the theory according to which the earth goes around the sun is foolish, absurd, and a heresy. I am charged, Mr. Galilei, with cautioning you to abandon these teachings. (*To the First Secretary*) Would you repeat that?

FIRST SECRETARY (*reading*)   "His Eminence, Cardinal Bellarmin, to the aforesaid Galilei: The Holy Office has resolved that the theory according to which the earth goes around the sun is foolish, absurd, and a heresy. I am charged, Mr. Galilei, with cautioning you to abandon these teachings."

GALILEO (*rocking on his base*)   But the facts!

BARBERINI (*consoling*)   Your findings have been ratified by the Papal Observatory, Galilei. That should be most flattering to you . . .

BELLARMIN (*cutting in*)   The Holy Office formulated the decree without going into details.

GALILEO (*to Barberini*)   Do you realize, the future of all scientific research is . . .

BELLARMIN (*cutting in*)   Completely assured, Mr. Galilei. It is not given to man to know the truth: it is granted to him to seek after the truth. Science is the legitimate and beloved daughter of the Church. She must have confidence in the Church.

GALILEO (*infuriated*)   I would not try confidence by whistling her too often.

BARBERINI (*quickly*)   Be careful what you're doing – you'll be throwing out the baby with the bath water, friend Galilei. (*Serious*) We need you more than you need us.

BELLARMIN   Well, it is time we introduced our distinguished friend to our guests. The whole country talks of him!

BARBERINI   Let us replace our masks, Bellarmin. Poor Galilei hasn't got one.

(*He laughs. They take Galileo out*)

FIRST SECRETARY   Did you get his last sentence?

SECOND SECRETARY   Yes. Do you have what he said about believing in the brain?

(*Another cardinal – the Inquisitor – enters*)

INQUISITOR   Did the conference take place?

(*The First Secretary hands him the papers and the Inquisitor dismisses the Secretaries. They go. The Inquisitor sits down and starts to read the transcription. Two or three Young Ladies skitter across the stage; they see the Inquisitor and curtsy as they go*)

YOUNG GIRL   Who was that?

HER FRIEND   The Cardinal Inquisitor.

(*They giggle and go. Enter Virginia. She curtsies as she goes. The Inquisitor stops her*)

INQUISITOR Good evening, my child. Beautiful night. May I congratulate you on your betrothal? Your young man comes from a fine family. Are you staying with us here in Rome?

VIRGINIA Not now, Your Eminence. I must go home to prepare for the wedding.

INQUISITOR Ah. You are accompanying your father to Florence. That should please him. Science must be cold comfort in a home. Your youth and warmth will keep him down to earth. It is easy to get lost up there. (*He gestures to the sky*)

VIRGINIA He doesn't talk to me about the stars, Your Eminence.

INQUISITOR No. (*He laughs*) They don't eat fish in the fisherman's house. I can tell you something about astronomy. My child, it seems that God has blessed our modern astronomers with imaginations. It is quite alarming! Do you know that the earth – which we old fogies supposed to be so large – has shrunk to something no bigger than a walnut, and the new universe has grown so vast that prelates – and even cardinals – look like ants. Why, God Almighty might lose sight of a Pope! I wonder if I know your Father Confessor.

VIRGINIA Father Christopherus, from Saint Ursula's at Florence, Your Eminence.

INQUISITOR My dear child, your father will need you. Not so much now perhaps, but one of these days. You are pure, and there is strength in purity. Greatness is sometimes, indeed often, too heavy a burden for those to whom God has granted it. What man is so great that he has no place in a prayer? But I am keeping you, my dear. Your fiancé will be jealous of me, and I am afraid your father will never forgive me for holding forth on astronomy. Go to your dancing and remember me to Father Christopherus.

(*Virginia kisses his ring and runs off. The Inquisitor resumes his reading*)

Scene Seven

> Galileo, feeling grim,
> A young monk came to visit him.
> The monk was born of common folk.
> It was of science that they spoke.

Garden of the Florentine Ambassador in Rome. Distant hum of a great city. Galileo and the Little Monk of Scene Five are talking.

GALILEO   Let's hear it. That robe you're wearing gives you the right to say whatever you want to say. Let's hear it.

LITTLE MONK   I have studied physics, Mr. Galilei.

GALILEO   That might help us if it enabled you to admit that two and two are four.

LITTLE MONK   Mr. Galilei, I have spent four sleepless nights trying to reconcile the decree that I have read with the moons of Jupiter that I have seen. This morning I decided to come to see you after I had said Mass.

GALILEO   To tell me that Jupiter has no moons?

LITTLE MONK   No, I found out that I think the decree a wise decree. It has shocked me into realizing that free research has its dangers. I have had to decide to give up astronomy. However, I felt the impulse to confide in you some of the motives which have impelled even a passionate physicist to abandon his work.

GALILEO   Your motives are familiar to me.

LITTLE MONK   You mean, of course, the special powers invested in certain commissions of the Holy Office? But there is something else. I would like to talk to you about my family. I do not come from the great city. My parents are peasants in the Campagna, who know about the cultivation of the olive tree, and not much about anything else. Too often these days when I am trying to concentrate on tracking down the moons of Jupiter, I see my parents. I see them sitting by the fire with my sister, eating their curded cheese. I see the beams of the ceiling above them, which the smoke of centuries has blackened, and I can see the veins stand out on their toil-worn hands, and the little spoons in their hands. They scrape a living, and underlying their poverty there is a sort of order. There are routines. The routine of scrubbing the floors, the routine of the seasons in the olive orchard, the routine of paying taxes. The troubles that come to them are recurrent troubles. My father did not get his poor bent back all at once, but little by little, year by year, in the olive orchard; just as year after year, with unfailing regularity, childbirth has made my mother more and more sexless. They draw the strength they need to sweat with their loaded baskets up the stony paths, to bear children, even to eat, from the sight of the trees greening each year anew, from the reproachful face of the soil, which is never satisfied, and from the little church and Bible texts they hear there on Sunday. They have been told that God relies upon them and that the pageant of the world has been written around them that they may be tested in the important or unimportant parts handed out to them. How could they take it, were I to tell them that they are on a lump of stone ceaselessly spinning in empty space, circling around a second-rate star? What, then, would be the use of their patience, their acceptance of misery? What comfort, then, the Holy Scriptures, which have mercifully explained their crucifixion? The Holy Scriptures would then be proved full of mistakes. No, I see them begin to look frightened, I see them slowly put their spoons down on the table. They would feel cheated. "There is no eye watching over us, after all," they would say. "We have to start out on our own, at our time of life. Nobody has planned a part for us beyond this wretched one on a worthless star. There is no meaning in our misery. Hunger is just not having eaten. It is no test of strength. Effort is just stooping and carrying. It is not a virtue." Can you understand that I read into the decree of the Holy Office a noble motherly pity and a great goodness of the soul?

GALILEO (*embarrassed*) Hm, well at least you have found out that it is not a question of the satellites of Jupiter, but of the peasants of the Campagna! And don't try to break me down by the halo of beauty that radiates from old age. How does a pearl develop in an oyster? A jagged grain of sand makes its way into the oyster's shell and makes its life unbearable. The oyster exudes slime to cover the grain of sand and the slime eventually hardens into a pearl. The oyster nearly dies in the process. To hell with the pearl, give me the healthy oyster! And virtues are not exclusive to misery. If your parents were prosperous and happy, they might develop the virtues of happiness and prosperity. Today the virtues of exhaustion are caused by the exhausted land. For that my new water pumps could work more wonders than their ridiculous superhuman efforts. Be fruitful and multiply: for war will cut down the population, and our fields are barren! (*A pause*) Shall I lie to your people?

LITTLE MONK   We must be silent from the highest of motives: the inward peace of less fortunate souls.

GALILEO   My dear man, as a bonus for not meddling with your parents' peace, the authorities are tendering me, on a silver platter, persecution-free, my share of the fat sweated from your parents, who, as you know, were made in God's image. Should I condone this decree, my motives might not be disinterested: easy life, no persecution and so on.

LITTLE MONK   Mr. Galilei, I am a priest.

GALILEO   You are also a physicist. How can new machinery be evolved to domesticate the river water if we physicists are forbidden to study, discuss, and pool our findings about the greatest machinery of all, the machinery of the heavenly bodies? Can I reconcile my findings on the paths of falling bodies with the current belief in the tracks of witches on broom sticks? (*A pause*) I am sorry – I shouldn't have said that.

LITTLE MONK   You don't think that the truth, if it is the truth, would make its way without us?

GALILEO   No! No! No! As much of the truth gets through as we push through. You talk about the Campagna peasants as if they were the moss on their huts. Naturally, if they don't get a move on and learn to think for themselves, the most efficient of irrigation systems cannot help them. I can see their divine patience, but where is their divine fury?

LITTLE MONK (*helpless*)   They are old!

(*Galileo stands for a moment, beaten; he cannot meet the little monk's eyes. He takes a manuscript from the table and throws it violently on the ground*)

LITTLE MONK   What is that?

GALILEO   Here is writ what draws the ocean when it ebbs and flows. Let it lie there. Thou shalt not read. (*Little Monk has picked up the manuscript*) Already! An apple of the tree of knowledge, he can't wait, he wolfs it down. He will rot in hell for all eternity. Look at him, where are his manners? – Sometimes I think I would let them imprison me in a place a thousand feet beneath the earth where no light could reach me, if in exchange I could find out what stuff that is: "Light." The bad thing is that, when I find something, I have to boast about it like a lover or a drunkard or a traitor. That is a hopeless vice and leads to the abyss. I wonder how long I shall be content to discuss it with my dog!

LITTLE MONK (*immersed in the manuscript*)   I don't understand this sentence.

GALILEO   I'll explain it to you, I'll explain it to you.

(*They are sitting on the floor*)

Scene Eight

> Eight long years with tongue in cheek
> Of what he knew he did not speak.
> Then temptation grew too great
> And Galileo challenged fate.

Galileo's house in Florence again. Galileo is supervising his Assistants Andrea, Federzoni, and the Little Monk who are about to prepare an experiment. Mrs. Sarti and Virginia are at a long table sewing bridal linen. There is a new telescope, larger than the old one. At the moment it is covered with a cloth.

ANDREA (*looking up a schedule*)   Thursday. Afternoon. Floating bodies again. Ice, bowl of water, scales, and it says here an iron needle. Aristotle.

VIRGINIA   Ludovico likes to entertain. We must take care to be neat. His mother notices every stitch. She doesn't approve of father's books.

MRS. SARTI   That's all a thing of the past. He hasn't published a book for years.

VIRGINIA   That's true. Oh Sarti, it's fun sewing a trousseau.

MRS. SARTI   Virginia, I want to talk to you. You are very young, and you have no mother, and your father is putting those pieces of ice in water, and marriage is too serious a business to go into blind. Now you should go to see a real astronomer from the university and have him cast your horoscope so you know where you stand. (*Virginia giggles*) What's the matter?

VIRGINIA   I've been already.

MRS. SARTI   Tell Sarti.

VIRGINIA   I have to be careful for three months now because the sun is in Capricorn, but after that I get a favorable ascendant, and I can undertake a journey if I am careful of Uranus, as I'm a Scorpion.

MRS. SARTI What about Ludovico?

VIRGINIA He's a Leo, the astronomer said. Leos are sensual. (*Giggles*)

(*There is a knock at the door, it opens. Enter the Rector of the University, the philosopher of Scene Four, bringing a book*)

RECTOR (*to Virginia*) This is about the burning issue of the moment. He may want to glance over it. My faculty would appreciate his comments. No, don't disturb him now, my dear. Every minute one takes of your father's time is stolen from Italy. (*He goes*)

VIRGINIA Federzoni! The rector of the university brought this. (*Federzoni takes it*)

GALILEO What's it about?

FEDERZONI (*spelling*) De maculis in sole.

ANDREA Oh, it's on the sun spots!

(*Andrea comes one side, and the Little Monk the other, to look at the book*)

ANDREA A new one!

(*Federzoni resentfully puts the book into their hands and continues with the preparation of the experiment*)

ANDREA Listen to this dedication. (*Quotes*) "To the greatest living authority on physics, Galileo Galilei." – I read Fabricius' paper the other day. Fabricius says the spots are clusters of planets between us and the sun.

LITTLE MONK Doubtful.

GALILEO (*noncommittal*) Yes?

ANDREA Paris and Prague hold that they are vapors from the sun. Federzoni doubts that.

FEDERZONI Me? You leave me out. I said "hm," that was all. And don't discuss new things before me. I can't read the material, it's in Latin. (*He drops the scales and stands trembling with fury*) Tell me, can I doubt anything?

(*Galileo walks over and picks up the scales silently. Pause*)

LITTLE MONK There is happiness in doubting, I wonder why.

ANDREA Aren't we going to take this up?

GALILEO At the moment we are investigating floating bodies.

ANDREA Mother has baskets full of letters from all over Europe asking his opinion.

FEDERZONI The question is whether you can afford to remain silent.

GALILEO I cannot afford to be smoked on a wood fire like a ham.

ANDREA (*surprised*) Ah. You think the sun spots may have something to do with that again? (*Galileo does not answer*)

ANDREA   Well, we stick to fiddling about with bits of ice in water. They can't hurt you.

GALILEO   Correct. – Our thesis!

ANDREA   All things that are lighter than water float, and all things that are heavier sink.

GALILEO   Aristotle says –

LITTLE MONK (*reading out of a book, translating*)   "A broad and flat disk of ice, although heavier than water, still floats, because it is unable to divide the water."

GALILEO   Well, now I push the ice below the surface. I take away the pressure of my hands. What happens?
(*Pause*)

LITTLE MONK   It rises to the surface.

GALILEO   Correct. It seems to be able to divide the water as it's coming up, doesn't it?

LITTLE MONK   Could it be lighter than water after all?

GALILEO   Aha!

ANDREA   Then all things that are lighter than water float, and all things that are heavier sink. Q.e.d.

GALILEO   Not at all. Hand me that iron needle. Heavier than water? (*They all nod*) A piece of paper. (*He places the needle on a piece of paper and floats it on the surface of the water. Pause*) Do not be hasty with your conclusions. (*Pause*) What happens?

FEDERZONI   The paper has sunk, the needle is floating.

VIRGINIA   What's the matter?

MRS. SARTI   Every time I hear them laugh it sends shivers down my spine.
(*There is a knocking at the outer door*)

MRS. SARTI   Who's that at the door?
(*Enter Ludovico. Virginia runs to him. They embrace. Ludovico is followed by a servant with baggage*)

MRS. SARTI   Well!

VIRGINIA   Oh! Why didn't you write that you were coming?

LUDOVICO   I decided on the spur of the moment. I was over inspecting our vineyards at Bucciole. I couldn't keep away.

GALILEO   Who's that?

LITTLE MONK   Miss Virginia's intended. What's the matter with your eyes?

GALILEO (*blinking*)   Oh yes, it's Ludovico, so it is. Well! Sarti, get a jug of that Sicilian wine, the old kind. We celebrate.
(*Everybody sits down. Mrs. Sarti has left, followed by Ludovico's Servant.*)

GALILEO   Well, Ludovico, old man. How are the horses?

LUDOVICO   The horses are fine.

GALILEO   Fine.

LUDOVICO   But those vineyards need a firm hand. (*To Virginia*) You look pale. Country life will suit you. Mother's planning on September.

VIRGINIA   I suppose I oughtn't, but stay here, I've got something to show you.

LUDOVICO   What?

VIRGINIA   Never mind. I won't be ten minutes. (*She runs out*)

LUDOVICO   How's life these days, sir?

GALILEO   Dull. — How was the journey?

LUDOVOCI   Dull. — Before I forget, mother sends her congratulations on your admirable tact over the latest rumblings of science.

GALILEO   Thank her for me.

LUDOVICO   Christopher Clavius had all Rome on its ears. He said he was afraid that the turning around business might crop up again on account of these spots on the sun.

ANDREA   Clavius is on the same track! (*To Ludovico*) My mother's baskets are full of letters from all over Europe asking Mr. Galilei's opinion.

GALILEO   I am engaged in investigating the habits of floating bodies. Any harm in that?

(*Mrs. Sarti re-enters, followed by the Servant. They bring wine and glasses on a tray*)

GALILEO (*hands out the wine*)   What news from the Holy City, apart from the prospect of my sins?

LUDOVICO   The Holy Father is on his death bed. Hadn't you heard?

LITTLE MONK   My goodness! What about the succession?

LUDOVICO   All the talk is of Barberini.

GALILEO   Barberini?

ANDREA   Mr. Galilei knows Barberini.

LITTLE MONK   Cardinal Barberini is a mathematician.

FEDERZONI   A scientist in the chair of Peter!

(*Pause*)

GALILEO (*cheering up enormously*)   This means change. We might live to see the day, Federzoni, when we don't have to whisper that two and two are four. (*To Ludovico*) I like this wine. Don't you, Ludovico?

LUDOVICO   I like it.

GALILEO   I know the hill where it is grown. The slope is steep and stony, the grape almost blue. I am fond of this wine.

LUDOVICO Yes, sir.

GALILEO There are shadows in this wine. It is almost sweet but just stops short. – Andrea, clear that stuff away, ice, bowl, and needle. – I cherish the consolations of the flesh. I have no patience with cowards who call them weaknesses. I say there is a certain achievement in enjoying things.

(*The Pupils get up and go to the experiment table*)

LITTLE MONK What are we to do?

FEDERZONI He is starting on the sun.

(*They begin with clearing up*)

ANDREA (*singing in a low voice*)
The Bible proves the earth stands still,
The Pope, he swears with tears:
The earth stands still. To prove it so
He takes it by the ears.

LUDOVICO What's the excitement?

MRS. SARTI You're not going to start those hellish goings-on again, Mr. Galilei?

ANDREA
And gentlefolk, they say so too.
Each learned doctor proves,
(If you grease his palm): The earth stands still.
And yet – and yet it moves.

GALILEO Barberini is in the ascendant, so your mother is uneasy, and you're sent to investigate me. Correct me if I am wrong, Ludovico. Clavius is right: these spots on the sun interest me.

ANDREA We might find out that the sun also revolves. How would you like that, Ludovico?

GALILEO Do you like my wine, Ludovico?

LUDOVICO I told you I did, sir.

GALILEO You really like it?

LUDOVICO I like it.

GALILEO Tell me, Ludovico, would you consider going so far as to accept a man's wine or his daughter without insisting that he drop his profession? I have no wish to intrude, but have the moons of Jupiter affected Virginia's bottom?

MRS. SARTI That isn't funny, it's just vulgar. I am going for Virginia.

LUDOVICO (*keeps her back*) Marriages in families such as mine are not arranged on a basis of sexual attraction alone.

GALILEO Did they keep you back from marrying my daughter for eight years because I was on probation?

LUDOVICO My future wife must take her place in the family pew.

GALILEO You mean, if the daughter of a bad man sat in your family pew, your peasants might stop paying the rent?

LUDOVICO In a sort of way.

GALILEO When I was your age, the only person I allowed to rap me on the knuckles was my girl.

LUDOVICO My mother was assured that you had undertaken not to get mixed up in this turning around business again, sir.

GALILEO We had a conservative Pope then.

MRS. SARTI Had! His Holiness is not dead yet!

GALILEO (*with relish*) Pretty nearly.

MRS. SARTI That man will weigh a chip of ice fifty times, but when it comes to something that's convenient, he believes it blindly. "Is His Holiness dead?" – "Pretty nearly!"

LUDOVICO You will find, sir, if His Holiness passes away, the new Pope, whoever he turns out to be, will respect the convictions held by the solid families of the country.

GALILEO (*to Andrea*) That remains to be seen. – Andrea, get out the screen. We'll throw the image of the sun on our screen to save our eyes.

LITTLE MONK I thought you'd been working at it. Do you know when I guessed it? When you didn't recognize Mr. Marsili.

MRS. SARTI If my son has to go to hell for sticking to you, that's my affair, but you have no right to trample on your daughter's happiness.

LUDOVICO (*To his Servant*) Giuseppe, take my baggage back to the coach, will you?

MRS. SARTI This will kill her. (*She runs out, still clutching the jug*)

LUDOVICO (*politely*) Mr. Galilei, if we Marsilis were to countenance teachings frowned on by the church, it would unsettle our peasants. Bear in mind: these poor people in their brute state get everything upside down. They are nothing but animals. They will never comprehend the finer points of astronomy. Why, two months ago a rumor went around, an apple had been found on a pear tree, and they left their work in the fields to discuss it.

GALILEO (*interested*) Did they?

LUDOVICO I have seen the day when my poor mother has had to have a dog whipped before their eyes to remind them to keep their place. Oh, you may have seen the waving corn from the window of your comfortable coach. You have, no doubt, nibbled our olives, and absentmindedly eaten our cheese, but you have no idea how much responsibility that sort of thing entails.

GALILEO   Young man, I do not eat my cheese absentmindedly. (*To Andrea*) Are we ready?

ANDREA   Yes, sir.

GALILEO (*leaves Ludovico and adjusts the mirror*)   You would not confine your whippings to dogs to remind your peasants to keep their places, would you, Marsili?

LUDOVICO (*after a pause*)   Mr. Galilei, you have a wonderful brain, it's a pity.

LITTLE MONK (*astonished*)   He threatened you.

GALILEO   Yes. And he threatened you too. We might unsettle his peasants. Your sister, Fulganzio, who works the lever of the olive press, might laugh out loud if she heard the sun is not a gilded coat of arms but a lever too. The earth turns because the sun turns it.

ANDREA   That could interest his steward too and even his money lender – and the seaport towns. . . .

FEDERZONI   None of them speak Latin.

GALILEO   I might write in plain language. The work we do is exacting. Who would go through the strain for less than the population at large!

LUDOVICO   I see you have made your decision. It was inevitable. You will always be a slave of your passions. Excuse me to Virginia, I think it's as well I don't see her now.

GALILEO   The dowry is at your disposal at any time.

LUDOVICO   Good afternoon. (*He goes followed by the Servant*)

ANDREA   Exit Ludovico. To hell with all Marsilis, Villanis, Orsinis, Canes, Nuccolis, Soldanieris. . . .

FEDERZONI   . . . who ordered the earth stand still because their castles might be shaken loose if it revolves . . .

LITTLE MONK   . . . and who only kiss the Pope's feet as long as he uses them to trample on the people. God made the physical world, God made the human brain. God will allow physics.

ANDREA   They will try to stop us.

GALILEO   Thus we enter the observation of these spots on the sun in which we are interested, at our own risk, not counting on protection from a problematical new Pope . . .

ANDREA   . . . but with great likelihood of dispelling Fabricius' vapors, and the shadows of Paris and Prague, and of establishing the rotation of the sun . . .

GALILEO   . . . and with *some* likelihood of establishing the rotation of the sun. My intention is not to prove that I was right but to find out *whether* I was right. "Abandon hope all ye who enter – an observation." Before assuming these phenomena are spots, which would suit us, let us first set about proving that they are not – fried fish. We crawl by inches. What we find today we will wipe from the blackboard tomorrow and reject it – unless it shows up again the day after tomorrow. And if we find anything which would suit us, that thing we will eye with particular distrust. In fact, we will approach this observing of the sun with the implacable determination to prove that the earth stands still and only if hopelessly defeated in this pious undertaking can we allow ourselves to wonder if we may not have been right all the time: the earth revolves. Take the cloth off the telescope and turn it on the sun.

(*Quietly they start work. When the corruscating image of the sun is focused on the screen, Virginia enters hurriedly, her wedding dress on, her hair disheveled, Mrs. Sarti with her, carrying her wedding veil. The two women realize what has happened. Virginia faints. Andrea, Little Monk and Galileo rush to her. Federzoni continues working*)

Scene Nine

> On April Fool's Day, thirty two,
> Of science there was much ado.
> People had learned from Galilei:
> They used his teaching in their way.

Around the corner from the market place a Street Singer and his Wife, who is costumed to represent the earth in a skeleton globe made of thin bands of brass, are holding the attention of a sprinkling of representative citizens, some in masquerade who were on their way to see the carnival procession. From the market place the noise of an impatient crowd.

BALLAD SINGER (*accompanied by his Wife on the guitar*)
When the Almighty made the universe
He made the earth and then he made the sun.
Then round the earth he bade the sun to turn –
That's in the Bible, Genesis, Chapter One.
And from that time all beings here below
Were in obedient circles meant to go:

Around the pope the cardinals
Around the cardinals the bishops
Around the bishops the secretaries
Around the secretaries the aldermen
Around the aldermen the craftsmen
Around the craftsmen the servants
Around the servants the dogs, the chickens, and the beggars.

(*A conspicuous reveller – henceforth called the Spinner – has slowly caught on and is exhibiting his idea of spinning around. He does not lose dignity, he faints with mock grace*)

BALLAD SINGER

Up stood the learned Galileo
Glanced briefly at the sun
And said: "Almighty God was wrong
In Genesis, Chapter One!"

Now that was rash, my friends, it is no matter small
For heresy will spread today like foul diseases.
Change Holy Writ, forsooth? What will be left at all?
Why: each of us would say and do just what he pleases!

(*Three wretched Extras, employed by the chamber of commerce, enter. Two of them, in ragged costumes, moodily bear a litter with a mock throne. The third sits on the throne. He wears sacking, a false beard, a prop crown, he carries a prop orb and sceptre, and around his chest the inscription "The King of Hungary." The litter has a card with "No. 4" written on it. The litter bearers dump him down and listen to the Ballad Singer*)

BALLAD SINGER

Good people, what will come to pass
If Galileo's teachings spread?
No altar boy will serve the mass
No servant girl will make the bed.

Now that is grave, my friends, it is no matter small:
For independent spirit spreads like foul diseases!
(Yet life is sweet and man is weak and after all –
How nice it is, for a little change, to do just as one pleases!)

(*The Ballad Singer takes over the guitar. His Wife dances around him, illustrating the motion of the earth. A Cobbler's Boy with a pair of resplendent lacquered boots hung over his shoulder has been jumping up and down in mock excitement. There are three more children, dressed as grownups among the spectators, two together and a single one with mother. The Cobbler's Boy takes the three Children in hand, forms a chain and leads it, moving to the music, in*)

*and out among the spectators, "whipping" the chain so that the last
child bumps into people. On the way past a Peasant Woman, he
steals an egg from her basket. She gestures to him to return it. As he
passes her again he quietly breaks the egg over her head. The King of
Hungary ceremoniously hands his orb to one of his bearers,
marches down with mock dignity, and chastises the Cobbler's Boy.
The parents remove the three Children. The unseemliness subsides)*

BALLAD SINGER

The carpenters take wood and build
Their houses – not the church's pews.
And members of the cobblers' guild
Now boldly walk the streets – in shoes.
The tenant kicks the noble lord
Quite off the land he owned – like that!
The milk his wife once gave the priest
Now makes (at last!) her children fat.

Ts, ts, ts, ts, my friends, this is no matter small
For independent spirit spreads like foul diseases
People must keep their place, some down and some on top!
(Though it is nice, for a little change, to do just as one pleases!)

*(The Cobbler's Boy has put on the lacquered boots he was carrying.
He struts off. The Ballad Singer takes over the guitar again. His
Wife dances around him in increased tempo. A Monk has been
standing near a rich Couple, who are in subdued costly clothes,
without masks: shocked at the song, he now leaves. A Dwarf in the
costume of an astronomer turns his telescope on the departing
Monk, thus drawing attention to the rich Couple. In imitation of
the Cobbler's Boy, the Spinner forms a chain of grownups. They
move to the music, in and out, and between the rich Couple. The
Spinner changes the Gentleman's bonnet for the ragged hat of a
Beggar. The Gentleman decides to take this in good part, and a Girl
is emboldened to take his dagger. The Gentleman is miffed, throws
the Beggar's hat back. The Beggar discards the Gentleman's bonnet
and drops it on the ground. The King of Hungary has walked from
his throne, taken an egg from the Peasant Woman, and paid for it.
He now ceremoniously breaks it over the Gentleman's head as he is
bending down to pick up his bonnet. The Gentleman conducts the
Lady away from the scene. The King of Hungary, about to resume
his throne, finds one of the Children sitting on it. The Gentleman
returns to retrieve his dagger. Merriment. The Ballad Singer
wanders off. This is part of his routine. His Wife sings to the
Spinner)*

WIFE

Now speaking for myself I feel

That I could also do with a change

You know, for me . . . (*Turning to a reveller*) . . . *you* have appeal

Maybe tonight we could arrange . . .

(*The Dwarf-Astronomer has been amusing the people by focusing his telescope on her legs. The Ballad Singer has returned*)

BALLAD SINGER

No, no, no, no, no, stop, Galileo, stop!

For independent spirit spreads like foul diseases

People must keep their place, some down and some on top!

(Though it is nice, for a little change, to do just as one pleases!)

(*The Spectators stand embarrassed. A Girl laughs loudly*)

BALLAD SINGER AND HIS WIFE

Good people who have trouble here below

In serving cruel lords and gentle Jesus

Who bids you turn the other cheek just so . . . (*With mimicry*)

While they prepare to strike the second blow:

Obedience will never cure your woe

So each of you wake up and do just as he pleases!

(*The Ballad Singer and his Wife hurriedly start to try to sell pamphlets to the spectators*)

BALLAD SINGER   Read all about the earth going round the sun, two centesimi only. As proved by the great Galileo. Two centesimi only. Written by a local scholar. Understandable to one and all. Buy one for your friends, your children and your aunty Rosa, two centesimi only. Abbreviated but complete. Fully illustrated with pictures of the planets, including Venus, two centesimi only.

(*During the speech of the Ballad Singer we hear the carnival procession approaching followed by laughter. A Reveller rushes in*)

REVELLER   The procession!

(*The litter bearers speedily joggle out the King of Hungary. The Spectators turn and look at the first float of the procession, which now makes its appearance. It bears a gigantic figure of Galileo, holding in one hand an open Bible with the pages crossed out. The other hand points to the Bible, and the head mechanically turns from side to side as if to say "No! No!"*)

A LOUD VOICE   Galileo, the Bible killer!

(*The laughter from the market place becomes uproarious. The Monk comes flying from the market place followed by delighted Children*)

Scene Ten

> *The depths are hot, the heights are chill*
> *The streets are loud, the court is still.*

Ante-Chamber and staircase in the Medicean palace in Florence. Galileo, with a book under his arm, waits with his Daughter to be admitted to the presence of the Prince.

VIRGINIA   They are a long time.

GALILEO   Yes.

VIRGINIA   Who is that funny looking man? (*She indicates the Informer who has entered casually and seated himself in the background, taking no apparent notice of Galileo*)

GALILEO   I don't know.

VIRGINIA   It's not the first time I have seen him around. He gives me the creeps.

GALILEO   Nonsense. We're in Florence, not among robbers in the mountains of Corsica.

VIRGINIA   Here comes the Rector.

(*The Rector comes down the stairs*)

GALILEO   Gaffone is a bore. He attaches himself to you.

(*The Rector passes, scarcely nodding*)

GALILEO   My eyes are bad today. Did he acknowledge us?

VIRGINIA   Barely. (*Pause*) What's in your book? Will they say it's heretical?

GALILEO   You hang around church too much. And getting up at dawn and scurrying to mass is ruining your skin. You pray for me, don't you?

(*A Man comes down the stairs*)

VIRGINIA   Here's Mr. Matti. You designed a machine for his Iron Foundries.

MATTI   How were the squabs, Mr. Galilei? (*Low*) My brother and I had a good laugh the other day. He picked up a racy pamphlet against the Bible somewhere. It quoted you.

GALILEO   The squabs, Matti, were wonderful, thank you again. Pamphlets I know nothing about. The Bible and Homer are my favorite reading.

MATTI No necessity to be cautious with me, Mr. Galilei. I am on your side. I am not a man who knows about the motions of the stars, but you have championed the freedom to teach new things. Take that mechanical cultivator they have in Germany which you described to me. I can tell you, it will never be used in this country. The same circles that are hampering you now will forbid the physicians at Bologna to cut up corpses for research. Do you know, they have such things as money markets in Amsterdam and in London? Schools for business, too. Regular papers with news. Here we are not even free to make money. I have a stake in your career. They are against iron foundries because they say the gathering of so many workers in one place fosters immorality! If they ever try anything, Mr. Galilei, remember you have friends in all walks of life including an iron founder. Good luck to you. (*He goes*)

GALILEO Good man, but need he be so affectionate in public? His voice carries. They will always claim me as their spiritual leader particularly in places where it doesn't help me at all. I have written a book about the mechanics of the firmament, that is all. What they do or don't do with it is not my concern.

VIRGINIA (*loud*) If people only knew how you disagreed with those goings-on all over the country last All Fools day.

GALILEO Yes. Offer honey to a bear, and lose your arm if the beast is hungry.

VIRGINIA (*low*) Did the prince ask you to come here today?

GALILEO I sent word I was coming. He will want the book, he has paid for it. My health hasn't been any too good lately. I may accept Sagredo's invitation to stay with him in Padua for a few weeks.

VIRGINIA You couldn't manage without your books.

GALILEO Sagredo has an excellent library.

VIRGINIA We haven't had this month's salary yet –

GALILEO Yes. (*The Cardinal Inquisitor passes down the staircase. He bows deeply in answer to Galileo's bow*) What is he doing in Florence? If they try to do anything to me, the new Pope will meet them with an iron NO. And the Prince is my pupil, he would never have me extradited.

VIRGINIA Psst. The Lord Chamberlain.

(*The Lord Chamberlain comes down the stairs*)

LORD CHAMBERLAIN His Highness had hoped to find time for you, Mr. Galilei. Unfortunately, he has to leave immediately to judge the parade at the Riding Academy. On what business did you wish to see His Highness?

GALILEO I wanted to present my book to His Highness.

LORD CHAMBERLAIN   How are your eyes today?

GALILEO   So, so. With His Highness' permission, I am dedicating the book . . .

LORD CHAMBERLAIN   Your eyes are a matter of great concern to His Highness. Could it be that you have been looking too long and too often through your marvelous tube? (*He leaves without accepting the book*)

VIRGINIA (*greatly agitated*)   Father, I am afraid.

GALILEO   He didn't take the book, did he? (*Low and resolute*) Keep a straight face. We are not going home, but to the house of the lens-grinder. There is a coach and horses in his backyard. Keep your eyes to the front, don't look back at that man. (*They start. The Lord Chamberlain comes back*)

LORD CHAMBERLAIN   Oh, Mr. Galilei, His Highness has just charged me to inform you that the Florentine Court is no longer in a position to oppose the request of the Holy Inquisition to interrogate you in Rome.

Scene Eleven

The Pope

A chamber in the Vatican. The Pope, Urban VIII – formerly Cardinal Barberini – is giving audience to the Cardinal Inquisitor. The trampling and shuffling of many feet is heard throughout the scene from the adjoining corridors. During the scene the Pope is being robed for the conclave he is about to attend: at the beginning of the scene he is plainly Barberini, but as the scene proceeds he is more and more obscured by grandiose vestments.

POPE   No! No! No!

INQUISITOR (*referring to the owners of the shuffling feet*)   Doctors of all chairs from the universities, representatives of the special orders of the Church, representatives of the clergy as a whole who have come believing with child-like faith in the word of God as set forth in the Scriptures, who have come to hear Your Holiness confirm their faith: and Your Holiness is really going to tell them that the Bible can no longer be regarded as the alphabet of truth?

POPE I will not set myself up against the multiplication table. No!

INQUISITOR Ah, that is what these people say, that it is the multiplication table. Their cry is, "The figures compel us," but where do these figures come from? Plainly they come from doubt. These men doubt everything. Can society stand on doubt and not on faith? "Thou art my master, but I doubt whether it is for the best." "This is my neighbor's house and my neighbor's wife, but why shouldn't they belong to me?" After the plague, after the new war, after the unparalleled disaster of the Reformation, your dwindling flock look to their shepherd, and now the mathematicians turn their tubes on the sky and announce to the world that you have not the best advice about the heavens either – up to now your only uncontested sphere of influence. This Galilei started meddling in machines at an early age. Now that men in ships are venturing on the great oceans – I am not against that of course – they are putting their faith in a brass bowl they call a compass and not in Almighty God.

POPE This man is the greatest physicist of our time. He is the light of Italy, and not just any muddle-head.

INQUISITOR Would we have had to arrest him otherwise? This bad man knows what he is doing, not writing his books in Latin, but in the jargon of the market place.

POPE (*occupied with the shuffling feet*) That was not in the best of taste. (*A pause*) These shuffling feet are making me nervous.

INQUISITOR May they be more telling than my words, Your Holiness. Shall all these go from you with doubt in their hearts?

POPE This man has friends. What about Versailles? What about the Viennese court? They will call Holy Church a cesspool for defunct ideas. Keep your hands off him.

INQUISITOR In practice it will never get far. He is a man of the flesh. He would soften at once.

POPE He has more enjoyment in him than any man I ever saw. He loves eating and drinking and thinking. To excess. He indulges in thinking-bouts! He cannot say no to an old wine or a new thought. (*Furious*) I do not want a condemnation of physical facts. I do not want to hear battle cries: Church, church, church! Reason, reason, reason! (*Pause*) These shuffling feet are intolerable. Has the whole world come to my door?

INQUISITOR Not the whole world, Your Holiness. A select gathering of the faithful.

(*Pause*)

POPE (*exhausted*) It is clearly understood: he is not to be tortured. (*Pause*) At the very most, he may be shown the instruments.

INQUISITOR That will be adequate, Your Holiness. Mr. Galilei understands machinery.

(*The eyes of Barberini look helplessly at the Cardinal Inquisitor from under the completely assembled panoply of Pope Urban VIII*)

Scene Twelve

> June twenty second, sixteen thirty three,
> A momentous date for you and me.
> Of all the days that was the one
> An age of reason could have begun.

Again the garden of the Florentine Ambassador at Rome, where Galileo's assistants wait the news of the trial. The Little Monk and Federzoni are attempting to concentrate on a game of chess. Virginia kneels in a corner, praying and counting her beads.

LITTLE MONK The Pope didn't even grant him an audience.

FEDERZONI No more scientific discussions.

ANDREA The "Discorsi" will never be finished. The sum of his findings. They will kill him.

FEDERZONI (*stealing a glance at him*) Do you really think so?

ANDREA He will never recant.

(*Silence*)

LITTLE MONK You know when you lie awake at night how your mind fastens on to something irrelevant. Last night I kept thinking: if only they would let him take his little stone in with him, the appeal-to-reason-pebble that he always carried in his pocket.

FEDERZONI In the room *they'll* take him to, he won't have a pocket.

ANDREA But he will not recant.

LITTLE MONK How can they beat the truth out of a man who gave his sight in order to see?

FEDERZONI Maybe they can't.

(*Silence*)

ANDREA (*speaking about Virginia*) She is praying that he will recant.

FEDERZONI   Leave her alone. She doesn't know whether she's on her head or on her heels since they got hold of her. They brought her Father Confessor from Florence.

(*The Informer of Scene Ten enters*)

INFORMER   Mr. Galilei will be here soon. He may need a bed.

FEDERZONI   Have they let him out?

INFORMER   Mr. Galilei is expected to recant at five o'clock. The big bell of Saint Marcus will be rung and the complete text of his recantation publicly announced.

ANDREA   I don't believe it.

INFORMER   Mr. Galilei will be brought to the garden gate at the back of the house, to avoid the crowds collecting in the street. (*He goes*)

(*Silence*)

ANDREA   The moon is an earth because the light of the moon is not her own. Jupiter is a fixed star, and four moons turn around Jupiter, therefore we are not shut in by crystal shells. The sun is the pivot of our world, therefore the earth is not the center. The earth moves, spinning about the sun. And he showed us. You can't make a man unsee what he has seen.

(*Silence*)

FEDERZONI   Five o'clock is one minute.

(*Virginia prays louder*)

ANDREA   Listen all of you, they are murdering the truth.

(*He stops up his ears with his fingers. The two other pupils do the same. Federzoni goes over to the Little Monk, and all of them stand absolutely still in cramped positions. Nothing happens. No bell sounds. After a silence, filled with the murmur of Virginia's prayers, Federzoni runs to the wall to look at the clock. He turns around, his expression changed. He shakes his head. They drop their hands*)

FEDERZONI   No. No bell. It is three minutes after.

LITTLE MONK   He hasn't.

ANDREA   He held true. It is all right, it is all right.

LITTLE MONK   He did not recant.

FEDERZONI   No.

(*They embrace each other, they are delirious with joy*)

ANDREA   So force cannot accomplish everything. What has been seen can't be unseen. Man is constant in the face of death.

FEDERZONI   June 22, 1633: dawn of the age of reason. I wouldn't have wanted to go on living if he had recanted.

LITTLE MONK   I didn't say anything, but I was in agony. Oh, ye of little faith!

ANDREA I was sure.

FEDERZONI It would have turned our morning to night.

ANDREA It would have been as if the mountain had turned to water.

LITTLE MONK (*kneeling down, crying*) Oh God, I thank Thee.

ANDREA Beaten humanity can lift its head. A man has stood up and said "no."

(*At this moment the bell of Saint Marcus begins to toll. They stand like statues. Virginia stands up*)

VIRGINIA The bell of Saint Marcus. He is not damned.

(*From the street one hears the Town Crier reading Galileo's recantation*)

TOWN CRIER I, Galileo Galilei, Teacher of Mathematics and Physics, do hereby publicly renounce my teaching that the earth moves. I foreswear this teaching with a sincere heart and unfeigned faith and detest and curse this and all other errors and heresies repugnant to the Holy Scriptures.

(*The lights dim; when they come up again the bell of Saint Marcus is petering out. Virginia has gone but the Scholars are still there waiting*)

ANDREA (*loud*) The mountain did turn to water.

(*Galileo has entered quietly and unnoticed. He is changed, almost unrecognizable. He has heard Andrea. He waits some seconds by the door for somebody to greet him. Nobody does. They retreat from him. He goes slowly and, because of his bad sight, uncertainly, to the front of the stage where he finds a chair, and sits down*)

ANDREA I can't look at him. Tell him to go away.

FEDERZONI Steady.

ANDREA (*hysterically*) He saved his big gut.

FEDERZONI Get him a glass of water.

(*The Little Monk fetches a glass of water for Andrea. Nobody acknowledges the presence of Galileo, who sits silently on his chair listening to the voice of the Town Crier, now in another street*)

ANDREA I can walk. Just help me a bit.

(*They help him to the door*)

ANDREA (*in the door*) "Unhappy is the land that breeds no hero."

GALILEO No, Andrea: "Unhappy is the land that needs a hero."

(*Before the next scene a curtain with the following legend on it is lowered*)

You can plainly see that if a horse were to fall from a height of three or four feet, it could break its bones, whereas a dog would not suffer injury. The same applies to a cat from a height of as much as eight or ten feet, to a grasshopper from the top of a tower, and to an ant falling down from the moon. Nature could not allow a horse to become as big as twenty horses nor a giant as big as ten men, unless she were to change the proportions of all its members, particularly the bones. Thus the common assumption that great and small structures are equally tough is obviously wrong.

— From the "Discorsi"

Scene Thirteen

1633–1642.
Galileo Galilei remains a prisoner
of the Inquisition until his death.

A country house near Florence. A large room simply furnished. There is a huge table, a leather chair, a globe of the world on a stand, and a narrow bed. A portion of the adjoining anteroom is visible, and the front door which opens into it. An Official of the Inquisition sits on guard in the anteroom. In the large room, Galileo is quietly experimenting with a bent wooden rail and a small ball of wood. He is still vigorous but almost blind. After a while there is a knocking at the outside door. The Official opens it to a peasant who brings a plucked goose. Virginia comes from the kitchen. She is past forty.

PEASANT (*handing the goose to Virginia*)   I was told to deliver this here.
VIRGINIA   I didn't order a goose.
PEASANT   I was told to say it's from someone who was passing through.
    (*Virginia takes the goose, surprised. The Official takes it from her and examines it suspiciously. Then, reassured, he hands it back to her. The Peasant goes. Virginia brings the goose in to Galileo*)
VIRGINIA   Somebody who was passing through sent you something.
GALILEO   What is it?
VIRGINIA   Can't you see it?
GALILEO   No. (*He walks over*) A goose. Any name?
VIRGINIA   No.

GALILEO (*weighing the goose*) Solid.

VIRGINIA (*cautiously*) Will you eat the liver, if I have it cooked with a little apple?

GALILEO I had my dinner. Are you under orders to finish me off with food?

VIRGINIA It's not rich. And what is wrong with your eyes again? You should be able to see it.

GALILEO You were standing in the light.

VIRGINIA I was not. – You haven't been writing again?

GALILEO (*sneering*) What do you think?

(*Virginia takes the goose out into the anteroom and speaks to the Official*)

VIRGINIA You had better ask Monsignor Carpula to send the doctor. Father couldn't see this goose across the room. – Don't look at me like that. He has not been writing. He dictates everything to me, as you know.

OFFICIAL Yes?

VIRGINIA He abides by the rules. My father's repentance is sincere. I keep an eye on him. (*She hands him the goose*) Tell the cook to fry the liver with an apple and an onion. (*She goes back into the large room*) And you have no business to be doing that with those eyes of yours, father.

GALILEO You may read me some Horace.

VIRGINIA We should go on with your weekly letter to the Archbishop. Monsignor Carpula to whom we owe so much was all smiles the other day because the Archbishop had expressed his pleasure at your collaboration.

GALILEO Where were we?

VIRGINIA (*sits down to take his dictation*) Paragraph four.

GALILEO Read what you have.

VIRGINIA "The position of the Church in the matter of the unrest at Genoa. I agree with Cardinal Spoletti in the matter of the unrest among the Venetian ropemakers . . ."

GALILEO Yes. (*Dictates*) I agree with Cardinal Spoletti in the matter of the unrest among the Venetian ropemakers: it is better to distribute good nourishing food in the name of charity than to pay them more for their bellropes. It being surely better to strengthen their faith than to encourage their acquisitiveness. St. Paul says: Charity never faileth. – How is that?

VIRGINIA It's beautiful, father.

GALILEO It couldn't be taken as irony?

VIRGINIA No. The Archbishop will like it. It's so practical.

GALILEO   I trust your judgment. Read it over slowly.

VIRGINIA   "The position of the Church in the matter of the unrest . . ."

(*There is a knocking at the outside door. Virginia goes into the anteroom. The Official opens the door. It is Andrea*)

ANDREA   Good evening. I am sorry to call so late, I'm on my way to Holland. I was asked to look him up. Can I go in?

VIRGINIA   I don't know whether he will see you. You never came.

ANDREA   Ask him.

(*Galileo recognizes the voice. He sits motionless. Virginia comes in to Galileo*)

GALILEO   Is that Andrea?

VIRGINIA   Yes. (*Pause*) I will send him away.

GALILEO   Show him in.

(*Virginia shows Andrea in. Virginia sits, Andrea remains standing*)

ANDREA (*cool*)   Have you been keeping well, Mr. Galilei?

GALILEO   Sit down. What are you doing these days? What are you working on? I heard it was something about hydraulics in Milan.

ANDREA   As he knew I was passing through, Fabricius of Amsterdam asked me to visit you and inquire about your health.

(*Pause*)

GALILEO   I am very well.

ANDREA (*formally*)   I am glad I can report you are in good health.

GALILEO   Fabricius will be glad to hear it. And you might inform him that, on account of the depth of my repentance, I live in comparative comfort.

ANDREA   Yes, we understand that the church is more than pleased with you. Your complete acceptance has had its effect. Not one paper expounding a new thesis has made its appearance in Italy since your submission.

(*Pause*)

GALILEO   Unfortunately there are countries not under the wing of the church. Would you not say the erroneous condemned theories are still taught – there?

ANDREA (*relentless*)   Things are almost at a standstill.

GALILEO   Are they? (*Pause*) Nothing from Descartes in Paris?

ANDREA   Yes. On receiving the news of your recantation, he shelved his treatise on the nature of light.

GALILEO   I sometimes worry about my assistants whom I led into error. Have they benefited by my example?

ANDREA   In order to work I have to go to Holland.

GALILEO   Yes.

ANDREA   Federzoni is grinding lenses again, back in some shop.

GALILEO   He can't read the books.

ANDREA   Fulganzio, our little monk, has abandoned research and is resting in peace in the church.

GALILEO   So. (*Pause*) My superiors are looking forward to my spiritual recovery. I am progressing as well as can be expected.

VIRGINIA   You are doing well, father.

GALILEO   Virginia, leave the room.

(*Virginia rises uncertainly and goes out*)

VIRGINIA (*to the Official*)   He was his pupil, so now he is his enemy. – Help me in the kitchen.

(*She leaves the anteroom with the Official*)

ANDREA   May I go now, sir?

GALILEO   I do not know why you came, Sarti. To unsettle me? I have to be prudent.

ANDREA   I'll be on my way.

GALILEO   As it is, I have relapses. I completed the "Discorsi."

ANDREA   You completed what?

GALILEO   My "Discorsi."

ANDREA   How?

GALILEO   I am allowed pen and paper. My superiors are intelligent men. They know the habits of a lifetime cannot be broken abruptly. But they protect me from any unpleasant consequences: they lock my pages away as I dictate them. And I should know better than to risk my comfort. I wrote the "Discorsi" out again during the night. The manuscript is in the globe. My vanity has up to now prevented me from destroying it. If you consider taking it, you will shoulder the entire risk. You will say it was pirated from the original in the hands of the Holy Office.

(*Andrea, as in a trance, has gone to the globe. He lifts the upper half and gets the book. He turns the pages as if wanting to devour them. In the background the opening sentences of the "Discorsi" appear:*
MY PURPOSE IS TO SET FORTH A VERY NEW SCIENCE, DEALING WITH A VERY ANCIENT SUBJECT — MOTION. . . . AND I HAVE DISCOVERED BY EXPERIMENT SOME PROPERTIES OF IT WHICH ARE WORTH KNOWING. . . .)

GALILEO   I had to employ my time somehow.

(*The text disappears*)

ANDREA   Two new sciences! This will be the foundation stone of a new physics.

GALILEO   Yes. Put it under your coat.

ANDREA   And we thought you had deserted. (*In a low voice*) Mr. Galilei, how can I begin to express my shame. Mine has been the loudest voice against you.

GALILEO   That would seem to have been proper. I taught you science and I decried the truth.

ANDREA   Did you? I think not. Everything is changed!

GALILEO   What is changed?

ANDREA   You shielded the truth from the oppressor. Now I see! In your dealings with the Inquisition you used the same superb common sense you brought to physics.

GALILEO   Oh!

ANDREA   We lost our heads. With the crowd in the street corners we said: "He will die, he will never surrender!" You came back: "I surrendered but I am alive." We cried: "Your hands are stained!" You say: "Better stained than empty."

GALILEO   "Better stained than empty." – It sounds realistic. Sounds like me.

ANDREA   And I of all people should have known. I was twelve when you sold another man's telescope to the Venetian Senate, and saw you put it to immortal use. Your friends were baffled when you bowed to the Prince of Florence: Science gained a wider audience. You always laughed at heroics. "People who suffer bore me," you said. "Misfortunes are due mainly to miscalculations." And: "If there are obstacles, the shortest line between two points may be the crooked line."

GALILEO   It makes a picture.

ANDREA   And when you stooped to recant in 1633, I should have understood that you were again about your business.

GALILEO   My business being?

ANDREA   Science. The study of the properties of motion, mother of the machines which will themselves change the ugly face of the earth.

GALILEO   Aha!

ANDREA   You gained time to write a book that only you could write. Had you burned at the stake in a blaze of glory they would have won.

GALILEO   They have won. And there is no such thing as a scientific work that only one man can write.

ANDREA   Then why did you recant, tell me that!

GALILEO   I recanted because I was afraid of physical pain.

ANDREA   No!

GALILEO   They showed me the instruments.

ANDREA   It was not a plan?

GALILEO   It was not.

(*Pause*)

ANDREA   But you have contributed. Science has only one command-
ment: contribution. And you have contributed more than any man
for a hundred years.

GALILEO   Have I? Then welcome to my gutter, dear colleague in
science and brother in treason: I sold out, you are a buyer. The first
sight of the book! His mouth watered and his scoldings were
drowned. Blessed be our bargaining, whitewashing, deathfearing
community!

ANDREA   The fear of death is human.

GALILEO   Even the church will teach you that to be weak is not
human. It is just evil.

ANDREA   The church, yes! But science is not concerned with our
weaknesses.

GALILEO   No? My dear Sarti, in spite of my present convictions, I
may be able to give you a few pointers as to the concerns of your
chosen profession.

(*Enter Virginia with a platter*)

In my spare time, I happen to have gone over this case. I have spare
time. – Even a man who sells wool, however good he is at buying
wool cheap and selling it dear, must be concerned with the standing
of the wool trade. The practice of science would seem to call for
valor. She trades in knowledge, which is the product of doubt. And
this new art of doubt has enchanted the public. The plight of the
multitude is old as the rocks, and is believed to be basic as the rocks.
But now they have learned to doubt. They snatched the telescopes
out of our hands and had them trained on their tormentors: prince,
official, public moralist. The mechanism of the heavens was clearer,
the mechanism of their courts was still murky. The battle to
measure the heavens is won by doubt; by credulity the Roman
housewife's battle for milk will always be lost. Word is passed down
that this is of no concern to the scientist who is told he will only
release such of his findings as do not disturb the peace, that is, the
peace of mind of the well-to-do. Threats and bribes fill the air. Can
the scientist hold out on the numbers? – For what reason do you
labor? I take it the intent of science is to ease human existence. If
you give way to coercion, science can be crippled, and your new
machines may simply suggest new drudgeries. Should you then, in

time, discover all there is to be discovered, your progress must then become a progress away from the bulk of humanity. The gulf might even grow so wide that the sound of your cheering at some new achievement would be echoed by a universal howl of horror. – As a scientist I had an almost unique opportunity. In my day astronomy emerged into the market place. At that particular time, had one man put up a fight, it could have had wide repercussions. I have come to believe that I was never in real danger; for some years I was as strong as the authorities, and I surrendered my knowledge to the powers that be, to use it, no, not *use* it, *abuse* it, as it suits their ends. I have betrayed my profession. Any man who does what I have done must not be tolerated in the ranks of science. (*Virginia, who has stood motionless, puts the platter on the table*)

VIRGINIA   You are accepted in the ranks of the faithful, father.

GALILEO (*sees her*)   Correct. (*He goes over to the table*) I have to eat now.

VIRGINIA   We lock up at eight.

ANDREA   I am glad I came. (*He extends his hand. Galileo ignores it and goes over to his meal*)

GALILEO (*examining the plate; to Andrea*)   Somebody who knows me sent me a goose. I still enjoy eating.

ANDREA   And your opinion is now that the "new age" was an illusion?

GALILEO   Well. – This age of ours turned out to be a whore, spattered with blood. Maybe, new ages look like blood-spattered whores. Take care of yourself.

ANDREA   Yes. (*Unable to go*) With reference to your evaluation of the author in question – I do not know the answer. But I cannot think that your savage analysis is the last word.

GALILEO   Thank you, sir.
(*Official knocks at the door*)

VIRGINIA (*showing Andrea out*)   I don't like visitors from the past, they excite him.
(*She lets him out. The Official closes the iron door. Virginia returns*)

GALILEO (*eating*)   Did you try and think who sent the goose?

VIRGINIA   Not Andrea.

GALILEO   Maybe not. I gave Redhead his first lesson; when he held out his hand, I had to remind myself he is teaching now. – How is the sky tonight?

VIRGINIA (*at the window*)   Bright.
(*Galileo continues eating*)

Scene Fourteen

> The great book o'er the border went
> And, good folk, that was the end.
> But we hope you'll keep in mind
> You and I were left behind.

Before a little Italian customs house early in the morning. Andrea sits upon one of his traveling trunks at the barrier and reads Galileo's book. The window of a small house is still lit, and a big grotesque shadow, like an old witch and her cauldron, falls upon the house wall beyond. Barefoot children in rags see it and point to the little house.

CHILDREN (*singing*)
   One, two, three, four, five, six,
   Old Marina is a witch.
   At night, on a broomstick she sits
   And on the church steeple she spits.
CUSTOMS OFFICER (*to Andrea*)   Why are you making this journey?
ANDREA   I am a scholar.
CUSTOMS OFFICER (*to his Clerk*)   Put down under "reason for leaving the country": Scholar. (*He points to the baggage*) Books! Anything dangerous in these books?
ANDREA   What is dangerous?
CUSTOMS OFFICER   Religion. Politics.
ANDREA   These are nothing but mathematical formulas.
CUSTOMS OFFICER   What's that?
ANDREA   Figures.
CUSTOMS OFFICER   Oh, figures. No harm in figures. Just wait a minute, sir, we will soon have your papers stamped. (*He exits with Clerk*)
   (*Meanwhile, a little council of war among the Children has taken place. Andrea quietly watches. One of the Boys, pushed forward by the others, creeps up to the little house from which the shadow comes, and takes the jug of milk on the doorstep*)
ANDREA (*quietly*)   What are you doing with that milk?

BOY (*stopping in mid-movement*)   She is a witch.
(*The other Children run away behind the Custom House. One of them shouts*) "Run, Paolo!"

ANDREA   Hmm! – And because she is a witch she mustn't have milk. Is that the idea?

BOY   Yes.

ANDREA   And how do you know she is a witch?

BOY (*points to shadow on house wall*)   Look!

ANDREA   Oh! I see.

BOY   And she rides on a broomstick at night – and she bewitches the coachman's horses. My cousin Luigi looked through the hole in the stable roof, that the snow storm made, and heard the horses coughing something terrible.

ANDREA   Oh! – How big was the hole in the stable roof?

BOY   Luigi didn't tell. Why?

ANDREA   I was asking because maybe the horses got sick because it was cold in the stable. You had better ask Luigi how big that hole is.

BOY   You are not going to say Old Marina isn't a witch, because you can't.

ANDREA   No, I can't say she isn't a witch. I haven't looked into it. A man can't know about a thing he hasn't looked into, or can he?

BOY   No! – But THAT! (*He points to the shadow*) She is stirring hell-broth.

ANDREA   Let's see. Do you want to take a look ? I can lift you up.

BOY   You lift me to the window, mister! (*He takes a sling shot out of his pocket*) I can really bash her from there.

ANDREA   Hadn't we better make sure she is a witch before we shoot? I'll hold that.
(*The Boy puts the milk jug down and follows him reluctantly to the window. Andrea lifts the boy up so that he can look in*)

ANDREA   What do you see?

BOY (*slowly*)   Just an old girl cooking porridge.

ANDREA   Oh! Nothing to it then. Now look at her shadow, Paolo.
(*The boy looks over his shoulder and back and compares the reality and the shadow*)

BOY   The big thing is a soup ladle.

ANDREA   Ah! A ladle! You see, I would have taken it for a broomstick, but I haven't looked into the matter as you have, Paolo. Here is your sling.

CUSTOMS OFFICER (*returning with the Clerk and handing Andrea his papers*)   All present and correct. Good luck, sir.
(*Andrea goes, reading Galileo's book. The Clerk starts to bring his*

baggage after him. The barrier rises. Andrea passes through, still
reading the book. The Boy kicks over the milk jug)
BOY (*shouting after Andrea*)   She *is* a witch! She *is* a witch!
ANDREA You saw with your own eyes: think it over!
   (*The Boy joins the others. They sing*)
   One, two, three, four, five, six,
   Old Marina is a witch.
   At night, on a broomstick she sits
   And on the church steeple she spits.
   (*The Customs Officers laugh. Andrea goes*)

METHUEN DRAMA
BERTOLT BRECHT PLAYS

WORLD CLASSICS

☐ COLLECTED PLAYS: ONE (*Baal, Drums in the Night,*
In the Jungle of Cities, The Life of Edward II of England
and five one-act plays)   £9.99

☐ COLLECTED PLAYS: TWO (*Man equals Man, The Elephant Calf,*
The Threepenny Opera, The Rise and Fall of the City of
Mahagonny, The Seven Deadly Sins)   £9.99

☐ COLLECTED PLAYS: THREE (*St Joan of the Stockyards,*
Lindbergh's Flight, The Baden-Baden Lesson on Consent,
He Said Yes/He Said No, The Decision, The Exception and
the Rule, The Horatians and the Curiatians, The Mother)   £10.99

☐ COLLECTED PLAYS: FIVE (*Life of Galileo, Mother Courage*
and her Children)   £9.99

☐ COLLECTED PLAYS: SIX (*The Good Person of Szechwan,*
The Resistible Rise of Arturo Ui, Mr Puntila and his Man Matti)   £9.99

☐ COLLECTED PLAYS: SEVEN (*The Visions of Simone Machard,*
Schweyk in the Second World War, The Caucasian Chalk Circle
and Brecht's adaptation of *The Duchess of Malfi*)   £8.99

MODERN PLAYS

☐ CAUCASIAN CHALK CIRCLE   £6.99
☐ THE GOOD PERSON OF SZECHWAN   £7.99
☐ LIFE OF GALILEO   £6.99
☐ MOTHER COURAGE AND HER CHILDREN   £6.99
☐ THE RESISTIBLE RISE OF ARTURO UI   £6.99
☐ THE THREEPENNY OPERA   £6.99

● All Methuen Drama books are available through mail order or from your local bookshop.

Please send cheque/eurocheque/postal order (sterling only) Access, Visa, Mastercard, Diners
Card, Switch or Amex.

☐☐☐☐☐☐☐☐☐☐☐☐☐☐☐☐

Expiry Date: _____ Signature: _____

Please allow 75 pence per book for post and packing U.K.
Overseas customers please allow £1.00 per copy for post and packing.

ALL ORDERS TO:

Methuen Books, Books by Post, TBS Limited, The Book Service, Colchester Road, Frating
Green, Colchester, Essex CO7 7DW.

NAME:

ADDRESS:

Please allow 28 days for delivery. Please tick box if you do not
wish to receive any additional information   ☐

Prices and availability subject to change without notice.